Caliban and the Yankees

Caliban and the Yankees

Trinidad and the United States Occupation

Harvey R. Neptune

The University of North Carolina Press · *Chapel Hill*

Set in Scala by Tseng Information Systems, Inc.
Manufactured in the United States of America

The paper in this book meets the guidelines for permanence
and durability of the Committee on Production Guidelines for
Book Longevity of the Council on Library Resources.

Library of Congress Cataloging-in-Publication Data
Neptune, Harvey R., 1970–
Caliban and the Yankees : Trinidad and the United States occupation /
by Harvey R. Neptune.
p. cm.
Includes bibliographical references and index.
ISBN-13: 978-0-8078-3080-2 (cloth : alk. paper)
ISBN-13: 978-0-8078-5788-5 (pbk. : alk. paper)
1. Trinidad and Tobago—Civilization—American influences.
2. Nationalism—Trinidad and Tobago—History—20th century.
3. Trinidad and Tobago—History—20th century.   I. Title.
F2121.N47   2007
972.983′03—dc22

2006027176

Some material in Chapter 6 appeared in somewhat different form
as "Manly Rivalries and Mopsies: Gender, Nationality, and Sexuality
in United States–Occupied Trinidad," *Radical History Review* 87
(Fall 2003): 78–95. It is reprinted here with permission.

cloth   11 10 09 08 07   5 4 3 2 1
paper   11 10 09 08 07   5 4 3 2 1

To the Two Santiagos

Contents

Illustrations

Acknowledgments

I could not complete this book without the patience, generosity, support, and hard work of many people, some of whose names I am sure I'll forget to mention here—to those individuals, please accept my forgiveness in advance. I count myself very lucky to have been trained at New York University by some of the most intimidatingly bright and bighearted scholars. Ada Ferrer has been as resourceful, caring, and sensitive a mentor as one could ask for. Her own scholarship, moreover, has been a constant guide for my thinking and writing. In so many ways, Ada remains a model academic. I belong, too, to that legion of students deeply indebted to Robin D. G. Kelley not only for his inspiring manner of doing history but perhaps more for his unwavering kindness and encouragement. Much gratitude also goes out to Sinclair Thompson, Martha Hodes, and Gerard Aching, close and keen readers of the work at earlier stages. Special thanks, too, to Jeff Sammons, Nikhil Singh, and Walter Johnson and, for more recent interest and engagement, Michael Gomez, Fred Cooper, Adam Green, and Jane Burbank.

No less important than teachers have been folks who ensured my survival during those "training days." I am happy to acknowledge Carmen Diaz, Ben Maddox, Dennis McNulty, Debbie Hall, Karin Burrell, Stephanie Lyle, and Nicole Davidson. At various stages of this history-making process, many friends and peers have sought to keep the work tight and my mind loose; wisely and generously, they have read, listened, commented, suggested, ignored, cheered, mocked, celebrated, and, yes, dissed. Boundless big-ups to Danny Widener, Jemima Pierre, Betsy Esch, Fanon Che Wilkins, Melina Pappademos, Taj-Nia Henderson, Paul Kramer, Deborah Thomas, Faith Smith, Tanya Huelett, and Jerry Philogene. They all read parts of this book, some back when it was a baby bawling out for attention and care. Two individuals, moreover, saw and heard more about this project than one can reasonably expect and deserve very special thanks: Donette Francis and Krista Thompson.

Researching for this study meant receiving help from (almost literally) perfect strangers. Thanks to Bridget Brereton; Rhoda Reddock; Fitz Baptiste; the staff at West Indiana at University of the West Indies Library, Saint Augustine (especially Ms. Bhodoo); the staff at the Public Records Office at Kew Gardens; the staff at Port of Spain and Arima municipal councils (especially Lindy-Anne Braithwaite); the staff at the U.S. National Archives in Maryland; the staff at the U.S. Army Center of Military History; the staff at the National Archives in Port of Spain; and Elaine Maisner and Stephanie Wenzel at the University of North Carolina Press.

At later stages in the project, I benefited immensely from the critical and generous support of several people and institutions. Thanks to Calvin Holder and the entire history department at the College of Staten Island; to the history department at Northwestern University, especially Paula Blaskovits, Sarah Maza, Nancy Maclean, Dylan Penningroth, Peter Carroll, Tessie Liu, Brodwyn Fischer, Ji-Yeon Yuh, Edward Muir, David Schoenbrun, Michael Sherry, Steve Hahn, and Stephany McCurry; to my crew at Northwestern University's Department of African-American Studies (don't think I'm not mad at you all for leaving me longing for yet another place and group of people!): Richard Iton, Mary Pattillo, Martha Biondi, Marsha Figaro, Celeste Watkins, Aldon Morris, Dwight McBride, Sherwyn Bryant, Barnor Hesse, Reul Rogers, and E. Patrick Johnson. Michael Hanchard and Bayo Holsey also helped make for a warm, productive time in cold Chicago. Most recently, I am grateful for the support from my new professional "home," the history department at Temple University, especially Patricia Williams, Arthur Schmidt, Richard Immerman, and Andrew Isenberg.

If I have been able to forget at times that research and writing is but a part of what my life is about, it is because I am lucky to have a big, warm, loving circle of family and friends. They, thankfully, have shown more interest in the lines on my forehead than in the lines in this book. Appreciation is due to a massive squad best labeled my "Soca Warriors." Because of them, I can feel at home whether in Trinidad, Brooklyn, London, or Washington, D.C. Then there are some very special shout-outs, individuals whom, to be honest, I could never thank enough: Michael "dbombo" Toney, La Tonya Pierre, Selwyn Williams, Perthrina Pegus, Jason Taitt, Lesley Nurse, Brian Thomas, Dexter Braithwaite, Clarissa Cummings, Andre Fergusson, Krista Thompson, Solomon Luke, and

Claudia Celestin. Finally, deep deep appreciation and love to the Neptunes—Juanita, Bernadette, Maralyn, Anthony, and Gabriel (and the bestest crew of nieces and nephews). In a life that has involved much moving, you all remain the constant center.

This book is dedicated to the memory of a passed teacher, Aida Santiago, and to the dreams of my favorite current teacher, Santiago Neptune.

Introduction
A Brave New World

For we have always been mixed up in America's business.
—George Lamming

A year into World War II, the British colony of Trinidad was conscripted to contribute to the cause of the Allies. By a quick diplomatic exchange on September 2, 1940, U.S. president Franklin Roosevelt and Great Britain's prime minister Winston Churchill agreed that the tiny Caribbean territory would accommodate extensive U.S. naval and air bases. For Trinidad's nearly half-million residents, this period of establishing and operating military installations (roughly 1941–47) proved to be epochal. What they would dub the "American occupation" witnessed the birth of a brave new world on the island.[1]

This world resembled neither the utopias nor the dystopias of epic fame; yielding no clear-cut narratives, occupied Trinidad amounted to neither paradise on earth nor hell incarnate.[2] In what were truly tempestuous times, rather, the colony presented a scene bristling with quotidian social conflict. Left little choice but to deal with the "America" lawfully in their midst, virtually everyone adopted a strategic approach, seeking in Yankee personnel, paychecks, and practices the means to realize and reenvision as well as deny and defend particular dreams and agendas.[3] Such purposeful local interaction with the U.S. occupation almost inevitably intensified internal struggles in a community as differentiated, indeed as fractious, as Trinidad. Already agitated by popular and nationalist mobilization in the previous decade, this colonial society endured dizzying new levels of contentiousness during these years. Employers condemned workers who rushed to offer their services to Americans; respectable folks renounced rebellious young dandies who dressed in the latest Yankee fashion; men upbraided women who consorted with U.S. servicemen; critics panned calypsonians for pandering to American patrons.

And this was but the beginning. For those who lived in wartime Trinidad, the close encounter with the U.S. empire meant more than anything else endless internecine friction and confrontation. This book is about that antagonistic time and place, about the clashes, subversions, and evasions that excited a small colonial island forced to engage a grand imperial America.

SETTING THE STAGE

Occupied Trinidad's palpably charged social atmosphere was certainly not what statesmen on both sides of the Atlantic intended when they crafted the bases-for-destroyers deal. In deciding to swap territory on several British West Indian islands for fifty old American destroyers, diplomats were responding to the exigencies of war- and empire-making.[4] Under fire from German blitzkriegs, Great Britain aimed to fortify its forces and to enlist the United States in the defense of its West Indian possessions. On the other side of the Atlantic, the still-neutral United States sought not only to better Allies' chances but also to prevent Axis powers from gaining a stronghold in the hemisphere.[5] Thus, as keen local critics understood, even if the wartime bout of American base construction was an immediate effect of the fascist peril, it did nonetheless help to make manifest abiding dreams of the U.S. imperial destiny in the Caribbean.[6]

Trinidad figured prominently as Washington resolved to build what military architects envisioned as a "Fortress America."[7] Strategically situated at the "crossroads of the Atlantic," the 1,900-square-mile territory guarded paths to North and South America, to the prized Panama Canal westward, and to the perilous combat zones eastward. This island would be called upon to do decisive sentinel duty and, indeed, was worth, the tale went, forty of the fifty destroyers. Apocryphal as it might be, this claim has the merit of highlighting Trinidad's distinction as host of the largest—by far—of the new military installations in the British Caribbean "base colonies" (as these islands would soon be labeled).[8]

By 1940 the imperative of bearing with newcomers, including those in the employ of empires, was more than a familiar feature of Trinidad's post-Columbian past; to a large extent, it was Trinidadian history. Claimed for Spain on Christopher Columbus's third voyage in 1498, "Iere"—as the natives allegedly called it—suffered the decimation of its indigenous people that defined the wider Antillean area. The island lacked silver and gold and, located a few miles off the legendarily alluring mainland, would remain sparsely settled until the 1780s when reform-minded Spanish policy-makers began courting French-speaking planters. Along with their African and African-descended chattel, they soon emerged as the prime developers of Trinidad's economy and composers of its cultural repertoire. Before long, though, came another crew of colonizers. In the heat of European revolutionary battles that inevitably bled into the Caribbean Sea, belligerent English ships sailed to the island in 1797 and, with very little ado, wrested it from Spain. Conquered, containing a nonwhite, non-British majority, and considered by English abolitionists to be a potential "experimental" slave society, Trinidad would be governed as a "Crown Colony" rather than granted representative government.[9] To be sure, this autocratic form of rule provoked endless protest (from calls for constitutional reform in the early nineteenth century to whispers of annexation to the United States at its end); stewardship of the state nevertheless would stay in British hands for the next 165 years.

Beyond the increasingly anglicized sphere of officialdom, though, the patchwork of peopling continued apace. In the aftermath of emancipation (1838), state-sponsored indentured laborers from South Asia, China, and Portugal joined Trinidad's hitherto predominantly African black workforce. Furthermore, having developed into a plantation society relatively late and hence holding out the possibility of landownership for prospective settlers, the island continued to attract migrants of all kinds and circumstances. At the dawn of the twentieth century, Trinidad counted among its residents the hopeful, restless, and exiled from as near as Venezuela and St. Vincent and as far as Germany and (present-day) Lebanon.[10] Thus by the time thousands of U.S. personnel began descending on the territory in 1941, its population was already what a wary President Roosevelt allegedly deemed an "ethnic potpourri."[11]

Roosevelt's characterization of the British colony, issued in the course of renouncing any interest in annexation, would have brought a sigh of relief in local political quarters. Racist rationale aside, the president's disavowal of expansionist ambitions would have assuaged not only anxious establishment loyalists, a group long apprehensive of Americanization, but perhaps, more important, Trinidad's increasingly potent assemblage of "Creole patriots."[12] The onset of occupation, it is hard to overemphasize, coincided with a watershed in the history of oppositional activity in the island (and the region, for that matter). On the verge of the bases-for-destroyers deal, the colony stirred with a defining double-sided cultural politics: the "banalization of Britishness" (to coin a phrase) and the invention of "Trinidadianness."[13] Against this backdrop of anticolonial nation-building, the struggles (over labor, dress, culture, and sexuality) that marked occupied Trinidad, while dramatic and salient in their own right, assumed even greater meaning and moment.

The story of the quest for nationhood in colonial Trinidad entered a decisive chapter in the interwar years. While the late nineteenth and early twentieth centuries certainly did produce a prologue, having thrown up trenchant detractors of Crown Colony rule, that period's critics never quite called colonialism into question, never quite suspended the presumption of Britain's imperial mandate.[14] Only after the Great War was the historical stage set for the appearance of political actors confident enough to doubt Great Britain's greatness. Not until the 1930s, especially, with the fig leaf rhetoric of "civilizing missions" increasingly unable to hide the moral and financial bankruptcy of empires in general and Britain's empire in particular, did local agitators begin couching their claims on the state in terms of a putatively essential difference between British and Trinidadian identities. To young, committed patriot intellectuals and activists like Albert Gomes, Ralph Mentor, Jean De Boissiere, Alfred Mendes, Lloyd Braithwaite, De Wilton Rogers, and Sylvia Chen, the notion of self-determination went beyond "home rule." They dreamed of a comprehensive decolonization, one that demanded tossing aside the conceit that culture was synonymous with English creative achievements and, instead, embracing a distinguished Trinidadian edition. To put it simply, politics and culture were virtually inseparable for these individuals, most of whom easily assumed multiple roles as gadflies, artists, organizers, and impresarios.[15]

These Creole patriots, it is worth stressing, were neither a tight-knit nor a homogenous group. Although they shared an antiestablishment spirit and subscribed to organs (like the *Beacon*, *People*, and *New Dawn*) and organizations that raised issues around peoplehood and politics, a range of differences obtained among them. Not all, to begin with, were even born in Trinidad. Black journalist, writer, and bibliophile Owen Mathurin, for example, joined and played an active role in the nationalist intelligentsia after coming from the nearby British colony of St. Lucia in 1935; political affinity rather than nativity inspired his contributions. Sylvia Chen, a "mixed" (Chinese, black, and white) dancer, had been abroad (in London, Moscow, and New York) for nearly two decades before returning to contribute to the choreography of nationhood for a brief but vibrant spell in 1940.[16] Furthermore, although a few of these activists hailed from the island's deprived black and Indian communities and could connect their oppositional work to personal experience, others boasted considerable privileges of gender, class, and color (for starters) and arrived at their radical views only through remarkable though not unproblematic leaps of empathy.

Indeed, Trinidad's patriot cadre did not lack for paradoxical personalities. In this regard no one was more compelling and conspicuous than Albert Gomes, who cast a huge shadow over protest politics in the period under consideration. A descendant of migrants from the Portuguese island of Madeira, Gomes was born to a Port of Spain shopkeeper who over the years had become sufficiently prosperous to send his son to study philosophy at City College in New York City. Returning to Trinidad in 1930, the brash youngster quickly earned a reputation as a perennial thorn in the side of the colonial establishment, a rebel journalist and firebrand who frequently advocated on behalf of the island's poor, nonwhite majority. Gomes, though, cut a deeply complicated and compromised figure. Hardly a model of ideological purity, he could and often did argue every side of an issue.[17] Extreme as they were, his inconsistencies were not exceptional within the nationalist coterie. During the 1930s and 1940s, patriot politics in Trinidad made for an uneven and at times ambiguous terrain.

WHAT'S IN A (SHAKESPEAREAN) NAME?

Centering the careers of a colonial nationalism along with two tensely collaborating imperialisms, this account of Trinidad's past is distinguished by a concern for the strong and varied U.S. presence, by a recognition, more specifically, that in the production of a postcolonial Trinidadianness, Americans featured as audience, actors, sponsors, and, always, behind-the-scenes forces sometimes powerful enough to cancel the entire drama. Thus one way of rendering this story—a rendering that retains terms appropriate to the stage—is as that of a colonial society in which the assumption of a blasphemous Caliban-like stance toward British rulers coincided with the intimate assertion of a powerful Yankee presence.

Mining the metaphoric riches of *The Tempest* has become commonplace in Caribbean studies. Following up on George Lamming's iconoclastic reinterpretation of the seventeenth-century play in the 1950s, scholars, poets, and writers have routinely appropriated Caliban as a personification of the region's "anticolonial riposte," as a symbol of the struggles of Caribbean people against the mastery of European Prosperos.[18] Here, however, the Shakespearean allusion aspires simultaneously to less and to more. This work does not pretend to contribute to the politically charged debates about deployments of the dramatic text—however productive these have been. It turns to *The Tempest*, rather, to call attention to a historical situation far more fraught than the dyadic arrangement often drawn in British Caribbean historiography. In casting Yankees alongside Caliban, this book means to foreground that in West Indian colonies (from Jamaica to Trinidad), the struggle for independence entailed facing not one but two Prosperos: Great Britain and the United States.[19] These islands belonged to Britain, but they lay in America's backyard, a geopolitical factor that the relevant scholarship has yet to adequately integrate. Extending the geographic purview of this insight, moreover, pushes toward a general recognition that colonialism and its countervailing historic force of nationalism have been beset by tensions that exceeded the domain defined by any single metropole and its possession. From this perspective, it ought to be clear, full accounts of the making and breaking of empires have to consider overlapping, connecting, and colliding imperial formations, their significance as well as their uses.[20]

There is yet more conceptual nuance to be gained from the Shakespearean cite. When the United States embarked on its colonizing mission at the end of the nineteenth century, influential observers south of the Rio Grande did not regard the northern republic as an awesome Prospero. To the contrary, they scorned the imperial newcomer as a base Caliban, with *Arielista* intellectuals, in particular, condemning Yankees as slaves to a utilitarian, materialist world and devoid of the arts of civilization.[21] In this anomalous allegorical relationship between the United States and the cast of *The Tempest* lies an almost irrepressible and insightful provocation. The plainly paradoxical figure of a colonizing Caliban virtually begs scholars to address the unstable and contested apprehension of America's role in struggles for self-determination across the rest of the hemisphere and the wider colonial world. This kind of contingent tack toward contemplating the meanings of the United States has particular pertinence for histories of the Caribbean. It is a region, after all, whose inhabitants have long found in the northern republic, especially in its black population, a potent source of inspiration for anticolonial politics. Indeed, Caribbeanists who trace stories of U.S. imperialism must be mindful for subplots of diaspora, for linkups (sometimes strained, sometimes successful) between descendants of Africans who were once literal—not literary—slaves.[22] *Caliban and the Yankees* strives to capture something of this uncertainty and complexity in exploring the possibilities and predicaments that attended the U.S. occupation of a British West Indian island.

What follows makes no pretense of telling the whole story. Yet far more than a clichéd acceptance of the all-too-human impossibility of omniscience, this caveat means to signal the decisive importance of the production of archives, the vital forces shaping historians' valid body of evidence. Accounting for the constraints governing academically credible claims about the past, "the power in the story" (to quote Michel-Rolph Trouillot), is especially crucial in this study of wartime Trinidad.[23] Set in a moment of virtually undisputed emergency, *Caliban and the Yankees* is based on an archive that bears the stamp of official authority even more impressively and scrupulously than in other, more routine times. Moreover, with court and police records and other such sources unavailable to the researcher of colonial Trinidad, newspapers constitute the primary documents for this account, and these organs, it has to be appreciated, suffered severe censorship during the occupation. For the island's "fourth estate," sanitizing and even muting stories that discredited, or raised doubts about, American occupiers were essential wartime duties.[24] This study thus relies largely on weaving and patching and, especially, on "reading against the grain." Even so, gaps remain, and at times, recourse has been sought in fictional sources. Despite registering a different order of evidence, these narratives possess indisputable historical value.[25] Not only were their authors engaged, contemporary actors, but also, as literary works, they were explicitly meant to capture the new world of occupied Trinidad.[26]

THE NEW WORLD OF OCCUPIED TRINIDAD

That some of the island's finest writers have been inspired by the years of occupation is hardly surprising; this, after all, was a period of indisputably dramatic remaking for Trinidadian society. Indeed, when U.S. military officials pledged to try to "minimise any disturbance in the normal life of the [local] community" on the eve of base installation, either naïveté or disingenuousness had spoken.[27] The myriad manifestations of their presence—from big, rumbling trucks to casual laboring, white men to abundant, well-paying work—all but guaranteed the era's chronic unsettlement.

To begin with, Americans made themselves virtually unavoidable by virtue of the sites chosen for their military installations. After reconnaissance missions in late 1940, the navy insisted (against the stubborn protests of Governor Hubert Young) on an eleven-square-mile spread of land in Chaguaramas, a village at the tip of Trinidad's northwestern peninsula and a mere twenty-minute jeep ride west of the capital city of Port of Spain. The army went east, securing eighteen square miles in the forested environs of Cumuto. Although relatively removed from the capital (twenty miles away), this settlement was practically contiguous with the eastern edge of Arima, the most recent of Trinidad's three boroughs. For shipping purposes, Americans acquired a sizable swath of the wharf on Port of Spain's Gulf of Paria coast, and for general convenience they extracted the immediate hinterland along Wrightson Road. The U.S. military subsequently procured sites elsewhere in the capital (St. Clair and Laventille) and the colony (Chaguanas), but it was the Port of Spain "docksite" and the two bases that proved most consequential. Taken together, these facilities traversed Trinidad's densest residential settlement, the "east-west corridor" that ran along the foothills of the northern range.[28] Establishing their presence within the colony's most urbanized county (St. George) and, moreover, aggrandizing the value of the area, American newcomers ensured their ubiquity and import.

Along with physical geography, a range of related societal ramifications virtually dictated the historic impact of the occupation. Undertaken on an island in a notoriously poor region—long tagged "the slums of empire"—this $90 million mission made Americans an immediately impressive source of employment and economic activity.[29] Compounding this effect was the bustling informal economy generated by servicemen and workers whose incomes dwarfed locals'; American carpenters and plumbers earned in one hour what skilled locals took an entire day to make (at least before the arrival of U.S. employment).[30] As embodiments of the powerful northern republic, moreover, Yankee personnel possessed compelling cultural cachet in Trinidad. Stationed in a colonial outpost where people's desires often betrayed a worldliness that belied its backward reputation, Americans were received as representatives of a metropolitan space storied for its "modern" achievements. As bosses, models, patrons, and partners, these occupiers landed on the island with doubtless currency.

Yet another undeniably sensitive aspect of the occupation's significance was its racialized profile. Notwithstanding the appearance of approximately 2,000 African American soldiers in the middle of 1942, base installation had

an overwhelmingly white face (total troop strength at that time numbered upward of 25,000). This demographic character held crucial yet contradictory
implications for a host society where whites comprised less than 3 percent of
the local population (around 15,000).[31] On one hand, these occupiers represented a formidably armed police force and thus contributed materially to the
defense of a preexisting white supremacist social order (albeit one less reliant on overt forms of physical violence than in the United States). Such a
reinforcement had particular poignancy given that only four years earlier the
tiny white ruling class had faced a deadly violent uprising of black and Indian
workers (the so-called Butler riots of 1937). Yet, on the other hand, Americans
embodied a serious ideological threat. With local whites already desperately
struggling to stage their superiority before an increasingly restless, disbeliev-
ing nonwhite audience, Yankees would come under acute pressure to properly
perform their racial parts. Failure to do so risked disrupting the social economy of prestige in the colony. On a range of accounts, then, from wage rates
to whiteness, the occupation was pregnant with possibilities that Trinidad's
residents could not afford to ignore.

If compulsory negotiation of the U.S. presence was the predominant plot,
transgressions of epochal proportions were the overarching outcome. As large
portions of the local population, nonelites in particular, purposefully worked
for, took fashion cues from, entertained, and established intimacies with
American sojourners, many of the society's fundamental organizing precepts
buckled or, in some cases, completely fell under a chain of challenges. The
conceit of an awesomely respectable Englishness and—more broadly—whiteness, the cushion of a reliable supply of cheap nonwhite labor, and the comfort
of masculinist control of women—all these and more underwent assault and
erosion during the period. Precious little indeed appeared invulnerable to rejection, subversion, or revision in the years that Trinidadians faced Americans.

This sweeping array of change, not surprisingly, sparked a panicked response within the establishment and, broadly, among those invested in the
status quo. Throughout the occupation, Trinidad's white plantocracy; its respectable, Anglocentric types; and more generally, its male population maneuvered to preempt, counter, and manage what they experienced as a period
of electrifying disorder. The colony was a veritable theater of social battle in
these years. By the time the dust cleared, the result was indisputable: those
dominant groups fighting to turn back the hands of time, to restore the society
to its prewar mores and conditions, ended on the side of futility. The island's

subaltern set, seizing the moment occasioned by base installation and operation, had wrought irreversible social unsettlement.[32] Such was the decisive-
ness of the upheaval that by late 1943 ubiquitous social observer Albert Gomes
could declare that the old Trinidad "will never return."[33]

Gomes arrived at this conclusion with an unmistakable and telling unease.
Like many privileged locals, he was tested and, at times, even stunned by what
transpired during the occupation, by what appeared to be a society swept up
in a "revolution" made from below. Given Gomes's political and ideological
commitments, his discomfort about the tenor and character of this change
assumed a particular poignancy. He was part of a nationalist intelligentsia
that over the course of the previous decade had elaborated a sense of Trinidadianness based on grassroots practices and priorities framed as inveterately
folksy and radically un-Western. Despite their own modernist manners and
affiliations, these dissident dreamers of nationhood pegged their postcolonial
futures to a non- or even antimodern vision of Trinidad's most downtrodden,
especially its black sector. This heavy investment in a traditionalist interpretation of popular cultural politics proved consequential during the occupation;
specifically, it precipitated among patriots a profoundly ambivalent reaction to
the world being born. Observing nonelites negotiate American money, men,
and modes of being in ways that questioned everything from the conditions of
domestic labor to the convention of tucking shirts in trouser, the colony's agitators were often torn. As antiestablishment critics, on one hand, they appreciated how the deprived majority enlisted U.S. resources toward empowering
themselves and subverting the Anglocentric status quo. These developments
accorded with their own demands. On the other, as patriots committed to a
notion of a Trinidadian community rooted in pristine—indeed, at times, near-
primitivist—virtues, they agonized over transactions with Americans that, to
them, helped refashion the colony's romantic folks into rebellious moderns.
The Yankee presence, these nationalists feared, not only facilitated the liberation of colonial subjects from British conventions but also sponsored a popular alienation from Trinidad's putatively indigenous values.[34]

The underlying story of occupied Trinidad thus presents a twist on the conventional tale about "modernity" in the colonial world. During these years, it
was the subaltern crowd (the poor, women, and youth) that found most utility
in, and moved most avidly to make something new out of, America. By contrast, the patriot intelligentsia, the constituency commonly singled out as aggressively intent on adopting and adapting the up-to-date ways of the Western

world, remained haunted by a hesitation at the signs of new times.[35] As Albert Gomes reflected on the state and fate of Trinidad in the middle of the occupation, he gave honest expression to the predicament of his intellectual coterie. Although "the conscious daytime mind is ever eager to profess its love of change and progress," wrote Gomes, "the deeper implication of being accepts with extreme reluctance all those portents of what seems new and strange."[36] This existentialist-sounding rhetoric is telling: a member of the modernist vanguard of the 1930s, Gomes betrayed at the height of the period a certain disenchantment with the rapid disappearance of the old. He was not alone. For many within the colony's patriotic cadre, activists who tended to imagine themselves as beacons in the remaking of an enlightened national order, the Yankee years presented a disturbing Trinidadian scene. It was one in which the tempo of "the people" appeared to be ahead, that is, more modern than that of the leadership.[37]

DISQUIETING REVOLUTION?

Rife with struggles over local reception of the U.S. presence, the story of occupied Trinidad has gone largely untold within academic groves. This reticence has its reasons. The most developed of the relevant fields, U.S.–Latin American relations, remained for a long time given to a moral and ideological tidiness that would have found such an unsettled episode difficult to assimilate. Initiated in the interwar United States, the literature first leaned toward judging the interests and effects of the republic's dealings with governments to the south. It featured Yankee citizens (especially state-connected and business-backed figures) as the real protagonists and fixed on interrogating instructive projects and projections of U.S. power: were they beneficently modernizing or exploitatively imperial? Into the postwar period, the institutional turn to "area studies" and the ideological (re)turn to radical Marxist-influenced scholarship spurred another tendency. This strain of writing, drawing inspiration from eruptions of armed Latin American resistance to the Colossus of the North, was animated by unequivocal, violent opposition to evil Yankee imperialists. Yet the effect of this historiographical reorientation was limited in an important respect. Despite reversing agency, these studies maintained a sharp dichotomy; they retained a premium on producing agonistic narratives, accounts marked by endless and uncompromising struggle between the United States and the rest of the Americas.[38]

Patently, neither of these perspectives was conducive to inquiry into occupied Trinidad. While part of Washington's larger geopolitical strategy to strengthen its hemispheric hegemony, the U.S. presence in the colony (and the Anglo-Caribbean more generally) conspicuously lacked the imperious and comprehensive reformist mission of early-twentieth-century ventures in Cuba, the Dominican Republic, or Haiti.[39] Americans had come primarily to guard a British possession, not to seize and reorganize an unruly republic. By regional standards, indeed, Trinidad's experience appeared to be a doubtful instance of occupation; it was one, after all, that proceeded not from a belligerent, arrogant invasion but from state-level diplomacy.[40] Equally pertinent (and perhaps as a corollary), the island's inhabitants mounted no overt challenges—armed or otherwise—to Yankee occupiers. Absent of any clear and totalizing battles between ambitious civilizers and recalcitrant "natives," this instance of U.S. intervention languished in historiographical obscurity.[41]

The episode has endured an equally forgettable fate among academic custodians of Trinidad's past, and the elision can only be partially attributed to the relative infancy and "underdevelopment" of British West Indian historiography.[42] More germane is the political logic guiding the production of knowledge about the colony's history, a logic that largely dismisses the period from 1938 to 1955 and thus leaves the years of occupation deep in a lacuna. The literature on colonial Trinidad has been underwritten by a post-1950s nationalism that tends to treat the achievement of "independence" in 1962 as the inexorable outcome. Such a presumption renders the past before this climactic moment as mere prologue and, in turn, has dictated a glaringly uneven coverage of a history in which the biography of nationhood appears to unfold not as a plot of progressive thickening but as one with temporary sclerotic spells, too. After beginning nobly with Captain Arthur A. Cipriani, the venerated Great War veteran who stood up for the colony's "barefooted" during the 1920s and then gaining massive heroic momentum with the Butler riots in the following decade, the story of Trinidad flounders. The 1940s and early 1950s stand out, rather sorely, as an era of inept leaders (epitomized perhaps by Albert Gomes) incapable of nurturing the nation to maturity. This decade and a half comprises a detour of sorts in the narrational order of things. Only the dramatic entry of Dr. Eric Williams onto the political stage in 1955 conspires to turn fortunes around, closing the curtain on a period trashed in one text as the "nadir of Trinidadian life."[43] A brilliant, charismatic historian, Williams founded in 1956 the People's National Movement, the party that "revitalized" the island's "depressing situation" and returned Trinidad to the path toward its appointment with national destiny.[44]

This emplotment has lost little authority since it first appeared in 1962, not least because of the auspicious circumstances of its inauguration. The plot was introduced in *History of the People of Trinidad and Tobago*, a book composed expressly for the occasion of independence by Eric Williams, who at the time was not only the country's first prime minister but also arguably the Caribbean's most acclaimed historian. Almost inevitably, *History of the People* earned acceptance as a—if not the—landmark statement on the island's history.[45] Ever since, as a result, an admitted "manifesto," a narrative authored with the postcolonial future in mind, has captivated the scholarly imagining of Trinidad's past.[46]

However satisfying ("the doctor's" rhetorical bite is no less sharp four decades later), the weight of Williams's unrepentantly nationalist interpretation has imposed an undue censorial burden on the historical imagination. Indeed, it has dictated the slighting and simplification of mid-twentieth-century Trinidad, and there should be little surprise that the most serious claims for the importance of occupied Trinidad appeared prior to the casting of Williams's shadow on the historiography. Lloyd Braithwaite's 1953 essay, though primarily a sociological analysis of the structures and values that "integrated" the colonial order, insisted on the U.S. occupation as a revolutionary event. Focused on race, Braithwaite (a prominent dissident during the 1940s) argued that by working in "humble capacities" and thus ending "the automatic association of whiteness with power and prestige," Yankees played "indeed the most important part in disrupting the pre-established order of the island society."[47] Subsequent renderings of twentieth-century Trinidad, to be sure, rehearse this contention about the occupation and the abrupt demise of white supremacy; still, they offer no more than a perfunctory treatment of these years.[48]

A NEW WAY OF SEEING

Caliban and the Yankees thus breaks new ground in Trinidadian historiography.[49] By resituating Trinidad squarely within the realm of the U.S. empire as well as reassessing the biography of its nationhood, this book opens new perspectives on the past of the colony, the region, and beyond. It illuminates for Trinidad a cultural politics far richer and, indeed, far more complicated than hitherto portrayed.[50] Alert to the utility people found in American ways of life, the work adds an important yet mostly ignored element to the dynamics of creolization: along with Europe, Africa, and Asia, the United States, too, offered material for the fashioning of ideas, practices, and identities that comprise the local cultural repertoire.[51] Furthermore, in highlighting that non-elites made their living, made their lives, and often simply made do by trafficking with "America," *Caliban and the Yankees* enables an alternative recounting of mid-twentieth-century Trinidad. Its recognition that "the people" displayed little compunction about looking beyond the strictly local and traditional so prized by Trinidadian patriots points to tensions and discrepancies between nationalists' project and subalterns' practices. Factoring these incompatibilities, in turn, invites a reframing of the 1940s and early 1950s not so much as an era of failure in the narrative of nationhood but as a period in which nationals-in-the-making publicly challenged, violated, and subverted patriots' priorities and prescriptions. Rather than a kind of interregnum to be carelessly dismissed, the years between Turbal Uriah Butler and Eric Williams, this account shows, ought to be viewed for all their vibrancy and complexity. A moment crossed by figures, fads, and practices (from Albert Gomes to saga boys to flagrant interracial intimacies), it demands nuanced recovery and reassessment. Indeed, this was a time and place in which both colonialism and nationalism came under question; as such it offers further evidence for the necessity of histories that attend to contingency, ambiguity, and especially the penetrating debates about political and cultural imaginations that occurred as the age of empire entered its twilight.[52]

As a meditation on the particular styles and strategies in the construction of Trinidadianness, moreover, *Caliban and the Yankees* brings onto the horizon other "fragmentary" views of the cultural politics of nation-making.[53] It underscores, for example, Indo-Trinidadians' doubtful interrogations of a patriotic discourse that from incipience presumed Africanness and marginalized Indianness. In the midst of the effusive rhetoric of nation-building in the 1940s, many "East Indian" observers, the study reveals, discerned and publicly disputed the decided "West Indianness" of the nationalist imagination. At the same time, though, this history cautions against easy segregationist assumptions about the significance of ethnicity in colonial Trinidad. In fact, instead of taking for granted any marked distinction between Afro- and Indo-Trinidadian in terms of everyday dealings with Americans, the book stresses that the "Indians," too, eagerly moved to take advantage of the circumstances occasioned by the occupation. Ultimately, in acknowledging both the discursive distancing of East Indians from African-centered nationalist representations and the practical indifference between Indo- and Afro-Trinidadian activities, *Caliban and the Yankees* deepens arguments for conceptualizing the society's "racial tensions" not in terms of timelessly plural cultural dispositions but as the product of struggles for hegemony.[54]

This work also has ramifications across the region by virtue of its skepticism toward the homogenizing ambitions and effects of nationalist narratives. From Cuba to Guyana, the imperatives of nationhood have organized and authorized conceited stories about the emergence of peoplehood, tall tales that vastly overstate the autonomy and persuasive powers of the nation idea. *Caliban and the Yankees* is premised on the notion that suspending belief in these plots promises a fuller comprehension not only of the Caribbean's history but also of its present. This study, indeed, suggests that there is a mistaken haste in the current Caribbeanist proclivity for presenting the contemporary popular disillusionment with nationhood as well as the salience of America as recent historic breaks. Although immediate to us, these dilemmas, this book shows, belong just as much to times too often disavowed as utterly past.[55]

Finally, this story of Trinidad's encounter with America offers yet more evidence of the Caribbean's ecumenical historical significance and reaffirms the value of viewing these tiny islands as theaters of globally momentous struggles.[56] Not only was the island a world during the occupation (to steal the title of Samuel Selvon's fictionalized account of the period), it anticipated a world. Often cast as an epoch called the American century, this world is one in which facing manifestations of U.S. power has become an inescapable fate.[57] *Caliban and the Yankees*, in fact, can be read as an urging to think of the Caribbean along with postwar Europe, a field in which students of Americanization have underscored local subalterns' capacity to appropriate select expressions of the United States toward subversive ends. Insofar as the reception and use of America went, what was true in Caribbean outposts, this study suggests, would soon be valid in European metropoles.[58] This book nevertheless parts with a Europeanist historiography that, in some cases, goes as far as to characterize its subjects' investment in America as a form of self-colonization. That literature, indeed, continues to argue about the propriety of the term "empire" in figuring the United States, making for a debate that sometimes appears bafflingly naive about power.[59] Such an appearance is especially true from the vantage point of the Caribbean, where, since the late nineteenth century, residents have been keenly cognizant of—to steal Ann Stoler's term—a "haunting" imperial force emanating from the north.[60] *Caliban and the Yankees* avers that no matter how much U.S. citizens have debated the character of the republic and its historic mission in the world, the region's people, living in America's backyard, have rarely ignored or euphemized their vulnerability to varied and uninvited forms of U.S. intervention.

Indeed, I hope that the perspective taken in this Caribbean study boomerangs to American studies and reinforces recent efforts to push the field out into the world.[61] Much of the history of the United States, after all, has happened beyond its territorial borders. As Rudyard Kipling, the imperialist poet laureate who famously urged Yankees to take up "the white man's burden," might have cautioned, What should they know of America who only America know? Adopting this "excentric" stance, fortunately, does not demand a conceptual invention from scratch.[62] Back in the interwar United States, a circle of scholars concerned with their country's interventionist role yet distrustful of too much theorizing about imperialism fanned out to various Caribbean sites to understand how American power operated in practice. In prefacing the resulting series of publications, radical intellectual and activist Harry Elmer Barnes provided an important gloss to the authors' methodology: "What a thing does," he counseled, "is more important than what it is."[63] *Caliban and the Yankees* amends Barnes's maxim; what people do with a thing, it postulates, might yet be more important.

OUTLINE

To fully appreciate this history of what people in occupied Trinidad did with America, the account first looks backward to portray the society that faced U.S. military installation in 1941. Chapter 1 addresses the preceding decade, and in the course of recounting the events and debates that shook the 1930s, it threads the emergence of nationalist priorities, thought, and personalities. Chapter 2 locates the British possession within the ambit of a longer history of U.S. expansionism, thus underscoring local preoccupation with the northern republic from the late nineteenth century through World War II. It is essentially an examination of how residents in a space inescapably subjected to Americanization apprehended and argued about its various manifestations— from encounters with roaming Yankee entrepreneurs to proposals of U.S. annexation to immigration to the northeastern seaboard.

The study then moves into occupied Trinidad, analyzing the contentious local negotiations of the U.S. personnel, paychecks, and practices then ubiquitous in the colony. Tackling in turn the subjects of labor, dress, music, and sexuality, these chapters plausibly can be read as separate essays. The division, however, is largely convenient and artificial, for they cohere thematically and analytically, each chapter moving—with varying emphases—along the overlapping axes of class, gender, race, sexuality, and nation. All, furthermore, relate subaltern activity as well as the conflicting responses it provoked among the establishment, patriot leaders, and indeed, nonelites themselves.

Set in the labor arena, Chapter 3 follows the island's population as a significant proportion flocked to what was generally more rewarding work with Americans and also tracks agitated local employers as they hatched various retaliatory schemes to combat laborers' new leverage. The occupation afforded men in colonial Trinidad alternative models of dress, and the fourth chapter foregrounds the spectacular contemporary changes in male fashions. Focusing on the emergence of local dandies, it shows how the young men who "made style" by adopting and adapting (African-)American fashion such as the jitterbug shirt and especially the zoot suit raised concerns about the very fabric of the social order. In Chapter 5, the attention turns toward the calypso, where Americans' overtly avid patronage did more than raise the profile and profitability of the song. This powerful Yankee audience, it demonstrates, also compelled singers to recompose their work, in the process aggravating the already vexed nationalist effort to construct Trinidad as the "Land of the Calypso." Women involved with Yankee men take center stage in Chapter 6. Recasting these "foreign affairs" too often reduced in the literature to matters of mercenary interests and immorality, it analyzes these liaisons as aspects of women's subversive capitalizing on the altered circumstance of occupied Trinidad.

Two decades after a quick exchange of notes had sanctioned American base construction and one decade after the Yankees had for the most part gone home, the British colony of Trinidad stirred with patriotic protest to reclaim the Chaguaramas naval base site leased to the United States for seventy-nine more years. The bases-for-destroyers deal and the American occupation had become compelling history again. Yet, in this retrospective mode, the episode risked assuming a historical meaning too simple and narrow to do justice to the lived experience of many. The memory produced in the intensely nationalistic moment of the late 1950s neglected the actual struggles and nuances of the wartime years, figuring American occupiers as little more than an exploitative foreign force. Still, competing recollections of the period could be heard, and among the most notable sources was the voice of George Lamming, a young West Indian writer who had moved to Trinidad just as the occupation wound down. Lamming, the coda emphasizes, adopted a sophisticated, dynamic perspective on the significance of America in the island and the wider region that resonates with the account that follows here. For him, as for this study, Yankees occupied an unavoidably complex and potentially useful place in the Calibanic lives and dreams of people struggling in Great Britain's Caribbean colonies.

I The Turbulent Thirties
Shaking Empire, Making Nation

*At the present time there is a wave of nationalism sweeping over the
civilized world and the West Indies cannot fail to be caught in its vortex.*
—*Labor Leader*, March 30, 1929

A new turbulence is at work everywhere[,] and Caliban is wide awake.
—George Lamming

The U.S. occupation of Trinidad coincided with what George Lamming would
have characterized as the Age of Caliban. The ink had barely dried on the
bases-for-destroyers deal when a local journal announced in its debut issue
that its mission was to move the island's "toilers" to "crash empires" and to
"shape their own destiny."[1] Inaugurated in November 1940, *New Dawn* was
a document of the times, a bellwether of the nationalist current that swept
across the British West Indies and, indeed, the rest of the colonized world.

A cultural projection no less than a political project, nationalism consoli-
dated itself in Trinidad during the 1930s. In that decade there emerged a feisty
young cadre of critics who insisted that the island community possessed its
own distinguished culture and thus ought to reject a British identity. In ad-
vancing this line of advocacy, these dissidents stood on decisively new ideological ground; more than protesting Great Britain's autocratic Crown Colony
rule and pleading for self-government, they were arguing for the existence
of a collective Trinidadian self that deserved self-government. Previous gen-
erations of dissidents had merely petitioned for "home rule," all the while re-
taining allegiance to the British Empire; for them, existing West Indian problems were indictments of incompetent administrators—not of the imperial
idea itself. The Trinidadian patriots who came of age after the Great War began
bidding goodbye to all that.

This crucial transformation of the colony's political culture in the 1930s is the subject of this chapter.[2] The story offered here defies straightforward or simple telling, for Trinidad in that decade did not offer one of those famously unambiguous "revolutionary circumstances" (like Haiti and France at the turn of the eighteenth century or Cuba at the turn of the nineteenth).[3] The island presented neither dramatic images of the "world turned upside down" nor triumphant claims of a clean break with the past. It featured no sustained scenes of insurgent subalterns armed against their legitimate rulers; opposition, moreover, did not climax in the displacement of an old regime. By the decade's close, British rule was embattled but hardly defeated.

What Trinidad underwent during the thirties might be best approached as a "passive revolution" that was simultaneously fought on two fronts.[4] In one instance, patriot agitators campaigned against the precepts that sustained the belief in Great Britain's greatness, constantly throwing Anglocentrism and the necessarily interrelated notions of white supremacy and respectability on the defensive. This attack on Britishness helped fuel the period's key political conflicts, from the controversy over divorce to debates over literary clubs and race-thinking, to exchanges on the history of emancipation. In the other, and tightly twinned to all this adamant anticolonial rhetoric, was the heady affirmation of indigenous peoplehood, in other words, the construction of nationality. Ardently over the course of the decade, the island's patriotic intelligentsia proposed the existence of a distinctly Trinidadian culture, claiming that its most eloquent expression was a musical form. These years thus witnessed the rechristening of Trinidad from the "Land of the Humming Bird" to the "Land of the Calypso."

Yet, for all its force, nationalist mobilization in this British Caribbean possession (as elsewhere in the colonial world) possessed neither absolute integrity nor resoluteness. It was strategic, uneven, and at times ambiguous. Illustrative was the controversy over divorce, a crucial and, indeed, an inaugurating event for the 1930s generation of patriots. Examining the affair, this chapter not only traces the emergence of Trinidad's defining set of patriots but also underscores their willingness to calculatedly collaborate with ostensible enemies in the British colonial administration. These agitators, it will also become clear, wielded an antiracism vulnerable to claims of white cultural—rather than biological—supremacy. Moreover, as they embraced the calypso as a national art, patriots proved guilty of romanticizing blackness in a manner that flirted troublingly with metropolitan primitivism. Far from pure and constant, these were figures compromised by both the particulars of their biography and the limits of their milieu.

The political potency of patriots did not simply inhere in the subversiveness of their ideas and activities. Essays, speeches, and poems penned by men (and a few women) for the most part schooled, relatively well off, and in many cases neither Afro- nor Indo-Trinidadian tell only part—the better-archived part—of the decade's turbulence. Indeed, only when set alongside strikes, demonstrations, and so-called disturbances authored by the predominantly darker and dispossessed laboring classes does the power of patriots' rhetoric register. Arresting, articulate, and occasionally violent episodes of grassroots protests played a pivotal part in delegitimizing British claims to an exceptional competence at government. The degree to which the imaginations of these "common people" were captured by the nationalist intelligentsia remains largely unknown and cannot be assumed. What is undeniable is that minus these popular attacks on the colonial order, the railings of dissident intellectuals against the demerits of Britishness would have lost considerable resonance. On the eve of the arrival of the Americans, the new dawn for which many labored and of which many dreamed was the product not only of enlightened patriot leaders but also of embattled laboring people.

THE DIVORCE BOMBSHELL

The decade began with a portentous political explosion. In February 1931 the colonial government served public notice of its intention to legalize divorce; a "bombshell," as one newspaper warned, was about to hit Trinidad.[5] Debated for a year, the proposed bill precipitated contention that reverberated throughout the society. From Catholic churches, where priests damned the colonial state for trespassing on sacred matrimonial ground, to the Legislative Council, where one antidivorce legislator literally took the fight into his hands, to the walls of Port of Spain, where engaged intellectuals plastered their support for the government, the colony convulsed with unprecedented conflict. This affair, improbably ignored by most historians (guilty perhaps of hastily divorcing the legislative from the political and cultural), was nothing short of historic.[6] Established over the course of the controversy were the political character and commitments of a "rising intelligentsia," a dissident crew that imagined itself to be tearing down the old social order and founding the new.[7] In retrospect, the dispute over divorce marked the political baptism of the defining generation of Trinidadian nationalists.

When colonial officials in London and their allies in the local Legislative Council concluded in 1930 that a "civilized" Trinidad would require legal divorce, they expected "a storm of opposition" from the powerful local Roman Catholic church.[8] They did not, however, anticipate the kind of tempest that led the acting colonial secretary to remark that "nothing in the political history of this colony has excited more controversy than this divorce bill."[9] And, perhaps, they could not. The introduction of divorce legislation on March 6, 1931, flared into such a fiery conflict largely because of the unexpected opposition put up by the most crucial elected member in the Legislative Council: Arthur Andrew Cipriani. Cipriani, as biographer C. L. R. James observed, possessed at the time political power that was rare for being so "real."[10] Cipriani was born into Trinidad's largely Catholic "French Creole" elite in 1875. He fell into the swirl of political dissent while seeing combat in Europe during the Great War. Upon returning to Trinidad, Captain Cipriani assumed the presidency of the colony's sole effective political organization, the Trinidad Workingmen's Association (TWA). With the introduction of elections (with qualified suffrage) for the legislature soon thereafter (1925), Cipriani sailed into a seat in the council, where he burnished his reputation as the "beloved rebel," the remarkable aristocrat who stood up for the colony's "barefooted man."[11] On the eve of the introduction of divorce legislation, the Captain was the undisputed champion of the people and hero of Trinidadian politics.[12]

Once Cipriani shocked onlookers by mobilizing against the bill (he had expressed support for it five years earlier) and, moreover, by joining forces with fellow Roman Catholics, the proposed legislation assumed dramatically new political proportions and meaning. What started essentially as a sectarian struggle between elites (Catholic Creole "aristocracy" versus Protestant British officialdom) developed into a wider Kulturkampf that opened an irreparable ideological breach within Trinidad's dissident camp, alienating the Captain from the young radicals who had hitherto revered him. Unlike Cipriani, who phrased his opposition to the bill in constitutional terms, as legislative evidence of the tyranny of Crown Colony rule, the emerging generation of agitators supported divorce as conducive to the secular, emancipated antiracist community they imagined for Trinidad. They thus deserted the Captain and entered a marriage of convenience—so to speak—with official supporters of the legislation.[13] Few might have foreseen it then, but a new phase in the colony's antiestablishment politics had begun.

A new organ heralded this era, and, instructively, it functioned as the de facto base for the prodivorce activism. Debuting just as the controversy detonated in March 1931, the *Beacon* would offer the defining forum for the increasingly assured nationalist voice. Insofar as the 1930s marked the critical decade for the imagining of Trinidadianness, this journal provided the critical domain. To be sure, its core contributors have been recognized as authors of a "Trinidad Renaissance." Underappreciated, however, is the fact that they were more than mere litterateurs. The figures affiliated with this monthly were also authors of political opposition; indeed, their twinning of politics and culture, their deliberate braiding of critiques of both state and society, underscores the centrality of the *Beacon* to the island's nationalist movement.[14] The bold contemporary claim that the coterie around the journal "criticize and question everything" contained more than a kernel of truth. The divorce controversy is instructive in this regard. For these dissidents, it was an opportunity to contest at once the religious, gendered, and racial authority that underwrote the colonial status quo.[15]

The *Beacon*'s founder and most visible figure was the young Albert Gomes, a famously mercurial and larger-than-life Portuguese Creole (he weighed more than 300 pounds) who came up from the "anonymous and underprivileged" shopkeeping class.[16] Recently returned from studying philosophy at New York's City University, Gomes attracted a remarkably diverse and gifted group of writers, artists, and critics, some of whom had already been making literary names for themselves. The journal's list of contributors included pedigreed names such as Alfred Mendes (Portuguese Creole), Jean De Boissiere (French Creole), and Hugh Stollmeyer (German Creole). At the same time, individuals from humble backgrounds also counted among its inner circle. Making up in talent what they lacked in family prestige, fine, versatile minds like Ralph De Boissiere (Jean's near-white French Creole nephew), C. L. R. James, and Ralph Mentor (both of whom were black) whetted the monthly's critical appetite. James, of course, would go on to international renown, but virtually all these figures would assume prominent roles on the local artistic and political scene over the next decade and a half.

Defiantly modernist, the *Beacon* set made anticlericalism or, at the very least, a certain secular insouciance central to their oppositional politics. For them, divorce advocacy was wrapped up in this disregard for church authority. This motivation manifested quite early in a piece by Alfred Mendes, a promising young writer who had earlier offended local Catholic leadership with a short story that appeared in *Trinidad* (a short-lived journal that in a sense anticipated the *Beacon*). On the heels of the first round of legislative debates in mid-March, Mendes submitted to the *Sunday Guardian* an essay on divorce that virtually begged further accusations of blasphemy. Titled "Revolt," it drew the Divinity recoiling at the introduction of divorce in Trinidad and thinking to himself, "Good God, I have my work cut out to do." Alongside such mischief, though, Mendes issued a serious call for pragmatism over piousness. Only people ignorant of real family life, the piece asserted, could oppose the proposal to legalize divorce. The legislation, it contended, was a worldly matter for the state and not the church to arbitrate.[17] Predictably, Mendes scandalized Christians (presumably Catholics, in particular) and provoked several outraged correspondences—one of which cleverly dismissed the op-ed as "mendacity." Even the pro-government and primarily Protestant *Sunday Guardian* (hence its willingness to publish the piece) subsequently carried a conciliatory editorial admitting that Mendes's writing should have been "toned down."[18]

Contrary and confrontational, Mendes and his *Beacon* confreres raised the tenor of their protests in the following months. They roamed the streets at night and clandestinely plastered posters on private and public property across Port of Spain. Their graffiti-like messages urged official bravery in the face of Catholics' increasingly militant opposition. "Stand Firm Your Excellency!" proclaimed an exemplary poster. Vigilance notwithstanding (they always had a lookout), Mendes and his peers were found out. The governor, in fact, warned Alfred's wealthy planter father that unless he got his troublemaking son out of the colony, the youngster would land in jail. Alfred Jr. did leave the island for a few weeks; his peers, though, persisted with the campaign. Trinidad's secularist patriots refused to surrender to the biblical zeal of the antidivorce crusaders.[19]

Prodivorce mobilization also illuminated that the era's emerging generation of agitators, though not quite bona fide feminists, stood ready to question the existing gender system. Insofar as they wielded their critical pens broadly, these dissidents routinely indicted female subordination, suggesting the need to modify the now-unquestioned scholarly wisdom about the "patriarchal politics of nationalism."[20] Telling in this regard is the short story, "Divorce and Mr. Jerningham," that appeared in the journal in the midst of the controversy. Its author was Percival Maynard, a young, black, primary-school teacher and regular *Beacon* contributor. Having previously come out in favor of divorce, he now penned a cautionary tale in which a cheating white husband corrects his ways only when faced with his wife's threat of divorce. The story climaxes with a frightened Mr. Jerningham paying off his content colored mistress and then reconciling with his wife. "Divorce," the narrator happily concludes, can "work wonders." The debated legislation, Maynard's piece of fiction was meant to imply, held the promise of moralizing men's patriarchal sexuality and meliorating women's impossible predicaments.[21]

One of the clearest links between *Beacon* patriotism and feminism was embodied in Beatrice Greig, a financier and contributor to the journal who, not surprisingly, strongly favored legalized divorce. A middle-aged, Canadian-born theosophist, Greig had earned a reputation as a tireless advocate of women's rights; within radical quarters, indeed, she was lionized as Trinidad's "leading theoretical suffragette."[22] (Greig, of course, might not have been unique in her opposition to a patriarchal system; whiteness and wealth, however, gave her exceptional space to articulate dissent.) In the days leading up to the final legislative vote (December 11, 1931), Beatrice Greig was one of three elite women (Audrey Jeffers and Alice Pashley completed the trio) who had prodivorce letters published in the *Labor Leader* (a strong supporter of the bill).[23] Promoting the legislation as an unambiguous "blessing" for unhappy wives whose marriages had gone "sour," she, like many advocates of divorce across the hemisphere, believed that such women were left in a virtual state of "legalized prostitution." Too many men, charged this woman, left their wives but returned only to "sponge" after the husbands had become old and sick. In the absence of divorce, Greig concluded, matrimonial bonds operated as "shackles" and sex as "nature's trap" for women.[24]

Also bared in the fight waged by *Beacon* patriots for legal divorce was their opposition to white racists' hypocritical claims to moral purity. These radicals recognized that an unstated but crucial reason for the explosiveness of the controversy was the fear held by elites that divorce cases would publicly dramatize their scandalous private lives (marriage, after all, was for the most part a concern of the affluent). Intent on fabricating their moral supremacy, Trinidad's "aristocrats," most of whom were white, quaked at the prospect of salacious revelations of their extramarital liaisons. Aggravating their trepidation was the fact that these illicit intimacies often involved less-than-respectable nonwhite women (as was the case with the fictional Mr. Jerningham). Yet, loyal to a British Empire that prided itself as color blind, local elites had an obligation to be discreet about this supremacist worry underlying their antidivorce position.[25] They could not openly admit that the fight against divorce was part of a larger racist struggle. Their discretion, it turns out, was imperfect, and *Beacon* critics were poised to pounce.

Their opportunity came in January 1932 when a three-man Catholic delegation—Captain Cipriani, Michael Hamel-Smith, and Gaston Johnson—traveled to England to make a last-ditch effort to derail divorce legislation. The bill had already been passed (on December 14, 1931) after three days of debates that included the spectacularly infamous scene in which an irate Cipriani slapped fellow legislator Sarran Teelucksingh. A high-ranking member of the Cipriani-led TWA, Teelucksingh chose, in defiance of the Captain, to vote for divorce. This "knock out," in fact, had climaxed a politically volatile week in which Catholic antidivorcists openly raised the prospect of riotous violence, and the government, in turn, preemptively called out the constabulary.[26] Yet even as "pro-Divorcists" rejoiced that "the king [had proved] mightier than the pope," their opponents looked to London for salvation.[27] Once in the metropole, Hamel-Smith and Johnson (the former was white; the latter, colored) disclosed their investment in upholding the status of whiteness—either that or they calculated that invoking race was an effective strategy in persuading white officials in England. Whatever the case, in meetings at the Colonial Office and in interviews with the English press, both men insisted that Trinidad's whites were sure to lose "prestige" if they sought divorce.[28] Much to the delight of *Beacon* dissidents, these arguments got back to the colony. For them, it was a rare opportunity to highlight and harangue local elites' antiblack racism. They thus gleefully reprinted the Hamel-Smith interview with an English paper in which he openly claimed that divorce threatened local whites' "caste"; alongside it, they also ran an editorial condemning the white Trinidadian as a racist and calling on Cipriani to renounce Hamel-Smith.[29] In a society where white supremacy sat like the proverbially uncited elephant, this story was a sensation; it provided one of the rare occasions in which heavy sales forced the publishers of the *Beacon* back to the press.[30]

In the end, the secretary of state remained unmoved. Despite Catholics' desperate efforts, divorce became legal in Trinidad in April 1932. After more than a year of unprecedented partisan struggle, Cipriani and the Roman Catholics lost. The real importance of the upheaval, however, lay not in legislative results but in political and ideological consequences. In the course of the controversy, antiestablishment activism in Trinidad shifted. In defying and breaking with Cipriani, prodivorcists helped close an era of agitation that had begun in the aftermath of the Great War. These young rebels ushered in the modern period in local oppositional politics. It was they who would lead the charge to dismantle British hegemony and construct Trinidadian nationality over the next decade.

BANALIZING BRITISHNESS: CULTURE, IDENTITY, AND HISTORY

Although *Beacon* patriots backed Great Britain's imperial agents during the battle over divorce, they had no doubt that in the war for self-determination, Englishness stood as the ultimate enemy. Trinidadian nationality, these critics recognized, remained implausible once "English," the solid foundation upon which the more expansive and relatively flexible "British" identity was built, signified some especial competence and unique virtue.[31] Throughout the 1930s, they thus undertook to banalize Britishness, to disturb its air of invulnerability and, indeed, inevitability. Race, of course, would rest almost ineluctably at the center of this move, for Britishness stood as an identity inextricable from the culture of white supremacy. Indeed, it was dependent on a contradistinctive blackness. The challenge for Trinidad's patriots, therefore, was not only to undermine the rhetoric of empire but, more complexly, to expose its complicity with tropes of whiteness.[32]

Although a broad band of dissidents enlisted in this struggle to "consciously decolonize consciousness," to bury a "belated Victorianism," *Beacon* intellectuals stood at the vanguard.[33] Forceful, insightful, and yet entertaining, their critiques epitomized the nationalist quarrel with the prevailing Anglocentric notions of culture, identity, and history. Trinidad's dominant artistic institutions, ideas of belonging, and narratives of the past, these patriots insisted, reflected a pathological idealization of Englishness. That in the end their challenge remained partial and Anglocentrism retained much of its allure should be taken as a testament not to nationalists' ineptness but to the knottiness of their task. Its incompleteness, in fact, only helps to confirm that in the Caribbean, any kind of Fanonian forgetting of Europe was, at best, excruciatingly difficult and, at worst, excessively fanciful.[34]

The thrust and tone of the rhetorical assault on Englishness during the thirties was exemplified in the *Beacon*'s relentless lambasting of Trinidad's literary movement. Pervasive and prestigious, literary societies and debating clubs littered the island's interwar social landscape; nearly every village and neighborhood had its own. These organizations, importantly, stood within the dominant quarters as the principal institutional purveyors of culture. Arnoldian to the core, the local establishment took culture to be virtually synonymous with an idealized Victorian literariness; it was "the best of which had been thought and said in the world," expressed in English literature and essential to the civilizing of all non-European people.[35] Opposition to this Anglocentrism galvanized Trinidad's nationalists. The literary movement, they sought to persuade the public, was a symptom of the unhealthy consciousness that flourished under British rule. For them, these clubs embodied not the bastion of culture but the "Cult of Imposture."[36]

The *Beacon*'s attack on these institutions bubbled with the vituperative glee for which Albert Gomes, in particular, was notorious.[37] The organ likened "the literary club-idea" to a "popular malady" and dismissed devotees as "simple souls" who spent hours listening to "bad manuscripts by nondescripts." Yet wrapped within this smug meanness was the substantive charge that these clubs illustrated the worst ills of colonialism. They were symptomatic, according to these patriot critics, of misguided local aspirations to Englishness; everything about literary societies, from subjects of debate to votes of thanks to aesthetics, captured a people caged in the "conscious apeing [*sic*] of another man's culture." The journal scorned members as "slaves" to an "English culture and tradition" from which it was necessary to "break away as far as possible" if any genuine literature was going to emerge in the colony. "The fact remains," concluded another editorial, "that the sooner we throw off the veneer of culture that our colonization has brought us the better for our artistic aims."[38]

Patriots' use of the word "slave" in denigrating the literary movement as pathetically subjected to Englishness signals the inherence of race in their critique of established culture. Foreshadowing a diagnosis made famous by Frantz Fanon, these intellectuals argued that colonialism had created in nonwhite subjects a unique inferiority complex that manifested in a desperate desire for the colonizer's recognition—hence the cultural mimicry, the "apeing."[39] The racial subtext of this discourse surfaced plainly at times. When, for example, Hugh Stollmeyer weighed in on the debate, he submitted a piece of correspondence meant to illustrate the putative self-loathing that plagued Afro- and Indo-Trinidadian affiliates of literary societies. One of these clubs, according to Stollmeyer's letter, had withdrawn a request for his painting after learning of his intent to do a mural "depicting scenes of native peasant life." "Certain of the members of that club who were of African and Indian descent," charged this white German Creole artist, objected to "a display of 'what those common Niggers and Coolies do upon the walls of their little Palace of Art and Culture.'"[40] For Stollmeyer, this incident was evidence of a "snobbish" and "pretentious" literary movement. In the end, he took poetic pity on the predominantly nonwhite literary types, submitting to the *Beacon* a verse that described club members as "self-despising, hating, spurning . . . [and] suffering for their lost pride of race."[41]

In Stollmeyer's critique lies an important ambiguity in contemporary patriotic rhetoric. Nonblack in many cases (as was Stollmeyer), these dissidents adopted a tone that made concern difficult to distinguish from condemnation. Their conviction that Trinidad's literary movement confirmed colonialism's especial victimization of nonwhites sometimes seemed barely distinguishable from the conclusion that nonwhites were essentially pathetic "mimic men" (to use V. S. Naipaul's later coinage). The *Beacon*, illustratively, disparaged literary clubs as the "monstrous caricatures," as the "grotesque" that invariably resulted when blacks attempted to appropriate the "paraphernalia of Western civilization." These intellectuals, it turns out, were not unaware of the perilously thin line between transgressively urging nonwhites to abandon the colonialist conception of culture and prejudicially deriding them as pathological. In the middle of the campaign against literary clubs, the journal acknowledged the need to preempt charges of antiblack racism by assuring readers that its critique was not "informed by race prejudice."[42] Rather, stated an editorial, the attack was launched reluctantly and regretfully and only because no Afro-Trinidadian had stepped forward and "spared" them the "pains" of execution.[43] This, to be sure, was a misrepresentation of black people's politics; yet, it was not meant to offer an empirical point about their priorities. The statement, rather, should be viewed as evidence of these dissidents' relentless determination to voice the "race question" in a colony where racial discourse remained closely and purposefully regulated if not muted.

Indeed, the embrace of "race consciousness" was fundamental to *Beacon* nationalists' struggle against the hegemony of Britishness.[44] Like many within the oppositional ranks, they fully appreciated the concept's profoundly subversive implications in colonial Trinidad. Signifying resistance to the seductions of white supremacy by wielding the conviction that, as one local advocate put it, "[the Negro] must remain a Negro and not think that he is white irrespective of the position he reaches," race consciousness was doubly dissident in the colony (and the rest of the West Indies).[45] In the first place, it endorsed a diasporic identification, a sense of belonging to a global community of Negroes; in this sense, it explicitly indicated a detour around British imperial identity.[46] Second, merely as a form of "race talk," it undermined the loyalist discourse of color-blind British rule and, as a corollary, the official insistence on the irrelevance of racial identity across the empire. Viewed in this light, "race consciousness" recast a British Empire that promoted itself as a "racial democracy" as no more than an empire predicated on "racial hegemony."[47] It was a notion that enabled patriots to call out a defining conceit of the British Empire.

So subversive were the politics and rhetoric of race consciousness that despite denunciations by loyalist intellectuals and censorship by a paranoid colonial state, dissenting voices such as the *Beacon* (as well as contemporaries like the *Daily Mirror* and, later, the *People*) seized every opportunity to deploy them. In what was perhaps the most provocative instance, critics at the journal contrived a debate meant to expose and attack the assumptions of white supremacy that prevailed among the colony's elites. In the middle of 1931, the monthly carried an essay written by Sydney Harland, an English geneticist teaching in Trinidad at the Imperial College of Tropical Agriculture. The professor had written what was for the most part a painstakingly recondite piece defending Afro-Euro hybrids and, by extension, racial mixing; his article, however, drew notoriety for its conclusion that whites ultimately possessed a natural mental advantage over blacks. "Negroes," insisted Harland, were on average inferior to Europeans in intelligence.[48] This white supremacist cant cloaked in scientific robes was meant as a cue for *Beacon* radicals to air their dissent and to confront the racism of English minds.

Yet what resulted was more complicated. While Harland's detractors rejected his notion of a biologically determined white supremacy, they were neither unanimous nor steadfast in challenging the professor's broader claims for a white (and English) supremacy grounded in culture. Essaying to upend the racial assumptions that maintained the prestige of Britishness, Trinidad's patriots betrayed the difficulty faced by their counterparts across the colonized world. "Provincializing Europe," they would discover, was a formidable ideological task.[49]

Alfred Mendes, Ralph Mentor, and C. L. R. James capture the range of responses to professor Harland, with Mendes and Mentor occupying the two extremes and James, meanwhile, inhabiting the shifting middle ground. By far the most concessive, Mendes could not even imagine intelligence and culture outside the history of white achievement. Despite distancing himself from Harland's biological arguments, this England-educated writer found the professor faultless in a key respect. "Only a rash man," Mendes submitted, could oppose the view that "with our present day standard of judgment" whites were superior in intelligence to blacks. "We have only to remember," he concluded, "what the nordic race has contributed to science and art for the fact of his superiority to become axiomatic."[50]

In stark contrast, Mentor mounted a vigorous objection to Harland, challenging both the fact of black futility and the truth of white triumph. Citing scholars such as W. E. B. Du Bois and Leo Frobenius, this young black intellectual pointed out that the art of making porcelain was an African contribution, that geometry and architecture were developed in Egypt long before they were known in Europe, and furthermore, that Europe had received its civilization from Egypt, which had its origins in Ethiopia. Then, even more radically, Mentor singled out the dubious history of racist imperialism in Africa rather than "Nordic superiority" in accounting for Europe's cultural achievements. Presenting a thesis that has become commonplace in critiques of "Western modernity," Mentor argued that Africa and Europe had showed no great developmental disparity until the fifteenth century and that only with the "molestations" of the West—the discovery of America and the enslavement of Africans—did Africa become a "backward" continent. Europeans' so-called achievements, he effectively concluded, came at the expense of African and African American development. Although Mentor did not go so far as doing away with the vocabulary in which Eurocentrism traded ("progress" and "backwardness"), this patriot participated in a critical rewriting of Europe's route to global dominance.[51] The underlying argument in this historiographical intervention, it is worth remarking, would be famously elaborated over the next decade by one of Mentor's *Beacon* collaborators, C. L. R. James, as well as James's student Eric Williams.[52]

At the time, though, James's contribution, "Reply to Doctor Harland," epitomized the ambiguous, ambivalent outcome of the nationalist battle against Britishness. Despite eloquently repudiating Harland's racial claims and conclusions, this well-reputed teacher, debater, and lecturer vacillated with respect to the professor's precepts about intellectual competence. On one hand, James stood firm in his antiracism: "I do not make excessive claims for West Indian negroes," he wrote. "I know only too well the shortcomings of my own people. But in one thing they are not inferior. And that thing is intelligence." On the other hand, he wavered with respect to contextualizing intelligence. To Harland's assertion that the "proportion of negroes with intelligence about equal to the foreman of an English jury is about 1 in 413," he responded with a strikingly uncertain "maybe. Maybe not." In this "maybe," James allowed for the possibility that the English, presumably Harland's exemplary whites, were on average more intelligent than blacks. Yet even this hesitant, young James offered a glimpse of the radically precocious imagination for which he would become iconic. Ridiculing the professor for having cited European travelers' claims as evidence of African inferiority, he retorted, "If I turned that argument round I wonder what Dr. Harland would say." Here James was suggesting that Africans possessed an autonomous intelligence, their own norms for assessment, which enabled a subversion of Europeans' supercilious claims to superiority.[53] It was a brief foreshadowing of the mind that would conceive a history in which enslaved Africans in St. Domingue give French republicans a lesson in revolution.[54]

Indeed, the reconceptualization of history comprised a critical aspect of local patriots' counterhegemonic mission during the 1930s. Advocates of Trinidadian nationality appreciated that if they did not publicly contest Anglocentric narratives about the past, British rule acquired an insuperable moral legitimacy. It was this recognition of the need to unsettle the assumption that Englishmen deserved exclusive credit for progress in the West and, specifically, in the West Indies that underwrote the contemporary revision of historiography in the colony (and the region).

In this patriotic quest to re-narrate the history of the British Caribbean, the subject of slave liberation assumed a central place. Such a thematic focus certainly owed something to calendrical logic. The year 1933 marked 100 years since the death of William Wilberforce, the Englishman who had headed the band of British abolitionists during the early nineteenth century and who had since been remembered as the "Great Emancipator." The arrival of August 1, furthermore, indexed the passage of 100 years since slavery had been abolished in these colonies. Still, it was more than simply some automatic marking of time that impelled the nationalist intelligentsia toward the subject of slave liberation. Their insistence on retelling the story of emancipation was rooted in an acknowledgment of the usability of history, of the intimate relationship between the ordering of the past and social order in the present. With Trinidad officially commemorating the death of Wilberforce on August 1, 1933, patriot intellectuals grasped that the prevailing practice of remembering slavery's end as the story of selfless, god-fearing English "saints" had the effect of empowering Britishness. For them, therefore, it was necessary to erase an established memory that sanctified Wilberforce and his British abolitionist collaborators and, instead, to compose emancipation narratives that downplayed the altruism conventionally ascribed to British antislavery activism.

Although Eric Williams's *Capitalism and Slavery*, first published in 1944 but based on a 1938 dissertation, represents by far the most celebrated example of this nationalist re-narration of the past, it had antecedents. In August 1933 the *Beacon* published a poem by Alfred Cruickshank, a well-known and prolific Afro-Trinidadian poet committed to what he once phrased as black people's "sad cause."[55] Anticipating Williams's historiographical intervention, Cruickshank's "Reply to a Message" questioned the triumphant Anglocentrism of the hitherto accepted history of emancipation. The piece, as the title implies, was a rejoinder; it replied to another poem, "The Message," penned by resident British artist and writer Stephen Haweis and publicly delivered by Beatrice Greig during the elaborate contemporaneous Wilberforce celebrations. Aimed at local blacks, Haweis's "Message" was both a critique and a wake-up call.[56] His verse scolded Afro-Trinidadians for not helping others—black and white—who remained unfree and questioned black people's sense of gratefulness. "What are you doing with this Freedom which Wilberforce gave you?" asked the poet. He wondered, too, if they "had thought or wish to pay [whites] back" after both the rich and poor among them had given so much to the cause for black freedom "without any thought of profit or return but solely for principle." And, again, "just what have cultivated black men done in the attempt to free [slaves in Abyssinia, Liberia and Arabia]?" This white man had a simple and unambiguous message for local blacks: a hundred years after Wilberforce, they performed no deeds that demonstrated their gratitude for the selfless whites who had emancipated them.[57]

The conventional pro-British, black-faulting historical sensibility informing Haweis's poetic message was not lost on Cruickshank, and he responded with a verse of pointed historiographical radicalism. Respectfully and directly, this black poet addressed the white messenger (Beatrice Greig):

> Madam, you read a little while ago
> A Message to my people. Would you know
> Our Answer? It is this: We owe no debt!
> That which you restored is really yet
> Withheld—our freedom. Lo, upon our limbs
> Still hang the shackles, clanking, hellish hymns
> To greedy Mammon, whom our masters serve
> On bended knees. But grant that we are free,
> As in the course of time all men shall be,

What is that debt we owe to Britain? And
For what? She but made clean her sullied hand,
Returning what she had no right to take
And could not hold with conscience wide awake!

But those who taught her to redeem her soul,
Who, sacrificing, fought to make her whole—
Great Wilberforce and Clarkson and the rest,
With her, their worth we proudly do attest.

If Englishmen now starve upon the dole,
Then shame to those who yet in millions roll!
And if barbarians still for filthy gold
Sell kith and kin, what power do we hold?
Yet, if your message smite us on the hip,
We know, madam, t'was love that plied the whip
To urge us on to win a worthier place
In the long pageant of the human race.[58]

"Reply to a Message" questioned the historical material from which Britishers proudly sculpted their image of moral greatness. The verse, to begin with, doubts the very achievement of emancipation; "shackles" and "masters" tellingly persist. More overtly, it treats freedom as first negative ("yet withheld") then only suppositive ("but grant that we are free"). Where Cruickshank does accept emancipation as a historical event, furthermore, he dismisses the interpretation that extols altruistic Englishmen liberating enslaved Africans. The poem thus rejects the implication that black people ought to be grateful to English justice for their freedom. Though acknowledging the virtues of English "saints" like Wilberforce and Clarkson ("their worth we proudly do attest"), Cruickshank refutes the idea that emancipation marked a gesture of English generosity. To the mind of this black Trinidadian, in supporting the cause of abolition, the English had merely redeemed themselves for having been greedy enslavers ("returning what she had no right to take").

The subversion signaled in this piece is difficult to overstate. With colonizers routinely legitimizing their rule by invoking histories of their selfless sacrifice on behalf of the ruled, notions of indebtedness and gratitude play a critical role in cementing colonial bonds. In such circumstances, any rhetoric that doubts the historical beneficence of colonizers possesses profound oppositional implications. It effectively questions the ethical rationale for colonial rule; in other words, it erases the debt owed by the colonized.[59] "Reply to a Message" was a verse of this liquidating kind. Boldly declaring that enslaved blacks had received nothing from Great Britain for which they should be grateful, Cruickshank authored a critical, if inchoate, counternarrative of British West Indian history.[60]

PLACING "THE PEOPLE": PROTEST AND IMPERIAL REFORM

Although a narrow and relatively privileged intelligentsia (largely identified with the *Beacon*) articulated critiques of a hegemonic Britishness and its cognate colonial ideologies, "ordinary" people occupied an integral place in the oppositional milieu of the 1930s. Their contribution, it should be stressed, did not necessarily derive from some putative popular nationalism; it stemmed, rather, from the effect of their mobilization during that famously depressed decade. Organizing themselves, seizing public space, and venting outrage at the period's extreme deprivation and blatant racism, Trinidad's nonwhite laboring classes (along with their counterparts throughout the British Empire) helped disrupt Great Britain's projection of imperial adeptness. These "poor people's movements" performed invaluable political labor.[61] They lent indispensable legitimacy to the discrediting of British rule, for the intelligentsia's counterdiscourse on Britishness, no matter how persuasive and pugnacious, drew decisive potency from the clamor of the colony's unhappy unlettered colonial subjects. Minus grassroots dissent, nationalist leaders could be desultorily dismissed by colonial officials as aberrant agitators. In fact, the imperial mind, in its twisted, self-serving logic, could conceive of the absence of popular demonstration as evidence of Trinidadians' political loyalty. In the end, the activity of the island's "barefooted" majority—strikes, "hunger marches," pro-Ethiopia protests, and "riots"—would play a critical part in compelling British rulers to take the epochal step of conceding legitimacy to nationalism.

The poor in Depression-era Trinidad (as in England, the United States and nearby Caribbean islands) waged endless war against joblessness and starvation. The first major eddy of what turned out to be a torrent of popular protest appeared in the middle of 1934. A full year before South African academic William Miller Macmillan traveled to the region and penned his famously ominous critique of the empire, Indo-Trinidadian workers from the island's sugar-producing central region issued their own "warning from the West Indies."[62] Provoked by increasing layoffs and underemployment, more exacting "task work," prolonged drought, and callous employers, laborers in the parishes of Caroni and St. George marched, struck, and ultimately resorted to violence to demand redress.

The disturbances came to wide public attention on July 20, after two weeks during which laborers had confronted district authorities. That day, more than 650 workers left for Port of Spain to bring attention to their plight. Hundreds more set out for the nearby town of Chaguanas, where they sought an audience with the warden. Still others walked to the home of the county's elected legislative member Sarran Teelucksingh. The marchers bound for Port of Spain were intercepted by the constabulary before they reached the city proper, and only a few were allowed to meet with the colonial secretary. But while these workers got no more than a sympathetic official ear, the Chaguanas contingent, who traveled unchecked, received money from the warden, a makeshift measure that troubled local elites. Promises, sympathy, and monetary relief, however, did not assuage sugar workers. During the following week, they turned to more dramatic tactics, stopping work, arming themselves with agricultural tools (such as hoes and shovels), and attacking estate personnel and property. Workers at one Caroni estate allegedly injured six policemen and two overseers, cut telephone wires, broke office windows, and even attempted to set the compound afire.[63]

Such violent labor protest, it is important to appreciate, quickly registered in the political realm. With the *Port of Spain Gazette* representing the conflict as "serious trouble," the governor promptly appointed a commission to investigate conditions in the island's sugar industry. As an immediate measure, Captain Cipriani, president of the reorganized TWA, which was renamed the Trinidad Labor Party, traveled to central Trinidad and pleaded with workers to peacefully return to work and join his constitutional agitation.[64] Yet during the next year, the island's "barefooted" folks defied such demands and continued to trouble the colonial establishment by remaining—in Arthur Lewis's apt phrase—"on the march."[65] The familiar spectacle of streets overflowing with discontented working people offered glaring demonstrations of the failure of Trinidad's ruling class to govern effectively. It provided damning evidence of their incapacity to provide what one protester profoundly labeled an "existence."[66]

The eagerness of people at the grass roots to dramatize their suffering had appeared in Port of Spain as early as 1933, when radicals affiliated with Cipriani's TWA—but soon to splinter off and form the Marxist Negro Welfare Social and Cultural Association (NWSCA)—led a "march of the unemployed" through the city. Predominantly urban, these demonstrators responded to a predicament not significantly unlike that endured by Indo-Trinidadian agricultural laborers. They had to contend with a decline in the quantity and quality of available work and in wages offered. For poor city folk, moreover, the situation was aggravated by the closure of customary emigration outlets and, indeed, the return of some emigrant workers no longer welcome abroad. The "hunger march fever" peaked in the middle of 1935, as during the first two days of August more than 600 men, women, and children besieged the governor's residence demanding relief. Led by the Unemployed Central Action Committee (UCAC), the marchers had met earlier and decided to petition the mayor concerning the "rotten and deplorable conditions into which the unemployed and their families are forced." Unable to see the mayor or the governor on August 1, a select deputation of UCAC leaders finally secured an "interview" with His Excellency Claude Hollis the following day. That morning they presented Governor Hollis him with a petition demanding, among other things, "enterprises and schemes" to create jobs; "food relief depots," free milk, and meals for the children of the unemployed; the payment of five shillings per day for each unemployed family; the opening of the Princes Building for the "shelterless"; and the "exemption" of all unemployed workers from payment of all taxes and rent.[67]

While these welfarist demands convey the economic hardships the colony's laborers endured during the Depression, the depiction of marchers' conduct in the establishment press underlines the emerging sense of political crisis generated by workers' self-mobilization. The *Trinidad Guardian* and the *Port of Spain Gazette* portrayed the demonstrations as a popular insurgency and provided descriptions of protesters' placards that signaled their determination to "live free or die" and warned that "every action has a reaction."[68] Indeed, nothing better captured the aura of danger and militancy attributed to the march than the *Trinidad Guardian*'s headline the day following the protesters' failed effort to see the governor: "Unemployment Army Invades Governor's House," it blared on August 2. Readers troubled by such a headline would have found little solace the next day, as both newspapers featured bold announcements of "clashes" between marchers and the law. According to their reports, after UCAC leaders met with an unresponsive governor and decided to take the protest to Woodford Square, some demonstrators had become "disorderly" and had stolen from roadside vendors, which invited police intervention. Officers subsequently charged a couple of the leaders with "behaving in a manner calculated to endanger public peace."[69] At the middle of the decade, British rule in Trinidad appeared to be unraveling.

Toward the end of 1935, the mood of popular belligerence moved to another front, as the race question became a demonstrably incendiary source of "ordinary" people's opposition to the British government. This episode of racialized discontent had roots in geographically remote events. In early October, after nearly a year of anticipation and negotiation, fascist Italian forces finally invaded Ethiopia. Like the rest of the world, colonial Trinidad followed Mussolini's actions and Europe's reactions with a strong sense of the portent of the invasion for global peace and security. Moreover, as in communities throughout black world, from Kingston to Paris to the Gold Coast, many Afro-Trinidadians took particular offense at the racist logic guiding the Italians' attack. What they called "Abyssinia," after all, boasted an exceptional nineteenth-century history of triumphant resistance to European rule and thus held a proud, centripetal place in their construction of an oppositional diasporic blackness. For the colony's "race-conscious," Mussolini's move to "civilize" Ethiopia was a signal piece of white supremacist atrocity. Little wonder that people responded with such impassioned outrage, sympathy, and commitment. It was a reaction that would contribute not only to the (re)construction of a militant global blackness but, more important here, to the deconstruction of Great Britain's claim to possessing a superior civilization.[70]

"The progress of the Italo-Ethiopian war," a local journal noted in August 1935, "is the all-absorbing topic of the hour."[71] Indeed, it was the intensity and ubiquity of interest in the Ethiopian conflict that brought British action under such broad and scrupulous scrutiny in Trinidad. From raising funds for Ethiopians to growing beards in the style of Haile Selassie, people in the colony presented a surfeit of evidence that the war in Ethiopia was not nearly as distant as depicted in physical cartography.[72] Once invasion seemed inevitable, a large cross-section of the community mobilized to assist the Ethiopians and protest the actions of the Italians. Alongside the existing Marxist NWSCA sprang the Afro–West Indian League and the Committee of Friends for Ethiopia (CFE). Led by Hugh Mentor (Ralph's brother), the league was comprised mostly of middle-class blacks and coloreds. The CFE, meanwhile, boasted some of the society's most respected whites and blacks (including Captain

Cipriani, Beatrice Greig, and Canon Max Farquhar.[73] Trinidad's prestigious secondary schools, too, were drawn into the swirl of political activity during these heady days. Young Afro-Trinidadians at Port of Spain's Queens Royal College, including future *New Dawn* founder Lloyd Braithwaite, formed a discussion group titled the Pan African Order of Shebisti.[74] Indo-Trinidadians also joined in the mobilization, with Adrian Cola Rienzi, a young radical lawyer and former TWA member recently returned from London, seizing the crisis to call for a "new movement for Afro-Indian unity" in the colony.[75]

Solidarity meetings proved insufficient for some, and there were locals who clamored for a chance to do battle on behalf of Ethiopians. Indeed, so eager were they for military action that Captain Cipriani felt compelled to caution one audience that fighting on behalf of Ethiopia was "outside the question." These "enterprising" Trinidadians, he advised, should choose a "practical form" of sympathy by making monetary contributions to his committee's Ambulance Fund.[76] Calypsonians and other literary types, hoping that the proverbial pen might prove as effective as the sword, waged their own campaign against the Italians and, in fact, against institutions and people associated with Italy. Songs like "The Gold," "Abyssinian Lament," and "Mussolini the Bully" registered outrage against the invasion. Several pro-Ethiopian and pro-black essays and poems appeared in the press, especially in the "race-conscious" *People* (which had replaced the *Labor Leader* as the voice of proletarian advocacy). Alfred Cruickshank enhanced his controversial image with the publication in the *Sunday Guardian* of his poem that scolded the Roman Catholic church.[77] Local stevedores also showed their solidarity with Ethiopians, refusing to unload Italian ships at the Port of Spain harbor.[78] Protest fever spread as well to the Public Works Department, where indignant employees forced the authorities to rescind their appointment of an Italian-born man named Mr. Giusto.[79] Even Cipriani, whose foreparents came from Corsica, came under suspicion and would have to publicly dissociate himself from Italy's actions. Although people "truthfully said that Cipriani has a lot of Italian blood," he explained at a CFE meeting that it was immaterial; according to him, he was "responsible" only for himself and not for his "relations."[80]

But no less important than the public projection of a radicalized blackness and the denunciation of things Italian, the Ethiopian crisis conditioned a deep and popular discrediting of the British Empire. In the minds of many protesters, Mussolini's mission was nothing less than a criminally bold-faced race war, and since Great Britain (the most powerful League of Nations member) did nothing to reverse the violation of Ethiopian sovereignty and, worse, adopted a policy of appeasement toward Italian aggressors, they took their British rulers to be racist accomplices. From grassroots radicals to regular observers, people in Trinidad drew from the Italo-Ethiopian crisis the critical lesson that the British Empire disregarded the very justice and fair play it trumpeted as its distinguishing ethic. Certainly, there were local loyalists who tried to shield their rulers against this charge by narrating the conflict and its diplomacy in nonracial terms. For the "race conscious," however, the invasion was at its core a case of white supremacist collusion. It was, as black activist Elma Francois declared, a concern of "Negroes throughout the world."[81]

Francois and other grassroots radicals, in fact, stridently claimed that the invasion constituted an act of racist imperialism that knew no national boundaries. During one of the "Hands Off Abyssinia" meetings held by the NWSCA, this Saint Vincent–born founding member presented to the League of Nations a resolution denouncing not just the Italians but, much more widely, "the policy of world imperialism." Revealingly, the diminutive but big-voiced woman had prefaced the resolution by reminding listeners that "in the last War we fought for the white race"; this time, she vowed, "we will fight for ourselves."[82] This was a doubly subversive performance. Not only did Francois address the League of Nations rather than the British secretary of state and refuse to except Great Britain from condemnation; she also slyly insinuated British betrayal. Invoking the Great War, Francois recalled an episode in which blacks risked their lives for the empire, indirectly accusing Great Britain of failing to reciprocate blacks' sacrifice.

Such racially charged rhetoric, not surprisingly, offended Trinidad's loyal subjects. Thus although the West Indian Youth Welfare League shared the platform with the NWSCA at the August meeting, it quickly and publicly divorced itself from the radical organization's sentiments. Godfrey Phillip, the league's secretary, condemned Francois's resolution as "rash and inconsiderate." The speech, according to Phillip, went against "the spirit of international peace which England endeavors to maintain and which emperor Selassie himself desires."[83] Like-minded apologies for Great Britain came from empire faithfuls, including Captain Cipriani and his supporters. Though these types —dismissed by patriot Ralph Mentor as "medieval minded demagogues"— sympathized with Ethiopians, they sought to salvage Great Britain's imperial reputation by denying the relevance of race in the conflict. For example, Randolph Mitchell, the president of the St. James branch of Cipriani's Trinidad

Labor Party, told his audience that they were witnessing not a racial war but an "unjust war."[84] A similar argument came from members of the CFE.[85] Cipriani himself contended that rather than feelings of racial superiority, it was the desire of strong nations to exploit the weak that generated the Ethiopian crisis. "At times like this," he told listeners, "the sympathy and feeling seem to get the better of men, and this occasion is no exception to the rule, and some of our enterprising would-be politicians seem to try to make out of this issue a question of color or creed. Let us look things squarely in the face: what is the question of color that arises when you find the powerful European nations, England and France, on the side of the Ethiopians?"[86] Mussolini, in the Captain's view, was simply a bully, and once Cipriani had rendered race insignificant, he could insist that in this conflict the British Empire once again stood on the side of justice.

But support for Ethiopia, even if it could only be expressed within the realm of "infrapolitics," continued to erode British prestige.[87] In early January 1936 the *Trinidad Guardian* reported as a comic curiosity a case involving a San Fernando haberdashery store clerk named Frederick William. Seeing some dogs on the street, William allegedly issued a loud declaration: "When I talk," he shouted, "no dog bark. I am an Abyssinian." The dog, it turns out, was not the only one to "take a hint"—to quote the title of the newspaper story—from this brash affirmation of Ethiopian omnipotence; so did a nearby police officer, who subsequently brought William before the court. Once there, however, the defendant told a revealingly different story: all he had said, William claimed, was that "the only faithful nation in the world today was Great Britain."[88] To embrace an Ethiopian identity, this fragmentary yet fascinating piece of evidence betrays, was to signify doubts about Britain's imperial competence. In wittingly emending himself from an amazingly powerful Abyssinian to an unswervingly loyal Britisher, Frederick William affirmed full awareness that in contemporary Trinidad, Ethiopianness operated as a challenge to Britishness.

Local interest in Ethiopia's fate persisted long after hostilities had ceased and Selassie had exiled himself in England (1936), but in the next year the popular challenge to Great Britain's imperial prestige shifted to new terrain and assumed graver, more spectacular proportions. For a week in late June 1937, workers in several industries across Trinidad engaged the police in bloody skirmishes that ultimately claimed fifteen lives and resulted in injuries for scores more. These "disturbances," as tactful British officials labeled the clashes, have been the subject of extensive and insightful historical scholar-

ship; they thus matter here only insofar as they crested a wave of popular protests that questioned the empire's legitimacy and thus strengthened the credi-
bility of patriots' challenge to colonial authority. Whatever the debates about
its origins or objectives, the main outcome of the episode remains indisputable: the Butler riots (as they are memorialized in Trinidad) contributed to a
crisis that provoked a sea change in British imperial governance.[89]

The roots of the confrontation lie most immediately in a disrupted oil workers' sit-in on June 18 that spilled into a protest meeting the following day
in the southwest "oil town" of Fyzabad. At this meeting the police moved
in to arrest the eponymous Turbal Uriah "Buzz" Butler, a Grenadian-born
preacher and agitator and, above all, the undisputed champion of Trinidad's
oil workers. The ensuing events have since become the stuff of history and
legend. What does seem certain is that in attempting to get to Butler, the law-
men were met by defiant followers, their target slipped away, and by night-
fall an exchange of gunfire between police and civilians had left casualties on
both sides. Most notoriously, a detective named Charlie King had been chased
and, once caught, burnt to ashes. Over the next week the rebellion spread
throughout the island "like a fire along a tinder track"; from Point Fortin in
the south to Rio Claro in the east to Port of Spain in the north, Trinidad flamed
with conflict.[90] Only with the arrival of British warships days later did the violence abate.

This deadly bout of disorder was historic, as it helped to impel imperialists
to take the crucial step of validating the claims of local nationalists. Part of a
pattern of unrest resonant across the empire (from the Caribbean to Africa),
the eruption of violent, popular opposition in Trinidad could not be credibly
dismissed by colonial officials as the handiwork of hooligans and fanatics.
These events thus had a chastening effect on British imperial architects, who
now felt compelled to reappraise the very structure of their edifice. Of course,
they did not permit the possibility that, at base, the problem was empire itself.
Officials nevertheless did accept the need for "reforming imperialism" and, in
this undertaking, made the decisive move of conceding a modicum of political
space to local agitators.[91] These dissident leaders, colonial agents calculated,
had become necessary in the efforts to efficiently discipline rebellion-prone
workers. The official hope, in Fred Cooper's elegant formulation, was to convert these "apostles of disorder" into "Men of Moderation and Modernity."[92]

In the aftermath of June 1937, then, the idea of nationalism circulated
within the colony (and region) with newly acquired force and legitimacy. Po-

litical and labor organizers (often one and the same at that moment) felt licensed to fire off fundamental and uncompromising criticisms at their rulers. Whereas British imperialists advertised themselves as exceptional tutors, patriots like Albert Gomes and A. C. Rienzi, who, as Butler's legal adviser, had quickly emerged as Trinidad's most powerful trade union organizer and politician, dismissed their rulers as "bad schoolmasters." Bursting with confidence, local activists demanded that the British Empire face up to "the fact of nationalism."[93]

CALYPSO, THE TRINIDADIAN TRADITION

Although this moment of imperial vulnerability raised patriots' hopes with regard to politics, it also provoked among them a heightened concern about culture. With self-government acquiring a certain imminence toward the end of the 1930s, many dissidents began to worry that the impending political dispensation offered no guarantee of a society freed from its "fetish" for Anglocentric notions of "respectability," no assurance, in other words, of a truly postcolonial Trinidad.[94] This anxiety compelled increasingly impassioned rhetoric around creative practices and forms that supposedly expressed a Trinidadianness that was autonomous from and, indeed, opposed to Britishness.

This notion of Trinidadianness, of course, was not simply awaiting discovery; it had to be invented. And indeed it was. Following a pattern found in nationalist movements across the globe, patriotic critics and artists turned to grassroots sectors long denied the capacity for artistry, reconceived the meaning and value of particular elements of these subalterns' expressive repertoire, and re-presented them as realizations of a unique, indigenous culture. Such an ideological project, though, was not without perils. Undertaken by a largely privileged and often nonblack class of "cosmopolitan patriots" and involving fulsome appropriation of forms associated with the poor, especially the African-descended element, the invention of Trinidadian culture proceeded within a climate with a worrisome affinity to primitivism. More than just vindicate the creative facilities of the colony's dismissed darker set (an imperative for most Caribbean nation-building), the island's nationalist intellectuals recast these subalterns' artistic imagination as radically and irremediably outside and against the Western world. True Trinidadian culture, as a result, would appear to be intrinsically "traditional." In this, needless to say, patriots were committing a severe simplification of reality; it was one with important implications for an occupied Trinidad in which Americans embodied a captivating market for the island's creative workers.[95]

This nationalist quest for "culture" as well as its questionable excesses made an impression on journalist Jean De Boissiere and provoked his puckish imagination. Well placed to comment on the patriots' ideological project, De Boissiere had begun his career in journalism at the *Beacon* (defunct by 1933) and remained a fixture on the local intellectual circuit throughout the 1930s. Around the time war broke out, in fact, he founded his own "magazine of Creole humor," *Picong*, and therein appeared his characteristically satirical piece, "Culture: With Me Rum in Me Head."[96] Best read as a kind of modest proposal, it began by announcing that in Trinidad "everybody was looking for native culture." De Boissiere, it turns out, had found the answer, and it rested in "the making of rum drinking from a degrading habit into a culture." Such a transformation, he declared, offered Trinidadians their "best chance to shine forth and let the rest of the world follow our culture instead of us pretending to other peoples' cultures as if they were our own."[97] The rest of the essay elaborated humorously on "the tenets" of proper rum drinking. "Culture" is a richly indexical text. It underlined the contemporary preoccupation with identifying a distinct Trinidadianness and illuminated that patriots met the challenge of affirming cultural originality by revalorizing disparaged practices. This, moreover, might not be all. The article's Swiftian style might have been meant as a register of doubt. In recommending rum drinking as Trinidadian culture, De Boissiere, it is likely, was slyly insisting that there was something unsober, something giddy about patriots' rush to elevate conventionally "degraded" forms as national art. The invention of an indigenous culture, it seems, struck him as a dangerously heady affair.

Although in the real world the search for Trinidadian culture led patriots not to rum but to the calypso, their approach to the song would have vindicated De Boissiere's mocking skepticism. As these intellectuals embraced and redefined the musical form as "culture," they were indeed guilty of unreasonable, unbalanced projection. As if intoxicated by the calypso, nationalists were unable to situate the expression (and thus, more broadly, Trinidadian culture) within the world of modern art, entertainment, and commerce where it belonged; instead, they re-presented the calypso as part of an exotic, timeless pit of "traditionalism."

Patriots' determination to nationalize the calypso demanded an act of radical rehabilitation. For three decades, the song circulated in the public sphere mostly as part of attempts by the establishment to discipline, co-opt, or exploit grassroots leisure and entertainment. Emerging in the late nineteenth century within a predominantly black yet inescapably cosmopolitan, lower-class urban milieu, the calypso initially served as a celebration of and inspiration for stick fighters and their carnival bands. During the interwar period, as the calypso (along with the annual pre-Lenten carnival) became one of the most recognizable features of the colony's festive scene, it underwent profound change. Patois-singing *chanterelles* tied to a *gayelle* gave way to individual performers who composed in English and performed in tents. Like other hemispheric "sounds" with humble beginnings, moreover, the calypso acquired transnational appeal.[98] By the early thirties singers like Atilla, Tiger, Lord Beginner, and Radio were recording and performing for audiences in large U.S. cities such as New York and Los Angeles. Yet conventional wisdom continued to dismiss the song as a moral danger or, at best, an entertaining ditty. It certainly did receive a dash of legitimacy around this time, as tourist-promoting profit seekers began advertising the genre as delightful and charming. These boosters were convinced that once the calypso was attractively packaged, foreign guests would take delight in the form's "peculiar, local rhythm."[99] This new tropicalized marketing notwithstanding, the calypso remained disqualified from the rarefied arena of culture.

Such a lowbrow estimation of the calypso came under deliberate assault by the decade's end, as the patriot intelligentsia determinedly undertook to define Trinidadianness. Whether they wrote, danced, or painted, artists and critics advanced a view of the genre as the most articulate expression of routinely denied indigenous values and virtuosity. Through the ideological work of these promoters, the calypso quickly acquired a reputation as "the voice of the people," to cite the title of a 1937 essay by a sixteen-year-old politically committed student named Lloyd Braithwaite.[100] By 1938 the expression was commonly considered, as one skeptical observer put it, the "reservoir" of the island's culture.[101] Increasingly typical were remarks like that of De Wilton Rogers, the young black teacher and playwright who, early in that year, urged research on the musical form, since it was part of the "germ" of the island's autonomous artistic creativity.[102] A researcher soon appeared in the person of C. L. Madoo, an Indo-Trinidadian teacher and literary critic whose June 1938 *Sunday Guardian* essay inaugurated serious discourse on the calypso. Attesting to the new political stakes in discussions of the musical form, Madoo concurred that it expressed the colony's "individuality" and, further, disputed the argument that the song's origins traced back to French *trouveres*. Even though it represented for the most part a fusion of the colony's Spanish and black influences, the music, according to him, was not simply derivative (of European culture).[103] For this local intellectual, the calypso was a Trinidadian original.

Visual artists, too, enlisted in the quickly overwhelming campaign to nationalize the calypso. Illustratively, about a year after Madoo's essay, a piece titled *Roas' Salfish* appeared at what hitherto was the island's biggest art exhibition. Drawn by a talented teenaged artist named Carlisle Chang, it paid eponymous tribute to one of the biggest calypso hits of the recently concluded carnival 1939 season and portrayed carnival revelers dancing and singing in the streets during the festival. Hanging on the walls of Port of Spain's Royal Victoria Institute, the work quietly had the effect of declaring the calypso (and its twin, carnival) at home in a hallowed space reserved for art. With *Roas' Salfish*, Chang invested the calypso and its subaltern celebrants with the currency and prestige associative with culture. Raising the Rabelaisian low to the very apex of the Arnoldian high, he was helping to realize the quintessential act of Trinidadian nationalism.

Not to be viewed in isolation, Chang's achievement had direct antecedents. Years before the youngster began exhibiting, Hugh Stollmeyer, most prominently, had already found a muse in the calypso and produced several pieces inspired by well-known songs like "Sly Mongoose" and "Ole Lady Tay Lay Lay." Chang acknowledged his indebtedness to the "electric" visual art scene of the early thirties, a scene energized by Stollmeyer and other local artists such as Amy Leong Pang, Ivy Achoy, and Sybill Atteck, who formed the Society of Trinidad Independents around 1930.[104] Shockingly bohemian (flouting, among other norms, the society's racist and heterosexist norms), the Independents were also decidedly nationalist. The group championed an aesthetic that was "an expression of [their local] environment," and tellingly, its inaugural exhibition in January 1933 inspired one reviewer to remark that the event evinced the emergence of an "amorphous consciousness of the island."[105] This show, in fact, marked a kind of coming-out party for Stollmeyer, the most prolific and outstanding of the Independents. Contributing pieces such as "Hosein," a tribute to local Muslims' festive practices, and "Carib Woman," which paid homage to the island's dwindling indigenous population, he announced that Trinidad's visual artists, too, had made the historic nationalist break with established representational conventions. Like their Caribbean and

Latin American counterparts, they now committed themselves to portraying and celebrating the virtues of the colony's "common people" rather than the prestigious and powerful. Art, the Independents guaranteed, would be at the foreground of representations of Trinidadian nationality.[106]

What was true for the field of visual expressivity was also true for the arena of dance. Whereas at the start of the thirties, no one took seriously the notion of Trinidadian dance, by the turn of the decade it had become a noticeably current element of public discourse on the society's cultural originality. Moreover, as patriotic dancers sought to project Trinidadianness, they too would move to the music of the calypso. Among the pioneers in this sphere of nation-making was Sylvia Chen, daughter of the famous Trinidad-born fighter for Chinese nationalism, Eugene Chen. Although ignored by posterity, Sylvia Chen was quickly recognized by contemporaries as a contributor to the local nation-building cause. Albert Gomes might have clashed with her on broader questions about art and politics, but this patriot did not hesitate to acknowledge that Chen had "started something and perhaps has stimulated us to a greater interest in ourselves."[107]

Born in Trinidad in 1909, Sylvia Chen left the island as a youngster and subsequently lived in England, Russia, and the United States. In London with her stage-loving Creole mother (Agatha Ganteaume), Sylvia developed a passion for dance. In Moscow with her father in the 1920s, she received further dance training (which included a stint at the Bolshoi) as well as discovering the notion of proletarian art. When she and her American husband (filmmaker Jay Leyda) moved to New York City in the 1930s, Chen joined the socialist New Dance Theater and gained experience in the production of politically conscious pieces. By the time racist U.S. immigration laws forced the dancer back to the land of her birth at the end of 1940, she was perfectly prepared to invigorate what might be phrased the choreography of Trinidadian culture, a project only just undertaken by local talents such as Beryl McBurnie and Boscoe Holder.

The first public expression of Chen's nationalist sentiments appeared not on the stage but in the pages of the *Trinidad Guardian*, where she published an essay urging people in the colony to "develop something we can call our own." Despite her "mixedness" (she was Chinese and "colored") and her admission that "the island consciousness" of Trinidad was "a very complicated business because [its] roots involve so many different elements," Chen, like most contemporary patriots, nevertheless singled out the "African" as the most crucial contribution. Soon practicing what she preached, the dancer staged at Port of Spain's Prince's Building in April 1941 a recital aimed at challenging what she considered the unfortunate social convention of keeping the African influences "hidden" and "denied." The production, according to Chen, was meant as a work that "really showed Trinidad."[108]

The concert's nationalist entanglements were inescapable. Chen, to begin with, titled the concert *J'ouvert*, a local phrase for the opening phase of the colony's annual carnival. Her choreography, furthermore, drew from a study of various grassroots styles. An attendee at the 1941 editions of both "Hosay" and carnival festivals in the island, Chen, in her words, strove to "accumulate dance facets of Trinidad's multi-faceted life" and to discover "the primitive sources" of local dance. This ethnographic sensibility manifested in a show that featured New World African dances like Bellaire and Shango. Instructively, too, Chen also included a piece called "Calypso," in which her movements were accompanied by the miming of popular singer Tiger (Neville Marcano). The dancer's choice of singer was in keeping with the concert's political goals: Tiger was well known for his antiestablishment material, and that night he stayed within character, offering a composition that voiced dissatisfaction with Trinidad's colonial administration as well as concern about the racial implications of the impending American occupation.[109] In putting on *J'ouvert*, Chen invited people in the colony to review and revalue local vernacular expressivity. Re-presenting movements and sounds associated with nonwhite, lower-class bodies in a highbrow space, she helped (re)deem as culture practices respectable people habitually dismissed. In enlisting the calypso, moreover, her performance (like Chang's *Roas' Salfish*) contributed to the gathering effort to forge this musical form into the foundation of Trinidadianness.

Chen's approach to staging Trinidadian identity helps to illustrate the specific manner in which patriots went about imagining nationality, betraying, in particular, the broader tendency to essentialize authentic indigenous culture as inveterately antimodern, as critically traditional. When the dancer expressed interest in "primitive sources," she echoed other patriots, who almost invariably cast Trinidadianness in primordial terms. For these intellectuals, real local culture was raw, crude, and uncorrupted by modernity. Indeed, they took the calypso's putative remoteness from "civilization" as indispensable to its capacity for astute political critique. Without Western reason but with a rude, African-derived wisdom, the song, boasted nationalist champions, spoke sly and often prurient truth to power. In their ears, it offered a kind of "hidden transcript" of folk-authored resistance.[110]

Little wonder, then, that when establishment types moved to "improve" the calypso in 1939, Albert Gomes promptly warned them away. Such an intrusion, worried Gomes, would cow calypsonians away from the low terrain of the vulgar and scandalous, their true métier, and into the lofty realm of "mind" and "urbanity."[111] In arguing against improvement, he instructively cited Growler's "Roas' Salfish"; this song exemplified the kind of artistry that, for Gomes, deserved protection from the sanitizing hands of local reformers.

> Doris, darlin' I'm so blue
> Seem as what the neighbor told me is true (repeat)
> Just give me the roas' sal'fish not the green t'ing inside the dish
> And girl I must say to you (?)
> Lord I don't want no more callaloo
> That kind of love wouldn't do for me
> To tie me down in necromancy
> I losing me sight, I losing me hair
> You getting me deaf, I can't even hear[112]

Steeped in the folksy appetite for food and sex, "Roas' Salfish" was composed of the kind of clever, earthy prurience Gomes and his intellectual peers idealized as the essence of the song. In one sense, Growler sang of a domestic affair in which the narrator suspects his woman (Doris) of culinary conjuring (she had put the mysteriously frightening "green t'ing" in his food). In another, more vulgar register, the bard was simply beseeching sex from his woman ("salfish" here has the same connotation of present-day "pussy"). Although Gomes was not explicit, it is almost certain that his appreciation for the song stemmed from Growler's skillful use of double entendre, his ability to exploit the theme of sex. Cunningly, this calypsonian flaunted a seamy subject in the faces of censors and reformers.

Patriots' investment in an exotic, primitivist interpretation of the calypso and of black expressivity, more broadly, appeared most explicitly and portentously perhaps in a Hugh Stollmeyer essay. Titled "Calypso and Politics" and published in 1939 in the briefly revived *Beacon*, this piece, too, is traceable to "Roas' Salfish"; it was Stollmeyer's direct response to a daring deconstruction of Growler's calypso authored by a Lewis O'Sullivan. O'Sullivan's *Sunday Guardian* article analyzed the composition in relationship to modernism, suggesting that the lyrics (in particular, "the green t'ing inside the dish") expressed a return to the mysterious, to the "superstition" and "awe" that had disappeared in a modern scientific age of "cold facts."[113] From New York City, where Stollmeyer had recently relocated, he objected to O'Sullivan's critique as ill conceived. The calypso, wrote this patriot in exile, was fundamentally African and simple; its appreciation required invocations of neither modernity nor Monet (to whom O'Sullivan had linked Growler). Not unlike Gomes, Stollmeyer proposed that the song's appeal lay largely in its "lusty and lewd interpretation of sex and uncivil life of the common people." Echoing Chen, he considered the calypso to be at its best when possessing a "primitive vitality"; superior songs, according to this painter, contained a "strange charm" and offered an "aesthetic thrill" found in African ceremonial masks.[114] Stollmeyer thus concluded on a note of worry. The expression, he felt, had arrived at "a dangerous age"; singers had become enthralled to "those in authority" and thus imperiled the authenticity of the form. Too enmeshed in the modern world, they had strayed from "traditions." For him, as for many of his patriot peers, the calypso, and thus authentic Trinidadianness, was imagined to contain at its core an antidote to modernity. Nationality was rooted in outright resistance to contemporary Western ways.[115]

CONCLUSION

The United States occupied a British colony in which nationalist mobilization and the popular protest that helped make it imaginable had swept and shaken the social order, unsettling a broad set of established conventions. Britishness and its defining whiteness had become increasingly banal; culture had gone from something embodied in British colonial rulers into something that "natives," especially the grassroots blacks, also possessed. Local society in 1940 was caught between colonial subjecthood and claims to independent nationhood. Caliban had awakened. It was during this tense uncertain new dawn that the Yankees came to Trinidad.

2 The American Preoccupation
Assessing the United States before the War

We cannot help asking ourselves if the West Indies were americanized if
such deplorable conditions would be existing?
—*The People*, January 20, 1940

The Trinidadian society that encountered American occupiers brought more
than a recent history of rising nationalism; it lugged, too, a long past of con-
tending with the effects of the formidable U.S. presence. Ever since the late
nineteenth century, inhabitants of the colony had had no choice but to confront the power of a republic arrogantly realizing long-held dreams of hegemony across the hemisphere, a republic, indeed, whose very name betrayed an
arrogation of hemispheric proportions. By the time base construction began
in 1941, people in Trinidad had already produced an impressive record of assessing, engaging, and arguing about America. This experience would inform
their apprehensions of the U.S. occupation as well as intimate some of the
issues and contentions that arose during the period.

As early as 1861, with the fresh outbreak of a civil war casting grave doubts
on the territorial integrity of the United States, one of its citizens doing business in Trinidad confidently urged that his nation assert itself in the British
Caribbean. "It is the policy of England," wrote Frances Bernard, "to africanize
the West Indies, it is our interest to americanize them." Indeed, "the only hope
of redemption for these beautiful and valuable islands," Bernard proposed,
was "in an influx of American settlers to take the place of the old white families
who are either emigrating or melting away."[1] This businessman's prescription
was more than precocious; it was also prescient. Over the next eighty years,
inhabitants of Trinidad, too, would regard Americanization through the lens
of imperial rivalry, economic development, and race-making.

From the Civil War to World War II, the colony's subjects almost always addressed America as the alternative to Great Britain—and with completely good reason: during this period, the United States assiduously went about the Caribbean earning its reputation as the Colossus of the North. It made Cuba and Puerto Rico colonies in everything but name, finagled Panama into existence, occupied the twin republic island of Hispaniola, purchased the Danish Virgin Islands, lured tens of thousands of West Indian migrants, and overall, efficiently imposed its capital, technology, and practices across the hemisphere.[2] That people in Trinidad cast the United States this way, a specter that shadowed Great Britain, had many consequences. Among its most crucial was that local discourse on America almost always implicated the merit of the British Empire. A round of applause for the republic sounded like resentment of Great Britain; condemnation of the Colossus bore a striking resemblance to congratulations of Great Britain. For the colony's residents, reflections on the United States were inseparable from their disposition toward the regnant British regime; such reflections, by extension, were inextricable from people's political projects and priorities.

Framed by imperial rivalry, local deliberations on America focused on race and the economy. These, of course, were perfectly reasonable preoccupations in a postemancipation British West Indian society simmering with serious, many-sided conflicts over white supremacy, black subordination, and the reorganization of the agro-industrial complex. Against this backdrop of struggles over what Thomas Holt termed the "problem of freedom," America would assume a complicated and contested set of local meanings.[3] For although few disputed the proposition that this economic juggernaut of a nation was crucial to West Indians' achievement of material progress, the racial ramifications of the republic's growing reach made for an endless source of anxious debate.

The image of the United States as a uniquely effective agent of economic development gained currency in Trinidad even before the twentieth century. In the late 1880s, no less than the colonial government, against the wishes of local and British capitalists, opted to grant a Philadelphia industrialist monopoly control of the island's asphalt deposit. Over the next three decades, America's reputation as a fount of progress soared as thousands of struggling but hopeful residents left the island (and region) to resettle in the United States. So vital did this quest for the proverbial better life up north become that soon even the colony's patriots acknowledged America as a critically important site. Indeed, with these dissidents increasingly invoking popular emigration to, and economic dependency on, America as part of their challenge to Great Britain's claims of civilizational supremacy, the republic also became a rhetorically effective cite.

Still, in Trinidad, considerations of Americanization were haunted by racial apprehensions. Regarding the United States, people in this Caribbean colony recognized a New World society with a past of European colonialism and African slavery and a present of efforts to shoulder the "white man's burden." They observed, in other words, a national polity consumed with color lines and race problems that could be drawn and worked out in an international arena. Events in the United States, these British subjects understood, deeply implicated their livelihoods and security. Little wonder that locals paid such rapt attention to the republic's racial ideologies and practices.

Their responses would prove to be complex and contentious. Trinidad's colonial establishment, for example, despite subscribing to white supremacy, worried about the potential of American images and ideas to subvert their own locally specific regime of racism. Whether confronted with Hollywood cinema or Yankee citizens, therefore, these elites turned into scrupulous screeners. On the dark side of the island's color line, residents challenged such racist exercises of censorship as well as nursed their own set of racially rooted anxieties. Wary of a peculiarly brutal brand of racism identified with the "American way," they feared not only for their racial reputations but also for their real bodies. In Trinidad, nonwhites along with those who could find themselves stuck with the label nervously wondered whether notorious lynch law would follow the "stars and stripes." Yet even this antiracist query did not generate straightforward reactions. The priorities of local agitators would encourage purposefully nuanced rhetoric about racial formation in the United States. Intent on discrediting British rule, patriots calculatingly tempered their denunciation of the northern republic's Jim Crow practices. Fearing that such criticism ultimately redounded positively to Great Britain's imperial reputation, Trinidad's dissidents frequently finessed the familiar proposition that U.S. citizens practiced an exceptionally abhorrent variant of white supremacy.

PAVING THE AMERICAN WAY:
ASPHALT AND U.S. ENTREPRENEURSHIP

By the late nineteenth century, Great Britain could offer its Caribbean subjects no more than partial protection from an imperiously expansionist United States. As in the rest of *nuestra America*, residents of the British West Indies were exposed to the "spreadeaglism" that brought Yankees eager to exploit natural resources and political weaknesses in the region.[4] In Trinidad it was mineral deposits—rather than an edible fruit, as in Jamaica—that beckoned profit-seeking Americans.[5] During the 1870s a Philadelphian named Amzi Lorenzo Barber edged his way into what was then a petty but promising asphalt trade in the island's southwest. Less than a decade later, Barber's company controlled Trinidad's burgeoning asphalt industry, in the process quickly establishing a reputation in America for the colony's asphalt and a reputation in the colony for America. "Pitch" from a sleepy little La Brea "lake," it turns out, paved not only streets in vibrant U.S. cities but also the way for the entrenchment of a powerful U.S. presence locally. Barber's career in Trinidad resonates across the hemisphere. His is a story, indeed, that helps illustrate how elites across *nuestra America*, from Chile to Cuba, came to accommodate Yanqui capitalists as virtually indispensable to the modernization of their economies and societies.

Lorenzo Barber was by no means the first to appreciate the commercial possibilities of Trinidad's asphalt. Mercenary interest in La Brea's bituminous deposits dated to Spanish colonizers in the late 1700s, and by the middle of the nineteenth century, the English colonial government had begun leasing lots, mostly to local prospectors. Portentously enough, at the time Americans had already recognized the economic potential of Trinidad's asphalt. A "new branch of industry," the locally based U.S. consul reported back to potential investors in 1842, had appeared in the island, and in his estimation, they would be wise to develop an interest.[6] Yankee involvement, however, waited a couple of decades, for despite early use in France and England, asphalt acquired little industrial consequence in the United States until the postbellum period. It was not until the 1870s that Columbia University researchers publicized findings that an exceptionally efficient and durable pavement could be constructed with La Brea asphalt.

Barber's rise to prominence in Trinidad's asphalt industry derived from his success at both the production and consumption ends of the business. After effectively consolidating local mining by the mid-1870s, through a buyout of nearly all the other lessees and the formation of the New York & Trinidad Asphalt Company (NY&TAC), this entrepreneur established himself as the biggest booster of the La Brea lake outside the island.[7] Determined to make Trinidad asphalt the exclusive material for U.S. road construction, his company, for example, published the tellingly titled *Genuine Trinidad Asphalt:*

The Standard Pavement of America (1885). Characteristic of Barber's bold sales-manship, this book bragged that even the man who sold granite blocks—a rival road-building material—went "out of his way" to appreciate the "comfort and smoothness" of asphalt. Thus, as with the Jamaican banana trade in the late nineteenth century, the incipient commerce in Trinidad's asphalt relied heavily on American promotion and consumption. Not unlike the fruit, more-over, La Brea pitch quickly found its niche in the United States. Leading cities such as New York, Washington, D.C., Philadelphia, New Orleans, and Louis-ville relied on Trinidad asphalt for road paving.[8]

So decisively entrenched had Barber become within the island's asphalt in-dustry that the colonial administration was soon compelled to offer his firm a formal monopoly concession. In the mid-1880s, with the existing government-issued leases about to expire and with extraction having grown ninefold over the previous decade, Trinidad's government proposed to increase its revenue by "throwing open" the La Brea lake. Certain to end Barber's de facto mo-nopoly, the measure, tellingly, never passed the colony's legislature. Despite the vigorous gainsaying of a group of British and local leaseholders who con-demned Barber's asphalt "ring" for adding little to Trinidad's treasury, mem-bers of the Legislative Council voted in September 1887 to legalize the Ameri-can's monopoly by granting the NY&TAC concession rights.[9] The progress of the industry, they acceded, depended on a U.S. capitalist.

This admission of dependence, however, was hardly arrived at naturally or freely. Barber helped prejudice the outcome by dangling both sticks and car-rots. His firm had promised to pay the attractive sum of £10,000 per year for up to twenty years in exchange for the sole rights to extract asphalt from the lake (this figure eventually increased to a little more than £15,000).[10] Next to this monetary incentive, moreover, hung a thinly veiled threat. As the govern-ment weighed the matter, Barber's backers leaked his intent to withhold in-vestments in new infrastructure and to cease purchasing local pitch if he did not get his way. The NY&TAC concession thus constituted an official acknowl-edgment of the American firm's overwhelming power. Trinidad's administra-tion recognized that given Barber's capital, expertise, and access to an "enor-mous" U.S. market, he possessed the power to punish the colony's incipient asphalt industry. Frankly admitting the administration's predicament, the at-torney general stated that it was "impossible" to defy Barber; his company was simply too "strong" and "established." Were the American "killed," concluded this government official, the local industry would expire.[11]

This resignation to the economy's dependence obtained beyond the walls of the Legislative Council. Despite worrying about monopoly in principle, the southern-based *San Fernando Gazette* considered the American concession sound practice. To refuse Barber, it editorialized, was imprudent, as "Trinidad requires in the infant state of its subsidiary industries some special care for the growth and substantial spread of its commerce by which these industries may be substantiated to be something more than a temporary expedient to weather the crisis of an exceptional depression in the market of this chief industrial staple."[12] As in so many other polities across the Americas, including the similarly mineral-rich nearby republic of Venezuela, policy-makers in colonial Trinidad conceded that the manufacture of modernity needed, or at least was most thoroughly carried out with, the involvement of U.S. agents.[13]

A decade later, Barber's company appeared to have vindicated the decision of Trinidad's government. Along with filling the colony's coffers, the La Brea operation exhibited what British observer T. B. Jackson in 1895 deemed (not without ambivalence) "the prevailing spirit of modern times." Instructively, Jackson attributed the sector's modernity to an exceptional Yankee trait; the colony's asphalt industry, he asserted, instanced "the American nation doing work which it thoroughly understood." By the turn of the twentieth century, the American way, for better or worse, was increasingly seen as synonymous with an awesome modernity.[14]

EMBARRASSING WHITENESS:
AMERICAN RENEGADES IN INTERWAR TRINIDAD

Discourse on America acquired a crucial new referent with the rise of Trinidad's closely related petroleum industry. After several fitful starts in the late nineteenth century, the exploration and production of oil in the island surged during the second decade of the twentieth century. As with asphalt, the commodification of this fuel also relied on investment and technology from the United States; far more than with asphalt, though, the petroleum sector depended on American expertise. Whereas the work of procuring asphalt was mostly in the hands of black men, women, and children resident around La Brea, prospecting for "black gold" came under the supervision of white men contracted in the United States. The conduct of these "drillers"—as they were called—while in the colony would play a signal part in local contentions about America and Americans.[15]

Notwithstanding their relatively small number (no more than 500 until the 1930s), white American sojourners commanded significant but dubious attention in Trinidad. Indeed, in their comportment, or, more important, in the impression it made on onlookers, lies an underappreciated chapter of transgression in the racial history of U.S. imperialism. Granted automatic respectability by virtue of their race and gender, drillers on the island were expected by their peers to be discriminating (if not downright snobbish), to adopt a demeanor that displayed and defended white prestige in the presence of social subordinates. Often, however, they did not, and their brazen violations of colonial racial norms imperiled the prevailing social order.[16]

Despite originating from places as varied as Baltimore, Oklahoma, and California and boasting a plethora of experiences that included university training and prior careers in other mining industries, drillers shared a fantasy of their job as a combination of masculine adventure and enterprise.[17] Imagining themselves as men embarking on manly missions in the tradition of Theodore Roosevelt (whom one of them tellingly lauded as a great and "virile" American), drillers viewed their work as one "big oil hunt"—to borrow a title from an industry history.[18] They might not have been participating in exciting African safaris or battling Spanish armies at San Juan Hill, but Yankee oilmen envisioned themselves as no less courageous than Roosevelt and his renowned Rough Riders. As they saw it, their task in early-twentieth-century Trinidad was turning perilous, uninhabited jungles into profitable industrial estates.

Such self-imagination and, more important, self-presentation struck many white witnesses in Trinidad as embarrassingly renegade. In a caste-like world where these elites obsessively took care to deport themselves at a respectable distance from the dark, poor, and dangerous classes, white American men embodied deviance. Yankee sojourners, moreover, seemed not simply indifferent to but frankly contemptuous of established colonial codes of comportment. Relishing their local reputations as "outcasts," they gave the impression of taking great delight in "escapades" that disturbed local elites. As one unrepentant petroleum industry pioneer declared, "You just can't make oil men adopt British customs."[19]

Although white Americans rarely left public confessions, the specifics of their transgressions as well as the anxious responses they provoked among colonial elites occasionally emerged. In late 1941, months into the occupation, an observer seeking to allay contemporaries' fears about the impact of the recent influx of Americans recalled in a letter to the press the stir drillers had caused decades earlier. Signed by the "rockhound from La Brea," a village in the oil-rich southwest, the missive appearing in the *Trinidad Guardian* began with a reminder that this "is not the first American invasion in our history."

> The first was way back in the early days of the oil industry. The tough guys of those sedate days took La Brea, Point Fortin and Fyzabad by storm and even shook San Fernando to its very foundations. Dear old ladies were shocked at the stories which came from down south. . . . [And] club members were aghast to learn that the manager of UBOT [United British Oil Company] had come to town in shirt sleeve and had done the trip from Point Fortin to Port of Spain in five hours flat in his 1917 sports Packard. The roads will soon be unfit for decent people to drive, said some. Local truck drivers tried to emulate their new bosses and addressed us all as "say boy," wages went up and housewives complained that they could not keep servants. But gradually out of evil comes good. The tough guys softened and their wives took to giving tea parties. Many a wild and woolly Texan of those far off days stayed on to become our friends and we remember with affection many of the very toughs who have passed on.[20]

Insofar as oilmen imagined themselves as modern conquistadors, as fearless agents on a mission to integrate a frontier society into an empire of industry, locals, suggests this correspondent, concurred. People in Trinidad accepted Americans' hypermasculine conceit, apprehending these Yankees as carriers of an unsettlingly aggressive and reckless sensibility, as men who threatened the femininely figured decent society ("dear old ladies") unless domesticated (signified through wives' tea parties). Drillers, according to the rockhound, stuck out as "tough guys," men who shocked both the etiquette and the economy of colonial society. They scared elites with their driving, scandalized them with their dressing, and stole domestic workers with their relatively high wages.

Importantly, the letter also alluded to competing assessments of these American drillers, letting on that the very maverick modernity that rattled the colonial establishment could impress local subalterns. Trinidad's truck drivers, reported the rockhound, adopted their Yankee bosses' penchant for using the term "say boy." However brief, this observation merits consideration insofar as it points to the crucial issue of popular appropriation and resignification. Given that the rockhound was most likely a male member of the local elite (claiming familiarity with "club members"), the anecdote regarding the use of "say boy" raises the possibility that, for less privileged black men, the slang might have signified sly subversion, an instance in which they used a normally racist phrase to practice insubordination under the guise of witless mimicry. Whatever the case, such strategic nonelite redeployment of American expressions would become characteristic of occupied Trinidad.

But whereas the rockhound rendered a narrative of an unnerving encounter mollified by felicitous assimilation, such a happy outcome was not always the case. White American drillers at times turned out to be embarrassments egregious enough to warrant expulsion from the colony. This misfortune befell Jack Briggs, a California native who in April 1934 found himself "dumped" in New York City by Trinidad's authorities with a mere $19. Briggs, explained the local U.S. consul,

> was employed as an oil well driller but became so dissolute and drunken that he could no longer secure employment. He would have gone to prison for selling a stolen auto if his former friends among the American drillers had not returned the purchase price to the purchaser. . . . [Further,] during the past year, Briggs went from bad to worse living with and being kept in liquor by a negro prostitute in San Fernando. His behavior became so scandalous that a number of his former friends approached me and gave me $69 with which to purchase a third class passage to New York and give the purser the balance of $19 to be given to him on arrival at New York. I made two attempts to get him away, but on each occasion he disappeared. Finally, I requested the assistance of the Inspector General of constabulary who was himself eager to get such a type of white man out of this colony.[21]

These panicked charges against Briggs betray some of the specific proscriptions placed on white male residents in colonial Trinidad. These men were not to publicly operate above the law, under the influence of alcohol, or across the color line. The stuff of scandal, such conduct stained the image of not only white Americans but, importantly, all white people. Tellingly the colony's British inspector general remarked that he was only too "eager" to deport this "type" of white man. Briggs, moreover, was not the only white American accused of neglecting to cultivate white prestige. Roy Shores, according to the U.S. consul, after an early tenure as an "efficient," "well-paid," and "well-liked" driller, had become a "dissolute," unemployed drunk who cohabited with a Venezuelan prostitute. Despite eliciting sympathy from his peers (unlike Briggs), he, too, exhausted his welcome and was kicked off the island.[22]

While both Briggs and Shores might indeed have been drunken rogues sharing residences with local women who sold sex, more than coincidence might have been at play here.[23] The recurring "prostitute" label, in particular, prompts speculation about Trinidadian elites' rigid opposition to open interracial intimacy. Is it possible that the pejorative classification was no more than a convenient designation for authorities seeking justification to deport white men who unabashedly breached the rule against publicly taking non-white partners?[24] If so, both drillers' fates presaged a major vein of the worry that preoccupied the colonial establishment during the occupation. Their removal previewed the alarmed intolerance with which local whites would react to white American men who challenged the colony's racially coded conventions, especially the unspoken insistence on secreting intimacies across the color line.

THE RELIGION OF AMERICAN RACISM

By the early twentieth century, Trinidad's nonwhites, too, were troubled over the racial implications of the growing U.S. presence in the region. Their concern, however, was of a decidedly different hue. Rather than the sullied public images of whiteness, the colony's black, Asian, and variously mixed populations bothered themselves about the importation of what was often cast as a singularly brutal brand of U.S. race-making. In this sense, Americanization was, for many in the colony, a grave matter—a matter, indeed, of life and death.

This coupled question of U.S. expansionism and racial politics compelled an insightful book-length essay: *Confederation of the British West Indies versus Annexation to the United States of America: A Political Discourse on the West Indies*. Written by Dr. Louis Meikle and appearing in 1912, this undeservedly overlooked text ought to be read alongside a celebrated list of Latin American and Caribbean works devoted to interpreting the United States.[25] In the post–Civil War decades, canonical *pensadores* such as Jose Martí, Ruben Darió, Enrique Rodó, and Manuel Ugarte produced what have since been enshrined as classic assessments of America. These authors, despite their differences in intent, style, and effect, shared a crucial circumstance of composition:

all wrote wary of a "Yankee Peril" facing what they collectively labeled "our America."[26] Meikle was no different in this respect. A colored doctor born in Jamaica, trained in the United States, and resident in Trinidad at the time of publication, he, too, took up his pen fearful that the "claws of the American eagle" were poised to shred any possibility for the achievement of genuine freedom in the British West Indies.

Confederation, it has to be appreciated, entered a broader contemporary discussion about the political fate of Britain's Caribbean colonies. As Meikle remarked in the introduction, the subject of annexation to the United States had "undergone most serious contemplation."[27] The concern, of course, was reasonable at that time, the dawn of what would be known as "the American century." It was the historic moment in which the United States brashly declared its imperial prerogatives, the era of "splendid little wars," Big Sticks, and diplomatic dollars.[28] The title of W. T. Stead's 1901 text *The Americanization of the World* candidly bespoke the times, and in it the eminent English author flatly regarded the "transfer" of the British Caribbean to the United States as a "foregone conclusion."[29] West Indians themselves were hardly unaware of their situation within this historic tide of imperialist jostling, and they increasingly saw themselves not simply as British subjects but as British subjects inhabiting Americans' "backyard." In Jamaica, this consciousness manifested dramatically when the unsolicited landing of U.S. marines in the aftermath of Kingston's 1907 earthquake produced a fallout that led to the recall of the governor.[30] In Trinidad, the sensitivity mostly assumed the form of abundant back-and-forth over "Americanism" in the press.[31]

Against this backdrop of anxious uncertainty and endless debate, Meikle's essay braided two related objectives: the advocacy of a self-governing West Indian federation and the refutation of proposals of U.S. annexation. Revealing on several grounds, this text is particularly illuminating about the extent to which the lens of race critically refracted images of America among nonwhite British West Indians. The author's anti-annexationist arguments betrayed a singular, almost obsessive focus on white supremacy. Meikle's sole grievance with Americanization was that U.S. whites practiced an exceptionally menacing brand of antiblack racism. Contemporary Hispanic American critics might have commonly denounced Yanquis' treatment of "Negroes," but for this West Indian, white supremacy was the original sin of fin de siècle U.S. society.[32] As Meikle emphatically cautioned, to get anywhere with the Americans, "you must be White! White!! White!!!"[33]

At the heart of *Confederation* was a critique of what the author characterized as white Americans' "inbred antipathy for alien races[,] and more especially the negro." Calling this attitude an "open secret," the essay meant to break the conspiracy of silence. Yet Meikle composed more than a mere exposé; he theorized and adduced, producing a discourse that was not solely political (as the title implies) but also ethnographic. The essay ultimately amounted to an authoritative study on the comparative significance of race under British and American sovereignty. Based on a considerable stretch (participating and observing) in the "fields" (Jamaica, the U.S., Panama, and Trinidad), *Confederation*, as a reviewer in Trinidad positively noted, reflected "first hand knowledge."[34] The resulting "write-up" offered a devastating critique of white Americans. They had developed, it concluded, a "religion" of white supremacy and practiced it devoutly wherever they went. This was carefully chosen language, for Meikle had no illusions that whites in the United States exercised a monopoly on racism. He, in fact, flatly stated that "of all the books written on the British West Indies, touching the negro, those written by Englishmen are found to be most venomous and scandalous." What *Confederation* aimed to underline was the deep passion and eschatological zeal with which white Americans believed in "the hue of the skin." The distinction between British and Yankee racism, proposed the essay, was social—deriving from society and politics—rather than natural. Unlike the "Briton in the West Indies," the white American, Meikle argued, shared a home with a considerable number of blacks. And according to him, this spatial and social arrangement left white Americans less secure than their British counterparts. The Englishman in the Caribbean, he claimed, "differs from the Yankee in the States in that being always placed in a superior position to that of the average native, he does not have him as a direct competitor."[35] Here was the reason English colonizers did not have to "attack and disarm the negro . . . and to relegate him forcibly . . . to a position of inferiority, where he is no longer a menace to the sovereignty of the white race." In Meikle's view, everyday social and political rivalry played a decisive role in determining the character of racist practices. Hence despite acknowledging racial prejudice among British rulers, *Confederation* nevertheless came to the apparently paradoxical conclusion that "the British West Indies have no race issue of any moment to solve."[36]

Along with its relative virulence, American-style racism, according to Meikle, constructed racial categories with a particular rigidity that spelled disaster for British West Indians. This characteristic had especial consequences, he warned, for mixed West Indians, a group given to guarding their privileges and "demand[ing] a place in the white circle." This hybrid class stood most at risk because it, explained the essay, would most threaten white Americans. As everyone knows, he wrote,

> over nine-tenths of the people of the West Indies are of negro descent, and consequently, of mixed blood. Their freedom of action and liberty has gone on unrestricted for generations. Some of these people have long forgotten that negro blood is discernible by the naked eye in their veins. They have taken up the guise and demeanor of the Europeans, with the title of "white" to boot. And imitating the "jackdaw in peacock's feathers," they "strut along" among the illiterate under the garb of "white men."
>
> To such the Americans apply the distinctive name of "West Indian Whites," which is interpreted to mean persons who are posing as what in reality they are not.[37]

In Meikle's frightening social prognosis, white American rule guaranteed demotion for the "passing" class of nonwhite British West Indians. Unlike under the prevailing dispensation, people with known African ancestry, he predicted, would be precluded from the privilege of assuming a white social identity. And once downgraded to the status of nonwhite, they would become vulnerable to a species of racial discrimination they had hitherto escaped. *Confederation* foretold an Americanized future in which mixed West Indians who in everyday life imagined themselves—and indeed lived as though they were—white would suddenly find themselves victims of new injustices.

Of these, lynching was the most spectacular and infamous, and Meikle invoked the practice as one of the likely and most fearful consequences of annexation. Lynching, he explained, represented a strategy for policing sexual intimacy between nonwhite men and white women, and, although the author conceded that Englishmen, too, castigated these interracial sexual relationships, they did not, he reminded readers, follow the American way of attacking such liaisons with mob justice. Thus to heighten the urgency of his argument, Meikle adapted the axiomatic question regarding the implications of imperialism: "Would lynch law," he asked, "follow the flag?" Predictably, the essay answered positively; *Confederation*, after all, meant to offer a terrifying presentiment of annexation to the United States.[38]

Still, Meikle never denied the validity of one key aspect of the pro-annexationist position. On the subject of economic development, he accepted that British West Indian supporters of U.S. rule stood on legitimate ground. Even if America comprised West Indians' worst "social enemy," the republic, acknowledged the essay, remained their best "commercial friend."[39] *Confederation* even conceded that ever since the decline in the sugar industry, the region's economic savior appeared in the form of the United States. It was Americans, as consumers and as entrepreneurs, the author agreed, who had provided the key to the economic redemption in England's Caribbean possessions. "Were it not for American markets and American capital," Jamaica, Meikle admitted, "would have long ceased to be of any more importance in the world's history than a stranded iceberg."[40]

Confederation explored the ground beneath the increasing ambivalence felt by many nonwhite West Indians toward the United States in the early twentieth century. They, the book showed, embraced America as a vibrant economic power but feared Americanization as the source of a terroristic racism. This juxtaposition of rampant racialized injustice and remarkable economic development continued to frame the tense discussion of America during the interwar period. Indeed, it assumed even greater starkness as struggling Afro-Trinidadians thronged ships bound for the United States in search of the El Dorado to the north.

EMIGRATION AND THE CRITICAL AMERICAN SITE/CITE

In the decade following the publication of Meikle's essay, emigration emerged as a prominent factor in local deliberations on America. As thousands from the colony, typically black and poor or middling, joined the swell of British West Indians flooding the U.S. eastern seaboard, they helped define not only culture and politics in the United States (in Harlem, most conspicuously) but also the significance of America back in Trinidad.[41] Their capacity to find succor and sometimes even success in the spectacularly racist republic and, moreover, their remittances of some of this good fortune deepened the profoundly Manichaean image of America. Indeed, with the rise of this migratory network in the interwar period, Meikle's thesis about British West Indians' dichotomous apprehensions of the United States—at once friend and enemy—only assumed greater sharpness.[42]

Increasingly over the first two decades of the twentieth century, people in Trinidad, especially those of African descent, faced the predicament of freedom by opting for flight. An island that historically lured workers, it now witnessed this constituency escaping by the shipload. Emigrants ventured to various places (from Panama to Cuba to Canada), but the northeast United States was by far their preferred destination. The absence of island-specific statistics makes accurate figures impossible to determine; but of the more than 100,000 nonwhite Caribbean people who relocated to the United States between 1900 and 1930, approximately 80 percent originated in the British West Indies, and within this group, Trinidad's contribution might have been bested only by those of Jamaica and Barbados. Middle-class types certainly rode this northward wave, but it was driven for the most part by working-class people. The unmistakably proletarian character of this traffic struck many observers, not the least a worried U.S. consul, who complained in 1919 that "practical paupers" in Trinidad were buying out first-class tickets, leaving elite American travelers stranded in Port of Spain.[43]

The northbound movement drew America into an even more remarkably integral and intimate place in the lives—real and imaginary—of the colony's inhabitants, especially the poor. They quickly came to view the United States as a source of employment, education, commodities, remittances, and even symbolic resources such as place-names (denizens of John John, Laventille, dubbed their neighborhood "Harlem").[44] The decisive social and economic ramifications of locals' "foreign" interests could not escape the attention of Trinidad's social commentators. "Thousands of young men and women," the *People* subsequently reflected, "have obtained education and their parents' security and independence through money earned and remitted from the United States." Another editorial in the same paper elaborated on the observation:

> For many a year America was a haven of refuge for the unfortunate
> of these islands, a land of opportunity for the ambitious. Many a West
> Indian family were rescued from threatened necessity by migration
> to the States and many who remained behind were supported by re-
> mittances from the relatives there. Many a West Indian owes their
> higher education, his profession, to the generous facilities affording in
> the United States, and it is only too true that every such West Indian
> on his return to his native home is an enthusiastic propagandist of
> the virtues of the sister republic.[45]

Although the precise terms in which people at Trinidad's grass roots assessed and argued about America largely escaped conventional archives, a piece of contemporary fiction by patriot Alfred Mendes left a few hints. *Black*

Fauns appeared in 1935 (a couple of years after Mendes himself had moved to the United Sates) and, in both subject and style, resembled the social realist "barrack yard" genre embraced by *Beacon* writers.[46] Set in contemporary Port of Spain, the novel tells a sympathetic yet unflinching story focused on the lives of a fractious community of wretchedly poor black women.

America, it turns out, figured prominently in their world.[47] Mendes's narrative opens with the arrival of a letter from New York City. Sent by Snakey, the son of a barrack woman and one among many poor Trinidadians resettled in "America," the correspondence announces his impending return for a vacation. Snakey, readers learn, had left the colony years earlier, pushed by police and paramours and pulled by what other emigrants had reported as "the new el dorado."[48] Now, he wrote to his mother, "the Trinidad itch in my blood is calling me back to the land of my birth." Returning near the novel's end, Snakey cues (among other things) a labyrinthine conversation filled with wonder, speculation, and discord about America. Following the initial stir created by his ironed hair, spanking suit, dandy walk ("Trinidad nigger don't walk like dat!"), and thick wad of dollars, the women eagerly gather around to learn "somet'ing about America."[49] Smugly, Snakey obliges and conjures up visions of America for what he saw as "ignorant" women on a "small island . . . far from everything." His America was synonymous with New York City; it was a place packed with millions of people who did not sleep at night, streets that lit up in the night as if it were day, and spectacular structures that dwarfed Trinidad's biggest buildings. America was all huge hotels and skyscrapers with elevators. The women were awed. They had never heard of elevators, and Snakey had to explain their function. The same was true for elevated trains, which the barrack dwellers imagined as "trains running on houses!"[50]

This informal symposium, however, soon went beyond America's "marvels." As so often happened in twentieth-century Trinidad, in *Black Fauns* the assessment of the United States soon juxtaposed material accomplishments with racist record. Having casually slipped a reference to white supremacy into his rave about New York City hotels, explaining that he was "ok" with segregation and now "accustom" to whites who "think they more better than nigger people," Snakey was forced by the women to elaborate. One of them, Etherilda, became angrily incredulous. Already annoyed by Snakey's glowing over what he had called the "white man's magic," she raged at his acceptance of another woman's contention that "white people more smart than nigger people." Etherilda was severe: "If you leave your own land, where you born and bring up, to go to crazy country run by crazy white people living in crazy city, to come back with de news dat white people more smart than nigger people it was more better your never born." An unfazed Snakey simply continued his boastful talk about the "great city [made] by white men."[51]

As the women's fascination with America rose, Etherilda shot at Snakey the single question that appears to have summed up their concern: "*Is de people in New York happy?*" To a question weighed down with doubt, Snakey replied with succinct certainty: "Sure." He saw no reason to justify his answer, and it was left to his mother to explain what seemed to her so obvious: "How you want them not to be happy," she asked, "with all them t'ings they got there!" Etherilda remained unconvinced; for her, the land of "t'ings," signified the exact opposite. "It looks like as if all them t'ings," she concluded, "bound to make people unhappy."[52]

In *Black Fauns*, the verdict was still out on America. Mendes's novel acknowledges and grapples with the important yet contested place the United States occupied within the imaginations of poor people in interwar Trinidad. The characters all agreed that America marked a bountiful material modernity; they all appreciated the "t'ings" associated with Yankees. As to the extent to which this rich republic enabled happiness for humanity, especially for those on the dark side of the color line, they remained divided.

Emigration, moreover, made America not only a critical site for the local grassroots Trinidadians but also a critical cite for Trinidad's anti-British agitators. In the huge outflow of laboring people from the island, the colony's critics found an effective cause to fault their rulers. At the height of the northward flight in the middle of 1923, a series of editorials in the pro-working-class *Labor Leader* declared that Trinidad's deplorable conditions had "forced" working people to leave the Union Jack in favor of the Stars and Stripes.[53] Workers, the paper argued, needed "inducements" to remain on the island, and, in closing, the editor demanded an economic commission be sent to Trinidad. Over the next decade, this strategy of invoking the indispensability of the U.S. economy to undermine British rule became more commonplace.

It was a rhetorical tactic, furthermore, with an intriguingly gendered inflection. Underlying a lengthy 1923 *Labor Leader* editorial on the "exodus" to the United States was the worry that "women [were] leading the way." Their departure and subsequent support of relatives back home, according to the organ, "radically" changed family dynamics; specifically, it attenuated male economic power in the household (already dubious in most lower-class families).[54] Although recent scholarship has begun to uncover women's pivotal place in this interwar travel, the *Labor Leader*'s claims are perhaps best read rhetorically. Editors of the paper most likely were convinced that analogizing emigration and emasculation would appeal to colonial policy-makers committed to the domestic authority of "manhood."[55] Whether the mass relocation to the United States actually comprised a gendered threat to local laboring-class men raises an important question in need of a definitive answer. Is it possible that while poor women optimistically imagined America as a place for leading more independent lives, their male counterparts apprehended the republic as a social setting for female subversion of their claims to patriarchal power?[56]

SCREENING AMERICA: CINEMA, RACE, AND IMPERIAL SUBVERSION

By the time the U.S. government effectively ended British West Indian immigration in 1924, people in Trinidad were increasingly encountering copious images of America without emigrating or relying on emigrants' reportage. Via the inescapably popular medium of motion pictures, America was coming to them. On the heels of the 1911 local debut of a film exhibition at the London theater in Port of Spain, Trinidad's inhabitants hurriedly took their place alongside the rest of a movie-struck world. In less than a decade, two permanent cinemas—the Olympic and the Empire—joined the London in the capital; six others, meanwhile, sprouted up outside Port of Spain. By World War II, Trinidad had become so "cinema conscious" that Port of Spain's population of around 80,000 comfortably supported nine theaters.[57] The United States, it is important to recognize, dominated local motion picture exhibition from the outset, accounting for around 95 percent of the films shown in interwar Trinidad.[58] For all intents and purposes, the island's cinema screened a world that was exclusively American.

Like other local manifestations of America, cinematic images generated public conflict. And once again, race marked a critical term of contention. Trinidad's white elite were troubled about Hollywood's racial representation. Notwithstanding their condescending discourse about vulnerable viewers of the "inferior race," they were alert to the gaze of a predominantly nonwhite audience and, in fact, worried that these patrons comprised a discerning, deconstructive spectatorship. As in other parts of the British Empire, therefore, local guardians of white supremacy discreetly formulated guidelines to screen "unsavory images of the white race" as well as subversive images of nonwhites, especially blacks.[59] Once exposed, though, this racially rationalized censorship faced opposition from dissidents, observers who recognized the insepa-

rable connection between on-screen racism and real-life racism and thus condemned the establishment's calculated labors to suppress positive, authoritative representations of blacks. These critics saw American cinema as more
than simply a source of escapist amusement; it was a diasporic resource in the
envisioning of a new social order.[60]

From the inception of cinema in Trinidad, colonial censors dedicated themselves to policing racialized representations. Principles they formalized in
1921 explicitly focused on the questionable light in which U.S. film cast white
characters, and included in the list of objectionable "political" scenes were
pictures of "white men in a state of degradation amidst native surroundings
or using violence toward natives, especially Chinese, negroes and Indians."
Immediately following this proscription was another against "equivocal situa-
tions between men of one race and girls of another race."[61] Indeed, underlying
much of the contemporary uproar around the cinema's reliance on "sex appeal" appears to have been a worry about the precode Hollywood habit of exploiting images of white women's sexuality.[62] When, for example, the Board of
Censors banned the 1933 film *Broadway Melody*, chief censor Colonel Mavrogordato explained that it was inappropriate because of "the number of women
appearing throughout the film half dressed or in otherwise scanty attire." This
show, he forewarned, revealed "the white woman in a degrading viewpoint before the large East Indian and Negro audiences." Such a situation, according
to this white official, should be "avoided at all costs."[63]

But whereas these moves to regulate portrayals of whiteness seemed to
have stirred little interest beyond official circles, efforts to censor black images
could provoke protest and controversy. Local censors, conscious of the inter-
pretative acuity of Afro-Trinidadian audiences, had long clandestinely though
conscientiously targeted films that, to their eyes, offered powerful, autonomous representations of blackness. In these pictures, they believed, patrons
might discern subversive visions of black disregard for, threat to, or mockery
of white priorities and supremacy. The Board of Censors rejected *Kongo*, for
example, arguing that this horror film set in Africa "contained voodoo worship which could not be shown to audiences so largely composed of African
race."[64] It banned *Hallelujah*, a picture that explored religious practices among
blacks in the United States, on the same grounds.

Local agitators took on the racialized premise of censorship policy quite
early, indeed, even when it was practiced thousands of miles away. Soon after
black American boxer Jack Johnson famously defeated white opponent Jim
Jeffries in July 1910, a column in the pro-black local weekly, the *Mirror*, chafed

at the widespread refusal to show reels from the fight. In a piece that paid poetic tribute to Johnson as "the nigger" who "did the job in proper style," the writer challenged censorship with the disingenuous declaration that the contest did not "matter to the race at large." It was a sly sign that critics in Trinidad discerned the subversive power of seeing America's "bad nigger" on-screen.[65]

No less than they welcomed the cinematic projection of "bad niggers," local dissidents denounced the featuring of what one dismissed as "good niggers." In 1926, for example, as English filmmakers and their political allies intensified their campaign against Hollywood's domination of Great Britain's imperial market, Tito P. Achong, a consistently outspoken opponent of British rule, bluntly denounced the efforts as complicit with a white supremacy fundamental to imperial rule. In a *Labor Leader* essay titled "Made to Order Patriotism: Americanism as Its Enemy," Achong accused Trinidad's censors of viewing U.S. pictures as if they were "the obstacle in the way of converting the natives into good niggers." The Anglophile local establishment, he charged, targeted Hollywood films because they featured fantastic visions of democracy. Meanwhile, they preferred to screen British films, which, according to him, were "emphatic that the 'unwashed' colored man's function is to provide good things for his 'lord' the white man to eat." A longtime booster of the United States, Achong elaborated on the contrast between national cinemas across the Atlantic: American films, he wrote, were "in the great part pleasing nonsense."

> Their pretensions are not unlike the boast of the ancient philosopher who claims that he would lift the world if only he could find a place to stand on. The jocund American film with its bizarre students always fascinates. . . . British films in the main invariable portray exasperating rubbish. If it is an English scene, only lords and dukes are credited with being worthwhile. It is therefore small wonder that the English workingman prefers the American pictures which tell of the possibility of a rail-splitter or tailor becoming president of the United States. The crown colony native prefers to be told that neither economic independence, manhood nor good citizenship is associated with color.[66]

In Achong's eyes, loyalist censors were watching to ensure that poor non-whites saw only those pictures aimed at persuading them to passively accept their subordinate status. This antiracist critique, of course, was far from unfounded. During the 1927 parliamentary debates that ultimately secured a quota for British films, a Conservative English MP condemned American films for projecting before the "coloured races . . . representations of the lives of white people which are completely contrary to the life the bulk of us live."[67] For many British imperialists, film policy was indeed an instrument for the projection of white supremacy.

Tito Achong was hardly alone in viewing the double feature of American cinema and colonial censorship as an important site of racial struggle. Throughout the 1930s, the "race-conscious" *People* weekly, in particular, scrutinized the depiction of black characters on movie screens, parsing and protesting films like *Emperor Jones*, *Imitation of Life*, and *Sanders of the River*.[68] The period's biggest controversy over censorship, though, involved not an exhibited film but one initially denied a local audience. In the middle of 1936, Trinidad's Board of Censors banned the much-ballyhooed *Green Pastures*. Based on a Broadway play and featuring an "all-Negro" cast, the film was essentially a comic reinterpretation of several Old Testament narratives. Local censors, however, remained unamused, claiming to have seen in the movie a slur on black people; *Green Pastures*, concluded chief censor Colonel Mavrogordato, stood to "offend the religious susceptibilities of a large section of the community." Rather than "contemporary black understandings," the picture, he argued, portrayed blacks as they might have been a long time ago when they were "fresh from Africa."[69]

Although there were local commentators sympathetic to Mavrogordato's purported rationale (some, after all, were susceptible to the Eurocentric premise that Africans on the continent were left "uncivilized"), not a few remained unconvinced. For these skeptics, the board's official position was no more than the transparent mask of white supremacy. Among this disappointed and disgruntled set was someone who sent a public letter to the *Sunday Times and Sporting Chronicle* and signed as "cinema-goer." The correspondence began by noting that with the banning of *Green Pastures* Afro-Trinidadians had been "denied" the chance to see yet "another all star colored picture." (*Hallelujah* and an Oscar Micheaux independent titled *Harlem after Midnight*, it recalled, had been previously banned.) But more than simply mourn the missed opportunity, cinema-goer discerned and denounced a racial reasoning underlying the board's decision.

> The common reason given for banning these films is that they will engender race strife and in the case of "Green Pastures" we understand it is deemed sacrilegious. Indeed the attitude of the board is

amusing. To picture the deity as white will in all respects be religious, as black—sacrilegious. To show the negro as an illiterate self-made king, exemplifying at first a powerful and vainglorious individual then later crawling and groveling in the dust as in "Emperor Jones" is quite in order and does not engender race strife, as probably the board feels that the colored man's mind is a blank in so far as racial pride is concerned. . . . The government should realize that it is bad psychology to try and coerce loyalty and patriotism from the people by cunningly striving to impress them of their inferiority. The colored man can only feel himself a loyal Britisher when he is allowed impartial participation in the much-boasted fairplay and justice of the British.[70]

Not unlike Tito Achong a decade earlier, this observer boldly accused the colony's censors of exercising their power in the interest of racist British imperialism—in other words, in the service of producing "good niggers." The board, according to this correspondent, systematically rejected films that presented authoritative, self-possessed black characters. Closing with a call for reform, cinema-goer urged the incorporation on the board of members of the "colored intelligentsia" who would be able to "represent honestly [colored people's] feelings and desires."[71] The protest registered, and Trinidad's colonial government appointed a special committee that included Canon Max Farquhar to reconsider the ban. Upon review, it reversed the board's earlier decision.

Green Pastures appears to have been anticlimactic, given all the pointed rhetoric around the film. Audiences reportedly gave it a "mixed reception," some viewers finding it "objectionable" and others "unexceptionable."[72] It was a tame ending to a critical debate that exposed the racial investments lurking behind the exhibition and viewing of American films in colonial Trinidad.[73]

DISPUTING AMERICANIZATION

The popularity of cinema, in fact, was often taken as an index of the broader local influence of U.S. culture, an issue that proved to be disputatious and even controversial on the eve of the occupation. On one side of this conflict over "Americanization" stood those loyalists for whom the phenomenon provoked a combination of scorn and defiance. Cipriani, for example, denounced Hollywood movies as an "americanising influence" and "insidious propaganda."[74] On the other side of the debate were those, not the least Trinidadian patriots, who appreciated that engagement with the United States had become too pervasive, too practical, and too productive to renounce. Rather than excoriating Americanization, the colony's young cadre of critics calculatingly embraced it as rhetoric that dramatized the failures of their British imperialist nemeses.

Certainly, the strong anti-American sentiment that coursed through Louis Meikle's pre–Great War essay survived into the thirties. In 1933, for example, A. H. V. McShine, who came from an affluent Afro-Trinidadian family, warned against annexation to the United States as "inimical to [Trinidadians] best interest"; federation, he advised, established the best guard against absorption into the American empire.[75] Cipriani, too, recoiled at the slightest whisper of annexation, and like Meikle, this "Crown patriot" invoked racist terror as reason enough to reject association with the United States. As long as "lynch law" prevailed in America, he declared, no one could dispute that the British Empire was a "freer community." Even mythically alluring Yankee dollars lost currency in the face of the Captain's devotion to self-government within the empire. There was no way, Cipriani insisted, that he could be compromised by the "almighty American dollar"; Britishness was too dear to be sold.[76]

By and large, however, Trinidad's rising generation of rebels refused to prize Great Britain over the United States. Their disposition derived to some degree from a pragmatic recognition of their interests, as the biographies of key *Beacon* patriots bear testimony to significant past and ongoing ties to the republic. Gomes attended New York's City University, Hugh Stollmeyer and Alfred Mendes left for New York in the 1930s, and by the end of the decade, C. L. R. James, who first migrated to London, had taken up residence in the United States. Dissidents who never left or returned to Trinidad, furthermore, closely followed progressive politics up north. They kept up with the ideas and activities of West Indian–born agitators and intellectuals based in the United States (people such as Alfred Maloney, Charles Petioni, and Oliver Cox) as well as turned to the broader American political scene for exemplary models. Tellingly, these patriots' first political party, founded in 1938, was dubbed the New Deal Organization.[77]

Over the course of the decade, indeed, local critics would grow increasingly explicit about their favorable disposition toward the United States. In late 1936, the *People* seized the opportunity of President Franklin Roosevelt's stopover to acknowledge that "America's stock has in the past decade risen considerably."[78] Titled "A Good Neighbor," the editorial in what had become the preeminent voice of Trinidadian nationalism attributed the newfound appreciation for the United States to various factors: Roosevelt's "personality," the withdrawal of troops from Haiti, the recent goodwill visit of black American pilots to the West Indies, and economic benefits derived from the United States. Despite admitting America's flaws (parenthesized as "failings"), the weekly concluded that British West Indians realized "more and more . . . that good neighborly relations with the colossus of the north are essential to the future advancement of these islands." By the late 1930s, the colony's oppositional circles displayed an unmistakably appreciative regard for America.

Yet these proclamations of pro-American sentiment should not be treated simply as testimonials. Voiced within earshot of British colonial rulers, they were meant as politically charged discourse, composed as rhetorical pulls of Britain's imperial tail. That these statements sometimes proved effective was evidenced in the controversy they generated, the most memorable and instructive of which flared up in the wake of a visit to the colony by English writer and critic Arthur Calder-Marshall. More than any other, this quarrel clarified the strategic character of local dissidents' endorsement of "Americanization."

Calder-Marshall arrived in Trinidad in March 1938 intending to expose the social conditions underlying the recent labor troubles. At the end of a three-month stay during which this socialist addressed literary gatherings, fraternized with labor activists, and partied with poor folk, he claimed to have happened into an important political phenomenon. The "feeling of loyalty or respect for Great Britain," the Englishman concluded, "is almost completely absent from the people of Trinidad."[79] Such sentiment, Calder-Marshall reported, held not only for workers but also for the middle class. He then drew a contrast with regard to local feeling for the United States. Trinidadians, according to him, greatly admired America; representative for the writer was a local taxi driver who pledged that though he would have to be "crucified" before he would fight for Great Britain, he was eager to bear arms on behalf of the United States.

This impeachment of Trinidadians' imperial loyalty sparked debate back in the colony. First publicized in October 1938 in an English newspaper piece sensationally titled "Trinidad Would Like to Be American," Calder-Marshall's claim immediately raised bristles within the local establishment. The *Trinidad Guardian*, most prominently, charged the English critic with casting an "unfounded aspersion" on the people of Trinidad.[80] It followed up with a publication of the results of its own survey demonstrating that "across all classes" Trinidadians desired to remain British. The organ trundled out, too, endorsements of imperial loyalty from several influential public figures, such as George McClean, the black president of the Shop Assistants Trade Union; Edward Bruyning, a well-known colored legal advocate of the poor; and Captain Cipriani. All bore witness to the vigor of British patriotism in the colony.[81]

But even within the loyalist crowd came concessions that Calder-Marshall's thesis had some validity. Cipriani, for one, admitted that while people in Trinidad had no desire to become American, they "admired" many things American.[82] Even more telling were the views of Aubrey Williams, a well-known black Port of Spain intellectual. Williams proposed that though essentially British ("British to the core"), Trinidadian society was superficially American. Any visitor to the island, he explained, would easily get the impression that people preferred the United States over Great Britain. Locals, after all, showed "nonchalance" in the presence of English personalities while, according to Williams, making a "big thing" for "unimportant" American tourists. Pointing to other examples of apparent imperial disloyalty and Americanophilia, he cited the post office, "where locals get money from relations in United States and sing praises of the almighty [American] dollar." The same was true, Williams stated, for the cinema, where patrons "stamped like wild prairie ponies for the exit just as His Majesty's picture was flashed on the screen and the playing of the national anthem begun." For this loyalist, the British colony was conspicuous for its absence of what might be labeled "banal imperialism," on one hand, and for its enthrallment with America, on the other.[83] In closing, Williams tried to etch a silver lining into Calder-Marshall's dark portrayal. The Englishman's essay, he expressed hope, would shame Trinidadians into "throw[ing] off a dubious disguise and let[ting] the world see us as we see ourselves."[84]

Instructively, though, Trinidad's patriots openly sided with Calder-Marshall. Even as loyalists continued to deny the Englishman's assertions in the early months of 1939, testifying that they would "fight to the last drop of blood to preserve our present protection under the British flag," local agitators agreed that Calder-Marshall had authored a proper indictment of British imperialism.[85] Still, they distanced themselves from the idea that people in the colony favored annexation. For them, support for Americanization expressed a demand for a social progress unaffordable under British rule.

Tito Achong, not surprisingly, was among the first to validate the English writer's claims. Calder-Marshall, wrote Achong, "has no new idea. He simply stated a current dominant economic notion among the people at large that they had no more faith in an exploiting [British] imperialism." Trinidadians, according to this dissident, saw America as an "economic paradise"; they simply "want bread and are not at all interested in any frothy patriotism, any five year plan unconnected with a full diner table or any other scheme contributing nothing to liberty or social happiness." He elaborated: "Look at the many houses built at Woodbrook, Baratoria and else where with money earned in that republic. See the number of pupils being educated on remittances from the union. . . . Think of the large number of West Indians who have risen above the bread line economically and morally in the American commonwealth. . . . Even if the people are prone to forget the degrading influence of Crown Colony absolutism their two hundred thousand and more fellows abroad would keep the mental pot boiling."[86] The *People* echoed Achong, complaining that the Englishman's critics were too "imperialist minded." In an editorial titled "Is Mr. Calder-Marshall Wrong?" the island's main nationalist organ explained that local support for the United States indicated an act of loyalty — not to empire but to Trinidad. The weekly, in fact, reasoned that it would be disloyal for Trinidadians to oppose association with the United States if the colony were better off linked to the republic. "To indulge in mere abuse of things American," the *People* warned, "is to betray crass ignorance."[87]

Throughout the debate, though, local patriots never accepted that people in Trinidad wanted to be American. Appreciation for America, they insisted, expressed local discontent with British economic policies. Achong, for example, dismissed as "superficial" the issue of annexation. "The people of Trinidad as a whole," he wrote, "love their native land above all other lands."[88] The *People*, too, disavowed any interest in a transfer of sovereignty across the Atlantic. "An exchange of British imperialism for American imperialism," the paper declared, "should not be the desire of any person in Trinidad." Rather, "complete self-government with universal suffrage [and] the total abolition of property qualification for membership of the Legislative Council" ought to be Trinidadians' ambitions.[89]

On the eve of the occupation, nationalists continued to tread the thin line between embracing the rhetoric of Americanization and endorsing the reality of American rule. In March 1940 the *People* wondered aloud "if the West Indies were americanized if such deplorable conditions would be existing" in the colony. Remarkably, the editorial went as far as discreetly hinting that there was something less intolerable about U.S. Jim Crow segregation than the British Caribbean status quo: "The American," the newspaper flatly stated, "will pay you what you are worth and let you know your boundary. That is what we like about the Americans." Yet no matter how much Trinidadian patriots regarded Americanization as an improvement, they remained resolutely against annexation to the United States. The colony, concluded the same editorial, desired not a "foster mother" but "progress."[90]

CONCLUSION

By the time the base construction began, British colonial Trinidad had spent more than four decades dealing with the United States as an imperial force. Capital, citizens, cinema, and modern marvels from America circulated as inescapable social facts in the island. Local residents treated (with) these powerful expressions of American power in ways that reflected as well as reinforced the conflicts that rent their society. Americanization was a site of struggle, real and rhetorical. The onset of occupation in 1941 would intensify —not inaugurate—Trinidadians' tactical and antagonistic engagement with the United States.

3 Laboring over the Yankee Dollar
Work in Occupied Trinidad

Those who were thankful were for the most part workers. Servants
ceased working for Madame, or compelled her to double and treble their
wages. Clerks out of work for years went to work on the bases, or got jobs
with Trinidadian firms which had lost employees to the Yanks with their
higher wages. . . . Those who were angered or dissatisfied were chiefly
property-owners whom the new masters had unceremoniously
dispossessed.
—Ralph De Boissiere, *Rum and Coca-Cola*

In September 1941, the *Trinidad Guardian* reported the appearance of a new
unofficial job category at the air base site in Cumuto. U.S. contractors had
hired thousands of local men to clear the forested area, and a few of the
more enterprising laborers allegedly came up with an ingenious scheme: for a
penny charged to each delinquent worker, they would keep an eye out for the
Yankee supervisors. Watching for a hundred base employees, these "spotters,"
as the piece pointed out, could earn a dollar a day, which was twice as much as
the average nonbase Trinidadian laborer.[1] Contributed by visiting American
journalist Hugh Hepner, this story went neither unnoticed nor unchallenged.
Victor Bryan, a rising pro-labor politician from the nearby borough of Arima
and himself a former reporter, quickly questioned its veracity. Americans,
Bryan countered in a letter to the *Trinidad Guardian* the following week, were
not so "impractical" as to leave one foreman overseeing a hundred workers.
He closed his dismissive missive with an Americanism; the "spotters" article,
concluded Bryan, was pure "bunkum."[2]

Apparently petty, this discrepancy indexes what was perhaps the most fundamental conflict arising from the U.S. occupation of Trinidad. Once plans
for base installation were announced, and especially once construction began,

the colony bristled with debates—sometimes openly vehement, sometimes deceptively diplomatic—about the price, availability, and ethics of local labor. On one side of the contest stood the island's hopeful majority, people who sold their skills and thus relished the opportunity to take advantage of the new market created by Americans' demands. From Indo-Trinidadian cane cutters to Afro-Trinidadian domestic servants, laborers set out to take advantage of what they expected to be more remunerative U.S. employers. Few captured workers' mood and mindset better than a fictional character who observed that "American people not cheap like British people, gul! From de time people hear about Yankee work, dey leaving everyting else, post office and treasury and government work."[3]

Squared off against optimistic workers was Trinidad's small but immensely influential class of employers. Reliant on a large, cheap labor force, they chafed at the prospect and, subsequently, the reality of locals readily deserting them for Yankee counterparts. Planters were particularly vociferous, bemoaning that they endured the worst of this abandonment. More than complain, though, these elites went to great lengths to combat workers' flight. Alarmed agriculturalists addressed the colonial state and demanded the depression of U.S. wage rates, access to immigrant labor, and as desperation set in, the conscription of labor. Their pressure forced the administration into a difficult situation, for along with assuaging plantocrats, colonial officials had to accommodate the base-building needs of Americans as well as mollify a Trinidadian workforce whose capacity for violence remained fresh in their memory. Thus despite trying, the government did not always comply with employers' wishes. In occupied Trinidad, the labor problem was highly charged and ceaselessly challenging.

The range of contestation over work is the subject of this chapter, and by its end, the stakes involved in the journalistic tiff over spotters should become clear. In the report about cunning but indolent workers, the pro-labor Victor Bryan discerned potential ammunition for local employers determined to portray the colony's economy as paralyzed by a labor force that had become perversely and intolerably idle since the onset of base construction. Whatever Hugh Hepner's intent, Bryan spotted in the piece a sly opportunity for conniving local elites. His rejection of the American journalist's story captured the general attitude within a patriotic circle that actively supported subaltern struggles to earn the Yankee dollar. In the midst of an American-made economic boom, leaders like Bryan backed those poor people who, after having lived long on very little, sought wages that would afford them "two pounds of beef and pork."[4]

FIXING WAGES, FIGHTING WORKERS

"The news that the Americans were coming," according to the narrator of *Rum and Coca-Cola*, caused Trinidad's working-class youth to entertain "the rosiest illusions about the chances awaiting" them. "Nigger have mo' chance with American than with Englishman," opined a black character in Ralph De Boissiere's social realist novel about occupied Trinidad. Not even an ominous query about Yankees' notoriously deadly racism dampened this young man's optimism about the impact of base construction: "They kean't lynch all-a we," he told off a skeptical East Indian interlocutor; "otherwise who goin' to work for them?"[5] This appreciation of workers' new value and leverage was widespread on the verge of base construction and would set off intense struggles over wages in the early years of the occupation. Though it never erupted into the kind of violence witnessed over labor prices as the United States contemporaneously built bases in the Bahamas, the conflict in Trinidad was nonetheless fierce and devious.[6]

Not everyone took for granted the coming of brighter days with the arrival of U.S. employers in the colony. The pro-labor *New Dawn*, for example, assumed a watchful stance, cautioning people not to confuse the military project with economic reconstruction. Base construction, it proposed, promised only a temporal shock, "tourist-type betterment." The monthly, moreover, warned that whatever gains were to be had from American employment would require vigilance. "The least we can do," *New Dawn* soberly observed in early 1941, "is to see that the people get work, as little v.d. [venereal disease] as possible and a guarantee that in the case of strikes etc. [Americans] will not interfere in our internal affairs."[7]

Dissidents at the journal had good reason to urge alertness and readiness for struggle. Ever since the announcement of plans for base installation, Trinidad's employers had begun agonizing over the prospect of Americans pricing them out of the labor market. Ever since then, too, they had begun conspiring to deal with the challenge. In early 1941 some planters tried to persuade their field hands to sign long-term contracts that would tie them to their current estates.[8] Around the same time, moreover, there were suspicious goings-on with American wages at sites where surveying had begun. In late January, when the Legislative Council convened to draw up ordinances regarding the U.S. acquisition of local property, two pro-labor elected members raised the subject of labor prices. But whereas longtime Butlerite Timothy Roodal was "ecstatic" that workers had been abandoning local employers paying $80 a month for Americans offering $120, Adrian C. Rienzi, the president of the Oilfield Workers Trade Union, had distressing news. The wages of two locals, Rienzi disclosed, had been inexplicably reduced by Americans from the healthy rate of $35 a month to $22.50 a month. It was, to his mind, a disheartening development, for although he was worried about Yankees' "objectionable" Jim Crow practices, Rienzi had been "optimistic" about their wages. The only consolation for this trade unionist was that both men had since "chucked" the job with Americans.[9]

No doubt these stories of locals ditching their jobs for high-paying opportunities with Yankees rang ominously in the ears of the colony's employers and their allies. The day after the speeches by Roodal and Rienzi, the *Trinidad Guardian* began what would be an implacable campaign on behalf of the island's employing classes, planters in particular. Unless checked, the establishment organ warned, base construction would disastrously destabilize Trinidad's economy. Though careful to register satisfaction at Americans' defensive military presence in Trinidad, the daily expressed grave doubts about the economic ramifications of the project. "It is to be hoped," the editorial advised, "that the government will make early announcements of a policy to save agriculture from . . . economic ruin."[10]

The *Trinidad Guardian* and its planter pals had no real cause for panic, for their ambitions, as so often happened, quickly morphed into the administration's mandate. When in January 1941 Governor Hubert Young left for the London conference where American and British diplomats worked out the specific terms of the lease arrangement, he prioritized the base wages issue. Resolutely set against the establishment of a dual wage system (local and American), Young insisted that his administration be granted the power to set pay scales for the colony's base workers. Already the governor had been deeply displeased about the terms of base construction—especially Americans' decision to use Chaguaramas instead of the Caroni site he had proposed.[11] Thus he must have felt a moment of rare relief to find U.S. officials cooperative on this matter. In February American authorities announced their intention to adopt the "prevailing wages" policy. They, in other words, agreed to adhere to the local pay scale that preceded their arrival in the colony.[12]

A blessing for Trinidad's employers, this policy was a curse for its workers. Disappointed and somewhat surprised, they had anticipated from Americans wage rates as high as three times the local standard. "Have you left the spirit of goodwill on the United States shores?" asked one unhappy local laborer. "Are you going to let [local workers] down after they have been boosting you up all along?"[13] Notwithstanding the addressee of this query, most people in the colony understood that the implementation of prevailing wages responded to colonial far more than American interests. *New Dawn*, for example, explained that "pressure has been brought to bear on the Americans to keep them in line with the local wage policy." That the island's base employees should earn "the same rate of wages as are paid to American workers," the journal sneered, "sounds like madness in the ear of those who seem to want to keep us eternally ignorant and eternally enslaved."[14] The Trinidad and Tobago Council of Trade Unions (TTCTU) also disclosed awareness that responsibility for "prevailing wages" rested squarely on the shoulders of selfish colonial employers. Tellingly, the council condemned "efforts to *induce* the United States Government to tie down the wages" (emphasis added). Pay scales, according to a TTCTU resolution, "had been influenced by the Local Government and Industrialists in a desire on their part to avoid raising the standard of living of the workers they employ."[15] This recognition of local elites' insidious role in Americans' adoption of the "prevailing wage" policy, suggests novelist Samuel Selvon, had popular currency and vernacular articulation. Selvon's *A Brighter Sun* has a base laborer's wife explaining to a neighbor that since her husband and other workmen had been "getting more money dan de government cud pay. . . . De government say, 'Eh-heh! Is so?' And now dey pass ah new rule, telling de Americans dey can't pay so much money to de poor people, dat it upsettin 'conomy and society!"[16] In occupied Trinidad, those who felt it, as the saying goes, certainly knew it.

Overturning this "new rule" regarding wages would preoccupy workers and their representatives during the early months of base construction. By the middle of 1941 the TTCTU had asked both British and American officials permission for "unfettered collective bargaining" with base authorities. This request seemed to have gone unanswered in Washington but prompted a tellingly intimidating response from the British Colonial Office. Along with the rote reply that prevailing wages represented established U.S. military practice, the secretary of state urged Governor Young to remind the island's labor advocates that agitation would make it "difficult for the United States Government to carry out their promise to employ local labor to the maximum extent practicable."[17] But perhaps confident in their belief that the wartime emergency left U.S. authorities with no real alternative to "native" employees, the colony's labor representatives continued to hammer away at what they deprecated as the "fixing" of American wages.

Another tack taken by labor advocates was to seek sympathy within the hearts of both empires. "An alliance with British and American workers [to] bring these injustices prominently before the British and American public," advised the trade unionist *Vanguard*, was absolutely necessary.[18] And although such lofty dreams of international mobilization remained largely unrealized, workers in Trinidad did find expressions of solidarity from abroad. Walter Citrine and Arthur Creech Jones, both members of the British Labor Party, urged imperial officials to alter Americans' wage policy in the Caribbean.[19] The London-based League of Colored Peoples, an organization that included many West Indian migrants, protested too, charging that instead of trying to raise the region's standard of living, Americans contributed to lowering living standards in the West Indies.[20] Across the Atlantic in New York City, meanwhile, the American West Indian Council on Caribbean Affairs and the National Association for the Advancement of Colored People approached influential U.S. statesmen in the hope of securing better terms of employment for British Caribbean base employees.[21]

Yet, for laboring people, diplomacy by itself has rarely ever worked, and notwithstanding local unions' pledge to refrain from strike activity during the war, base employees challenged the "prevailing wages" policy through direct action.[22] Indeed, while Americans were still surveying construction sites, workers struck on the grounds that their daily wage of 72 cents (the average for a local unskilled laborer) was too low. Hostile colonial authorities responded with truckloads of replacements ("blacklegs"), but the stoppage ultimately proved effective; strikers won a higher rate of $1.20 per day.[23] On June 6, 1941, base workers again withdrew their labor. Led by the Public Works Trade Union, more than 2,000 men hired by Walsh-Driscoll (the American firm contracted to build the army facilities at Cumuto) went on strike. Explicitly calling for a revision of the "prevailing wage," they demanded increased rates of 29 cents per hour for unskilled laborers and 40 cents an hour for skilled workers; they also requested double time on Sundays and holidays and time and a half for overtime work. The stoppage lasted three days, a significant shutdown for a construction project in which speedy completion was essential; still, strikers did not win the requested raises—not in a colony where unskilled laborers rarely earned more than 10 cents an hour and skilled workers got around 25 cents.[24]

Fortunately for workers in Trinidad, the wartime pressure on U.S. authorities to complete base construction as quickly as possible often dictated a departure from formal policy. Military officials and contractors could ill afford an inadequate or irregular workforce, and in the hopes of securing sufficient supplies of reliable laborers, they often revised rates upward. In early May 1941, for example, Americans asked the colonial administration for permission to increase wages, arguing that the hike was necessary because of the difficulty of base labor.[25] At other times, they simply ignored the colonial administration and upgraded local workers, paying unskilled and semiskilled laborers at rates reserved for the skilled.[26] The willingness of these foreigners to increase wages should be put into proper perspective. It did not reflect "the goodness of [their] heart," as *New Dawn* observed; rather, it was evidence that unable to employ coercive tactics on British subjects, American employers had to resort to something more like seduction.[27]

Yankees' departure from the policy of paying "prevailing wages," not surprisingly, distressed Trinidad's employers as well as the broader establishment. Indeed, at the very top of the colonial administration, Sir Hubert Young "deprecated" Americans' attempts to revise pay scales. Informed at one point of their desire to ratchet up rates, the governor had the colony's industrial adviser remind these foreigners that it was of "greatest importance that the government should continue to set the standard thus precluding the possibility of United States authorities driving up government rates." A most "embarrassing" situation, Young warned, would result if base employment paid more than its colonial counterpart.[28] This executive's language suggested a concern that went beyond economic dislocation; "embarrassing" betrayed that British imperial prestige, too, was at stake. In the eyes of the local representative of the Crown, colonial employers' inability to match American wages must have appeared to be part of a broader usurpation of British supremacy. To the governor, it must have appeared as yet another harbinger of what the narrator of *Rum and Coca-Cola* characterized as the "unceremonious dispossession" of Trinidad's old ruling class.[29]

TOWARD THE BASE

However much the colony's employers maneuvered to diminish the appeal of U.S. employment, people in Trinidad marched toward the bases. Six months into construction, more than 15,000 of them had found formal positions with Americans. (The number then working informally for Americans, from shoe-

Locals (in the background) observe as Americans' modern infrastructure becomes part of the island's landscape. (U.S. Army Signal Corps)

shine boys to portrait artists, is incalculable but, of course, significant.) Half a year later, that number had swollen to 25,000.[30] Included in this drove of base-bound locals were not only so-called unskilled laborers but also clerks, teachers, and policemen—people, in other words, who gave up "good" jobs. The appeal of American work, furthermore, transcended ethnicity, too; Indo-Trinidadian agricultural laborers streamed to the bases no less purposefully than Afro-Trinidadian clerks. In the world of work, as in virtually every aspect of the social sphere in occupied Trinidad (dress, music, and sexuality), the notion of an ethnic divide was well-nigh negligible.

It was the Yankee dollar, to a large extent, that lured locals to American employers. Although base construction did not offer the high wages anticipated by workers and although there is merit to the claim that rates for manual labor on the bases did not significantly exceed the rates in off-base local sectors, laboring for U.S. bosses nevertheless turned out to be relatively lucrative.[31] For one, abundant overtime and holiday work as well as the "dependability bonus" augmented income.[32] In the realm of nonmanual labor, moreover, a considerable discrepancy did obtain between base and nonbase wage rates. One local

Black American soldiers going through drills. (U.S. Army Signal Corps)

who worked for Americans at their docksite facility recalled leaving his cleri-cal job in a San Fernando firm at a rate of $8 per week to take up a comparable position with Americans at the rate of $5 per day.[33] The average cook earning $6 after a month of sweating in a local kitchen could make that in one week under Americans. And whereas the colony's trained teachers had starting sal-aries of around $30 a month, they could make between $80 and a $150 dollars per month clerking for Americans.[34] Little wonder that teachers in occupied Trinidad readily turned in their chalk for American-issued stationery in num-bers disturbing to the government. By September 1941, as the press carried stories of teachers working as carpenters on the bases, concerned officials at the Education Department began demanding a month's notice and salary from teachers intending to quit.[35] U.S. employers also poached the island's police service, leaving it "extremely short handed" by late 1942. A quick com-parison of annual resignations hints at the larger tale of turnover; whereas in all of 1940 only 5 officers left the service, the number for 1941 was 21; for the first two months of 1942 alone, the figure had already reached 24.[36]

Wages alone, however, cannot fully account for people's choice of work. The social meaning of American employment—its challenges and luxuries, its thrills and threats—helped shaped locals' disposition toward base labor. For some in Trinidad, working for Americans presented the opportunity to participate in an exciting new world. Instructively, one of the colony's planters charged that locals abandoned agricultural estates for Americans not so much on the basis of superior wages as on the autonomy and adventure their employment offered. Under these foreigners, he stated, the "younger section of our agricultural community" could work "without adequate supervision." They could partake, too, of "the novelty of a long bus drive in convivial company to parts hitherto unvisited and the excitement of being together with thousands of strangers. This was better than the [horse] races or a fair."[37] These observations, to be sure, might have been no more than convenient justification for this planter's—and his peers'—refusal to pay competitive wages. They do point nevertheless to the need to go beyond narrowly economistic interpretations of workers' flight toward American employers. Base work, by this view, satisfied young people's desires for liberty and novelty. It was for them exhilaratingly modern leisure.[38]

Samuel Selvon's *A Brighter Sun* also alludes to how U.S. employment could satisfy ambitions for progress into a modern world. In a story in which employment with Yankees proves central to plot and character development, an Indo-Trinidadian called Bunsee becomes comically pompous because he has secured an "office job" with the Americans.[39] Riding in a jeep with Yankee soldiers, wearing new suits and panama hats, and smoking American-issued Lucky Strike cigarettes, Bunsee quickly fancies himself a man of prestige. Tiger, another young Indo-Trinidadian and the novel's main protagonist, also eagerly goes to work for Americans. He, significantly, does so not because of their wowing $20-per-month wages but because of the fascinatingly worldly values of their construction project. "Afterwards, when everything finish," he confessed to a friend, "I could look and say, 'Tiger help to build that road.'"[40] The American-built road had special meaning for Tiger. It was, as one literary critic noted, "a symbol of all [his] aspirations," his desire for "knowledge," for ties to "the outside world," and for all that "village life has denied him."[41]

Yet Yankee dollars and modernity did not uniformly enchant Trinidad's workers (even the fictional Tiger eventually became discontented with base work). They grasped the grave undersides to laboring for these American bosses, with nothing perhaps giving them more pause than the specter of a violently arrogant white supremacy long regarded as a definitive element of society in the United States. Whatever racially rooted fears that haunted locals could not have been allayed by the conduct of the white Americans on the island. Whether manning the gates at the bases, driving trucks, ambling down the street, or dancing at parties, they showed scant respect for the interests, bodies, and indeed lives of the colony's nonwhite population. The vast majority of unsavory incidents, to be sure, was suppressed or misrepresented, but locals had no illusions about the public appearance of harmony. Afro-Trinidadians especially understood that many of these sojourning Americans had little compunction about summarily lynching any insubordinate "Negro."[42] In one of the rare openly reported episodes, a U.S. army private attending a dance hall party in Arima found the antics of a drunken "native" patron annoying and simply shot him to death. Certainly, this outrage as well as others that dramatized what, according to one local, was white Americans' "belief in being the supreme race" did not go unprotested.[43] But as a nonwhite native base worker named Prince Kagan soon learned, deep-rooted racist habits die hard—or, in some cases, kill easily. Kagan had been hired by the U.S. Engineers Department as a security guard and apparently had left his post on the night of March 24, 1943, when Byrd Nix, a white American superior, made his rounds. A Texas native, Nix eventually found Kagan, whom he promptly fired and ordered into his jeep. The local man, however, repeatedly refused to get into the vehicle; for this he received from the barrel of Nix's gun four fatal shots into his back. Such an act, though extreme in its brutality, would surely have frightened off many Trinidadians from working on the bases.[44]

Another drawback to American employment was its impermanence and questionable claim to status. Many people in Trinidad appreciated that it was unwise for them to give up jobs with secure tenure. Like Hat in V. S. Naipaul's *Miguel Street*, they were cognizant that "Americans ain't here forever and ever."[45] Others stayed away or were kept away from base labor because of its dubious esteem; in the minds of many locals, base work did not accord with traditional notions of respectability. (By contrast, indeed, it appeared more reflective of what anthropologist Peter Wilson famously theorized as "reputation.")[46] Alfred Lalla, then a teenaged assistant teacher, got this sociology lesson in August 1941 as he tried to join many of his young Arima friends who had begun working at the nearby Wallerfield site. Once word of the boy's movements reached the school where he taught, the principal chastised Alfred and turned him away from base labor. He then personally secured for Alfred a place in the island's teacher's training colleges. The older man's actions were not surprising; as a principal, perhaps the ultimate embodiment of a conventionally respectable occupation, he was guiding the young man toward traditional decency rather than doubtful new money.[47]

IMMIGRATION AND THE BAJAN INVASION

For the most part, though, the colony's less privileged residents showed little such reserve about going to work for Americans, and this massive flight sent employers, especially planters, scrambling. Quickly and unsurprisingly, these hirers responded with strong demands for migrant labor. Estates in Trinidad (and the region) had long relied on imported workers; in previous centuries it was the sweat of African slaves, Asian indentures, and West Indian migrants that fueled the island's agro-industrial complex. By the time the occupation got under way, however, recruiting extraterritorial labor was not a doubtless proposition. Existing laws restricted migrant workers (stipulating, for example, that they first deposit a fee); to get access to outside labor, plantation owners would require sympathy and collaboration from Trinidad's colonial administration.[48] Unfortunately for them, the government did not always share their assessment of the labor situation; these employers would thus expend plenty of energy trying to persuade local officials that the U.S. occupation had drained the local supply and left them in financial ruin.

Plantocrats and their allies wasted no time urging the introduction of workers from other British West Indian islands. As early as January 1941, when U.S. authorities had hired only a handful of "natives," the *Trinidad Guardian* called on the government to relax immigration laws so as to ensure estates' access to an adequate labor supply. By the time land-clearing had begun in March, the daily voice of the colony's planters was issuing what would become a familiar cry: "labor shortage."[49] The notions of crisis and emergency, however, were hardly self-evident. Indeed, they demanded invention, and herein lies the explanation for the full-page ads in daily newspapers publicizing the availability of "regular" work soon after the onset of base construction.[50] Taken out by the colony's leading estates (Caroni, Woodford Lodge, and Trinidad Sugar Estates Limited), they aimed less at workers than at the colonial state. These notices comprised part of an effort to induce governmental intervention, intending to substantiate plantocrats' arguments that estates were genuinely and thoroughly but in the end futilely in pursuit of Trinidadian labor.

Such claims and schemes faced challenges. Heaping scorn on the notion that Trinidad faced an acute labor shortage, the island's labor advocates attacked the agitation for immigration as no more than a pathetic "sugar baron" plot to enlist the state in its attempt to sabotage workers.[51] A *New Dawn* editorial, for example, explained that "scared at the thought of having to face a new setup in the economic life of the island, [planters] are pressing—god and government knows how hard—to bring laborers from the other islands to keep the army of unemployed as large as possible."[52] Furthermore, having recognized the persuasive power of statistical discourse in a modernizing administrative moment, resourceful trade unionists presented figures to disprove the existence of a labor shortage. Their report to A. V. Lindon, the colony's industrial adviser, submitted the availability of more than 60,000 local workers, a number, as Lindon pointed out, sufficient for the efficient operation of Trinidad's agricultural estates. In the end, not surprisingly, the colonial government disregarded this figure. By the middle of 1941 restrictions on immigration to the island had been loosened.[53]

Yet, for planters, the new legal facility for contracting British West Indian labor proved inadequate, and they continued to express their dissatisfaction. Indeed, the issue of immigration policy opened between Trinidad's plantocrats and the administration a rift that helped to hasten Governor Young's departure from office. Throughout 1941 Young deflected estate owners' complaints of a labor shortage as "greatly overstated."[54] Thus, whereas owners demanded a deluge of British West Indian migrants, the governor proposed a program of regulated immigration. Young had arrived in Trinidad in the aftermath of the 1937 labor unrest, and he feared that the flood of West Indian migrants would turn into a sea of unemployed wardens of the state or, worse, flotsam for overzealous labor organizers. Only under specific conditions would he agree to the suspension of the migrant deposit fee. The governor stipulated that each planter be allotted a quota of migrant workers who would sign contracts prior to arrival and that planters, moreover, would assume responsibility for migrant workers' welfare, especially housing. Until estate owners accepted these terms, he refused to budge. Frustrated, planters could do no more than complain to the Colonial Office. Young, they cried, was intent on overseeing the ruination of the local agricultural industry.

In time, though, the governor gave in. At the high point of base construction in 1942, when U.S. authorities recorded over 25,000 locals on their payrolls and estate managers ominously forecast fields of unharvested crops, planters and their advocates intensified their remonstrations against the Young administration. The West India Committee, in particular, charged the executive with taking a contemptuous attitude toward the plight of the estates; the governor, this London-based planter lobby told the Colonial Office, had adopted a policy of "evasion" with regard to the labor situation in Trinidad.[55] Around this time Young bowed, pushing the legislature to pass another immigration ordinance. This one, significantly, permitted the entry of migrants to work for Americans; the governor had initially opposed such a measure, preferring to reserve base employment for the island's workers. Planter power thus won in the end. Young had to backpedal and endorse a measure meant to return the colony's workforce from the bases back to the estates.[56]

Although authorities entertained the idea of procuring workers from as far north as Jamaica, they turned to a nearby and familiar source.[57] From Barbados, beginning in early March 1942, arrived the first batch of what would eventually total nearly 2,000 laborers. Contracted by the Walsh-Driscoll Company, they started at a rate of $1.19 daily (a little over 25 percent more than the average nonbase local laborer), found housing in U.S.-built barracks on the outskirts of the army base, and (on their employers' advice) brought their bicycles for transport.[58] This immigration scheme, though, would come to an abrupt and violent end. Brought at the behest of planters, "Bajan" workers were confronted by Trinidadians keenly conscious of the invidious roles these migrants came to play. Indeed, with Americans laying off more than a hundred "native" employees the very week the Barbadians arrived, many locals saw in their fellow West Indian colonials favored rivals.

The result was resentment and friction that flared into violent conflict on Good Friday night, April 3, 1942. Around 11:00 P.M. a group of these Barbadian workers interrupted the show at Arima's Princess cinema and ordered all their countrymen out; they then proceeded to attack and injure scores of the remaining local patrons. The Bajan Invasion—as it was quickly dubbed—unnerved colonial authorities, who over the next few days placed Arima under curfew. The city's inhabitants, too, became consumed by the fray; finding a lighter side to the incident, they, according to the *Trinidad Guardian*, took up a new teasing form of greeting: "are u a bajan?" and "look a bajan!" were commonly heard across the eastern municipality.[59] The immediate cause of the clash remains unclear, but there is no doubt that antagonism between "native" and Barbadian workers provided the backdrop. Tellingly, when colonial and U.S. authorities sought to defuse the tension in the aftermath, they issued a public notice insisting that Barbadians were not stealers of Trinidadians' jobs but loyal British subjects assisting in the war effort.[60] Such reassurance was a clear case of bolting the stable door after the proverbial flight of the horse. To reduce the risk of further violence, the colonial government soon began repatriating Bajan workers.

CONSCRIPTING HOOLIGANS

With "prevailing wages" and immigration schemes offering little salve to Trinidad's plaintive employers, they got desperate enough to advocate conscription. So dire a measure, though, demanded not only conscious discretion but also cogent justification. Thus alongside mostly quiet calls for conscription was a purposeful plantocrat smear campaign against the island's workforce. Recognizing the imperative of convincing the state of the necessity of coerced labor, Trinidad's agricultural interests cried that the colony crawled with lazy, immoral, and even criminal young working-class males. "Hooliganism," their chorus went, was holding the society hostage, and conscription was the only effective policy response.

Talk of conscription first surfaced in early 1942, but the embattled Governor Young quickly rejected it as unworkable.[61] By the middle of the year, however, the proposition received new life as the increasingly ornery Young found himself replaced by Bede Clifford. Then the governor of Mauritius, Clifford had an American wife (Alice Gundry) and had earned a reputation for easy relations with Yankees during his tenure as governor of the Bahamas (1932–37).[62] Much to the encouragement of the local employing class, Clifford's maiden address to the Legislative Council in June included supportive, even euphemistic references to the policy. Conscription, the new governor explained, should be viewed not as "coerced labor" but, rather, as "getting the best men for the best job."[63] The executive "on the spot," moreover, had the support of his superiors back in London; the secretary of state informed him that the imperial government was quite "prepared to agree if necessary to the adoption of conscription subject to satisfactory detailed arrangements being worked out."[64] In the colony, of course, Clifford could count on the unwavering endorsement of planters and their establishment sympathizers. People such as H. Neal Fahey, a landowner and Department of Agriculture official, argued that given workers' determination "to make all the gain out of the emergency that they can," which left "essential industries" to suffer, coercion had become necessary. Anticipating pro-labor retorts couched in terms of democ-

Trinidad's governor Sir Bede Clifford talking to U.S. military commander General H. C. Pratt. (U.S. Army Signal Corps)

racy and rights, Fahey's essay in the *Trinidad Guardian* characterized workers' actions as "democratic" only insofar as the word meant "the right of being left alone and doing within reason what you like."[65] From his invested perspective, labor's flight to American employment abetted anarchy; it was, as a result, an unassailable cause for conscription.

Despite vehement opposition from patriotic dissidents such as Ralph Mentor, who accused Fahey and his cohorts of libeling workers under the "guise of patriotism," Trinidad's administration discreetly mobilized for the policy of coercion.[66] In July 1942 the government gave notice of an impending registration of the island's population, even though at this preliminary stage officials remained tight-lipped about any links between the proposed register and the "labor crisis." The notice simply stated that teachers would have to forgo part of their August vacations to help with the registration and offered no further explanation. Days later, however, another press report suggested that the exercise was a response to the government's interest in the population's nutritional needs: "no registration, no ration," according to the *Trinidad Guardian*, was the administration's official slogan to encourage public participation.[67]

But as the dates (August 26, 27, and 28) neared, it became clear that the measure had implications for labor policies. Registration was carried out under the Compulsory Training and Service Ordinance; it was administered, furthermore, by a committee that included Labor Adviser A. V. Lindon, prominent planter Captain Watson, and the increasingly isolated ex–trade unionist A. C. Rienzi. Removing all doubt, newspapers began admitting that in addition to the coordination of rations, registration stood to contribute to "compulsory service" if the need arose. Every "man woman and child," implored a *Trinidad Guardian* editorial, should register to help in the collection of unemployment statistics for the colony's Manpower Committee.[68] The *Port of Spain Gazette* also carried a revealing report in which Hugh Wooding, the lawyer in charge of carrying out the exercise, was quoted as reiterating that registration would serve the important task of collecting vital labor statistics. Finally, the official form itself reflected the priority accorded to labor. Whereas only one question addressed food preferences, no less than four focused on labor issues: occupation, special skill, last job, and name of employer.[69]

In the end, although islandwide registration went smoothly, conscription turned out to be a nonstarter. In mid-1943 Clifford advised the secretary of state to inform planter lobbyists in London that the measure was "impracticable."[70] The governor did not elaborate on his reasoning, but perhaps with Americans at the beginning of the year signaling their intent to lay off base workers, it had simply become unnecessary. That conscription even came under serious consideration, however, remains instructive. Planters, it underlines, were terribly desperate to reverse any gains workers might have achieved in occupied Trinidad.

Coupled with the demand for conscription, it is important to appreciate, was a deliberately pernicious portrayal of the colony's workers. Ever since the arrival of liberal-spending Americans, argued establishment and even mainstream types, the laboring classes, especially those who were young and male, had degenerated into nuisances and criminals. Such aspersions about the proletarian character, to be sure, had a long and dubious past in the colony and region; the postemancipation period, in particular, witnessed relentless attacks on the integrity of laborers whose ambitions often crossed with that of ex-slaveholders.[71] But public defamation of Trinidad's "common people" acquired a new stridency during the years of the occupation. This, not coincidentally, was the very moment in which planters and their advocates pressed and even began to mobilize for conscription.[72]

Throughout 1942 and 1943, especially, the plantocracy and even members of the mainstream tirelessly trashed Trinidad's workers as indolent, dissolute, and dishonest. It did not matter, argued one sugar magnate and member of the British Parliament, if workers' wages rose; such an increase, according to Leonard Lyle, only "had the effect of reducing the number of hours worked."[73] Echoing many planters in the colony, the London-based Lyle also questioned the ethics of locals employed at the U.S. bases. These workers, he privately informed the secretary of state in London, would easily refuse honest agricultural jobs in the face of corruptible American alternatives. "While the West Indian may not have a highly developed sense of the ridiculous, he does have a sense of humor: but he is not merely trying to be funny when he tells one that he is working at the American base for the 'good old firm of Steal and Dolittle.' . . . To the workers, this is the nearest thing to plenty for nothing which is ever likely to come their way. It is appreciated that it will not last forever but while it does the workers intend to make most of a heaven sent opportunity."[74]

The rhetorical attack on the demeanor and discipline of the colony's laboring men soared to extreme heights in the trope of "hooliganism." The term was hardly new to Trinidad, as even before the arrival of Americans, it had been employed by respectable people when condemning poor people's anti-establishment displays.[75] By late 1942, however, hooliganism assumed new alarmist salience; it became the name for a social epidemic. Trinidadian society, according to elites' diagnosis, was now afflicted by a new (anti)social disposition. The island had succumbed to a "new evil," in the words of veteran conservative journalist Charles B. Mathura.[76] Admittedly, hooliganism was not simply a convenient elite invention; yet, it must not be mistaken for an accurate marker of a new criminal propensity. Best viewed as a "moral panic," it has to be set against the backdrop of planters' anxieties about securing a workforce that openly deserted them in favor of more remunerative base employment. Ultimately, it was inseparable from the struggle between employers and employees in occupied Trinidad. Hooliganism was an index of respectable people's fears in the face of unsettling American-influenced changes in the local labor market.[77]

The panicked discourse about the deportment of the colony's workingmen ever since the arrival of the Yankee dollar was particularly audible in courtrooms. Representative were the remarks of a Port of Spain magistrate at the end of a trial involving a group of young men who worked at the Cumuto air base site. They stood accused of stoning a filled train as it passed them, and according to the jurist, the incident of disorderliness derived from the current wave of Yankee-funded prosperity. After mocking one defendant's use of the

Americanism "guy," he concluded that "American money had made all those people crazy."[78] In another courthouse, this one in Arima, the magistrate decried Yankee dollars for relieving local youth not only of "training" but, worse, a sense of remorse. He was struck by the complacent insolence of a crew of young men found guilty of "misbehaving" at parties. They, according to this stunned official, greeted the verdict with the boast that "we have money, we can pay, Uncle Sam is here!"[79]

As with so many moral panics, the phenomenon of hooliganism was to a large extent driven by the establishment press. Law, order, and discipline, drummed the two main dailies, had broken down in the colony. Editorials and articles railed every day about terrible "gangs" of young men garbed in colored shirts and armed with sticks and stones. The *Trinidad Guardian*, in particular, chronicled what it christened a "wave of lawlessness" and routinely treated readers to outraged reports about local toughs—the period's infamous "robust men."[80] These types, alleged the paper, stole food, stoned bystanders, and assaulted anyone impeding their progress.[81] The organ also published numerous pieces of public correspondence on the subject; one, for example, mockingly advised that, to become a member of the hooligan gangs, all one had to do was "to beat up on someone, supposedly with a lead pipe."[82] Other missives took a sincere stance, appealing for the eradication of the "evils" of hooliganism. "We women of Port of Spain," began one letter to the editor, "have been suffering molestations for a long time in silence not only by the native element of the population, but by the personnel of the various forces established here." Yet whereas "American defenders" had learned better and amended their ways, "native marauders," the writer contended, continued where these foreigners left off.[83]

Indeed, although hooliganism almost always entered public discourse as inseparable from the presence of Americans, public opinion tended to blame native working-class men. Patriot journalist Jean De Boissiere was rare in attributing the phenomenon primarily to locals' mimicry of Yankee "tricks."[84] The mainstream tendency was to explain hooliganism as a product of the terrible twinning of American money and lower-class Trinidadian immorality. From this perspective, the root of the new social evil lay in Yankee dollars placed in the wrong hands, the hands of young local rogues. When, for example, the commissioner of police unveiled the administration's anticrime program in November 1942 (which included banning the public consumption of alcohol, increasing the difficulty in procuring licenses for recreation clubs, and deploying more police on the streets), he explicitly identified laboring people's "abnormal purchasing power" as one of the fundamental causes of hooliganism. The island's "top cop" further underlined the connection between hooliganism and a sense of inappropriate working-class empowerment by characterizing the colony as caught in a "chronic state of carnival."[85] With American wages available, the "common people," suggested this phrase, now mocked the established order. To the establishment, the colonial world had been turned upside down in these years.

Not all commentary on hooliganism, however, degenerated into a harangue against Trinidad's working people. Patriots, in particular, questioned the quick recourse to condemnation of the colony's impoverished youth as criminals running amok. Though conceding that Yankees had produced a pattern of worrisome conduct among the populace, dissidents like Tito P. Achong and Albert Gomes subscribed to a diagnosis more sociological than moralistic. In late 1942, both these municipal politicians (Achong was then Port of Spain's mayor) opposed a convening of the city council meant to discuss hooliganism for fear that that the "city fathers" would endorse increased punishment and other "drastic remedies." These, it is worth recalling, were the days when calypsonian Lord Invader's call to "bring back the cat" echoed the establishment's clamor for the government to reinstate flogging.[86] Achong subsequently elaborated on his reasons for challenging the dominant interpretation of the troubling phenomenon, asserting that "what is now described as hooliganism" was for the most part "simply an emotional reaction to economic phenomena." He went on: "The people who work with their hands in Trinidad have never been able to satisfy their recreational wants on account of the wage slavery of which they are still, in the main, victims. Now that they are economically better off, there is not enough encouragement given to them to fulfill that want; nor are there enough centers where they may congregate for social and recreational purposes."[87] Thus although Achong, too, correlated the trouble with American money, this longtime socialist absolved local workers in the end. As he saw it, the U.S. occupation had funded popular desires that the colonial society neglected to satisfy. Trinidad's real social problem, this patriot argued, was a suddenly flush but frustrated working-class population.

OCCUPIED WITH THE "SERVANT PROBLEM"

Women, too, labored to take advantage of the phalanx of foreign employers in Trinidad. This was especially true for the females who made a living cooking, cleaning, washing, and performing sundry domestic duties in other people's households. Customarily subjected to low wages and humiliating conditions and acutely conscious of the new possibilities enabled by sojourners from the United States, they eagerly and defiantly sought to renegotiate the terms on which they offered their services. Threatening either to turn to Yankee hirers or to completely withdraw their labor, they not only demanded better wages but also resisted the expectations of subservience. Their new assertiveness, not surprisingly, struck "madams" and "masters" as no more than greed, impudence, and depravity. These employers, immersed in the "ideology of service" and thus given to trampling on the rights of their "girls," fussed and fumed about a so-called servant problem when confronted with what was no more than their employees' struggle for material betterment and dignity.[88]

Domestic work offered one of the most reliable sources of a regular income for poor women in colonial Trinidad. Employing more than 10,000 (approximately 36 percent) of the island's wage-earning females in the 1930s, paid household labor proliferated for reasons stemming from factors of both supply and demand.[89] In the first place, the work required skills that the majority of females were compelled to cultivate quite early in life. By her teenage years, the average working-class girl had already mastered the tasks of cooking, cleaning, ironing, and laundering. Menial work, moreover, frequently guaranteed food and shelter, appealing perquisites for women often drawn from the pool of poor, urban migrants. On the other side of the market, families that aspired to respectability tended to view a servant as essential. Fastidious about their status, Trinidad's wives (predominantly middle and upper class), as one novelist mocked, "never thought it was possible to do without a servant."[90]

But despite their indispensable service in the hearth of colonial society, household workers endured depressingly dreadful conditions. Whether "living in" or doing "day work," they earned meager wages performing miserable toil. For tasks that began at dawn and did not end until late in the night, these women made no more than $10 a month and sometimes as little as $4. This work, moreover, was not only physically but also psychically taxing, and the harrowing inner lives of servants constantly captured the critical attention of Trinidad's anticolonial agitators. Albert Gomes's semiautobiographical *All Papa's Children*, for example, presents a black servant Dorothea as a tortured victim of an affective uncertainty essential to her occupation. She, as the narrator observes, could never "really decide whether she cared for or heartily disliked" her Portuguese Creole employers.[91] Both C. L. R. James and

Alfred Mendes also acknowledged the predicaments of these "girls," in particular, their vulnerability to the unwanted sexual advances of their "masters."
James's *Minty Alley* includes an account of Wilemina, a young servant aggressively groped by her employer despite her protests.[92] And, most dramatically, Mendes's *Pitch Lake* explores how a naive servant's sexual involvement
with the brother of her "madam" leads to her murderous end. This novel, in
fact, amounted to a tragic critique of the miseries faced by Trinidad's poor
nonwhite household workers.[93] These domestics' desperate need for amelio-
ration certainly did not go unrecognized. At the end of the 1930s, women
trade unionists walked from house to house seeking to enlist servants for
the colony's nascent labor movement.[94] Even members of the visiting Moyne
Commission, scandalized by what they heard of these workers' plights, recommended greater rights for them to cope with their arbitrary employers.[95]
By 1941, however, little had improved for the island's domestics; they thus figured prominently among the thousands eager to capitalize on the arrival of
American employers.

Although no statistics exist for the number of servants who abandoned
old employers—either for Americans or for their own homes—the endless
public despair about occupied Trinidad's "servant problem" suggests a consequential figure. As early as March 1941, chatter about servants' "quitting"
on their British housewives began to surface.[96] In the following months, as
more Americans arrived on the island and offered double and triple the going
wage rate, droves of domestics began deserting colonial employers to turn
up on visitors' doorsteps. With no "prevailing wages" policy in the domestic
sphere, the colony's housewives, according to one report, were "in a frenzy."[97]
By the end of the year, there was palpable "social friction" between Americans
and "shorthanded" Trinidadians, who, according to the U.S. consul, charged
Yankees with "spoiling the servant class."[98] But local hirers of menial labor did
more than whine about the exodus of their girls. They urged the administration to establish a vocational education committee that, among other things,
would oversee the training of domestic workers. Moreover, as an immediate
(and more fruitful) measure, they persuaded the colonial government to procure more than a hundred household workers from Barbados.[99]

Domestics in occupied Trinidad served up a "problem" not only by walking out but also by contesting employers' contemptuous attitude. Admittedly,
evidence of their new defiance comes from an inherently dubious source:
"madams" and "masters"; complaints by these employers hardly constitute

objective descriptions of laborers' conduct. Yet they possess indexical value; expressions of dissatisfaction about the quality of domestic labor attest to an intensification of the contest between household workers and their hirers. More specifically, they register a sense of employers' decreasing control and authority and, conversely, a gain, however minute or fleeting, for menials who sought commensurate remuneration and self-determination.

Public records of domestic workers' new oppositional mood are rare but not entirely absent. In April 1943 the *Trinidad Guardian* reported the trial of Emelda Francis, a San Fernando washerwoman who beat up a client named Mrs. Jean Moreley during a dispute over wages. The presiding jurist and, no doubt, many local employers of domestic labor were shocked by Francis's behavior. Indeed, in sentencing Francis to prison, the judge incredulously wondered what kind of "state" Trinidad had reached. A washerwoman had demand a higher wage rate, refused to leave when turned down, and worse, assaulted her client when attempts were made to remove her from the woman's premises.[100]

Such defiance and self-possession among servants in occupied Trinidad appear most startlingly in Ralph De Boissiere's historical fiction of the period. Virtually every reference to domestic workers in *Rum and Coca-Cola* conveys their conscious efforts to secure favorable conditions and to undermine the authority of their employers. With the onset of base construction, one of these women declares to her madam, Mrs. Goodman, that since "her man was working for the Yankees she need no longer slave." It was "high time," she announced, "that she stayed home to look after her own children." Another servant character chooses not to withdraw from the market but to demand more wages. Earning only $8 monthly with the aristocratic French Creole Du Coudray family, Marie requests a $12 wage increase. That amount, she tells her stunned madam, was what American employers paid for even fewer hours. But like Mrs. Goodman, who raged that "it was ridiculous" that "these niggers getting so much," Mrs. Du Coudray objects to the increase and releases her employee of eight years. Marie, revealingly, moves next door to work for the newly arrived Americans.[101]

In De Boissiere's account, open insubordination offers another gauge of household workers' heightened struggle against employers and especially of employees' new sense of empowerment. When Mr. Belle-Smythe, a senior white government official, asks his Barbadian-born cook to procure fresh meat from the butcher, Betty simply replies that she "ain't able," citing the wartime shortage and the resultant pushing and shoving at the shop. To Belle-Smythe's stern reminder that he pays her $22 a month, Betty boldly retorts, "You ain't bound and 'bloige to pay me that. . . . You could get a nex' body to cook for you." For Belle-Smythe, furthermore, the cook rubbed outright injury on top of rank insult by keeping a white American man in her quarters. His discovery of this bold case of interracial intimacy proved to be the final straw, and he promptly fires Betty.[102]

For the majority of Trinidad's nonfictional employers, however, terminating insubordinate domestics would have been like cutting off their proletarian noses to spite their bourgeois faces. They thus did what must have seemed the next best thing: railed and ranted. In late 1943, as frustration and discontent mounted, the colony's hirers of household labor seized the press to sound off about the putatively lazy, brazen breed of servants with which they were now forced to treat. The vitriolic attack began with a letter titled "The Servant Problem" published in the *Port of Spain Gazette*. Signed by "Suffering Celia" from the wealthy Port of Spain suburb of St. Anns, it fulminated that "maids," despite their increased wages, had become "most miserable and impossible." The correspondent then submitted a veritable laundry list of the deficiencies and discredits of servants. "Coarse of manners and crude of speech," they indulged in "dumb insolence and mastery of inactivity when set to their household task." They "must bathe when it is time to serve the breakfast." They must have their "siesta" between 2:00 P.M. and 5:00 P.M. They "pretend that they cannot or that they will not wash or iron, but clandestinely use your starch soap and electricity to keep themselves and their relatives and boyfriends cleaner than you and your family can appear." Indeed, domestic workers, according to Suffering Celia, took "a secret delight in seeing [her] working to exhaustion while they dawdle around." Immoral and insensitive, they "speedily try to convert [their room] into a filthy bawdy house or rendezvous for all their host of relatives coming from far and wide." Untrustworthy, too, they forced this madam to keep "a vigilant eye" and her property "under lock and key." Household workers, Suffering Celia ultimately declared, exercised "tyranny" in Trinidad.[103]

This searing attack struck a chord among hirers of household labor and inspired a chorus of complaints. The colony, these correspondents agreed, was littered with careless, unscrupulous household employees. "Suffering Celia," claimed a follow-up letter, "has penned a true picture of todays domestic servants." It then provided a tally of improprieties. "The boy whistles outside and the girl will go even if she has to leave the baby taking the feeding bottle—and that isn't once in a while." Though "tired and sick" during the day, servants were always "fit and fresh" to go out at night. They also entertained guests and, last but not least, pilfered property. Other exasperated employers chimed in, lamenting about household workers who could not cook and who preferred to "wander from place to place" in search of entertainment and "easy living." What they needed, concluded one correspondent, was conscription.[104]

But just as Trinidad's supposedly idle, criminal, young working-class men found sympathizers, so, too, did servants (who, it should be clear, were portrayed as if they were household hooligans). More moderate commentators hoped the current discord would inspire in the future a spirit of sympathy and harmony between masters and servants. Toward this end, they counseled the formation of a housewife association and the education of domestics. A writer named Iris Alcantara advised wives and their girls to ally with one another on the basis of gender and downplay the class conflict. She asked housewives to be cognizant that "servants have been denied the advantages of an education and had little or no cultural background to equip them for the task of pleasing their employers." Thus although Alcantara, too, agreed with the call for housewives to "blackball the real incorrigibles," she urged that employers also "humanize" the conditions of domestic service.[105]

More radically, some observers openly denounced employers and sided with servants. Criticizing Suffering Celia as "uncharitable" and dismissing the cascade of complaints about household workers as no more than "exaggerated humor," they saw the so-called servant problem for what it was: an altering of the terrain of struggle that promised to favor domestics rather than employers. The American presence, these correspondents contended, brought a measure of justice to a historically lopsided struggle. In their eyes, bitter protests against household workers were simply the grievances of the greedy forced to sacrifice some of their selfish ways. After all, argued one letter, "madams" and "masters" "sweated" their girls "from 6 to 9 for four and five dollars a month" and got away with treating their "maids" like "beasts of burden." For such critics there was a felicitous turn in the debate about domestics: "We are righting quite a lot of wrongs [now]," this correspondent happily concluded, "and this is one of them."[106]

Not surprisingly, patriot Albert Gomes figured among these locals ready to view the situation from the servants' perspective. Gomes, moreover, approached the standoff with the kind of sympathy, measure, and ambivalence characteristic of the general nationalist disposition toward the conduct and fate of the disadvantaged in occupied Trinidad. The day after the appearance of a *Trinidad Guardian* editorial despairing that scarcity and increased rates had all but doomed families dependent on domestic workers, Gomes submitted a column titled "That Trinidad Will Never Return." His essay recast the so-called servant problem as a by-product of the modern times thrown up by base construction. In ranting about etiquette and ethics, the colonial establishment, he wrote, had ignored the fundamental societal forces underlying their predicament. The "servant problem," Gomes insisted, lay not in a lack of "personal decorum, discipline and responsibility"; it was symptomatic, rather, of important "social economic and psychological changes" under way in the colony.

> The class from which the domestic servants have been always drawn has undergone certain social economic and psychological changes that render its adaptability to [domestic labor] a steadily lessening factor. . . . The domestic servant or the quondam domestic servant is loath to do work not consistent with her more recent notions about herself: she is resentful dissatisfied and sullen. Perhaps she is at times annoyingly perverse. Perhaps she is no longer a domestic servant because, since the work on the bases began her husband or her paramour insisted that she became a housewife and do his work at home. Perhaps too she has become friendly with some member of the armed forces local or foreign and has grown sensitive about the work she has been accustomed to do.[107]

Where most elites inveighed against insolence and impudence, this patriot stressed neither ill will nor flawed character but the circumstance that conditioned new subjectivities and values among laboring women. Gomes was certainly not unambivalent about these drastic transformations; he conceded, for example, that at times servants could be "annoyingly perverse." For him, though, the most crucial issue was to recognize that the prosperity generated by the American occupation had availed to poor young women and their male partners a consciousness of new possibilities for labor and living. Many "girls" were now determined to inhabit a world unlike the one they knew; they imagined as well as aspired to more. "It might have been all well and good with the old folks we know," he commented, "but these young girls have ideas." Occupied Trinidad, this patriot believed, had bred a new generation of working-class subjects; it was a generation that frowned on compulsory cooking, cleaning, and washing for others as a thing of the past.

CONCLUSION

Gomes's observations about domestic servitude bespeak one of the defining dynamics of occupied Trinidad. Despite noting that some "girls" might have independently withdrawn from domestic service, he allowed that others had been compelled to leave. Some of them no longer worked for their madams because their male partners "insisted" that they "do his work at home." Alongside a narrative of household workers resisting drudgery, therefore, Gomes also offered a glimpse of females confronted with the patriarchal process of "housewifization."[108] He thus acknowledged that poor women's progress toward accessing long-denied privileges of respectability was complicit with, perhaps even indistinguishable from, men's desires to assert and augment their authority by restricting women to the household. This kind of ambiguity and paradox was not limited to the field of domestic labor where female servants moved to capitalize on the presence of Americans. It was, as will be seen in the following chapters, evident everywhere during the years of occupation: in the spheres of dress, music, and intimate relationships.

4 From Barefooted Men to Saga Boys
Gender, Class, and Clothes in Occupied Trinidad

Sagaboy—a chap who works little but is always well dressed and well fed.
As in "he got plenty ooman boy, he is a real sagaboy."
—Robert Carlton Ottley, *Creole Talk*

In June 1946, as Trinidad's cricket team prepared for an upcoming match against Jamaica, a letter signed by "a saga boy" appeared in the *Port of Spain Gazette*, the daily voice of the colony's socially conservative Catholic elite. The correspondence expressed deep dissatisfaction with the current composition of the squad and proposed some urgent changes. After announcing its rationale that "modern ideas demand that I do away with everything that appeared correct in the past," the letter listed the inadequacies of the present players. They were too "courteous," devoid of "aggression"; the batsmen didn't hit the ball into the "stratosphere," and, at the other end, the bowlers didn't try to "maim" opposing batsmen. Trinidad's side, in short, lacked individuals who played for "the amusement of the crowd." The writer, significantly, closed by advising that when these kind of cricketers were assembled, they ought to sport a new uniform: instead of the traditional white flannel outfit, the team would flash pink, blue, or green zoot suits.[1]

This was wickedly sharp lampoonery, for in occupied Trinidad, as local men modeled themselves after figures from the oppositional culture of the American jazz dance scene, they were seen as bearers of a salient and contested style (of) politics. Their fondness for the zoot suit, in particular, signified a rejection of Anglocentric precepts not only about fashion but, more profoundly, about manhood. Swaggering in the extravagant "drape shape" pants and knee-length, square-shouldered coat favored by "hep" young Americans (especially African Americans and Mexican Americans), the island's seminal saga boys posed daring affronts to British colonial conventions that demanded of them a masculinity defined by humility, discipline, and respectability.[2]

Herein, then, rests the explanation for the correspondence satirizing the colony's new dandies through cricket. A privileged ground for the cultivation of the traditional ideal of British manhood, the game could not accommodate the novel saga boys, aggressively modish men who lived for the showy present rather than by the time-honored rules of restraint.[3] These stylists, indeed, embodied the very antithesis of the game. "Saga boy cricket" was a veritable contradiction in terms and thus made for wonderfully effective mockery. Colorful and reckless, it simply "wasn't cricket"; played in saga style, the sport was a spectacle (specter, perhaps) absurdly beyond the boundary. Contemporary sartorial shifts, the letter to the *Port of Spain Gazette* poignantly indicates, signaled far more than a superficial turn in taste; indeed, in the eyes of respectable society, they betrayed trends that troubled the very fabric of the social order. These trends and troubles are the subject of this chapter.[4]

Men in Trinidad had struggled to style themselves in the image of Americans even before the start of the occupation, but in a colony where they could scarcely put shoes on their feet, fashion was largely out of the question. This situation underwent a dramatic transformation with the deluge of Yankee men and dollars that accompanied base construction. In occupied Trinidad, the quest for sartorial splendor suddenly assumed a new sense of possibility. American attire became readily available and, more important perhaps, affordable for many men. Yet these newfound fashion sensibilities won few raves within the mainstream; to the contrary, they provoked palpable opposition. The disfavor around fashion grew especially vociferous in late 1941 when the government's new relaxed employee dress codes permitted up-to-date local men to don the jazzy "jitterbug shirt." For respectable onlookers, the new fad for casualness along with the official reform that sanctioned it was a deplorable case of following American fashion. Patriotic agitators, not surprisingly, saw things differently and endorsed this appropriation of contemporary Yankee styling insofar as it undermined British colonial priorities. Eventually, however, even these dissidents, too, expressed reserve about dress trends in occupied Trinidad. Confronted with the ultra-hip saga boys, they discerned a threat to their own ambitions for national leadership. "Making style," these aspiring local leaders recognized, meant more than just dressing up; as in the Trinidadian vernacular understanding, the phrase signified an act of bold refusal to acknowledge any and all conventional authority.[5]

THE STRUGGLE FOR STYLE

Though the pursuit of stylish dress by local men attained the pitch of genuine controversy during the occupation, their sartorial ambitions were not nearly novel. In the interwar period, the 1930s especially, Trinidad's populace hankered after the latest wear; indeed, the increasingly fashionable aspirations of the colony's poor fueled political contentions, for however much they wished to be modish, local subalterns ran up against policy-makers and administrators who counseled modesty.

Despite possessing what patriot journalist Jean De Boissiere phrased a "fashion formula" of their own, people in Trinidad made patterns from the United States integral to their dress solutions. Like many communities the world over, they turned to American motion pictures in particular for stylistic cues, confirming that fashion did indeed follow the film. Once impressed with outfits sported by cinema stars, the island's avid Hollywood fans either purchased similar attire if they could afford to or, more likely, paid someone to craft approximations of what they witnessed on-screen.[6] These appropriations, of course, did not always achieve the desired effect; in some cases, in fact, the outcome appeared to be comic. De Boissiere mockingly recalled the misfortune of one such figure: "There was one man who taking a trip to New York had the very latest in suits made for him at one of the best tailors in town [Port of Spain] at a very high cost. He nursed his grand garment on board to 'make style' when he landed. Once there, he was met by friends who offered to take him to lunch but insisted they first take him and buy him a ready-made suit as most of the people on the avenue where they were to take the meal had never been in the Caribbean. And their curiosity would certainly be aroused by his queer rigging as he sailed up the street."[7]

For the most part, though, Americanized sartorial elegance remained beyond the pockets of the vast majority of people in Trinidad before the occupation. Laboring in an economy where employers and government officials held little regard for and, in fact, actively opposed their sumptuary desires, few could afford the luxury of discarding their worn-out garments, far less to keep up with foreign fashion. An essay by left-leaning activist Rupert Gittens related the plight of the colony's impoverished, exposing a pitiable situation in which they were forced to "hoard" their "old clothes" for reuse. Most workingmen, Gittens reported, did one of three things: they passed these retired pieces of attire on to a wife or younger person, patched them on to some torn piece of attire, or packed them to make "bedding."[8] Such were their options in a colonial society where those in power had depressingly sparing notions of workers' wants.

Elites' dismissal of subalterns' interest in making style was to some degree part of a generalized intolerance of the entire cornucopia of popular culture imported from the United States. Long before the occupation, establishment types betrayed a tendency to see subversion in everything American, especially black American. Typical was the attitude of Roman Catholic columnist Captain C. Longridge, who in 1932 denounced jazz from the United States as "primitive music" and summoned fellow believers to "taboo the jazz dance in every shape and form." These dances, according to Longridge's tirade, were "relics of a very ancient negro fetishism, . . . fantastic gyrations of savagery" that ultimately threatened colonial subjects' respect for England.[9] As the decade wore on, even less conservative voices joined the chorus of condemnation of an American youth culture increasingly steeped in black forms and styles of expressiveness.[10]

Yet there was more to the resistance to popular style-making in interwar Trinidad than a racially inflected anti-Americanism. By the 1930s, imperial policy had taken a pivotal turn with serious implications for workers' efforts at self-fashioning in the British Caribbean. Rather than the century-old worry about stimulating acquisitiveness among the region's reluctantly emerging proletariat, officials now feared that this class had become inordinately interested in consumption. Gone was the establishment's Victorian-era conviction that West Indian workers needed to develop "habits of greater expense in respect of living, dress and dwelling." To the contrary, colonial agents now viewed laborers' excessive desire to acquire goods their primary nemesis.[11] Among Trinidad's ruling classes, such a disposition was scandalously bared in the mid-1930s when the government set up the Wages Advisory Board to help determine a minimum wage for manual laborers. Composed mainly of employers, the board issued in 1936 a report that turned out to be nothing short of notorious.[12] Heedless to laboring people's flair for fashion, it suggested that, at best, the working classes should dress for the sake of "self-respect" and "cleanliness"; normally, they should strive only for "decency." Laboring men, the board presumed, purchased one dress suit every three years and a khaki suit and three dress shirts per year. As for workingwomen, cosmetics never even figured into the board's computation of their expenses, despite women's fondness for them. Indeed, allowing these females only four pairs of underwear annually, even the board's definition of "decency" was dubious. The "bloomer report," as critics mockingly dubbed it, was condemned in antiestablishment circles as an instructively gross insult to Trinidad's working classes.[13]

Policy-makers' concern with what should be viewed as humbling workers intensified in the wake of the 1937 "disturbances" and other contemporaneous instances of unrest across the empire. This is hardly surprising given that, as Lord Moyne and his imperial troubleshooters searched for an underlying explanation for the turbulence in the British West Indies, they concluded that, along with the economic depression, laborers' increasingly ambitious demands were fundamentally at fault. As the Moyne Commission put it, "The discontent that underlies the disturbances of recent years is a phenomenon of a different character, representing no longer a mere blind protest against a worsening of conditions but a positive demand for the creation of new conditions that will render possible a better and less restricted life."[14] In this context, imperial administrators and colonial elites envisioned their major task as reconciling the growing discrepancy between the worldly desires of West Indian laborers and the provincial designs they had in mind for West Indian economies.[15] Not yet committed to an economic policy that would develop a substantial industrial sector to challenge the preeminence of agriculture, they focused on diminishing workers' ambitions. Illustratively, the 1938 report on West Indian labor conditions, which included notes on workers' patterns of expenditure, disparaged "extravagant" budgeting. Clothing, makeup, and cinema, it observed, constituted far too great a proportion of workers' expenditures.[16] As far as the official diagnosis was concerned, the region's laborers suffered from misplaced priorities, valuing trends over thrift.

Contemporary colonial policies were explicit about the determination to rusticate West Indian workers, to mold them into simple, stable sellers of labor.[17] Although the Welfare and Development program formulated at the end of the thirties was immediately geared toward preventing further unrest by improving the social conditions of laboring people (in the form of better housing and medical facilities, for example), it comprised more than a package of short-term, conciliatory measures. Constructive in the long run, the program was part of a comprehensive vision of a British West Indian future in which the majority of workers would become agriculturally oriented, efficient, and humble. At its core, Welfare and Development sought to settle workers in rural villages near agricultural estates rather than in towns.[18] Despite recognizing planters' needs for steady labor, imperial policy-makers, haunted as they were by memories of the impact of the Great Depression, stressed the value of peasant-type farming and noncash-crop production.

This imagined peasant lifestyle, moreover, possessed a moral appeal insofar as it was touted by imperial architects as conducive to strong family life, a social feature they meant to cultivate in a region where they found it sorely lacking. This view was clearly expressed by the agricultural adviser A. J. Wakefield when he was asked to formulate policy for Trinidad in 1941. It was crucial, according to Wakefield, to foster a "spirit of sturdy independence and self reliance" in the laborer. Toward this end, he argued, it was necessary to engineer new social communities in which "father and son work together in the field, mother and daughter in the home and the interest of the whole family is centered on the homestead and its stock."[19] This "back-to-the-land" solution for Trinidad's social problems, it should be noted, received local approval, with endorsement coming not only from predictable quarters like the conservative *Trinidad Guardian* but also from moderates such as Canon Max Farquhar. In early 1941, this prominent commentator condemned the colony's education system as an "admirable recruit for urban life." Although he was sensitive that his view might be regarded as "reactionary," this black clergyman nonetheless mourned the situation where, according to him, increasingly "in spirit and mind the average laborer has become estranged from agriculture."[20]

This official effort to reconstitute a peasantry in the British Caribbean, needless to say, did not redound well for workers concerned with consumption. The policy, after all, demanded the delineation of a new, lower social standard of living for the region's laboring class. No longer would the conditions and lifestyles of working people in the industrialized countries of Europe and North America be valid references for West Indians.[21] Such a consequence was spelled out by sociologist T. S. Simey, appointed as the region's social welfare adviser in 1941. Surveying the challenges of "rebuilding" West Indian society, in his seminal *Welfare and Planning in the West Indies*, Simey warned that "the initial uncertainty must thus be faced of having to define some sort of 'West Indian,' rather than 'Western,' objective for social and economic policy in the West Indies." As he saw it, "the scaling down of standards applicable both in public administration and in private life appears to be inevitable before the new colonial policy can be put into practice in the West Indies."[22]

Thus just when colonial subjects in Trinidad (and other British Caribbean possessions) became increasingly attuned to the trends and styles fashionable in the contemporary West, and in the United States especially, policy-makers explicitly discouraged them from cultivating Western-type desires. Their "West Indianness," officials insisted, warranted lifestyles defined by diligence, simplicity, and thrift. It is against this backdrop of colonial elites' attempts to shackle poor laborers with a new regime of humility that concerns about their struggle to dress up in occupied Trinidad ought to be appreciated.

DRESS REFORM AND JITTERBUG REDRESS

The onset of the occupation presented an enormous boon for local men of modest means bent on making style. Base construction brought not only the latest Yankee fashions made manifest on the bodies of occupiers but also the Yankee dollars that would enable working-class people to acquire such attire. U.S. patterns of men's dressing were on public display as never before as well as more affordable than ever before. Yet however dramatic the improvement of the situation for the colony's "barefooted men," elites' attitude toward their sartorial desires remained stubbornly unaltered. As local workingmen quoted American-accented apparel to compose bold fashion statements, intense conflicts ensued. Arising in occupied Trinidad was unprecedented public debate about the relationships between clothes and the overlapping precepts around class, gender, race, and empire.

It was only with the advent of Americans, according to Lloyd Braithwaite, that members of Trinidad's working class were exposed to "unconventional" dress and began styling themselves to "show their different standards of taste." Slightly overstated perhaps, this popular enthusiasm for contemporary U.S. fashion not only garnered attention; it also generated considerable disapproval and antagonism within the mainstream. Even Braithwaite, though a leftist, betrayed a bourgeois suspicion with laborers' new emphasis on fashion. His pioneering sociology of colonial Trinidad included the casual remark that "in good times, the worker tends to spend an inordinate amount of money on clothes."[23] It was the kind of normative statement that hinted at the society's broader and deeper discomfort with style-making among the poor.[24]

Braithwaite's critique proved to be relatively benign, as in occupied Trinidad elites and, more generally, the mainstream openly condemned the pursuit of style among laboring men. In August 1941, less than six months into the occupation, a public correspondent to the *Trinidad Guardian* excoriated the new fashion expressions among working-class males. Writing from the upscale Port of Spain neighborhood of Maraval, Charles Barcant complained that these men were dressing up in "silk shirts and striped flannel pants" and taking "delight in flouting their independence." They and their families, Barcant believed, should pay for their flashy taste; he thus advised Audrey Jeffers, the president of Trinidad's Child Welfare League (who had recently appealed to the government for financial assistance), to withhold support from these people. If such laborers could afford to dress up, reasoned Barcant, they should be able to ensure, too, that "their children are provided for."[25] In the eyes of this witness, who was almost certainly well-off, only the humble among the disadvantaged merited welfare; making style was not to be a poor person's prerogative.

Barcant's rebuff merely marked the beginning of the conflict over popular male dress in occupied Trinidad. A month later the politics of fashion moved to the fore of the public imagination and debate as the colonial government issued a circular laying out the terms of dress reform. Publicized on September 16, 1941, the new policy brought a hoary tradition of sartorial respectability to an end by, on one hand, declaring coat, tie, and long pants optional work wear and, on the other, deeming open-neck shirts and short pants acceptable. Demands for such a change dated back to November 1939, when a few Port of Spain office workers issued a plea for "cooler dressing." Their request, however, went unnoticed until the influx of Yankees. Although the local administration admitted no link between newly arrived Americans and its amendment of the established dress code, framing the decision as a wartime measure to conserve fabric, the U.S. presence undoubtedly spurred the new policy.[26] Yankees, after all, had introduced de facto dress reform for themselves; American employers, in fact, had encouraged native employees to follow fashion and wear open-necked shirts. In opting for reform, officials, it turns out, were not initiating as much as acknowledging change. The measure, as a local journal observed, was little more than a governmental means of preempting the wider adoption of Americans' "common sense" style of dress.[27]

The new code provoked an immediate conservative backlash. Although some skeptics tolerated it as "a good measure for war, not a fashion statement," many in the mainstream mourned the "breakdown of the 'coat and tie' standard of respectability." Dress reform, they despaired, was government-supported social disorder.[28] For them, moreover, it was official endorsement of subversive American fashion. Exemplary was the reaction of Leo Pujadas, a Port of Spain lawyer and the city's deputy mayor. Steeped in the prim Anglocentric conventions of literary societies and bearing a reputation as one of the best-dressed men in his profession, Pujadas immediately vented his displeasure at the policy. "Such a radical change," he told a newspaper reporter the day after its announcement, "would lead to undermining the social standard which forms part of the tradition of the people." Pleading that "there must be order even in attire," Pujadas denounced reform as an unwelcome "revolution in dress standards." Tellingly, this elected official saw the new code as an extension of the unfortunate Americanization of local fashion already under way. Scandalized that Yankees committed the inexcusable fashion faux pas of going to church on Sunday without coats and wearing short-sleeved shirts that hung outside the pants, Pujadas panicked at the postreform vision of local men emulating irresponsibly dressed Americans. In the end, he could only look to the future and hope that Trinidad's fashion would "remain under European influence."[29]

Letters protesting the government's decision poured into the press over the next month. People who cultivated and were committed to British colonial values stridently rejected the change in dress standard as a "retrograde step" that warranted resistance.[30] Much like Pujadas, moreover, they consistently paired the policy change with Americans' style. Noting that these foreigners went to church in casual dress, one opponent of reform charged that Yankees broke "certain customs and traditions that no community may break with impunity." Despite conceding the importance of "broadmindedness" and of allowing people to live "according to their own taste," this correspondent could not help but wonder if Americans recognized the "sacredness of God's place."[31] For other critics, the fear was not divine but social. If men wore shorts, declared one letter, there would be no way to distinguish "the lads from the grownups."[32] Some detractors went so far as to foresee in reform the decline of civilization. When the debate about the policy shifted to teachers, one scandalized reader reminded them that they had to raise children and thus ought to remain "conventional." Indeed, this commentator predicted that if the new dress code came into "vogue for teachers, then the next generation of teachers will propose going to school with bare backs."[33]

In the midst of the contention, one particular element of Yankee style stood out for special attention: the so-called jitterbug shirt. The bête noir of many antireformers, these shirts were all the rage in 1941. On the very day that the *Trinidad Guardian* announced the implementation of the new code, the daily reported that many young men had "happily turned" to their "jitterbug shirts" as work wear.[34] Appearing on the local scene just prior to the occupation, they were brightly colored (sometimes in two tones), made of light fabric, and most significantly, worn outside the pants.[35] Until then, untucked shirts were publicly unacceptable. Undoubtedly, the appeal of the jitterbug among young Trinidadian trendsetters derived in part from its provenance in the brave, antiestablishment, black American youth culture.[36] "Jitterbug" was the name given to an African American dance innovated during the early thirties.[37] Closely related to the Lindy Hop, another popular step in Depression-era America, it went with the hottest swing music of the time and demanded of the male-female pair superb displays of coordination, athleticism, and energy. As a social dance, jitterbugging was a joyful expression of youthful creativity that helped to maintain various solidarities, from community to street gang. The craze, moreover, also crossed racial lines and seized white American youths; doing what was considered a "black" dance (one that expressed the "hedonism and uninhibited exhibitionism of African-American culture"), they were often condemned as rebels against their race.[38]

In Trinidad, too, the dance trend captured the imaginations of the young and hep. Even some of the not-so-young, one calypsonian mockingly suggested, stood ready to "cut the rug." In 1941 singer Growler (Errol Duke) did a number called "Ol' Lady Yuh Mashin' Meh Toe"; poking fun at the attempts of a senior to join in the youthful jitterbugging, the chorus went as follows:

> De new dance dey got in this town
> Making ol' women feel dat dey young [repeat]
> Old lady yuh mashing me toe
> Old lady stop it isn't so
> Yuh crazy, leave de people dance
> Read yuh bible and give de young girls a chance.[39]

Unlike the senior in Growler's song, many older and more reserved onlookers maligned young people's latest moves. Demonizing the dance, the island's "stiff shirts"—as some were pejoratively called—declared the jitterbug "barbaric" and claimed that it concealed a kind of "hooliganism." According to one observer, in fact, the step did not even deserve to be called a dance; it was, rather, a "menace" and an "insult" to the terpsichorean art.[40]

Little wonder, then, that when young Trinidadian men decided to wear their jitterbug shirts to work, they stoked fears of social subversion within the establishment. The *Trinidad Guardian* might have tolerated dress reform and thus distanced itself from what it deemed "ultra-conservative" opinion; it nevertheless warned against those "monstrosities" known as jitterbug shirts.[41] Likewise, many private employers—banks, for example—who followed suit and instituted reform specified that jitterbug shirts were unacceptable. Indeed, as the debate raged, critics consistently counterposed the jitterbug to decency, responsibility, and even manliness. One letter contended that wearing the shirt to visit the governor or to go before a magistrate was an act of "disrespect" and "contempt."[42] When some of Port of Spain's elected municipal representatives inquired whether the new policy applied to them, the *Trinidad Guardian* seized the opportunity to take a jab at both the jitterbug style and the city council. Exasperated with what the newspaper considered the annoying, juvenile twists and turns of municipal politics, an editorial quipped that "there was enough jitterbugging in there already."[43] Some detractors of the shirt even raised questions about gender. Replying to a local male who had earlier complained that women's clothes had begun to take on a masculine appearance, one female correspondent shot back that, quite the contrary, it was men's dress that was guilty of effeminacy.[44] Her primary exhibit, it turns out, was none other than the jitterbug. This piece of apparel, according to this woman, was so "feminine" that it brought to mind a "maternal coat."[45] With the jitterbug fad, it seemed to some, there was no longer a guarantee that clothes would make the man.

Yet in spite of all the fuss and antagonism, dress reform, in general, and the jitterbug, in particular, won endorsement within some local quarters. Patriot dissidents, especially, largely greeted the measure as an alternative to Anglocentric conventions they regarded as ridiculously inappropriate imperialist impositions. Observing local men making style in their jitterbug shirts, these critics saw individuals challenging the established social order, fashionable figures flouting an obsolete British colonial tradition. In their eyes, reform was entirely enlightened policy, and in advocating it, they repeatedly invoked the rhetoric of "freedom," "modernity," and "liberty." In a sketch of the interaction between two Trinidadian men, Jean De Boissiere, for example, reported that when one young man started to wear his jitterbug shirt "Yankee fashion outside of his trousers," the other commented that "at last you can express yourself freely."[46] Similarly, a correspondent endorsing reform argued that it signified "liberty" and testified that he now felt "like a bird freed from a net." Only people who were insufficiently "broadminded" and "progressive," according to this letter, opposed the new policy of reform; they, the writer thus concluded, needed to accept that "the old order changeth, giving place to the new."[47]

In an equally modernist register, the antiestablishment *Teacher's Herald* pleaded with locals to welcome the shift as part of the process of fashioning a Trinidad in which reason and pragmatism rather than sentiment and tradition determined action. With a few teachers already "dressing down" even before they were officially cleared to do so and prompting clashes over the propriety of applying dress reform to teachers, the monthly openly supported the new code. "Conservatism," argued the journal, "is as much due to mental laziness as it is to fear of change. Its great danger in any community is the arrest of progress and the tendency of the intellect to degenerate into an instinct. . . . This is precisely the attitude of those who say we should wear in the tropics clothes designed for the temperate regions." In an era defined by "emancipation and freedom," changes, concluded the *Teacher's Herald*, should not be evaluated on the basis of "the habits of our ancestors but must be governed by reason and intellect."[48]

Other defenders of dress reform and the jitterbug shirt emphasized the practicality of their position, reminding the public that the new American style suited Trinidad's tropical climate. A letter signed by "Professor Shaw" lectured that reform promoted the wearing of "tropically sensible, economic and democratic" clothing and, therefore, need not elicit a "fuss."[49] Patriot Albert Gomes, too, applauded the new policy and encouraged the Port of Spain city council to "fall in line" and implement it. Declaring that clothing ought to be suitable to the climate, Gomes expressed hope that dress reform would be a permanent and not just a war measure.[50] Agreement no doubt would have come from Eric Williams, a celebrated young scholar then at Howard University completing what would soon become a classic work of scholarship. In *Capitalism and Slavery*, as much a vigorous indictment of British colonialism as an economic history, Williams included what might be read as a patriotic contribution to the contemporary debate about colonial traditions and dress: "Like the Englishman and unlike the North American in the colonies," he wrote, "the Caribbean colored middle class today still apes the fashions of the home country in its preference for the heavier materials which are so ridiculous and uncomfortable in a tropical environment."[51] For the future "philosopher of West Indian nationalism," dress patterns in the region reflected British domination and indifference to local needs. Fashion, according to Williams, offered yet another pathetic expression of colonial exploitation.[52]

The Indo-Trinidadian intelligentsia added a revealing dimension to the discussion of dress reform and the jitterbug style. For them, the debates availed an opportunity to mock not only British colonialism but also the broader orientalist view, held by many patriots, too, that the colony's "East Indian" community constituted a culturally irrelevant minority in need of Westernization or "creolization." The *Indian* remarked on the new "jitterbug" trend with a biting sense of irony, posing the following question in its regular "Do You Know" column: "Do You Know . . . that the bright colors that have become very fashionable now had been characterized a few years ago as 'Indian colors?' . . . that what is now called the jitterbug was the fashion of Indians—keeping their shirts outside their pants or dhoti?"[53] With amused self-satisfaction, this Indo-Trinidadian observer exposed the "Creole" craze for the jitterbug shirt as no less than an unremarked instance of Indianization, the very opposite of the process of creolization so often demanded of Indians. If jitterbug shirts were now en vogue, the rhetoric implied, then the island's Indians had been hip all along; whimsical Western fashion was only now catching up with the East.

Another Indo-Trinidadian monthly, the *Observer*, adopted a strikingly similar perspective regarding the controversy over dress. Arguing that their colonial society exhibited a "distortion" in its fashion sense, young progressives at the organ contended that most locals wore clothing "copied wholesale from Europe and America" (imported wool suits, for example) even though it was blatantly unsuited to Trinidad's tropical climate. Meanwhile, the essay related, "the more suitable clothes which were worn by Indians, cotton shirt, kurtah, loincloth and the dhoti were made the laughing stock of respectable society." This state of affairs, according to the *Observer*, was attributable to "a very efficient system of education in early years and by a subtle propaganda later." Both, it explained, ensured that people in the colony "were influenced to look upon such unnecessary dress and habit as being one of the primary aims of life—an end in itself." In the debate about reform, Trinidad's East Indian intellectuals found a chance for pointed criticism; it offered a moment to indict the society's dominant economic and ideological priorities, exposing how these foolishly discriminated against the sensible tastes of their community.[54]

By the middle of 1942 the public debate about dress reform and jitterbug shirts faded away. Having had government sponsorship and having met with ineffective elite opposition, the policy was a fait accompli. Still, it was a revealing episode of contention, clarifying that during the occupation American dress styles constituted a battleground for the fashioning of local manhood. This conflict would soon sharpen as daring young dressers began appropriating a particularly fabulous mode of American sartorial style: the zoot suit.

FOLLOWING ZOOT WITH SAGACITY

Appearing first in the United States in the early 1940s, the zoot suit emerged as the period's most spectacular sartorial sign of young, male, ethnicized, urban hipness (contemporary female wearers were exceptional). Defined by the draping trousers that tapered at the ankle and the broad-shouldered, knee-length jacket, but including a range of accessories such as the hanging gold watch chain and the broad-brimmed hat, the outfit proclaimed glamour. "Zooted up" young men, though, issued more than just a fabulously loud fashion statement; their clothes and comportment encoded complex, contradictory, and at times even inscrutable oppositional politics.[55] Wartime and even postwar wearers of the suit composed rhetorical figures of youthful rebelliousness; in circumstances where state and society demanded denial and selflessness, they symbolized a commitment to excess and individualism. This contemporary form of "style warfare" surfaced in occupied Trinidad, too, as men in the colony incorporated the zoot as part of their battle fatigues in fighting established convention and imposed humility.

Though it is impossible to identify precisely when and how the suit first came to the colony, it might have arrived as early as 1941 with the white American civilians working for base contractors. Another likely conduit was the black soldiers deployed on the island beginning in the middle of 1942.[56] Whichever the channel, the new fashion was certainly evident by the end of 1942. The "zoot suit craze," according to the December issue of the *Trinidad News Tips*, had "hit Trinidad," and a few U.S. servicemen, it reported, anxiously awaited a shipment of these garments from home. Three months later (March 1943), the army organ carried the story of an inauspicious local debut:

> Trinidad's first "zoot" suit exponent appeared at the personnel section
> of the district engineer office in Port of Spain recently. The wearer,
> fresh from the States and not knowing what the prevailing mode of
> apparel would be in Trinidad thought this irresistible bit of man's
> toggery was certain to be appreciated. However, much to his dismay,
> these stupid people just stood and stared, some just laughed out loud
> (maybe they've been away from the States too long). But the wearer
> has decided to auction off the zoot suit to some admiring Joe for the
> remainder of his stay in Trinidad. A great loss to the personnel
> section we say.[57]

Stylistically ahead of his compatriots, this hep American would have fit in perfectly among Trinidad's fashionable set. By January 1943 the zoot suit, according to a keen local commentator, numbered among the Yankee trends eagerly embraced by locals. Before long, moreover, the cinema ensured the outfit's familiarity among a considerable proportion of the colony. *Stormy Weather*, the "all-Negro" musical film whose closing scene featured Cab Calloway in a splendid white zoot suit, opened in Trinidad in October. Boasting some of the most outstanding contemporary black American musical and dance talent, the film was a huge success among local cinemagoers.[58] "Caterwauling and yelling" throughout the show, they so enjoyed it that motion picture exhibitioners brought it back for a second run a month later.[59] By the end of 1943, few on the island would not have at least heard about Calloway's marvelous style-making bit at the end of the movie.

In a premonitory sign, though, even on-screen the zoot provoked debate. Weeks before the official release of *Stormy Weather*, Albert Gomes penned a panegyrical preview that predicted the suit's transformative effect on local fashion. "The grand finale," wrote Gomes, "features a zoot suit dance which is sure to influence styles in male dress in Trinidad for a long time." Yet although this young dissident looked forward to the colony's young dandies (the local "Beau Brummels," he dubbed them) sporting the outfit at the Prince's Building Monday night dances, he anticipated objections from local conservatives ("blue stockings" and "simon pures," according to him). Gomes was right; against his view that the suit was essential for giving "local interpreters of jive the proper background for their music," a reviewer at the *Sunday Guardian* remarked that *Stormy Weather* "displayed to full advantage, or in my opinion, disadvantage the famous zoot suit."[60] The zoot style, according to the writer, "suited as it were to musical comedy, ceased to be funny in everyday life."[61] Perhaps the reviewer was aware of the link between the suits and a series of riots in the United States.[62] At any rate, it was an early sign that, for many local onlookers, the pursuit of this glamorous style was a serious matter.

Gomes's forecast wound up being a fashion understatement. The men who adopted the zoot suit in occupied Trinidad managed to do more than effect a scenic inspiration for local jazz musicians. Local aficionados of the outfit fashioned a new figure of infamy and, furthermore, a new figure of speech. They achieved a historic piece of eponymy: these zoot suiters were Trinidad's original "saga boys." Precisely how this novel label came to be attached to these men remains unknown. The rechristening, though, was audible in a Lord Invader (Rupert Grant) calypso called "Saga Boys in Town" (ca. 1942). Drawing attention to a spectacularly appealing new trend in local men's dressing, the composition offered tips to those desiring to join this bevy of the fashionable: "Your pants," went the choral advice, "must be fittin' you to your chest. . . . Your pants bottom mus' be very small an' your coat mus' be fittin' you to your knee." The young man flashing this look, sang Lord Invader, was promised not only the adoration of young girls but also a new term of endearment: "saga boy."[63] This sartorial guarantee of desirability, of course, was none other than the zoot suit.

"Saga," however, signified more than a flair for fashion that meant ready-made success with the girls in occupied Trinidad; it marked a subcultural lifestyle distinguished by a mode of dressing idealized in the glamorous zoot suit.[64] That the neologism defined not only a look but also a way of life was underscored in an unresolved contemporary etymological debate. Early in 1945 young journalist J. O'Neil Lewis took up the subject of Trinidadians' distinctly "quaint" Creole speech in a short *Trinidad Guardian* essay. Included in Lewis's list of peculiar local slang words was "saga," yet because he offered nothing by way of origins or use, readers soon volunteered their own etymologies.[65] The inaugural correspondence, signed by "Mr. English," objected to Lewis's insinuation that saga was a Creole creation. The word, this letter insisted, was a U.S. import, evolving from the Americanism "sag," which Yankees used to refer to countrymen who had abandoned their jobs at the base; rather than working, they were sagging. These idle American men were nicknamed "saggers," and since they paraded in Port of Spain wearing zoot suits, the amended term "saga" (an abbreviation), Mr. English explained, came to describe both them and their suits.[66] Another letter quickly took issue with this genealogy. "Saga," Ernest Graham contended, was indigenous rather than American. It was a reinterpretation of "swagger," a word for style-making, and had been in local use even before the occupation. Zoot suits, he added in closing, were "fashionable" not so much among American men as among a "certain class of local men."[67] One of the last statements on the origin of the word came from someone who signed as "Creole" and amounted to a compromise between the two competing explanations. According to this letter, "saga" did emerge in 1941 and was employed with reference to Americans. Despite supporting Mr. English in this respect, Creole, however, sided with Ernest Graham in identifying the term as Trinidadians' phonetic rendition of the word "swagger."[68] This dispute about "saga," however unsatisfying for those set on getting to the etymological truth of the term, is nonetheless enlightening insofar as it confirms a key point: the word described both daring dress and unconventional conduct.

If the origins of the label remain uncertain, the image of the saga boy could hardly be sharper. Traveling through Trinidad soon after the war, English writer Patrick Leigh Fermor produced a fetching (almost fetishistic) portrait of the dandyesque figure. It is arguably the most stunning and vivid literary rendition of a zoot suiter.

> The basis of the whole outfit is the trousers, the saga pants. They are usually held up by transparent plastic belts, and pleats like scimitars run down to an unusual fullness at the knee where they begin to taper, reaching almost ankle tightness where the turn up rests on the two colored shoe; peg top trousers, in fact, but so neat and clean and beautifully ironed that they are nothing like the floppy inexpressibles of *La Boheme*. The jacket too, the Bim Bim or Saga-boy-coat, has an eccentric and individual cut. There is no padding in the shoulders, a wasp waist a vent up the back and lapels that descend in some cases— and this gives them their distinctive character—as low as the volumi-nous trousered knee. They are sometimes cut square in front, so that the whole lower part forms a kind of elongated bell. A broad snap-brim hat is worn with this costume, absolutely straight on the head, or tilted rather forward. The shirts may be severely cut out from some pastel shade material with a high collar and deep cuffs fastened with glittering links, or in patterns of crossed Coca Cola bottles, mando-lines, palm trees, hearts transfixed with arrows, peonies or masks of Tragedy or Comedy; or even of *toile de Jouy*, with quiet pastoral scenes of rustics and grazing cattle, against the background of a water mill or ivy-hung ruins. The ties, secured with gold pins or chains, have the splendor of lanced ulcers. A rare but notable affectation is the wearing of a long gold Cab Calloway watch-chain, running from the belt in a loop that may fall below the knee before curving up again to the left hand trouser pocket. The effect of all of this, on the Trinidadians with their wide shoulders long legs and diminutive middles is flamboyant certainly, but at the same time elegant and imposing beyond words. The magnificent Negro carriage comes into its own at last.

As with sporters of the zoot elsewhere, moreover, the spectacular appeal of Trinidad's saga boys lay as much in the strut of its wearers as in the structure of the outfit. Saga boys, observed Fermor, carried themselves with a swagger of profound semiotic value. "The *ensemble* is, exactly as it should be, ineffably foppish and *voulu*, but worn with a flaunting ease and a grace of deportment that compels nothing but admiration; and like the authentic dandyism of Baudelaire and Constantin Guys, it is much more than a mere point of fashion. It is a philosophy and a way of life: the symbol, the outward and visible sign of the Saga *Weltanschauung*."[69] Although he was sufficiently discerning to recognize that saga style represented "more than a mere point of fashion," Fermor stopped short of elaborating on the *Weltanschauung*. Failing to specify the oppositional context of the saga worldview, he did not show how and why in those social and political circumstances to live the saga life was to live otherwise.[70]

In occupied Trinidad, where elites attempted to humble laboring-class men, to discipline them into a peasantlike agricultural way of living and make them hard-working farmers and breadwinning husbands, saga boys signified an uncompromising gesture of refusal. Even more specifically, in the face of an establishment that touted labor conscription as the solution to the colony's economic and social crises, these dandies embodied the triumph of urban leisure and pleasures. If work, village, and family formed the holy trinity constructed by the colonial establishment, leisure, town, and gang shaped saga boys' parallel (and impious) construction. Whereas the one focused on efficient production, the other luxuriated in excessive consumption. For disadvantaged local men, slipping into the saga suit was part of a move to slip the responsibilities imposed on their masculinity.

Hailing largely from the disempowered working classes yet seeking redress by daring to pose as power players, saga boys did all in their power to minimize labor in order to maximize leisure. "He does nothing more than pose," one contemporary recalled.[71] If not earning the relatively high wages offered by Americans, they were quite comfortable living off or exploiting other people's labor to fund their pursuit of the glamorous life. Sometimes these other people were women who labored in the sex trade; sometimes they were peers with whom the saga boy gambled. And although a newspaper editorial about "saga beggars" who, in reality, were pickpockets was consistent with elites' politically driven calumny, it is not impossible that some saga boys resorted to petty crime.[72] Ultimately, by easing through the city, these figures composed spectacular repudiations of authority. Putting on performances of elegance and excess, saga boys challenged that which was prescribed for their race, class, and gender.[73]

THE SAGA OF BOYSIE SINGH

Boysie Singh epitomized the heroic figure of the saga boy in occupied Trinidad. On the eve of the arrival of Americans, this young Indo-Trinidadian had settled into a combined career as a petty thug, gambler, and recreation club owner in Port of Spain. All of this, however, would change with the occupation. With monied American men combing the city in search of tropical pleasures, the resourceful Singh remade his small-time gambling clubs into emporiums of nocturnal pleasure. Aiming to offer Yankees a range of entertainment, he refurbished old properties and bought new ones. The Dorset, the Sunrise, and the Baltimore, according to biographer Derek Bickerton, were all popular Singh-owned Port of Spain spots that supplied a Yankee clientele with women, alcohol, drugs, and music. As an entrepreneur, moreover, he had ambitions not only toward scale but also toward style. It was Singh, Bickerton claims, who fashioned Trinidad's "modern prostitute." Unlike the shabbily dressed women who peddled sex in Trinidad before the occupation, the "girls" working out of Singh's establishments were encouraged to wear "high heels," "skin-tight dresses," and "elaborate hair-dos."[74]

Instructively, Boysie Singh's sensational rise manifested materially in a new sartorial taste and expression. During the occupation he gave up his simple dress code for more glamorous gear, specifically for the zoot suit. "Gone now," writes Bickerton, were "the merino and shorts which he had worn."

> A visit to the Cab Calloway film, "Stormy Weather", is supposed to have influenced his style of dressing; he blossomed out in the shoulderpads, drape-cut jackets and voluminous trousers that set the style for a whole generation of saga-boys. He wore a different-colored suit for every day of the week. . . . His accessories were still more startling. From his fob pocket a gold chain swooped dizzily to within inches of the floor, almost tripping him as he walked; this chain had cost him fifteen hundred dollars. Another chain with a gold star hung round his neck. On each finger were two gold rings, each ring worth eighty or ninety dollars. A gold-topped walking stick—one of a set of forty— had usurped the place of the too-rugged "Three Little Trees."[75]

Boysie had become a saga boy; his biographer, in fact, credits Singh for having "initiated the vogue for wearing completely matching outfits—hat, suit, shirt, tie, socks, shoes and cane all in an identical shade." So legendary was his commitment to making style that one time when supplies were scarce, Boysie, claims Bickerton, "bought an entire shipment of hats for his own use."[76]

As much as dress, demeanor and lifestyle defined Singh as a saga boy. Public appearances were synonymous with public performances. Recognizing that he was a showman, Singh carried out his duty to impress if not awe audiences. Bickerton describes how, when tired of being followed by youths and children, he would "fling handfuls of silver on the ground and walk on." He would also generously receive men who "came to him, flattering him, begging for a raise." Reportedly earning up to $3,000 a week during the occupation, Singh made money no object and splurged sensationally. His wedding reception in July 1941 lasted for weeks and featured live music and legendary quantities of food each night.[77] This husband, moreover, not only supported his family and in-laws; he also "kept" several mistresses and ex-mistresses. In occupied Trinidad, Singh's saga was a supreme expression of the saga life.

CONFRONTING SAGA

Although Boysie Singh's career outlined the contours of the saga life, he was rare. Few such figures had as much entrepreneurial energy and power or were as deeply entrenched in Trinidad's "underworld" of vice and crime. Indeed, it would be misleadingly simple to extrapolate from Singh's life and equate the saga boy with illicit activity. As the keen Fermor acknowledged, some men simply dressed the part but rejected the role, and the English writer accounted for these "virtuous saga boys" by issuing the caveat that though many tended to live off "immoral earnings" and had a "philosophy and a way of life," the term could also be "purely sartorial."[78]

Still, although some saga boys held down legitimate jobs and lived well within the law, they rarely got into the realm of respectability. Some local onlookers, no doubt, simply remained nonplussed by the new characters in their midst, by men whose lives seemed synonymous with theatrical performances. Mystified observers would have been not unlike the narrator in Earl Lovelace's *The Wine of Astonishment* who confessed that "what women see in [saga boys] I don't know; but these are the new heroes."[79] For the most part, though, the mainstream viewed saga boys as males who displayed an inordinate and inappropriate interest in making style, men who posed an unmanly challenge to responsibility and duty.[80]

Evidence of opposition to these notoriously natty men was everywhere in occupied Trinidad. In August 1946 a local magistrate expelled from his court a defendant dressed in a zoot suit. And although the jurist's action provoked a couple of sympathetic letters of protest (including one that mocked it as a "curtailment of liberties"), public efforts to validate the style were rare and largely futile.[81] Along with being thrown out of spaces of "respectability," saga boys were mercilessly mocked. Much like the correspondent who (in the chapter's opening anecdote) satirized these figures through the game of cricket, many locals viewed them as ideal grist for their humor mills. An *Evening News* column, despite acknowledging that the zoot suit did fashion men in Trinidad into Don Juans, ridiculed it. The outfit, suggested "Feste," was perfect for "knock-kneed" men and fit like gloves—boxing gloves! Turning to the saga boys themselves, this columnist concluded that "only foolish people are such slaves to fashion." Journalist J. O'Neil Lewis adopted a similarly derisive stance toward the zoot suit wearers and the hep cats who hounded them. Explaining why he was out of place in such circles, Lewis confessed that he lacked the requisite "mental vacuity" to join the "cult."[82]

But where some people saw fashionable farces, others found something far more sinister. In the middle of 1943 an anonymously penned letter to the *Trinidad Guardian* reported on the conduct of a male defendant. This young man, according to the correspondence, broke out into a song in the course of being sentenced. The lyrics were nothing short of the celebration of the "saga life."

> Number one, ah en' working no way
> Number two, ah en' drawing no pay
> Number three, ah en' got no wife
> Number four, is a saga life
> So I'm a robust man
> Don't talk 'bout no brave dange[83]

True or false, this allegation trenchantly testifies to the subversive significance of saga. Both lyrics and setting confirm saga as a subculture of deliberate and dangerous indifference, indeed, of boastful challenges, to decent manhood. The demands of neither work, woman, nor law could compromise the saga boy's worldview that life was a game meant to be played fully, richly, and fearlessly. The saga boy styled himself irremediably and unrepentantly against the conventional wisdom (otherwise) of colonial society. In the end, no image better conveys the arrogance, insouciance, and defiance of the saga life than that of a convicted man lyrically paying tribute to his deviance in the face of judicial power.

As this letter suggests, saga boys sometimes generated a fearful fascination; this mystique helped invest the label with considerable rhetorical currency during the period. Thus although the term was associated most immediately with laboring-class dandies, it was also effectively deployed to slander or question any ethos that appeared to brazenly transgress colonial conventions of dress and, more broadly, conduct. Indeed, addressing a man invested in established modes of respectable masculinity as a saga boy amounted, at times, literally to fighting words.[84] The effect, in other instances, was not provocative but regulatory, compelling deviant individuals to return to "proper" forms of comportment. There was a tendency, as a local journalist explained, to wield "saga boy" as an epithet against the colony's white men who dressed comfortably and casually—one who abandoned wrist neck, for example.[85] Used in this way, the term expressed "so much opprobrium," the article went on, that the white men in question "would scurry back to their comfortless portable Turkish baths with all haste."[86] As if to illustrate the point, the conservative *Indian* magazine shortly thereafter deployed the "saga" label in precisely this censorious manner. In an editorial titled "Saga Boys at Government House," the organ complained about the public "appearance" of some judges and a "general loosening of morals" among officials who occupied high government posts. Saga lifestyle, it charged, had "entered the heads and hearts of the more educated class," and as a result, the "dignity" of important offices had disappeared.[87] Ultimately, in occupied Trinidad, any stylish challenge to accepting one's place in the social order lay vulnerable to being attacked as saga.

A "COSQUELLE" CONCLUSION

The antiestablishment aura of saga should have easily recommended the style to the colony's patriots; yet the trend drew neither unanimous nor unambivalent raves within dissident circles. Less than a year after Gomes's eager endorsement of the zoot suit, in fact, came Jean De Boissiere's despairing deconstruction. However sympathetic he was to the interests of the laboring poor in making style, De Boissiere expressed grave doubt about the spectacular contemporary aesthetic. Voicing a concern that obtained to varying degrees within Trinidad's nationalist quarters, he questioned whether the refashioning of the old order left the society with any redeeming features. According to this patriot, Trinidad had become overdone, incoherent, and unattractive during the occupation; saga, in this regard, was iconic of the modern times.

De Boissiere's most developed critique of local taste in general and dress in particular appeared in a 1944 essay titled "Cosquelle Is the Word for It." Since the onset of the occupation, it argued, Trinidad had become stricken with a distorted tastelessness. Americans, their images, and their money, De Boissiere was convinced, had made "the people" pathetically imitative and hence embarrassingly unconcerned with their own environment. The majority of them, he believed, were vainly obsessed with an Americanized appearance of personal luxury, for however much they struggled to model themselves after Yankees (seen on the colony's streets and on cinema screens), most Trinidadians ultimately achieved little more than "mock display." Locals, as De Boissiere saw it, succeeded in copying only the superficial aspects of Americans' lifestyles. They could neither appreciate nor reproduce the full, authentic setting of the United States.[88]

To capture this distressing shift in appearance and attitude, De Boissiere reached for a word from the local argot: "cosquelle." Carrying all the snobbish connotations of an adjective like "gaudy" (or the phrase "ghetto fabulous"), it referred to what the piece defined as tastelessness marked by "a contrast of luxury and squalor."[89] Illustrating "cosquelle," he invoked "base workers home for the weekend in dinner jackets escorting their women folk dressed in satins that swept around the heels of silver evening shoes along the *mud path that led from the house to the road*" (emphasis added). These houses, furthermore, were frequently made of tapia, wrote the journalist. Other Trinidadians, he lamented, did not even own a home but insisted nonetheless on appearing in splendor. Even more scandalous, some possessed nothing but a $50 suit and a $20 pair of shoes but remained untroubled. After all, their "raison d'être," according to De Boissiere, was to "make style at the Prince's Building in their gaudy expensive clothes."

Despite appearances, this critic aimed to author more than an aristocratic harangue of the nouveaux riches. It was not De Boissiere's style to regard Trinidad's poor with easy contempt. Indeed, he did not fault the people for leading what he called a "cosquelle existence." Ultimately politicizing the matter, this patriot discredited local elites for having failed to create local aesthetic standards to which the common people would subscribe. Rather than shoulder the responsibility of establishing indigenous notions of taste, Trinidad's ruling classes, De Boissiere contended, preferred to look to London. And without the guidance of the elite, the subordinated set was abandoned to imitate Yankees. For him, "cosquelle" was in the final instance the unfortunate result of subalterns being left to their own stylistic devices. In the face of the glamorously appealing American fashion, Trinidad's poor majority managed no more than miserable mimicry.

In De Boissiere's eyes, dress styles indexed just how deeply and dangerously American modes of being and money had stirred local imaginations. Yankees, he believed, struck fantastic images and paid fabulous wages; they had made their styles affordable for many in the colony. By his view, though, these foreigners had failed to fundamentally alter the substance of most Trinidadians' lives. De Boissiere thus saw the local society as one in which the gap between working-class reality and working-class imagination had become dangerously wide. This is what he mourned in writing about poor locals' "lack of interest in [their] surroundings." This is what he despaired of in claiming that the poor lived in a world of "make believe" and achieved "greater and greater flights of imagination." The majority of people in occupied Trinidad, according to Jean De Boissiere, chose not to engage but to escape their everyday realities.

This interpretation of local aesthetics reflected the particular anxieties of a Trinidadian patriot witnessing what he believed to be a society in limbo between the past and the future. "We are still thunderstruck and a bit uncertain as to where we stand," Gomes poignantly stated in late 1945.[90] De Boissiere's doubt was consonant with the broader nationalist commitment to forging a Trinidadian community out of "tradition." For this dissident, as for many of his patriotic peers, zoot suits, jitterbugs shirts, and other saga appropriations might have signaled the coming of a time free of British colonial rule. Troublingly, though, the styles also appeared to foreshadow a future filled with the seductively colonizing commodities of American modernity.

5 Yankees in the Land of the Calypso
Promoting and Patronizing
Trinidadian Nationality

Trinidad people don't know good thing. They just born stupid. Down at
the base it have Americans begging me to sing. They know what is what.
The other day, working and singing at the base, the colonel come up and
tell me I had a nice voice. He was begging me to go the States.
—V. S. Naipaul, *Miguel Street*

[The] marriage of Burlesque and Bacchanal will, we believe, end happily
in a divorce. They are incompatible.
—Jean De Boissiere, "Canned Carnival"

On May 16, 1944, two Americans attached to the military forces in Trinidad,
Tedd Joseph and Richard Knight, produced and directed *Land of the Calypso*.
A three-and-a-half-hour revue put on at Port of Spain's Empire theater, the
show was a dramatic "condensation" of the colony's carnival. It began with
a "J'ouvert" scene, the traditional opening of the two-day pre-Lenten festival, and moved into "Street" and "Backyard" before closing with "Las' Lap,"
the customary conclusion to the carnival.[1] Conceived with an American audience in mind, this presentation of what was fast being accepted as Trinidad's
national bacchanal strove for authenticity. It featured well-known calypsonians as singers, scores of nonprofessionals as dancers, and performances that
flowed down into the aisles among patrons. *Land of the Calypso* displayed a
deliberate determination to introduce Yankees to true Trinidadian culture, to
showcase what patriot Alfred Mendes tellingly termed the "real McCoy."[2]

Whether the American impresarios (who had help from Albert Gomes and
another local journalist and amateur musicologist, Charles Espinet) achieved
their ethnographic ambitions was a matter of interested debate. On one side,

Mendes raved. His review, "Something Trinidadian on Stage," thrilled that for the first time the colony witnessed "a completely proletarian cast" in a "completely indigenous" work. Despite its indebtedness to Yankees (its "odd paternity," in Mendes's words), the bill, he concluded, was "Trinidadian to the marrow."[3] Jean De Boissiere could not disagree more; for this critic, the event was anything but "trini to the bone." His pointedly titled review, "Canned Carnival," panned the program as abysmally inauthentic. The dancing, music, and singing, according to De Boissiere, were more an "idea" of Trinidadian culture than an honest portrayal. Reaching for an analogy, he likened the revue to a doomed wedding of "incompatible" Trinidadian "bacchanal" and American "burlesque." Divorce, cheerily predicted this patriot, awaited the "marriage."[4]

In the production and reception of *Land of the Calypso* lie themes central to the career of Trinidadian culture during the period of occupation. Staged by and for U.S. citizens yet considered by some locals to be "Trinidadian in every sense," indeed, even too "sincere" by one local reviewer, the event highlights Americans' active role in the cultural projection of nationality in the colony.[5] At the same time, De Boissiere's scathing review reveals that the presence of foreign hands in the forging of indigenous identity did not go unquestioned; his dissatisfaction, in fact, indexed the wider worry that attended Yankee involvement in this act of patriotic invention. This close yet contested relationship between U.S. occupiers and the construction of Trinidadian nationality is the primary subject of this chapter.

Americans, it is important to appreciate, arrived in the island at a moment when locals, as one commentator mocked, had "suddenly discovered" the concept of "culture."[6] The giddiness about this discovery (as shown in Chapter 1) manifested with particular force around the calypso, the epitome, according to the patriotic intelligentsia, of Trinidadian culture. Yet, as in many New World societies, this effort to nationalize a form associated with blackness was plagued by anxieties about race and the capacity for genuine artistry. Considerable debate thus surrounded the project of promoting Trinidad as the Land of the Calypso.[7]

The stationing of U.S. personnel in the island—more specifically, the impressive interest these occupiers showed in the song—profoundly affected this situation. It would endow the calypso not only with money but also with legitimacy; many locals, after all, took Yankees to be cultural authorities, people, in the words of a V. S. Naipaul character in *Miguel Street*, who "know what is what." The ramifications of Yankees' entry into the local calypso scene,

however, proved even more complicated and more ambiguous. Besides cata-
lyzing the validation of calypso, Yankees dramatically reconfigured the market
for the music. Bearing financial and artistic currency, these men captured the
imaginations of local singers. And these calypsonians, struggling yet savvy,
quickly recomposed themselves and their craft to capitalize on the relatively
prosperous, powerful consumers from the United States.

This preoccupation with the sojourning American audience affected not
only the performance but also the reception of the songs heard in occupied
Trinidad. The colony's patriots, not surprisingly, stood at the center of the
extensive public discourse about the period's calypsos, and they adopted a
deeply ambivalent response to contemporary developments. While, on one
hand, these advocates appreciated the investment of Yankee currency, they
were concerned, on the other, that calypsonians had begun to "sell out" the
island's artistic soul. Nationalists, moreover, were not the only listeners doubtful about the course of the musical form during the occupation. At the other
end of the political spectrum, establishment and respectable types also raised
objections; under the sway of profitable Yankee patronage, these critics argued, the genre had degenerated into obscenity. Americans' and patriots' zeal
notwithstanding, the calypso did not impress them as genuine art. The song,
however, was only part of the problem for this set unmoved by Creole patriotism. Their critique transcended the calypso and ultimately articulated a
deep distrust of the rhetoric about a distinct Trinidadian culture. In retrospect, it was, "postcolonial" critique *avant la lettre*.

PORTRAITS OF TRINIDAD: DRAWING THE LAND OF THE CALYPSO

Beyond the urgent wartime work of installing and operating bases, Yankees in
Trinidad seriously occupied themselves with the pursuit of leisure and entertainment. In so doing they almost inevitably encountered the calypso, not only
one of the colony's most visible and viable attractions at the time, but also one
of its most politically freighted.[8] The nationalist "transformation and appropriation" of the song inaugurated during the thirties continued apace in the
early forties. Patriotic discourse on the music in fact grew more energetic and
more explicit during the occupation. It would culminate in 1944 with the publication of a book proclaiming Trinidad the Land of the Calypso.

A text that effectively cemented the calypso into the foundation of Trinidadian nationality, "Land of the Calypso" had immediate origins in an infor-

mal symposium that began with a letter from the nearby British colony of St. Lucia. Sent in March 1943 by Harold Simmons, one of that island's foremost intellectual figures and a real "renaissance man," and published in the *Trinidad Guardian*, the correspondence requested clarification about the "development and history" of the calypso. Instructively, Simmons explained his query by asserting that West Indians needed to understand their distinctive musical traditions if they were to ever achieve a "true conception" of themselves. He, in other words, presupposed an intrinsic relationship between music and the orchestration of a national identity. Nations needed not only narrations but also serenades; no less than literature, songs, for Simmons, were essential to the projection of nationality.[9]

This call from across the region elicited a quick response, cuing within the local cognoscenti a chain of exchanges about what might be termed the biography of the calypso. Almost inevitably this was a politically pregnant conversation. With patriots zealously nationalizing the song, notions of its past and politics held profound implications for the representation of Trinidadianness. The story of this expression, participants recognized, was the narrative of nationhood writ small; to depict the calypso was to implicitly present a portrait of Trinidadian peoplehood. It was the awareness of these high ideological stakes that animated the extensive and exacting contentions about the musical form, about whether it was fundamentally African or Creole and whether it was a site of opposition to or reconciliation with the dominant social order.

First to respond to Simmons's inquiry was Edric Connor, a highly regarded young black actor and singer then employed at the Chaguaramas naval base. The "local Paul Robeson" set the political tone for the subsequent discourse by casting the calypso as essentially an expression of New World African resistance.[10] Inaugurating what might be considered the black radical approach to studies of the song, Connor's letter to the *Trinidad Guardian* proposed that although it had been "impressed" by European influence, the musical form belonged properly within the cultural sphere of Afro-America. Invoking years of research, which, according to him, included discussions with his octogenarian grandfather, the singer explained that the expression derived from West Indian spiritual and folk forms that were themselves "closely related" to the African American plantation musical tradition. Indeed, it was Connor who publicly pioneered the proposition that the appellation "calypso" was a West African derivative. The term, he contended, was a corruption of the West African "kaiso," a shout of appreciation meaning "well done" that was once used

for the singers who accompanied stick fighters. Connor, moreover, went beyond assigning the song an overwhelmingly African genealogy and invested
it with a rebellious impulse. The calypso, he asserted, grew out of a militant
musical tradition in which enslaved Africans registered their "resentment of
their massas."[11] Over the next few months, Connor continued to disseminate
this interpretation of the musical form. In July and September he organized
recitals meant to display the profound influence of African forms on local creativity, and at these shows, which featured didactic performances of dances
such as the bongo and limbo, Connor's rich baritone could be heard lecturing
on the calypso's insurgent past. Another kind of musical history, it is worth
noting, was made at the recital's July edition. That evening a novel indigenous
musical ensemble consisting of metal drums, containers, and other "junk"
materials appeared onstage; for many who lived beyond earshot of Port of
Spain's "slums," it was the first opportunity to hear the latest craze among the
city's young grassroots men, especially the "robust" and "saga" ones: the "steel
orchestra." This musical invention would eventually find a place in the pantheon of national artforms; at the time, though, such unapologetically subcultural sounds struck most listeners as hopelessly unrespectable.[12]

· Connor's activities provoked within the colony's intelligentsia an engagement that evidenced the salience of culture in general and of the calypso
in particular. Albert Gomes, Jean De Boissiere, Canon Max Farquhar, and
Charles Espinet recognized the critically pertinent politics in the knowledge
disseminated by the young artist. They discerned in Connor's rhetoric propo-
sitions about the past, present, and future character of Trinidadian society,
especially its racial order. Yet their contributions did more than affirm the
political currency of cultural matters; they also highlighted among patriot
intellectuals the existence of competing assumptions about the place of race
within the imagined community. Although all of these commentators carried
ambitions of nationhood for the colonial community, they expressed varying
opinions on Connor's labors in the field of cultural politics.[13] Gomes, for instance, warmly endorsed the recital's approach to the calypso and to Trinidadian aesthetic practices in general. Connor, in Gomes's mind, had made an
"important contribution to the cultural advancement of our people." A longtime romantic advocate of "race consciousness," Gomes described the event
as "most exciting" and, in the end, urged that Connor's lecture be published
so that it could be read by every Trinidadian.[14] De Boissiere saw far less to cele-
brate. His reasoning is not so obvious, for not only was he somewhat icono-

clastic, but as a descendant of an old aristocratic French Creole family, the writer was also given to nostalgia for a supposed pre–World War I golden age of French Creole hegemony in Trinidad.[15] Even more pertinent perhaps, De Boissiere had a rare capacity to resist the patriotic proclivity for romanticizing blackness.[16] Whatever the explanation, he was skeptical of Connor's perspective. The entire production, according to him, suffered for stressing the "exclusive African origins" of local creativity. Though quick to appreciate the genius of the steelband, boasting that it was "the most original and interesting entertainment that we have ever seen presented in Trinidad," De Boissiere deplored Connor's attempt to "make calypso African." Tellingly, too, he contested the etymological argument that "calypso" came from "kaiso," tracing, instead, a francophone genealogy that derived the name from the verb "to carouse."[17] As De Boissiere heard it, Connor's discourse represented an overzealous redemption of Africa and, as a corollary, a wrongheaded erasure of non-African contributions in the elaboration of Trinidadianness. This was a portentous line of criticism, one that the colony's East Indians especially reiterated with increasing urgency.

Canon Max Farquhar, too, felt moved to comment after attending the September version of the recital. Reacting not so much to the politics contained in Connor's rhetoric as to its effect on the audience, he confirmed the radical racialized implications of the lecture's particular portrait of the calypso. As Connor's account reached the point where it identified an old folk song as a commemoration of a slave plot to murder European masters, "instantaneous and spontaneous applause," reported Farquhar, erupted among some members of the audience. For these patrons, evidently, the portrayal of the calypso as a historic voice of violent rejection of white domination merited commendation. For the canon, however, this outburst brought deep chagrin. "Many natives like myself," he confessed, "were not a little embarrassed and conscious of a sense of deep humiliation. It was unpardonably bad manners and ill became the generous spirit which is the more natural heritage and instinct of the African race."[18] Such a shamefaced response was not surprising coming from this older, black, churchy type. Though an advocate of his people, Farquhar remained devoted to respectability and thus prized moderation and reserve. A believer in the potential of blacks, he nevertheless insisted that it was necessary for them to "assimilate" the best of European culture. He envisioned nationhood as rooted in reconciliation—rather than confrontation—between Africans and Europeans; developing Trinidadianness did not demand disavowing Europeanness. Indeed, for him, the articulation of nationality presumed a silencing of race.[19] Against such an ideological background, there is little wonder that Farquhar was troubled by the calypso as it appeared in Connor's frame.

Discomfort with Connor's black radical account contributed to what turned out to be the most consequential contemporary piece of writing on the calypso: *Land of the Calypso: The Origin and Development of Trinidad's Folk Song.* A book-length essay authored by journalist Charles Espinet and entertainer Harry Pitts, this 1944 work was far more polemical than suggested by its desiccated academic subtitle. However preliminary ("an interim report on research," according to the authors), it set out to contest Connor's portrait of the calypso as essentially and violently anti-European.[20] Aiming quite literally to moderate the debate, Espinet and Pitts (Espinet was mixed and Pitts was black) set out to de-authorize arguments for a radical, racially exclusive portrait of the song. For them, the calypso encased inclusiveness; it was a creative expression through which a colonial history of racial difference progressed felicitously toward a Creole blend of Trinidadian unity. Again, however, as in almost all contemporary constructions of nationality, the essay restricted its concerns to African and European ingredients. *Land of the Calypso* all but ignored the Asian presence in the society.[21]

Espinet and Pitts announced their opposition to a racialized casting of the calypso from the outset, complaining in the preface that there was a "complete lack of unbiased writing on [the calypso]. . . . Almost every work to which the authors referred contained altogether too many selfish opinions or all too few facts. They were either written by Europeans who had no 'use' for the creole or by the creole who had no 'use' for the European; they unearthed petty defects of one or other of the racial groups on the island, discovered mountainous mole hills of discrepancies, but sadly enough failed to find any traces of a common culture where it would have been so evident to the unbiased mind."[22]

Against such partisan perspectives, the authors strived to present the history of the calypso as the story of increasingly egalitarian mixing. Far from being the property of oppressed blacks, the musical form, they argued, was the product of "syncretism," a concept they had appropriated from American anthropologists Melville and Frances Herskovits. (*Land of the Calypso* acknowledged the help of the Herskovitses, whom Espinet had met while they did field research in Trinidad just before the war.) The origins of the song, Espinet and Pitts asserted, lay in the process of acculturation, in the creative combination of New World Africans' adaptations (of European forms) and retentions that accompanied the commingling among African, French, and to a lesser degree, Spanish cultures on Trinidadian soil. By their account, the island's blacks "listened" and "grafted" melodies from the music of social superiors, fused it with their traditional songs, and ultimately, created the calypso.[23] Creoleness rather than blackness was the key in *Land of the Calypso*.

The authors' opposition to Connor's portrayal of the calypso as an essentially black and radical expression was perhaps most pronounced in a chapter ironically titled "What's in a Name?" Studiously denying "calypso" a West African etymology, Espinet and Pitts dismissed the "kaiso" thesis on the grounds of inadequate linguistic evidence, assembling, instead, an alternative etymology favoring French roots. In this tack, they relied heavily on the work of Dom Basil Matthews, a respected, Fordham-trained, local black scholar who earlier had concluded that "calypso" came from the French word "carrouseaux." Trinidadians' difficulty with rolling double *r*'s, Matthews argued, had led them to say, first, "cayisseau," then "calliseau" and, eventually, "calypso."[24] Still, Espinet and Pitts confessed that they did not mean for theirs to be the last word on the word "calypso." The origins of the appellation, they allowed, would remain a "matter for conjecture and theorising."[25] Doubtlessly, their primary interest lay not in affirming their proposition but in discrediting Connor's.

As with history, so, too, with politics: *Land of the Calypso* conscientiously expunged the idea that the song expressed resistance to or alienated local whites. The authors, indeed, celebrated the music as intrinsic to the modern reconciliation under way in a traditionally divided and distrustful colonial Trinidadian society. By the 1920s, wrote Espinet and Pitts, the calypso was no longer exclusively enjoyed by the colony's blacks; it had begun, in fact, to attract many white and colored patrons who sought to break with the hegemony of Britishness. Following World War I, according to the essay, "the younger generation was breaking away from the apron strings of Victorianism, and with the new spirit of the independence of youth deliberately did 'naughty things'—daring to go into the former taboo calypso tents where they rubbed shoulders with the less respectable inhabitants of the backyards."[26] Cast this way, the calypso constituted the ideal political vehicle. Not only did it record a break with the old Anglocentric order, composing, in this sense, an instrument of anticolonial protest; the song also set the stage for a democratic order. In tandem with the island's carnival, the musical form, claimed Espinet and Pitts, yoked people across "every class and every section" of the society. Indeed, "to listen to and understand the calypso," they declared at the beginning, "is to get an appreciation of the mentality of the Trinidad Creole."[27] From their perspective, the calypso was essential to the expression of a raceless Trinidadian nationality.

A final indication of the essay's conciliatory motivation registered in its reserved regard for the new steelband phenomenon that Connor had openly validated. Though acknowledging that these "orchestras" did "create their own particular brand of music," Espinet and Pitts offered no more than a note about what they characterized as a "combination of empty steel drums, bits of old iron, disused garbage pails, empty tins, and a host of other paraphernalia to be picked up in any city dump." The authors, moreover, characterized the orchestra as a source of "discomfort" for many people in the colony.[28] This unflattering appraisal of the steelband is not surprising given the Espinet's and Pitts's intent on imagining a Trinidadian community devoid of racial and class antagonisms. They could not contemplate nationalizing a practice still subjected to such intense hostility because of its unambiguous ties to the subversive black culture of Port of Spain. Indeed, only their more radical contemporaries could embrace "music thumped out of old iron" as more than what Canon Farquhar, for example, censured as "savage sounds."[29] Trinidad's respectable people typically dismissed members of the steel orchestra as "hooligans." For decent folks, it was unthinkable that the young, mostly black men who took advantage of the Yankee boom to sport zoots suits, dance the boogie woogie, and lounge in cinemas were capable of creating genuine music. The emergence of the steelband thus captures a marvelously instructive story revealing the complex, unpredictable ties between the U.S. presence and local creativity during the occupation.[30] From what the mainstream maligned as a muddy pond of American mimicry blossomed music that many later would — but few then could — hear as "original art."[31]

Thus as sojourners from the United States began filling up the colony's calypso tents (the makeshift, open-air forum where singers plied their trade during the carnival season), the song continued to gain remarkable political capital; indeed, it was becoming nearly synonymous with the emerging idea of a postcolonial Trinidadianness. This, though, was a fraught process of nationalization, for in a colonial society long built on white supremacy, projecting a national community through a musical form rooted in lower-class, black life raised troubling questions. This already vexed situation around the calypso was only aggravated during a period marked by avid Yankee endorsement and dollars.

YANKEE CURRENCY: PROMOTION AND PATRONAGE

Within the local music scene, the arrival of U.S. personnel had an immediate and dramatic impact that can be neatly captured in the aptly bifunctional word "currency." Powerful promoters and patrons, Americans invested the calypso with unprecedented social acceptability and commercial profitability. This doubled sense of Yankee valorization would prove crucial in the creation and critique of the expression in occupied Trinidad. The interest of these foreigners in the calypso, it should be recognized, was neither natural nor inevitable. To be sure, some of them might have been caught up in the calypso "vogue" before they arrived in the island; what one newspaper in the United States deemed the song's "strange charm" had touched many in the north during the 1930s.[32] Tangible official policy nonetheless played a pivotal part in leading American occupiers to the calypso "like kids to chewing gum."[33] U.S. authorities consistently proffered the song to their personnel as a virtuous alternative to the vicious forms of recreation that existed in the island. Like everyone else in Trinidad, American officials observed that left unregulated, Yankee servicemen often became unruly, drunkenly thronging the streets soliciting prostitutes and brawling. Such public malfeasance was intolerable not only because it offended and generated resentment but, more significantly perhaps, because it stained the reputations of the United States and, more generally, of whiteness. Calypso, military leaders hoped, would help solve this "problem."[34]

Instructively, local singers routinely appeared before U.S. personnel following the 1942 opening of the United Service Organization (USO) on Wrightson Road, a facility meant to serve as a haven of healthful recreation.[35] These performers also found regular work on the Port of Spain–based U.S. armed forces radio station, WVDI, established in St. Clair in May 1943.[36] Also set up as part of an official effort to regulate the behavior of American servicemen, WVDI pioneered radio broadcasting in Trinidad and quickly became a vital forum for calypsonians. Such was the value singers placed on the American station that when a late-arriving rival began pressuring the colonial legislature to lower WVDI's signal strength in 1947, leading exponents such as Atilla (Raymond Quevedo) and Lion (Rafael Deleon) joined the swell of protest against the proposal.[37]

This official embrace of the calypso by Americans was crucial insofar as it positioned them as privileged promoters of the form. In the course of persuad-

The newly built USO on Wrightson Road in Port of Spain.
(U.S. Army Signal Corps)

ing their personnel to patronize local performers, U.S. authorities contributed to the artistic and ethical legitimacy of the song, in other words, to rendering it credible as culture. In March 1943, for example, the *Trinidad News Tips* advertised an upcoming calypso concert at the USO with a front-page piece titled "Voice of the People." More than publicity for the particular show, the article conferred authority and prestige on the local expression. Celebrating it as Trinidad's "folk song," the organ of the U.S. army explained that the calypso represented the "native" practice of putting "into song the happening of the day and the exploits of the strong." Along with "popular history," the music, according to the essay, offered political critique, for when singers reported on governmental goings on, they were rarely ever "complimentary."[38] In occupied Trinidad, Yankees joined the local patriots in validating the calypso.

The very presence of Americans as part of the audience for the calypso lent considerable force to its projection as Trinidad's offering to the banquet of world culture. Seated in tents and, moreover, lauding singers' achievements, these men, most of whom were white, from the Great Republic of the North introduced a new tone of respectability to the calypso milieu. That Yankees assumed a key part in helping to recast Trinidad's "native music" as world music did not escape Atilla the Hun, not only a prominent singer but also one of the most serious students of the song. His history appreciatively recalled these sojourners' "stupendous effect on the trends that governed the kaiso's subsequent development." The song, wrote Atilla, "almost immediately ceased

*Calypsonians Invader, Growler, Atilla, and Lion. This well-known picture
is often cropped in a manner that edits out the white American men who occupy
the front-row seats. (U.S. Army Signal Corps)*

to be endemic to Trinidad or the West Indies. Parochialism fled the scene.
The tens of thousands of American G.I.'s were coming and going and moving among us. What warmed the cockles of our hearts more than anything
else was that their response to the native music was refreshingly exhilarat-
ing, proving conclusively that 'music knoweth no geography.' New horizons
appeared and alluring vistas beckoned."[39] Applauded by U.S. personnel, the
calypso, Atilla asserted, gained a new level of international recognition. The
globalization of the genre that had begun during the interwar years acceler-
ated in the period of occupation.

The newly acquired American-made prestige manifested in the sudden acceptance of the calypso among the island's hitherto contemptuous colonial
elite. It is hardly coincidental that the carnival season of 1942 marked the first
time that an English governor in Trinidad set foot in a tent. Indeed, Ralph
De Boissiere remarked on the effect of Yankees' demonstrative power. The
island's upper classes (St. Clair and Maraval), he observed in 1944, began visit-

ing calypso tents mainly because Americans were doing so and because the song "achieved a certain respectability by going on the air and becoming the subject of numerous articles in American newspapers."[40]

U.S. citizens also helped legitimize and globalize the calypso through their participation in its production. The first taste of major international success for the genre, it is worth recalling, took the form of a song remade by an American group: "Rum and Coca-Cola." Yet the overseas saga of this calypso uncovers a cautionary flip side to the record of Yankees' entrance into Trinidad's cultural scene. Their power to endorse, the tale of this song testifies, proved inseparable from their power to exploit. In 1943 Lord Invader introduced the colony's audiences to a song titled "Rum and Coca-Cola." A composition that updated an old melody with new and topical lyrics, it told of scandalous sexual relationships between mercenary local women and moneyed American men. On the island, claimed the chorus, "both mother and daughter [were] working for the Yankee dollar." Quickly enjoying "phenomenal success," the song caught the fancy of Morey Amsterdam, an American emcee who had come to work at the Port of Spain USO in late 1943.[41] Upon returning home, Amsterdam altered some of the lyrics in the verse and presented Lord Invader's composition to the Andrews Sisters as his own. The Minnesota trio then recorded a version of the calypso in October 1944; famously racing up the Billboard charts, it spent ten weeks at the top in the middle of 1945. Word of the amazing fortunes of "Rum and Coca-Cola" on foreign soil soon reached Trinidad, and Lord Invader and his handlers scrambled to mount what would prove to be a protracted—though eventually successful—legal campaign to secure a share of the earnings.[42] Lord Invader's ordeal underlines that in turning to Americans, Trinidad's calypsonians made themselves no less vulnerable than the rest of the colony's inhabitants who engaged the U.S. presence. Singers, too, would have to be vigilant lest they suffer the consequences of dealing with powerful foreign actors largely indifferent to local interests.

THE AMERICANIZED TASTE OF RUM AND COCA-COLA

Yankees certainly deserve their lasting infamy as piratical appropriators of the calypso; yet in contemporary Trinidad they most impressed people in their capacity as rewarding patrons of the song. Largely ignored by a historiography more concerned with art and politics than marketing and economics, the phenomenon of profitable American audiences animated calypsonians, managers, critics, and even those who cared little for the local music. Once base construction began, singers and their impresarios quickly appreciated the enormous commercial potential of the massive American presence. Occupiers, they recognized, represented consumers prepared to multiply the demand for as well as the price of calypsonians' services.[43] Sojourning U.S. personnel, after all, disregarded the religiously rooted seasonality of calypso singing (in a society where Catholicism heavily influenced public culture, the local calypso business practically shut down on Ash Wednesday). With Yankees in Trinidad, singers found themselves in demand year-round.

For artists hailing mostly from poor and working-class backgrounds, the perennial, high-paying patronage promised by Americans was no less than the proverbial pot of gold. Everyone, notables as well as unknowns, flourished in this new Americanized economy of calypso production. The recollections of two singers, one then a youth on the verge of stardom and the other a venerated veteran, captured the wider sense of wonder that characterized the musical milieu. Lord Kitchener (Aldwyn Roberts), the period's most auspicious newcomer to the calypso stage, remembered occupied Trinidad as a time of surreal recompense:

> It seem to me like a dream, when the Yankees was here. . . . Oh, we had a wonderful time in this country. Money in the tents . . . I remember singing calypsos in the tents, and the Yankees would just take out their dollars and throw to the singers. We had a lovely time. And the tent used to be packed with people. As a matter of fact, the native of Trinidad couldn't easily get into a tent. The tourists took up the entire tent. You had just a few places for the native. . . . That show you how much calypso was in those days. . . . Then people start to quarrel and say, "Well, we can't get in." But of course we, the tent, looking for money, and we had to look for money. Therefore we had to entertain the foreigners. For that's where the money was.[44]

Kitchener was candid about the value he and other singers placed on deep-pocketed American patrons. Their romance with the Yankee dollar, this calypsonian confessed, drove him and his fellow performers to put the "foreign" ahead of the "native" audience. Atilla recalled the years of occupation in strikingly similar terms, describing it as a historic era of unprecedented prosperity. "The economic impact," he wrote, "was wonderful and encouraging. . . . The kaisonians were in such great demand that not only the top-notchers like Lion, Atilla, Tiger, Radio, Growler and Executor (who still thrilled the crowds sporadically), but even B-class singers who were soon to reach the top were avidly sought after. In the words of the great singer Douglas, '*tout ti cannar ka bembem*' (all the little ducks are bathing)."[45]

In a situation where calypsonians considered it imperative to "entertain the foreigners," there were crucial implications for the kind of songs produced. As with all expressions of art, to be sure, the music made in occupied Trinidad cannot be simply reduced to the vicissitudes of demand. Nevertheless, viewing the period's compositions through the lens of market-conscious calypsonians catering to the tastes of their American audience is insightful. It is thus worth asking, in a somewhat bald formulation, to what extent savvy singers like Lord Kitchener produced lyrical stories that—in their minds—Yankees desired to hear.

Generalizing about the demands and preferences of U.S. patrons is certainly hazardous, but some illuminating clues exist. In March 1942, for example, on the heels of what effectively was Americans' first calypso season in the colony, a soldier's epistolary essay appeared in the *Trinidad News Tips*. This "letter" was addressed to a fictive friend ("Louie") back in the States. "The calypsos," it admiringly began,

> are the ballads and the Calypso singers are the guys that sing the ballads and write them. Yeah, can you imagine that? They write their own songs and then sing them too. Lots of times they can just look at you and make up a song right out of their heads. It's really amazing, Louie, the stuff they can do. . . . There's nothing that's sacred to them. They write about the King and President Roosevelt, and they write songs about the American soldiers and sailors in Trinidad, and about how they're taking their "Mopsies" away from them and about the officers and the General. Chris', Louie, they even tell about going home and finding a soldier and his "Mopsie" in the place that's supposed to be used for sleeping.[46]

Americans stationed in the colony, suggests this writer, comprised a narcissistic masculinist audience. Prizing the calypso insofar as it carried clever, courageous, and above all, risqué reportage of their manly adventures, they took particular delight in being regaled with lyrics about their cuckolding of local men. This interpretation of the calypso's appeal to U.S. occupiers was echoed by Wenzell Brown, an American travel writer who visited the colony during the 1946 carnival season. Brown's observations deserve especial attention, since he not only zealously frequented Trinidad's calypso tents but also had the benefit of close association with seasoned calypso connoisseurs such as Albert Gomes and Alfred Mendes. Brown offered two telling observations about the relationship between Yankee audiences and calypsonians. These foreigners, he wrote, were always "rewarded" with compositions; they received these numbers, furthermore, as "good-natured" expressions through which they and local men "laughed" off their rivalries.[47] Fellow Americans, this visitor confirmed, were partial toward, and indeed treated to, entertaining odes to their manhood.

There is a surfeit of lyrical evidence that enterprising calypsonians created material aimed at satisfying the vainglorious narrative desires and earning the rewards of Americans. As early as the 1942 carnival season, a U.S. journalist on the island observed that nearly all of the calypsos being sung carried "an American twist"; if servicemen wanted to know how their "invasion" had affected Trinidad, he advised, they "should go down to the tents to hear calypsonians rehearse."[48] Wartime restrictions on pressing records have made it nearly impossible to know exactly what songs the reporter had in mind, but for the overall period there is ample documentation of local singers' readiness to exploit Yankees' preference for narratives centered on their sexual escapades. It was in 1943 that Lord Invader first released the historic "Rum and Coca-Cola," the era's defining song.

> Since the Yankees came to Trinidad
> They have the young girls going mad
> The girls say they treat them nice
> And they give them a better price
>
> [Chorus]
> They buy rum and coco-cola
> Go down Point Cumana
> Both mother and daughter
> Working for the Yankee dollar
>
> I had a little mopsy the other day
> Her mother came and took her away
> Then her mother and her sisters
> Went in a car with some soldiers

Conventional approaches notwithstanding, this calypso cannot be fully comprehended minus consideration of the taste of American audiences. For a long time, scholars have narrowly analyzed the composition, taking it as a commentary on the "disastrous impact" of Yankees on the "moral and social life of the island" and as a betrayal of local men's "psychic stripping." Despite admitting of a certain irony that "Rum and Coca-Cola" was a favorite with the very soldiers it supposedly criticized, critics have refused to consider the song from the perspective of the Yankee patron.[49] The reluctance is particularly striking in light of Atilla's poignant remarks; present at the point of performance, he explained that the calypso "was ostensibly a denunciation of the moral decay of certain of the natives, but some persons were of the opinion after listening to it and analyzing it that it was in fact a terrible indictment of the Americans in Trinidad." According to Atilla, then, it was only in retrospect and only by "some persons" that "Rum and Coca-Cola" was considered a criticism of Yankee occupiers. This contemporary performer thus draws attention precisely to the limits of interpretations that ignore the audience and, more poignantly, presume calypsonians to be pitted against their Yankee patrons.[50]

Far from exceptional, "Rum and Coca-Cola" was only one drop in a stream of calypsos that have been reductively read as expressions of anti-Americanism but that should be interpreted, too, as appeals to the ribald taste and, more important, rewarding pockets of U.S. personnel. That very season (1943), Invader performed a song about Trinidadian women who tried to foist upon local men babies fathered by American men.

> This Daisy she had ambition
> And she was friendly with a Yankee man
> But they sent the fella back to America
> So she want to put it on the Invader
> But me head is hard and knotty
> I can't make no straight hair baby
> When the baby born stick your grind
> No, darling, that child ain't mine[51]

In that same year Lord Beginner (Egbert Moore), too, embraced the subject of American men and Trinidad's women. In "Yankee Money," he offered a warning to local men.

> Since the Yankees came to this colony
> There's a difference in society
> Women have changed their lives

> Husbands have lost their wives
> Everybody happy and gay
> Tumbling down on the USA
> All the coloured girls come out their hiding hole
> And don't ask how they fearless and bold
> It is trouble now in the town
> You cannot tell the old from the young
> All the women have made a vow
> Their bodylines have no behaviour now
>
> A good girl today is hard to find
> If you have one today you must treat her kind
> Try to please in every way
> Before the Yankees take her away[52]

Not to be left out of the fray was Growler (Errol Duke), who also tackled the subject of Yankee cuckoldry in "No More Darling and Joe." The song's chorus and final verse substituted jealousy and anger for Beginner's resignation and appeasement.

> You planning your wedding
> Tina, who you think fooling
> Gimme back me damn kimona
> Before they try me for murder
> I don't want to go no further
> You could make you name with your Yankee soldier
>
> Young men when you loving
> You must be always dodging and peeping
> When it ain't a sailor
> It's an officer or an aviator[53]

Yankee scandal soaked the following season's crop of calypsos, too. Noting the continuing trend, the *Trinidad Guardian* observed that Americans "figured" in many of the songs released in 1944. Less neutral about the practice was the editor of the newspaper's social page who reported that, despite being better than the previous year's, the season's calypsos "again dragged [Americans] into the limelight."[54] Lord Invader took up where he left off in "Rum and Coca-Cola" with a composition titled "Until the Yanks Came."

> I was living wit' a decent and contented wife
> But the soldier came and broke up my life [repeat]
> For every Sunday she go Arima
> Heading for treat with a soldier
> And when she leavin' she'll tell me darlin'
> Kiss me on me cheek, I would be back in the mornin'[55]

That year Lion performed at least two calypsos addressing U.S. servicemen and local women: "The Soldiers and the Mopsies" and the notorious "Pam Palaam." Allegedly composed in the wake of a rumor about the imminent transfer of locally based American servicemen to the European theater, "Pam Palaam" spat a wicked delight in the anticipated reversal of fortune for Trinidad's women.[56] As with so many popular calypsos, moreover, Lion's composition drew its appeal from naughty double entendre: "Pam Palaam" referred both to the song's fictional female addressee and to the vernacular term for a woman's genitals.

> Pam Palaam, you too smart
> But note I'm no rubbish cart
> And, if you enter my bachelor
> You'll be paid a penny in silver paper
>
> For the sake of a couple dollars
> They had turned their backs on their own loyal lovers
> Denying their own people their favors
> For the Yankees who had the dollars
>
> And all at once they're only throwing crop
> Bit by bit, their jewels are in the pawn shop
> But I'm not sorry for them, not a bit
> For like a dog, they must return to their vomit[57]

In 1944 even Atilla, the "solid citizen" among singers, mined the subject of Yankees' manly exploits in his composition lamenting that American men "took all our girls and had a glorious time / and left us blue-eyed babies to mind."[58] Over the next couple of seasons, furthermore, there was no shortage of numbers belonging to this genre; these included huge hits like "Now the Yankee Harvest Is Over" (Lord Beginner), Yankee Sufferer (Lord Kitchener), and best known, perhaps, "Brown Skin Gal." Taking off from a Grena-

dian folk song and recasting it in late 1946 to suit the new Americanized situation, Radio (Norman Spann) featured a Yankee occupier as the protagonist and
delivered the chorus with a "pronounced American accent" (note the phrase
"what the heck").

> Brown skin gal, stay home and mind baby [repeat]
> I'm going away maybe on a sailing boat
> And if I don't come back, what the heck?
> Throw away the damn baby[59]

Calypsos like these have been subsequently interpreted as documents of deep
local discontentment with the American presence. Contemporary listeners,
though, heard something more and acknowledged that these songs were also
musical vehicles in pursuit of Yankee dollars.

PATRIOTIC DISAPPOINTMENTS

Some in the colony did more than merely note the pecuniary interest at work
in the island's calypso milieu; they condemned it. Patriots, not surprisingly,
were among these doubtful commentators. Deeply invested in the idea of the
calypso as a genuine artistic expression of a distinguished Trinidadianness,
they voiced concern that performers' mercenary interests compromised the
integrity of the song. The influence of American consumers, lamented these
critics, was drawing the music away from its authentic roots. Thus rather than
hailing compositions like "Rum and Coca-Cola" as heroic expressions of anti-
imperial protest, an observer such as Albert Gomes censured such lyrics as
products of crass commercialism. And although Gomes was by no measure a
representative figure, his misgivings about the period's calypsos are nonetheless instructive. Ultimately, they help to underscore how the issue of Yankee
patronage had moved to the center of debates about the politics of the musical form.

Gomes (as shown in Chapter 1) had long worried about elites' capacity
to compromise the subversiveness of the calypso through appropriation and
co-optation. By 1943, with Americans emerging as the most prominent consumers of the song, he was convinced that his worst fears had been realized.
Reflecting on the state of the art in his weekly column, this patriot articulated an acute anxiety that singers had "sold out" to Yankee audiences. Under
the influence of American patrons, calypsonians, he complained, were ne-

glecting their essential function of poetic criticism. His despair at the song's fate surfaced with particular force after Gomes attended a Prince's Building show in September. The music, he mourned, "was going down the ladder at a swift rate." The night's compositions betrayed an obsession with the "American invasion"; they were "monotonous" and at times almost "offensive," wrote Gomes (other local patrons, he reported, agreed). For him, moreover, the problem went further than lyrics; in the Prince's Building setting, too, this critic saw troubling signs that calypsonians and promoters sought to reimagine their performances to meet the expectations of an American audience. The "microphone, potential torch singer, tap dancer, and all," Gomes declared, "the whole thing [was] objectionable." In the end, he wished for a heroic reversal of the form; at the time, however, this patriot could offer no more than a sad assessment. "The calypso judging from the new compositions sung at the building that night was losing its basic primitive rhythm. . . . Unless some new star appeared on the horizon, someone emphasizing the old forms with perhaps more vigor, the calypso as we know it is doomed."[60]

More pertinent than Gomes's identification of the disease afflicting the calypso was his diagnosis. The source of the song's downward spiral, he reasoned, was American largesse and Trinidadian "toadyism." Anticipating the patronage of easy-spending American men, calypsonians performed material that catered to these foreigners. And although Gomes claimed he had no objection to singers who operated as a "business team" to make money, this patriot worried nevertheless that commercialization had compromised the art of calypso.[61] His assault on local performers continued in 1944. Upon leaving the Victory tent in early January, a disheartened Gomes took on Lion for repeating "They Took Me for Bing Crosby," which Gomes had already condemned as "pathetic." This time he poured on the vitriol. "Lion's inability to resist Bing Crosby," according to him, "has produced a calypso that is neither calypso, Bing Crosby nor anything else and eludes all attempts at classification. It is a freak most agonizing to listen to. Will some good friend please convince Lion that he is not a crooner and that every attempt he has made so far to imitate Bing Crosby has produced a dirge that is monotonous to the point of pain?"[62]

Yet calypsonians did not go undefended. There were commentators in the colony who understood that these predominantly poor artists routinely, strategically, and indeed, necessarily gave in to the demands of the "market." In the face of strident criticism like that of Gomes, fellow dissident journalist

Owen Mathurin sympathized with singers. Weighing in on the dispute between Lion and Gomes, Mathurin argued that it was not his place "to worry about the artist prostituting his talent"; calypsonians, as he saw it, had to either "please" their clients or "starve."[63] For him, in other words, "putting culture to work" was a common and often a practical course of action within Trinidad's laboring classes. Mathurin understood that what nationalist critics like Gomes approached as "art," singers counted, too, as "labor."[64] Another local essayist soon put it even more poignantly in the course of a discussion of indigenous arts: "culture without cash," he warned, "is a joke."[65]

SLACKNESS HIDING IN CULTURE?

Patriotic champions such as Gomes were not the only detractors of the calypsos composed in occupied Trinidad. Criticism also came from those in respectable circles, who complained that ever since the arrival of Yankee patrons in the tent, the song had become "slanderous" and "objectionable." Scandalized, these mainstream listeners railed that Trinidad's bards, in their eagerness to satisfy salacious American consumers, had become "corrupters of manners and morals," pornographic peddlers who casually transgressed the line that separated the vulgar from the amusing.[66] For these local "puritans," as Atilla dismissed them, no one would have been truer and timelier than the *Trinidad Guardian* columnist who mockingly urged singers to compose a number titled "calypso gives Yankeemen and mopsi the sack."[67]

Exasperation and disgust at the calypso's vulgarity hit a high pitch in 1944. Early in the season, illustratively, a scornful *Port of Spain Gazette* editorial declared the music to be "degraded" and no more than an "abortion" of Trinidad's genuine folklore.[68] Echoing the daily's sentiment, a correspondent to the *Trinidad Guardian* pleaded for singers to return to providing an "interpretation" of local life, the imperative that gave the calypso its "popularity" in the first place.[69] Respondents to a survey in the afternoon newspaper, the *Evening News*, agreed, condemning contemporary compositions as lewd and low in morals.[70] Lion's "Pam Palaam," with its pun on women's genitals, came in for especial criticism; indeed, it helped push the police to warn calypsonians away from lyrics that were "profane, indecent or obscene or . . . which [were] insulting to any individual or sector of the community."[71]

The moral panic around the song intensified in late January when Captain A. A. Cipriani controversially interrupted a "calypso drama" at the Victory tent. Featuring singers in comic acting roles, these skits debuted in the early 1930s and quickly became crowd favorites. For the Captain, however, the performance that night offered no humor and, in fact, fell below the limits of the acceptable. Centered on a Roman Catholic clergyman's efforts to raise funds, the drama showed the "man of the cloth," when all else had failed, successfully resorting to the use of a barely clothed rumba dancer. An old, staunch defender of the Roman Church (recall the Captain's leading role in the divorce debate), an offended Cipriani demanded that the show come to a halt. At first, calypsonians submitted; some even began to apologize, but "loud protests" from the audience brought the apology as well to a premature end. The proportion of American patrons in the audience on that particular night is impossible to determine, but doubtless it was significant. After all, 1944 was the year in which Trinidadian fans could not get into the Victory tent and eventually "crashed" the gates.[72] Order, at any rate was eventually restored, but only when Atilla, the tent leader, emcee, and an old Cipriani ally, explained to patrons that they would discontinue the drama not "to bow to the man but to the principles for which he lived and fought."[73] This was a telling episode: Cipriani's critique suggests that even among local listeners long sympathetic to the calypso (as the Captain had been), there was a sense that singers now violated the boundaries of decency in the colony.

At the same time, that calypsonians eventually deferred to Cipriani's "principles" underlines the need to temper arguments for the ultimate force of Yankee patrons in occupied Trinidad. The decision to halt the skit affirms that, for all their currency, Americans did not exercise unchecked power over the composition of expressive culture in Trinidad. These foreigners could not completely free the island's creative workers from obligations to local political constraints and causes. On that night, caught suspended—literally—between satisfying the demands of patriotism and Yankee dollars, the island's singers chose to identify with the former.

This incident along with the wider clamor for censorship placed the contemporary calypso in what Albert Gomes characterized as a "grim paradox" during the 1944 carnival season. While foreigners, as he put it, were "coming to inquire into our culture," locals were "persecuting it." Endorsed and elevated by Americans, the music was derided and denounced by the colony's "respectable" residents. In this situation, Gomes and other patriots passionately defended Trinidad's performers. Despite concern for what they saw as singers' creative decline in the face of American money, these nationalists insisted that the song was genuine art and, moreover, an essential source of Trinidadian identity.[74]

Practitioners themselves, it should be acknowledged, affirmed the merits of the calypso through the medium they knew best. The young Pretender (Aldric Farrell) advanced the case against governmental intervention in a composition titled "What Is an Obscene Calypso?" Meanwhile, his senior colleague Atilla performed "Ubiquitous and Kaiso"; marked by Quevedo's characteristic eloquence, the lyrics defiantly declared, "never mind whatever measures are employed / calypso is art and cannot be destroyed."[75] Along with these odes, moreover, came avowals of the song's values from within the patriot intelligentsia. Owen Mathurin maintained that despite "commercialization" the calypso remained genuine art. "However much some may dislike them," the colony's singers, he insisted, "deal with life in the community as it is lived." They should be left to sing of vulgarity, Mathurin concluded, because, after all, it was "to be found everywhere." Entering the partisan public discussion with a long newspaper essay, Alfred Mendes deemed the calypso an "unequivocally Trinidadian" musical expression. It was only because of local "bourgeois proprieties" and "snobbery," sneered the writer, that the song went unrecognized.[76] Joining in, Ralph De Boissiere conceded that given the calypso's "stickly limited" range, it was not "art" on the same level as the novel; singers, he nevertheless insisted, were artists. Not unlike Mathurin, this patriot stated that insofar as the songs expressed vulgarity and crudity, they simply reflected real life. For De Boissiere, calypsonians created art insofar as they approached their work as a way to "transcend and transmute obscenity."[77]

The most exuberant exposition on the subject, not surprisingly, came from the pen of Albert Gomes. In a column that an Atilla composition lauded as a "wonderful dissertation," Gomes began by posing the question, "Should we doctor our calypsos?" His answer was a predictably resounding no; what is remarkable, though, was the essay's elaboration of the song's defining qualities. In defending the right of singers to free expression, he seized on a current Lion composition to elucidate what he believed cathected the calypso form, what sustained it as a distinct and distinguished art. The particular Lion number to which Gomes referred was a "picong" of a reply to his earlier swipes at the calypsonians; this composition, unfortunately, has escaped documentation, but it was most likely one in which the chorus cleverly closes, "oh what an awful thing / To see Gomes in a lion skin."[78] At any rate, it is Gomes's interpretation of the song rather than the song itself that matters here. And according to the gleeful critic, Lion's lyrics were "vitriolic and astringent," emphasizing his "physical attributes and reprehensible characteristics" (Gomes, it should be recalled, weighed more than 300 pounds). The patriot also praised the singer's style of delivery as proper to the genre; juxtaposing it to Lion's earlier tribute to Bing Crosby, he dismissed the latter while lauding the former as "clear and unmistakable." In the end, then, though standing at the receiving end of Lion's wit, Gomes expressed great satisfaction in not being "crooned" into calypso fame.

As the essay got deeper into its celebration of Lion's composition, Gomes's broader interpretive project became clear: he had set out to reaffirm that the calypso was essentially the expression of what can be termed a "primal masculinity."[79] For this patriotic critic, Lion's pugilistic return to lyrical form represented a welcome re-emasculation of the calypso following a crisis of manhood. It is "not possible," he wrote, "to marry the calypso to the sob song without destroying the very integrity and spirit of the former." Opposing the wedding of the calypso and American pop, Gomes condemned it as an ill-advised arrangement; in his mind, after all, the local song "was intrinsically masculine! Its mood satirically sensual and even satanic. It recognizes a lady but still receives a woman. . . . The calypso is a swashbuckling gypsy, ill mannered perhaps but a healthy honest animal of a fellow free of the façade of pretense."[80] This construction of the calypso, it should be clear, was founded on a knot of assumptions about class, race, gender, and civilization. Just as Gomes had done at the end of the thirties, he held up the ideal calypso, the essence of Trinidadianness, as a declaration of defiance against what might be seen as modern Western values. For him, the authentic calypso flirted comfortably with the devilish, the dirty, and the demimonde. Little wonder that this nationalist continued to condemn censorship as well as American influence. Both, in his view, spelled the unwelcome domestication and feminization of an inherently Hobbesian expressive form, one that thrived best in a brutish state of manly combat.

POSTCOLONIAL DOUBT IN THE LAND OF THE CALYPSO

The more patriots and Yankee occupiers alike generously invested currency in the calypso, the more they provoked charges of wanton inflation from doubtful interlocutors in the colony. For locals unmoved by the legitimizing rhetoric of Trinidadian nationalism, the proposition that the musical form marked the quintessential expression of Trinidadian culture was at best dubious. These commentators, secure with European hegemony, or at least uncertain about the possibility of escaping its expansive arms, resisted the proposition that a song identified with the black lower classes could achieve the rare distinction of culture. Americans' support notwithstanding, these critics found it difficult to comfortably dwell in a Land of the Calypso. They, it is important to note, did not necessarily dislike the song; these observers simply questioned patriots' claims about its genius and gravity. For their skeptical ears, the calypso offered mere entertainment. Outside the colony's heady nationalist circles, it turns out, the notion of Trinidadian culture beyond the reaches of colonialism—postcolonial culture—was less a liberating prospect than an impossible predicament.

During the 1944 season, several of these unconvinced commentators took on the enthusiastic nationalist discourse on the calypso. In the midst of the glowing tributes from Gomes and other patriots, Eric Burger, a foreign-born *Trinidad Guardian* columnist, detoured from his usual discussion of international affairs to plead with the song's champions to regain a "sense of proportion." There was no need, according to Burger, to subject the expression to such inflated theorizing. Mocking local intellectuals for following the American way of "invading" the tents, he complained that they only attributed an "exaggerated importance" to the calypso. To dramatize what he viewed as misplaced critical energies, Burger turned to analogies: he likened the colony's patriots to men who "hung lead weights on a balloon and then wonder why the thing does not rise into the air." The columnist also compared the calypso to a "brightly feathered bird": it was fun to view but "nonsense to put the bird on an operating table and dissect the feather work. It leads only to killing the bird and all the feathered fun." Ultimately, for this commentator, the expression was best left freed from the political and intellectual minding of patriots.[81]

Local musician and critic McDonald Carpenter, too, opposed what he found to be an unwarranted elevation and overzealous promotion of the calypso. In the process, moreover, this white Trinidadian contributed a profoundly prescient commentary on nationalist discourse in the colony. Although acknowledging that the form had found fervid fans in Americans, who, according to him, were "vitally interested" in the calypso, Carpenter questioned the tendency to refer to the song as art and to the singers as artists and poets. Indeed, for Carpenter, who believed Americans to be "naturally" and "tremendously partial to novelty and good entertainment," Yankee ardor only confirmed that the music did not express art in any serious sense of the term. In his mind, the calypso deserved comparison with the music of Bing Crosby and the jitterbug dance: diverting it was, but certainly not art. "If a calypso does not amuse," he wrote in a reply to Alfred Mendes's earlier essay, "it simply flops." Thus despite agreeing that people should support the calypso, Carpenter deemed it "ridiculously enthusiastic" to define the genre as art. "We should not," he warned, "deceive ourselves."[82]

But Carpenter's intervention aimed at more than denying the calypso genuine artistry; more fundamentally, it sought to underline the dubious character of nationalist claims in a colonial context. Prefiguring what might be marked as a "postcolonial" mood, he drew attention to the contradictions inherent in patriots' discourse on culture. For him, it was an inescapable paradox that these intellectuals who trumpeted the calypso as true art and "typically Trinidadian" were themselves entangled in Eurocentrism. We are "colonial children," Carpenter wrote in a piece poignantly titled "Europe's Culture Cast Our Own." As he saw it, when Gomes (whom he counted as an old friend) and his patriot peers constructed expressions associated with the black lower classes (calypso and carnival, for example) as truly Trinidadian, they were building a nation to which they could not comfortably belong. Gomes, Carpenter declared, was "not typically characteristic of a creole by any stretch of the imagination." This was eerily prophetic, for Carpenter, it turns out, had provided Gomes a political epitaph. Three decades later, when Gomes came to account for his public demise, this Portuguese Creole reasoned that his career had been undone by racial difference, mainly by the emergence of Black Power. In an autobiography revealingly titled *Through a Maze of Color*, he insisted on the fatal force of "complexion—skin not political." Gomes, by the end of his career, had become convinced that his long-standing ideological romance with the "black masses" mattered less than his epidermal estrangement from them. In crafting a political autobiography, Gomes ultimately composed a story in which he tragically "dug his own grave."[83]

At any rate, Carpenter meant to issue a societal rather than a personal critique, aiming to emphasize local patriots' inextricable entrapment within European notions of culture, art, and beauty. "We walk in borrowed clothes, we play on borrowed instruments, we paint with borrowed brushes and we write with borrowed pens and words," he declared. Thus although "a politician can create his own zeitgeist and then argue about it," contended Carpenter, "it is a meaningless process to a musician in Trinidad." For him, in other words, even if the project of political decolonization was debatable, cultural decolonization was delusional. He thus ended on a rhetorical note registering his pessimism about the possibilities of "discard[ing]" Europeanness in Trinidad and the wider region. "Can Mr. [Albert] Gomes," asked Carpenter, "suggest a basis for what for convenience we might call a West Indian art and the sources from which our basic formulas may be drawn? I certainly cannot."[84] To his mind, there was no Trinidadian art or artistic values independent of the European tradition.

Such resignation to Trinidadian (and West Indian) derivativeness resonated within the colony's East Indian intellectual circles. Observing the nationalistic embrace of the calypso as Trinidadian culture (and, at times, more broadly West Indian culture), they were justly sensitive to their marginalization if not exclusion.[85] Their sense of fatal detachment from the Land of the Calypso shot through a 1946 *Observer* editorial addressing what the monthly characterized as the "glib" talk about the subject of culture. Explaining that in the colony the term "culture" had begun to signify a sense that people had had "enough of English culture" and "demanded [their] own," the Indo-Trinidadian monthly adopted a decidedly skeptical attitude. The *Observer*, indeed, counseled silence, reasoning that since "culture" was "the sum total of our material and mental (ideological) heritage," people in Trinidad ought to accept that they were "by the facts of history and geography a borrowing people. From China, Africa, India, Portugal, and America, where we draw heavily—and we are still drawing." The organ ended with a brusque admonition: "In a hasty desire to become a nation we are out to grab a culture, but when the situation is analysed we find ourselves rather denuded. The fact is we are cultural apes and the sooner [we] stop talking about a West Indian culture, the better."[86]

CONCLUSION

The main plot of the story told in this chapter can be seen as having coursed toward a remarkable epilogue. In 1960 V. S. Naipaul, the son of Seepersad Naipaul, a journalist and writer active in occupied Trinidad, returned to the West Indies from London. Having made himself into a critically acclaimed man-of-letters, the younger Naipaul now essayed to describe the region he had left a decade earlier. The product was *The Middle Passage*, a travel narrative in which he assuredly submitted that "nothing has been created in the West

Indies." This book has since secured a uniquely infamous place in the intellectual history of the postemancipation British Caribbean (bested perhaps only by James Anthony Froude's *The English in the West Indies* [1888]). Yet its local precedents and resonances have gone unnoticed. Students have thus ignored the delicious irony that Naipaul practically mimicked the language of his boyhood intellectual world. Indeed, the main ideas in *The Middle Passage* read like an impatient yet ingenious précis of competing critical positions staked out in occupied Trinidad. Not unlike the colony's Creole patriots, Naipaul praised the calypso as a privileged creative space in which locals approached "reality." Like these nationalists, too, he indicted the effect of powerful American consumers on the song. Yet, at the same time, in the spirit of skeptics of Trinidadian nationalism, the "East Indian" Naipaul dismissed the concept of Trinidadian or West Indian "culture" as restricted to rituals of "borrowing" and "aping."[87] That V. S. Naipaul continues to exercise critics and scholars attests to the intellectual significance of the encounter between Yankees and the Land of the Calypso. These years, it should be appreciated, produced a manner of framing arguments about culture and nationhood that anticipated the challenges of the postcolonial present.[88]

6 Love American Style
Race, Gender, and Sexuality in Occupied Trinidad

Slow walk soft hum and then a pause
About in step business the cause . . .
. . . Quick talk price set away in pair
No moon no love dark hidden lair
Far east Far west this once forget
The bond is tied the twain has met
—*Trinidad News Tips*

The girls and the women got together in the shade.
"Girl, how yuh would like to sleep wid ah Yankee man?"
"Ha ha, yuh better don't let Rajnauth hear yuh, he go cut off yuh head
*   wid de cutlass!"*
"Ah hear dey does have money like fire, and good cigarette. Ah hear Rita
*   say how dey nice, dat dem girls in Port ah Spain going wild over dem."*
—*Samuel Selvon, A Brighter Sun*

Around the time that Lord Invader released "Rum and Coca-Cola" (ca. March 1943), Trinidad buzzed with a trial whose details bear a striking similarity to the calypso's scandalous claims. A woman named Beatrice Springer stood accused of using her Point Cumana beach house for "immoral purposes," indeed, for running "one of the biggest rackets" in the colony. As with the song, too, Springer's operation paired American personnel and local women. Furthermore, although this light-skinned wife and mother did not quite belong to the set of "aristos" exposed by Lord Invader, she did hail from Woodbrook, a bastion of Port of Spain respectability. Like the chorus of the calypso, moreover, the case called into question a mother and daughter. Beatrice, according to testimony by police officers and a parade of prostitutes, reserved part of the premises for her "exclusive use"; her married daughter, meanwhile, appeared as the only witness on her behalf.[1] "Rum and Coca-Cola," it appears, did not excessively tax the imagination of its composer.

The trial of Beatrice Springer, though, offers more than a titillating footnote to a historic calypso. Featuring allegations of nonwhite women entertaining American sexual partners across the color line, of wives defying husbands' exclusive claim on their sexuality, and of putatively decent females investing their bodies in commercial sex, it captured the subversive visions of femininity that proliferated during the occupation. It was a period saturated with stories of women daring to violate the overlapping conventions of white supremacy, patriarchy, and respectability. In this regard, Springer's ordeal provides a well-placed window onto the web of transgressions spun as local females pursued intimacies with U.S. servicemen.

The arrival of tens of thousands of American men, most of whom were moneyed, white, and without female companionship, roused in Trinidad's women what elsewhere has been phrased "the desire for a yank."[2] This, of course, was no simple desire, and doubtless it had innumerable, intricate, and sometimes inscrutable sources, from the genuinely emotional to the calculatedly commercial. Yet whether it was real love, "money like fire," or something in between that had women "going wild over" Americans, their carnal associations with these occupiers stimulated a complex of conflicts and anxieties. These antagonisms and worries, the present chapter shows, had everything to do with the virtually inseparable precepts around race, gender, and sexuality. ("Queer" liaisons, though certainly part of the social scene in occupied Trinidad, produce a different set of conceptual and methodological demands and are not addressed here.)[3]

Frequently coupling individuals across the color line, relationships between local women and Yankee men undermined Trinidad's racial hierarchy. Whiteness was jealously guarded property in this British Caribbean society (as in virtually all European colonies), and white people viewed disavowing affective interest in nonwhite bodies as a decisive aspect of its guardianship.[4] Thus despite customarily embracing nonwhite partners, whites (the men especially) were held responsible for denying these "tender ties" the legitimacy that came through public acknowledgment and, more so, through marriage. For them the quip about counteracting their lusty integration by night with strict segregation by day was not just mischievous humor; it was also a moral imperative. This imperialist injunction seemed lost on many American servicemen in occupied Trinidad; appearing to "forget" about the Kiplingian conceit that sexually the "twain" never met, they flagrantly associated with local women of color. These indiscretions, it will be seen, left a long trail of chagrined white witnesses (American and especially British colonial) anxiously attempting to remedy what some Yankees facetiously self-diagnosed as "color blindness."

These "foreign affairs" embodied other challenges deeper perhaps than the privilege of white skin.[5] In liaising with Americans, local girlfriends, wives, and "mopsies" often left old boyfriends, husbands, and suitors in the lurch. During the occupation, as a result, many of the colony's males suddenly found themselves decidedly disadvantaged competitors in the masculinist quest for female bodies and affections. Resentful toward this development, these local men, not unlike their counterparts in other military theaters that accommodated Americans, sometimes responded hostilely and even violently, targeting not only rival Yankee men but also enterprising Trinidadian women. As the epigraphic female character in *A Brighter Sun* jokingly warned, "To sleep wid ah Yankee man," indeed, to talk about such an adventure, could drive a jilted lover to "cut off yuh head wid de cutlass."[6]

For some women, dealing with American men risked not literal but social death. In a society largely unforgiving of "fallen women," they were the ones who dared to undertake fundamentally commercial intimacies with U.S. occupiers. These relationships have since become iconic of the period; in fact, it often seems like the proverbial "world's oldest profession" was new to occupied Trinidad. Yet, despite acquiring unprecedented salience with the arrival of single, well-paid, Yankee servicemen, the contemporary world of commercial sex signified something far more complex and ambiguous than a scandalous novelty.[7] And although evidence for these subtle and uncertain aspects of the sex trade rarely found a way into conventional archives (few documents, for example, match Selvon's fictional nonprostitutes who nevertheless took American men primarily as trading partners), instructive apprehensions and observations of prostitution do exist. This discourse, the chapter reveals, figured the practice not only as a straightforward issue of morality but also as a far more vexing question of women's labor and independence in a quintessentially modern moment.

WHITE LIES AND COLOR BLINDNESS

The arrival of thousands of American occupiers engendered a serious anxiety for the overwhelmingly white set perched at the pinnacle of Trinidad's social order. Completely sold on the heterosexist presumption that, as males, these foreigners required female intimacy, U.S., and more so colonial, elites had to deal with the embarrassing possibility that these couplings might violate one of the key conventions upon which white prestige rested: the proscription against publicizing interracial affairs. This worry was not unwarranted; in occupied Trinidad, many white Yankees casually disregarded the color line in pursuit of female company.

To be sure, these white men did not suddenly and mysteriously dispense with their racist assumptions once they reached Caribbean shores. Indeed, countenancing the host society, they could spew some of the most fantastic white supremacist rhetoric. Barely two months into the occupation, for example, an unhappy member of the 252nd Coastal Artillery disclosed that his distress stemmed not only from the island's enervating tropical climate but also from the population's fatal racial composition. In a May 1941 letter sent to folks back in North Carolina, this soldier complained that Trinidad was 95 percent "Negro" and 80 percent infected with venereal disease. If not the heat then certainly the nonwhite women, according to this American, made the colony a white man's hell.[8]

Everyday practice, however, did not live up—or perhaps down—to such apocalyptic preaching. Negrophobia notwithstanding, it was not uncommon to witness white Americans openly fraternizing with nonwhite local women. On city sidewalks and beaches, in taxis and bars, interracial affairs assumed a frank, public profile in the island, especially in the east-west corridor between Arima and Chaguaramas.[9] These couples, needless to say, defy definitive parsing. Nonwhite women might have been motivated by romantic desire, by covetous demand, or by amorphous mixes of both. The reasons of American men are equally refractory; exoticist fascination and genuine romance merely mark the extremes of a spectrum that contained myriad intermediates. Foregrounding the social setting, though, is essential in accounting for the men's willingness to enter into these transgressive trysts. Away from the supervisory influences of home and surrounded for the most part by nonwhite people for whom they held little regard, many white Yankees simply felt licensed to ignore the established rules around race and public intimacy.

Whatever the reasons, cross-racial couples fast became a feature of occu-pied Trinidad's social landscape. Most of these liaisons fell outside the public record, yet some left traces of their presence insofar as they became the sub-jects of judicial proceedings. In late 1941, for example, when two Trinidadian women suffered violent attacks from their lovers, these females' involvement with white Americans emerged at the heart of the defense. Fined for beating common-law wife Olga Thomas, Topie Mahon sought exoneration by telling the court that although he had been living with her for four years, Thomas simply "left him and was living with a soldier man."[10] Another local woman paid more dearly for her interracial dalliances. When Rufemia (Fanny) Turton was stabbed to death by her husband Charles, he cited his wife's recent asso-ciation with Americans as mitigation for his murderous rage. Before a Port of Spain court in November, Charles testified that Fanny had boldly declared that she no longer had "regard for [him] when there are Americans in the land."[11] White American men, both trials disclosed, stood at the center of fierce and sometimes fatal battles over the hearts and bodies of the colony's nonwhite women. It was a dubious measure of the men's integration into Trinidad's social scene.[12]

Yankees, though, did not always emerge unscathed when their exploits across the color line came to violent climax. In October 1942 a white soldier named Vincent De Boer attended an all-day "souse and dance" party in Santa Cruz, a village within miles of the Wallerfield air base. Much remains un-clear about precisely what transpired, but subsequent court testimony estab-lished that at some point, De Boer met a local woman named Marie Watson, to whom he gave $10. For some unknown reason, a heated argument ensued between them; unfortunately for the soldier, the woman's son was nearby and overheard the dispute. Finding his mother sobbing and claiming that she had been insulted, Frank Watson slipped outside the house and waited for De Boer. When the American appeared, a scuffle broke out, and by the time it was over, he had been stabbed to death. For Yankees, the pursuit of local women could come at a grave cost. The very power and privilege that made white Americans desirable could also render them detestable. And although the son did not refer to De Boer's whiteness in defending himself (he cited his mother's honor), racial difference might have partially inspired his action. Frank, it is plausible to surmise, imagined himself not only as a son protecting his mother but as a nonwhite man attacking the embodiment of white male privilege.[13]

Whereas the foregoing accounts are silent about the racial salience of couplings of Yankee men and local women, other narratives affirm that race did indeed matter. These, furthermore, often acknowledged both the transgression that inhered in interracial affairs and the secrets and lies that went with them. This was the case with an unsigned piece of short fiction published in *New Dawn*. Appearing less than six months into the occupation (October 1941), "Beach Scenes" is told from the perspective of a black Trinidadian man whiling away at a Port of Spain bay when a light-skinned couple, their daughter, and her white American date (dressed in a jitterbug suit, not surprisingly) show up. The young woman quickly escapes the party and stumbles upon the protagonist. But just as she discloses her dislike for her suitor (he's "too crude"), the white American appears. Angered at the sight of his delinquent date talking to the "native," the Yankee picks a fight; sadly for the visitor, though, he collects a sound beating from the local black. At this point the parents arrive, and here the story twists into more than a stock nationalist narrative of raced masculinist resistance in which a heroic indigenous black man triumphs over a white foreigner in the contest for female affections.[14] As the mother exits the scene, she turns and shouts to the milling crowd that "wherever niggers go, they make trouble." To her charge comes a remarkably pointed rebuke: "You ain't white either! You can fool the Yankee. But you can't fool me!"[15] "Beach Scenes," it turns out, was also a tale of racial subversion. Seeking a partner for their daughter, the light-skinned Trinidadian parents had quietly embarked on a quest for whiteness.

Although this short story portrays locals dismissing the parents' effort to "pass" as doubly vain (self-aggrandizing and futile), it leaves unanswered the question of the American's visual acuity. Had he seen through the family's racial act? Or, as somebody in the crowd believed, had he been fooled? There is no doubt that in Trinidad's unfamiliar racial mélange, some white sojourners might have been genuinely confounded by people who took advantage of their ambiguous appearance to claim the privileges of whiteness. Convinced of the colony's inherent exoticism, Americans expressed endless fascination with its cosmopolitan makeup, with its "admixture of races."[16] Yet for the most part, the transgressions committed by U.S. occupiers hardly seemed the result of naïveté and disorientation.[17] Rather, based in a Caribbean island that many white men took to be a jungle, a "strange ground" devoid of "civilization," they simply imagined themselves beyond conventional proscriptions. This conviction that Trinidad presented a radically different "moral topography" found poetic voice when *Esquire* journalist Martin Torrence reported on the base colony.[18] The island, insisted Torrence after only a brief visit, was "extra sinful"; it breathed "an air of glamorous wickedness. . . . Blood flows faster here, spirits are higher. . . . You feel it in the way people look at one another."[19] If ever there was a place that seduced white men across the color line, surely this tropical colony was it.

White servicemen, moreover, repeatedly acknowledged awareness of their breaches. In writings replete with anxiety, they continuously mocked one another and at times themselves about their weakness for violating established rules regarding race and dating. A *Trinidad News Tips* profile penned by Sergeant Bob Flynn, for example, noted that fellow soldier Leo Heyman had several Port of Spain girlfriends of a ludicrously dubious complexion. These girls, Flynn joked, were "so dark that all [he] could see was the whites of their eyes." Stretching the humor, he quipped that Heyman "looked like a ghost between a set of black sheets." The profile, though, ended on a tellingly different rhetorical note: "What," asked Flynn, "would Jean say if she knew you kept that kind of company?"[20] Whoever Jean might have been (Heyman's white girlfriend? in Trinidad? in the United States?), the question intimated at impropriety and scandal. White Americans, it let on, recognized the racial subversion implied in their affairs with nonwhite local women.

The traffic across Trinidad's color line inspired one serviceman to poetry. Poignantly titled, "White Lies" was easily the most provocative and funniest reflection of the sensitivity of white Americans to their subversive choice of female partners. Appearing in the *Trinidad News Tips* in early 1942, the verse provided a lyrical send-up of both nonwhite local women who passed for white to pair with Yankees and these "color-blind" white men who indulged the comically conceited female counterfeits.

> Let's take a trip through Port of Spain
> The city fair and kind—
> Where every soldier from the States
> Is growing color-blind
>
> See the Damsel Standing there
> Whose skin's—well, rather tannish?
> I asked her what she was last night
> She answered: "Boss, Ah's Spanish!"
>
> And see the Girlie on the Square,
> Say, She's a comely wench,

And if you ask her pedigree
It's: "Honey Chile, I'se French!"

And pipe the Gal with the Corporal there
She has a delicate touch
I overheard her say to him,
"Oh Yah, Suh, Boss—I'se Dutch!"

And note the Broad with the vacant stare
Who has such shapely knees—
She whispers low to have you know
That she "Am Portuguese!"

Let's venture to the Country Club
Where all the white folks meet
Where entrance gained by the soldier boy
Is quite a noted feat

Oh, Gosh! Oh, Gee! Just looky here
Standing in the shade,
Never yet into my life
Come more attractive maid!

I steal across the velvet lawn
As softly as a kitten
And the first darn thing I hear her say:
"Ah sho does miss Great Britain!"

And so it goes with Port of Spain
The City fair and kind,
Where every soldier from the States
Is growing color-blind [21]

The color line, according to "White Lies," was losing its prohibitive significance in occupied Trinidad. Racial boundaries, to be sure, still existed; instructively, the U.S. personnel inquire about the racial identities of their dates
throughout the narrative, and the women, following proper form, insist that
they are white (European). In the end, the humorous truth in the lyric is that
these white men cared little about race when it came to establishing intimacies. Thus while the poem, in one sense, offers a commentary on Trinidad's

past of multiple imperial and immigrant "arrivants" and the bewildering racial results, its real appeal lay in its provocative betrayal of white men's purposeful deviance. U.S. servicemen, the poem suggests, did not grow incapable of accurately recognizing race but simply closed their eyes to it. Read this way, "passing" local women are hardly the only liars in the verse; so, too, are the American men, who appear to be ignorantly (or innocently) crossing the racial boundary between white and nonwhite but who are knowingly subverting social norms. "White Lies" was ultimately a sly mockery of this subversion, posing it as a problem of perception rather than deliberate rebellion. Being blind, the poet winks, fellow whites could not see that the women with whom they associated were in fact nonwhite.

Another Yankee soldier frankly confessed what "White Lies" parodied. An epigrammatic piece appearing in the *Trinidad News Tips* in early 1942 read as follows: "If black is white is white is black then I am color-blind. I never met a girl down here I wouldn't leave behind [go after]."[22] In Trinidad, declared this white soldier, racial distinctions dissolved in the face of desire; blackness marked no reason to refuse the opportunity for female intimacy. If in other places where white American servicemen encountered nonwhite women their revealing inside joke was that "the longer you stay, the lighter the women become," the Trinidadian variant would have been "the longer you stay the less their color mattered."[23]

Cartoons, too, offered a space in which white Americans laughed at their and their peers' proclivity for finding female partners across the color line. In one *Trinidad News Tips* sketch, a white soldier is shown making an advance toward a well-dressed white woman walking down the street; the caption carried her indignant response: "What do you mean 'hello mopsy'?"[24] The humor here was rooted in a ridiculously reckless case of racial misrecognition. Used primarily among local laboring-class men, "mopsy" was the sympathetic contemporary slang for a girlfriend or sexual partner; as such it was a horribly inappropriate form of address for a white woman, effectively disregarding her respectability and superior status. White American men, this cartoon implied, no longer registered the whiteness of white women—yet another case of color blindness.

These tales of racial transgression parading as cases of failed vision might have tickled many white American occupiers, but they could upset white relatives back home in the United States. Indeed, one Pennsylvania parent was driven to absolute despair upon discovering that her nineteen-year-old son—

her only boy—might have gone color blind in Trinidad. Henry Erben's disturbed and desperate mother wrote to the locally based U.S. consul in August 1942 relating news of her Henry's marriage to a local woman named Nita Milan. Claiming to have heard the story from a Red Cross volunteer stationed in the colony, she reported that the couple was expecting a child soon. All she wanted, the mother confessed, was to "assure his associates and everyone concerned regarding [his wife's] color," specifically, to get "information showing [the wife] is pure white." Word of the marriage, according to the letter, amounted to a "very serious accusation," and she "would like it cleared up." Until her daughter-in-law's whiteness was verified, the correspondence concluded, there would be no "peace of mind."[25] For those who cared deeply about whiteness, crossing the color line was depressingly dangerous business.

Had this Pennsylvanian woman traveled to Trinidad, she would have found many local whites equally troubled by what they would have seen as "race suicide." Even though their blood relatives were not involved, these mindful white onlookers, for the sake of skin prestige, were only too eager to guide and guard color-blind Yankees.

GUARDIAN ANGELS

The colony's white elites had long betrayed an alarmed intolerance of "tender interracial ties" in the public sphere. Yet whereas they could once choose to deport indiscreet American drillers (see Chapter 2), with a war on and with bases to build and operate, such unceremonious send-offs had become impossible. Trinidad's defenders of white prestige would have to devise a less dramatic and more delicate remedy for those white Americans susceptible to color blindness. The abstemious solution, it should be clear, was virtually unthinkable. Proscribing all intimacy between male personnel and females would have crossed purposes with authorities' investment in a "militarized masculinity." The most effective fighting men, according to official wisdom, displayed a cocksure manliness. Unequivocally heterosexual, their ability to strike fear in the hearts of enemies was seen as transposable with their ability to strike favor in the hearts of women. In occupied Trinidad, as in so many military theaters, the provision of male personnel with female companionship received near-unquestioned approval.[26]

In this circumstance, the only recourse for concerned whites was regulatory: all they could do was try to ensure that white American servicemen seeking access to women stayed on the appropriate side of the color line. This meant in practice providing Yankees with what might be termed an "education of desire."[27] Racial boundaries, after all, are neither natural nor self-evident and require routine marking and re-marking (about) lest they go unrecognized. This teacherly task of offering Americans the necessary "local knowledge" about race and dating was willingly undertaken by Trinidad's whites, quiet but deep investors in white supremacy.[28] The lessons they gave were private and hence remain unknown, but an incident from contemporary British Guiana suggests what American guests in Trinidad would have learned from their local counterparts. The demographics of British Guiana closely resembled those of Trinidad, and the arrival of white American military personnel in this South American colony provoked comparable racial anxieties. To address them, U.S. authorities offered their servicemen stationed in British Guiana explicit instructions about securing the racial order while seeking female companionship. Leaked to the local press in late 1941 (no doubt by dissidents intending to embarrass white supremacists), the document clarified local expectations of Yankees when it came to dating. "There is a strong color line observed in British Guiana," it began.

> While it does not in any way affect interbusiness relations among the local inhabitants, it is very strongly marked in social contacts.
> Generally speaking social life in town maybe divided in the following categories:
>
>   a) British white
>   b) Portuguese
>   c) Mixed Portuguese
>   d) Mixed colored.
>
> Officers' dates should derive from [group] a above and to a very limited extent from the upper group of b above. Officers are advised that they are not expected to associate with groups in this colony with which they would not associate at home. British officers and police have certain fixed social contacts. The American officer is categorized similarly and should conform to this social demarcation line. It has been observed in the past that officers have been seen in Georgetown with eminently undesirable companions. This situation reflects discreditably on the command and on the US and will be discontinued at once.

These guidelines indicate that, placed in an unfamiliar racial formation, white Americans had to be schooled about the significance of race in assessing the desirability of female companionship. What they were taught included not only a review of familiar prohibitions (they were "not expected to associate with groups . . . with which they would not associate at home," a reference no doubt to "Negro" women) but also an introduction to new proscriptions pertinent to British Caribbean colonial space. For the region's whites, this document emphasizes, pleas of ignorance would be no excuse for U.S. occupiers who crossed the color line.[29]

But pedagogy alone could not suffice for the effective carnal segregation of white American men; assuring racially exclusive dating, Trinidad's whites understood, demanded not only the dissemination of principles but, on a practical level, active policing. Local white women would play a pivotal part in this preemptive effort. Volunteering their selves, households, and daughters, they sought to offer Yankees an alternative to interracial liaisons. White colonials such as the Hugginses (one of the colony's wealthiest families and owners of the *Trinidad Guardian*) cooperated with U.S. officials to establish the Home Hospitality program. Essentially social occasions for local whites to entertain American guests in their homes, it involved young white women who were invited to help accommodate these servicemen. Seen broadly, Home Hospitality certainly offered a way for established colonial elites to cement ties with Yankee newcomers; the program did nonetheless serve the more immediate and narrower purpose of surveilling the social lives of white American men.[30]

In a similar spirit, an upper-class British resident named Mrs. L. Fahey began coordinating events for Yankee servicemen to meet young, white Trinidadian women soon after the occupation began. Overseeing almost every aspect of these occasions, Fahey took care of the printing and mailing of invitations as well as the provision of transport for the women. Despite dismal early results, she persisted; her labor eventually paid off, as by the end of 1941, Fahey was attracting hundreds of white girls to servicemen's dances held all across the island. Appreciative American soldiers would soon hail the "indomitable" Fahey as their "guardian angel."[31] She, it is important to grasp, was serving interests deeper and broader than soldiers' recreation. Helping to design racially exclusive social spaces, Fahey contributed to the fabrication of the supremacy of white skin in Trinidad.

Fahey soon organized a group of young white girls to serve as affiliates of the USO and, in this effort, enlisted help from among her peers.[32] The

*Senior hostesses, the local white women charged with recruiting younger
white women to socialize with white American soldiers at the Port of Spain USO.
(U.S. Army Signal Corps)*

systematic provision of occupying forces with "proper" female company had
been publicly requested by these men, for whom limited contact with women
seemed synonymous with low morale. Implicitly appealing to fears about interracial relationships, a *Trinidad News Tips* editorial had advocated a "dating
bureau." Many soldiers, it explained, felt like "they were cast out in a totally
strange land with no opportunity to uphold the rearing they have had at
home."[33] This "rearing," no doubt, referred to the customary refusal to publicly associate with nonwhite women. Fahey agreed that U.S. servicemen
would be well served by a "kind of clearinghouse" of local women and re-
cruited other white women of her standing to form a group of "senior hostesses." They would undertake to attract, screen, and supervise young girls—
"hostesses"—to socialize at the USO.[34]

Although these young white women were mobilized for the task of pro-
tecting the race, they could formulate and advance their own interests. These
could be more conventionally feminine, as with local white women who ended
up marrying Americans.[35] But they could also be of a transgressive ilk, as with
those who used ties to Yankee men to access hitherto unavailable or denied
freedoms and liberties—from jeep rides to jitterbug dancing. In this respect,

Local hostess gets USO award from military officer. (U.S. Army Signal Corps)

the fictional character Yvette Du Coudray in Ralph De Boissiere's *Rum and Coca-Cola* is illuminating. The unmarried thirty-two-year-old daughter of a wealthy local white (French Creole) family, Yvette experiences in the coming of Americans the "birth of a new life," and soon after the onset of the occupation she happily takes up with an American officer named Harry.[36] It is a choice, tellingly, that distresses her father, who loathes the American's casualness (Harry addresses Mr. Du Coudray as "Pop"). Beyond dating the Yankee, moreover, Yvette makes his "outlook on life her own," which turns out to be an unbearably rebellious decision.[37] In a scene that dramatizes the challenges posed by Yvette's adoption of the "American way," Mr. Du Coudray happens upon Harry and Yvette having sex in the house. He is shocked and scandalized, his disenchantment deepens, and soon thereafter he dies.[38] This death is symbolic in De Boissiere's narrative, marking the passing of a traditional Trinidad. It was a Trinidad fatally unsuited to the modern American ways desired by so many among the colony's youth, not the least its relatively privileged white members.

VOWS OF SILENCE

Yet neither anxious guidelines nor white hostesses proved to be thoroughly effective preemptions for white American men stationed in Trinidad. Many persisted—almost blindly, as it were—with open interracial relationships. Some men, indeed, grew sufficiently serious about their nonwhite partners to take their hand in marriage. Such a decision, however, precipitated another set of problems; marital ties triggered concerns that went beyond the social question of the colony's racial order and into the legal matter of U.S. citizenship. Racist to the core, many states in the republic (especially in the South) refused to recognize marriage between women of African decent and white men. There were laws, furthermore, denying "Asiatic and East Indian" women automatic citizenship, so that even after marriage to occupiers, many local women could be prohibited admission to the United States.[39] In taking native women as wives, Yankees in Trinidad threatened the white supremacy upon which their home society was founded.

These marriages thus sent authorities in the colony scrambling to craft an appropriate policy response. After months of deliberations that began in April 1942, U.S. officials and their colonial counterparts came up with a measure that, significantly, would reverberate around the world. Settling on an essentially supervisory solution, they made it mandatory for locally based U.S. personnel desirous of marriage to first receive permission from their commanding officer.[40] Presumably, if the woman in question was nonwhite and the man was white, the officer denied approval. Established to deal with the color-blind conduct of white Yankee personnel in Trinidad, this policy soon became the norm for American troops stationed across the globe.[41]

Yet a purposeful silence surrounded this new marriage measure. In a British Empire that prided itself on dispensing color-blind justice, officials recognized and respected their obligation to be reticent about any kind of racial policy-making. It was "impolitic and unnecessary," explained a ranking U.S. officer, to publicize the racist legal premises that supported the new restrictive marital policy.[42] The result was mystery and confusion within the Trinidadian public. Some locals came under the impression that marriage itself had been banned in the colony. Aware of the circulation of such a false belief, the two leading dailies (the *Trinidad Guardian* and the *Port of Spain Gazette*) ran editorials in late October 1942 reassuring readers that references to the banning of all marriages were nothing but "absurd" rumors.[43] The *Trinidad*

Guardian subsequently urged the colony's women to become aware of the relevant U.S. law on the subject but went no further than to say that marriage to American men did not necessarily entitle wives to enter the United States as citizens.[44]

Uncertainty about marriage nevertheless persisted. In late November 1942, a priest from Princes Town in central Trinidad wrote to the U.S. consul inquiring about the validity of the proposed marriage between one of his parishioners, Lenora Young Hoi, who was partially of Chinese descent, and a white American, John Trueman. Young Hoi worked at the American docksite in Port of Spain and planned to marry Trueman, an electrician from Chicago. Before taking the oath, however, she asked her priest to ascertain the legitimacy of her proposed marriage. The U.S. consul, not surprisingly, offered a terse response: the union, he replied, was ill advised.[45] The dubious status of marriages between Trinidadian women and American occupiers continued to attract public attention in the following year. Even then, the racial assumptions underlying the issue remained unuttered. At a public meeting in May 1943, Captain Cipriani attacked the government, the church, and parents for the "temporary marriages that were taking place between Americans and the local girls." These agencies, Cipriani charged, were "blinding their eyes," for it was "well known that the local girls who married the Americans could not go to America with their husbands."[46] A week later, the *Trinidad Guardian* published a pointed piece of correspondence. A writer who signed as "Father" reported that he had been forced to stop a marriage between his daughter and a Yankee soldier even after banns had been put up. The American, according to the letter, had not received permission to marry. This experience, hoped Father, would serve as a cautionary tale, a warning for all Trinidadians to find out about the marriage policy in order to "save our women."[47] Perhaps had Father known better, his letter would have acknowledged that more than female honor was at stake in this marital policy. As white American men publicly embraced and, furthermore, married nonwhite partners, white supremacy, both in the colony and back in the United States, was imperiled.

Plotted with telling lies and silences, this episode of transgressive conduct involving white Americans and nonwhite local women resists full recounting. It nevertheless warrants attempts at recovery, for ultimately these kinds of stories help reveal how the reproduction of the social order in colonial Trinidad depended on careful patrol of those intimate spaces touched by gender, race, and sexuality.

BLACK ARRIVALS AND MANLY RIVALRIES

In a move that should have offered a sliver of assurance to locals troubled by the rash of interracial intimacy, U.S. military authorities opted to station African American soldiers in Trinidad beginning in April 1942.[48] After all, the approximately 2,000 black men who made up the 99th Anti-Aircraft Coastal Artillery could pair with local women without prompting either racial "passing" or prevarication. The arrival of these "Red Diamond Boys" (their military nickname), however, was not without its own problems. Insofar as these servicemen were beholden to a public presentation of heterosexuality and found accommodating local females, they engendered a passionate rivalry with their Trinidadian male counterparts.

In theory, of course, African Americans were no different from their white peers insofar as they challenged local men's claims on the colony's women. In practice, however, they appeared to have represented more potent figures of encroachment. Among Trinidadian "girls," according to a military source, black personnel proved particularly "popular."[49] Their superior appeal, if more than fanciful, might be partially explained by, of all things, racially rooted privileges. Along with the benefits common to all American servicemen (relatively prestigious jobs and easy access to food and drink), the Red Diamond Boys had the advantage of escaping the surveillance visited upon their white peers. Indeed, having segregated black soldiers, U.S. authorities encouraged them to socialize with the nonwhite local community. African American servicemen put on public drills and artillery exhibitions in Port of Spain; they even participated against locals in athletic meets, boxing matches, and other social events.[50] Compared with white servicemen, they enjoyed greater liberty to connect and conduct public affairs with "native" women.[51] This increased opportunity for intermingling might explain why it was black — rather than white — Americans who figured in the most dramatic instance of a manly clash over females in the colony.

Local women wasted no time in seizing on the possibilities presented by the men of the 99th. Affairs with these foreigners, they grasped, offered a route to basic needs, modern pleasures, and even romantic dreams. Traces of the purposefulness of these females appear in the writings of African American soldiers who chronicled their social experiences in the *Trinidad News Tips*. These men, of course, had no intentions of paying tribute to enterprising local girls. Rather, drawing on a literary style that many learned back in the

Members of the 99th Coastal Artillery Regiment in classes. Remarkably, these classes appear to be integrated. (U.S. Army Signal Corps)

United States, black servicemen meant to entertain themselves with reports and riffs that buzzed with hep slang. Representative was an inaugural column announcing its intent "to tell you exactly who was seen out with whose mopsy. This is not to cause any disturbance," declared the soldier-turned-journalist, "but merely to keep you cats on the beam."[52] Yet for all their marks of self-congratulatory sexism (females often figured as no more than prizes in manly contests about who was the best dancer, dresser, and jive talker), these jottings and commentaries betray something of local women's savvy.

African American soldiers documented their own zealous pursuits as well as those of the women. A serviceman identified as Wallace Matthis, to cite just one case, was portrayed as a "sharp glamour boy (known here as a saga boy)" who "played" local females "the American way." Though unreported, Matthis's imported approach appeared to be successful (at least in the eyes of his peers); neighborhood girls, the writer approvingly pronounced, sought him out with candlelight.[53] Columns referred as well to the enthusiasm displayed on the other side of the gender divide, stressing the lengths to which black soldiers went to secure female companionship. In some instances, it

Members of the black 99th Coastal Artillery Regiment, stationed in Trinidad for about a year beginning in April 1943. (U.S. Army Signal Corps; courtesy Schomburg Center for Research in Black Culture, New York Public Library)

was not the lengths but the heights. According to a member of the 99th stationed at the Laventille cantonment, the shiny new fence erected by authorities in early 1943 was not a hindrance—as authorities had hoped—but merely part of a surmountable obstacle course for soldiers determined to meet local women.[54] In other instances, black personnel found that the real impediments to their search for female partners were not installed by authorities but personified in their peers, and throughout their stay in Trinidad, soldiers vied vigorously with one another for women. Three Laventille men (a sergeant, a corporal, and a private), according to a gleeful columnist, were "in love" with the same woman. The outcome, he predicted, would be determined by rank, as "the man with the most stripes will win."[55]

But this simplistic suggestion that the colony's interested women were passive pawns easily moved by men's military rank did little justice to the complex reality. Like most associations in which romance, sex, and material exchange play indeterminate roles, these affairs involved negotiations that prohibit straightforward invocations of "sexual imperialism."[56] Some of these unions, to begin with, bespoke genuine commitment. Six months after the arrival of the 99th regiment, one soldier reported that two of his peers were so "enthused over the local girls that they are thinking seriously of taking the final vows."[57] Another columnist reported that one particular corporal believed that "every man in our regiment would be married if the government hadn't walked in with that handicapping regulation on marriage."[58] Marriages, moreover, did occur between black soldiers and local women. And even if they sometimes were no more than convenient responses to desperate circumstances, these unions at the very least ought to belie the notion that women in Trinidad witlessly fell victim to black visitors.[59]

Even if sincerity, moreover, sometimes comprised a doubtful component of these liaisons, the women proved themselves forces to be reckoned with. The colony's "girls" could ably assert themselves and their desires, customarily extracting gifts from the men of the 99th who sought their company. Chewing gum (cherished at the time), fruits, chocolates, cigarettes, and money all passed from the hands of Americans to local women.[60] These presents, moreover, were not always adequate to gain a woman's undivided attention. One black soldier reportedly had been spending his hard-earned cash on a woman for three months only to find out that she had been seeing another soldier all along.[61] Some mopsies simply refused to wait for gifts from their black American boyfriends and appropriated what they coveted. A particularly amusing case involved a serviceman who returned to camp one night minus his wallet and money, claiming to have been the victim of a robbery by a gang of notorious "robust men." The following day, though, a woman—"a beautiful young squaw," according to one *Trinidad News Tips* columnist—showed up at the Laventille barracks with the missing wallet, but no money. The alleged robust man was perhaps no more than a cunning local woman.[62]

Finally, despite boasting about being able to "master" local women, black soldiers often revealed that their mastery was far from complete and, indeed, constantly challenged. One columnist rebuked another serviceman for cowardice in the company of his girlfriend, chiding that he was much too big to be "crossing his knees" whenever his woman became angry.[63] Others apparently even ended up on the receiving end of assaults. One black soldier chastisingly inquired of another why he had allowed his girl to use him as a punching bag; another columnist, meanwhile, observed that the girlfriend of a certain Private Betts had dealt him a black eye.[64]

These Port of Spain mopsies, it turns out, could mean trouble not only for African American boyfriends but also for their Trinidadian male counterparts. Neighborhood men, feeling displaced to the sidelines, became increasingly resentful at the intimacies that developed between black foreigners and local girls. The result was a masculine tension that eventually erupted into a violent climax. Around 9:00 P.M. on the night of April 16, 1943, scores of black servicemen took to the streets of Laventille, one of Port of Spain's toughest black proletarian neighborhoods. Helmeted and bare-chested in some cases and bearing weapons in nearly all, the men had set out on a seek-and-destroy mission, taking the neighborhood's "robust men" as the object of their exercise. How many of these toughs they eventually found remains unknown; what is clear is that soldiers rained sticks, bottles, and stones on homes and shops on Basilon Street and on anyone in their way. By the end of what outraged municipal representatives condemned as a "wave of homicidal fury," marauding members of the 99th had broken windows, dented walls, and left twenty-four local men, including four special reserve police officers, hospitalized.[65]

Though quickly deemed a "riot," this episode reflected a premeditation and purpose that belies the label. Testimony at a court-martial held six weeks later placed the Basilon Street attack against the backdrop of brewing hostilities between the black soldiers and young neighborhood men over women. "A preference of the girls of the district for the American boys," according to one eyewitness, "raised the jealousy of the boys of the district who in turn threatened violence to the girls."[66] Several accounts, in fact, claimed that the night before the riot, a neighborhood man (identified in one instance as Donald Steadman) had accosted a black American soldier and his Laventille girlfriend. After inquiring if the man belonged to the U.S. army and receiving an affirmative answer, Steadman threw a blow at the Yankee that missed the intended target and landed instead on the girlfriend.[67] This confrontation, apparently, sparked the following night's havoc.[68]

On that fateful Friday, furthermore, women appear to have been more than voiceless props in a male drama. Authoring the violent script, the girlfriends, it seems, were the ones who made up the vengeful minds of the black soldiers. A couple weeks after ten of the Red Diamond Boys had been tried, ten Laventille women stood before a Port of Spain magistrate accused of inciting the riot that shook Basilon Street. Witnesses at that trial testified that these girls had identified particular neighborhood men and then sicced their American boyfriends to assault them. "Joe, look some of the robust men here," one

In Trinidad to ward off a possible Nazi invasion, African American soldiers like these here found themselves engaged in hostilities with jealous local men. (U.S. Army Signal Corps; courtesy Schomburg Center for Research in Black Culture, New York Public Library)

woman reportedly told her black serviceman friend, "beat them."[69] Other girls allegedly joined in the assault. Eerily, one of the young men fingered as deserving of a thrashing was a self-confessed abuser of women named Mano Benjamin.[70] Two decades before the Trinidad public at large would learn of this legendary misogynist (dubbed "the Beast of Biche" in the local press during the 1960s), Port of Spain women had decided to deal with him. In retrospect, they might have exercised too much leniency.[71]

This decision to employ Yankee men as avengers was hardly the act of feminist revolutionaries; yet it was reasonable given the gendered norms in mid-twentieth-century Trinidadian society. Females who aspired to sexual self-possession customarily faced violent male policing that, moreover, often found sympathetic ears in the courts.[72] However provisional and partial, resorting to vicarious physical vengeance would have given these women the visceral satisfaction of retribution. This, in the end, was considerably more than what the judicial system offered. At the conclusion of the court-martial held in early June, the ten African American soldiers were found guilty of rioting. As their punishment (prison time and dishonorable discharges) was pronounced, some of the women in attendance openly expressed anguish. "The sentence of the court," a newspaper reported, "was the signal for loud screams from several girlfriends of the convicted soldiers who witnessed the closing stages of the trial."[73] It was an understandable response. Here, after all, were among the colony's most vulnerable individuals facing the abrupt end of relationships through which they sought to extract a measure of security difficult to attain in Trinidad.

THE OLDEST PROFESSION IN MODERN TIMES

In occupied Trinidad, the search for material security led some women to candidly commercial sexual transactions with American men. Notorious in the eyes of most, their conduct sparked prodigious commentary. But although much of this discourse carried the expected marks of anxiety around moral decline, apprehensions of the sex trade were complex and diverse. "Prostitution" meant different things to different people.[74] From respectable urban denizens to American officials to patriot intellectuals, its broad range of observers came away with competing interpretations of its significance. What the practice meant to the female protagonists, not surprisingly, remains hidden; as almost everywhere else, in Trinidad the women engaged in this kind of labor have been rendered practically voiceless. Indeed, the absence of firsthand testimony manifests even more profoundly for this colony, where, unlike in many twentieth-century metropolitan sites, no reformers, social workers, or politicians viewed sex workers as subjects worthy of interrogation.[75]

The conduct of the world's oldest profession in colonial Trinidad certainly predated the arrival of U.S. personnel during World War II. For the 1930s, illustratively, local and foreign observers of the social scene remarked on the vibrant commerce. Along with several calypsos, Calder-Marshall's *Glory Dead*, a polyphonous narrative that included an exposé-like account of "imaginary but typical incidents" in Port of Spain, recognized "rats" (the local pejorative label for sex workers), "pimps," and their male clientele as a ubiquitous urban presence.[76] Even pro-imperial advisers, who would have been reluctant to publicize unfavorable images of the colony, conceded the existence of a local skin trade. The Moyne Commission, despite its dubious charge that "promiscuity" made prostitution a "luxury profession" in the region, noted that many working-class females in Trinidad supplanted their wages through commercial sex. "While carrying on her own work as well in the daytime," Port of Spain's poor women, the report submitted, could be found "by nights at the docks when ships put in."[77] As with almost every modern society, prewar Trinidad contained spaces for the overt commodification of sexuality.[78]

Yet virtually no one would have honestly disagreed with the U.S. official who concluded that it was during the occupation that prostitution broke out in Trinidad on a "large and lucrative basis."[79] The arrival of thousands of American men injected new vigor and profit into the local trade. Each day, according to one official source, between 600 and 700 prostitutes plied their trade in Port of Spain. To some extent, the colony's social world of commercial sex simply assumed new scale rather than structure. The dominance of the tandem of "nightwalkers" and brothel proprietors persisted.[80] In many ways, too, the cartography of the trade maintained its contours, with the downtown Port of Spain stretch on Park Street between Edward and Charlotte streets acquiring a more intensely red-lit reputation. Anchored by the notorious "Green Corner" (Trinidad's Times Square), this strip was "filled with men and women of the lowest strata of society molesting and in other ways accosting men for their own purposes."[81] Little wonder that respectable Port of Spain people reported being appalled during the period.

There were, nevertheless, visible changes associated with the conduct of commercial sex during the occupation. The center of gravity of soliciting, for one, shifted toward the Wrightson Road USO recreational facility. It was a reorientation that outraged many Woodbrook residents, who publicly charged pimps, prostitutes, and "procuring" with ruining their prized middle-class neighborhood, with degrading it into a disreputable rendezvous point. Streetwalkers, complained one dweller, had become so commonplace in the area that policemen could be seen "chatting" with them.[82] By late 1943, disgusted, fed-up denizens began demanding that police mop up what one paper agreed was a "blot" on their community.[83] The establishment of the army base in Cumuto, furthermore, fueled a flourishing sex trade beyond Port of Spain and toward northeast Trinidad. By early 1942 the Arima city council had acknowledged the proliferation of these "deplorable" activities. Once a "clean town," mourned the deputy mayor, the city had become "the 'mecca' of all sorts of lewd women from all parts of the island."[84] Although this depiction of prostitutes as an external danger is certainly consistent with a conventional rhetorical strategy, the councilor made a pertinent sociological point. In occupied Trinidad, sex workers often migrated to the "east-west corridor," coming not only from remote parts of the island but in some cases from as far as Venezuela. Finally, taxi drivers appeared to have assumed a new salience within the economy and geography of prostitution. Performing varied and often pivotal tasks, they chauffeured, touted, and at times, let their cars out to be used as "rooms." Tellingly, when the administration formulated measures to crack down on commercial sex in late 1942, it proposed tighter regulation of the taxi industry, requiring for the first time that drivers wear photo identifications.[85]

But whereas the establishment panicked at the expanding sex trade, renouncing it as a nuisance and insisting on its suppression, there were observers who adopted cooler analyses, who apprehended in prostitutes more than "fallen women." Prominent among this set was the colony's nationalist intelligentsia. Willing to approach the trade as an economic and sociological matter, they saw sex workers as disadvantaged but pragmatic figures. A similar assessment emerged from within the ranks of U.S. officialdom, but sometimes for reasons distinct from those of Trinidadian dissidents. Concerned primarily with the health and morale of their troops, these foreigners often had no investment and, in some cases, simply no faith in local morality.

Patriots such as Albert Gomes and Ralph Mentor, for example, urged people in Trinidad to accept that the presence of thousands of relatively wealthy American men in the colony made commercial sex an obvious route for local females seeking a path to financial independence. In the face of Port of Spain city councilors' call for "punitive" measures to deal with prostitution in mid-1941, Gomes pleaded with his peers to address the matter in a "realistic way." Indeed, warning that the issue was fraught with "sociological difficulties" and emphasizing that policing would result only in "simplifying" the matter, he advocated the "regulation" of prostitution.[86] Mentor, too, argued explicitly for suspending moral judgments against women who traded sex for American money. Commenting on a sensational trial in which an older woman had been found guilty of tricking a teenaged girl into working in her brothel, this trade unionist reminded readers that Trinidad was filled with "thousands of well-fed American men with cash and plenty of time and no special training or reason to transmute the natural desires to perform a normal biological function into ascetic or mystic practice."[87] It was Mentor's long-winded way of stating that the mix of masculinity, money, and local poverty made for a virtually inevitable explosion of commercialized sex.

This view that the sale of sex was simply one of the ways poor women sought to eke out a living in radically transformed economic circumstances obtained, too, within American circles. In 1942, State Department official Henry Field, following his investigative trip to the island, accounted for Port of Spain's high incidence of sex workers in terms of labor cost. With wages for domestic servants set at about $12 per month, "it can hardly be wondered," Field concluded, "that almost any girl will practice prostitution."[88] A less explicit but no less telling instance of this understanding of sex as merely another category of labor appeared in a *Trinidad News Tips* cartoon. Depicting a soldier addressing a black woman who had done his laundry, the sketch carries a caption that reads, "That's reasonable — now how much for my laundry?"[89] Besides obviously mocking American men's relentless lust, this cartoon gestured at how this lust made commercial sex a possibility for a broad range of working women — not only for the so-called prostitute. For many Yankee occupiers, it is clear, the occupational classification of "service provider" assumed an amazing amorphousness.

Although the recognition by white Americans of the fluidity of the category of prostitute could reflect to a large degree their racist assumptions about the "easy virtue" of the island's nonwhite females, not all were devoid of a genuine understanding of the predicaments of these impoverished women.[90] Colonel Oliver Wenger distinguished himself in this regard. Not only did Wenger stand out as remarkably sympathetic toward the colony's women; he was positively radical when it came to drawing out the gender politics of their sex work. An officer in the U.S. army and a veteran of Chicago's anti-VD campaign during the 1930s, Wenger joined the Caribbean's anti-VD program in 1943 as a codirector.[91] By then, military authorities had declared VD the "most important and the most difficult health problem facing [their] armed forces in the region."[92]

As Wenger lectured and wrote about policies regarding disease and sexuality, he consistently and candidly downplayed questions of female morality. "There should be no mixing up of morals with this," he flatly told a Port of Spain audience. Indeed, this official admitted that it was his "personal opinion that men and women should select their own sex standards as they do their food, religion, occupation or their style of hair cut."[93] Unconstrained by questions of ethics, Wenger was able to appreciate the decision of women to participate in the skin trade as fundamentally economic. For him, they were people in search of relief, not outcasts beyond the moral pale. Troubling the moralism of the "prostitute" category, he pointed out that once it became clear the amount of money to be made from sexual encounters ($3, then $5, then as much as $10), the "professional prostitute" found herself with much competition from thousands of "girlfriends," "occasionals," and "clandestines." In fact, so committed was Wenger to the view of sex workers as ordinary people, no more than "victims of their circumstances," that he resolutely opposed the repression of commercial sex. To the proposal (from a U.S.-based military official) that sellers of sex be arrested, the colonel posed the following question: "What plans and provision were made, during and after their jail sentence, to equip these women for and provide them with a legitimate livelihood, at regular employment, with adequate wages, in lieu of their illegal occupation of prostitution?"[94] According to him, "To exercise stern law enforcement against prostitutes without providing legitimate employment in its stead is not only inhumane but short sighted from every standpoint." Wenger thus continued: "It's a double crossing of the worst kind. It makes a woman even more antisocial, causes her to feel she is an enemy of society, makes her a fugitive from justice and any and all health officers, who she associates from then on with law enforcement agencies."[95]

It was this sympathy with the perspectives of female participants that led Wenger to the radical insight that the problem of purchased sex lay primarily not with poor local prostitutes but with the moneyed American men. Underscoring that the male clients ought to be held accountable for the prevalence of prostitution, this American questioned how many "property owners, pimps, procurers, and CUSTOMERS were arrested and given the full penalty of the law?" In his assessment, policing prostitution remained unfair unless there was a nonsexist redefinition of the crime. "All repressive programs," he wrote, "penalize the woman—first, last and all the time. You never seem to reach the buyer, this soldier, sailor, or citizen, even though he is caught in the act." Wenger thus commended "repressive measures" under one condition: "if [authorities] really mean business and suppress BOTH BUYER AND SELLER." He proposed a redefinition of "prostitute," stating that it should be understood as "any person of either sex, who engages in the act of fornication or any of its substitutes outside of the marital state." The dominant discourse, this American ultimately clarified, elided the gendered and material oppression that conditioned women's decisions to participate in commercialized sex.

Many within the nationalist intelligentsia would have found nothing objectionable in Wenger's framing of prostitution; yet they did not—perhaps could not—go so far as to relinquish all interest in the moral significance of the trade. However sympathetically these dissidents viewed poor women pushed into sex work, they remained committed to imagining a "Trinidadian community" deeply invested in the folksy, "traditional" virtues and ethics of "the people." This commitment would lead them to produce a discourse decidedly ambivalent about prostitution. On one hand, local patriots recognized in the commerce the pursuit of independence for underprivileged females that was inseparable from the new conditions sponsored by the American presence. On the other hand, they read the skin trade metaphorically, taking the practice as an expression of a new alienation and uprootedness inherent in the embrace of this Americanized modernity.

The observations of Jean De Boissiere are instructive in this regard. In 1941 this patriot published an essay deeply sympathetic and sensitive to women who sold sex. Titled "Very Public School" and appearing in De Boissiere's *Picong* magazine, the piece presented them as females laboring over the liberties of modern life.

> Interesting are the girls (they range from 14 to 40) who are returning home after working the town for several nights. The bright crimson paint on their faces is scaling off but they have put on so much that even now if they stood in a two-day rain there would still be some left. They sit in their crumpled two shilling satin surrounded by gramophones, thermos flasks, records and gold earrings; all looted from England and America via Sa Gomes. For the most part they are too exhausted by their labors to utter a sound but occasionally one with terrifically animal spirits will give a lecture in a voice keyed to a pitch so as to let the locomotive driver in on the class. Her subjects include pure anatomy, finance and public relations as they are to be conducted in Frederick Street, Marine Square and a taxi-cab. By the time the train has arrived you will know all there is to know about these things and how much money the lecturer has made in the course of a night as well.[96]

Prostitutes, according to De Boissiere, were first and foremost diligent laborers. However daunting their lots, moreover, they found their efforts rewarded. By virtue of their hardly virtuous work, they could afford to be enthusiastic consumers, purchasing commodities (radios, records, jewelry, and more) that provided quintessentially modern pleasures. For De Boissiere, furthermore, these working girls were neither naive nor innocent; they were knowing subjects, individuals fully aware of every aspect of their jobs. Indeed, he drew them as veritable public intellectuals, women well versed in various vernacular disciplines and emboldened enough to conduct "classes" on government trains. Commercial sex, in the eyes of this patriot, was profoundly edifying labor.

This, at least, was his view during the early days of occupied Trinidad, for De Boissiere would soon develop a less benign impression of commercialized sexuality. Revisiting the subject less than three years later, this journalist offered a dubious review of the impact of Americans. Not pretending that Trinidad was somehow previously chaste, De Boissiere nonetheless was convinced that the availability of the Yankee dollar had degraded the colony. The society had gone from a place of "healthy" promiscuity to one of untreatable pathology. Whereas locals, according to this patriot, were once innocently extravagant with regard to sex, they had become mercenarily wanton. "Hundreds of military men," he charged "would come into the street with nothing on their minds except trying to hypnotize the population into an erotic state."[97] De Boissiere thus ended his reflection on a pessimistic note. Whereas "religious and social precepts can more or less control promiscuity and amorality," he argued, "it will take a generation to make back what the island has lost to commercial vice and immorality."[98]

This anxiety that the swelling local sex trade signified the sad disappearance of all that once defined Trinidad's society had wider currency within the patriot intelligentsia. As Albert Gomes, for example, grew increasingly nervous that the social order was unraveling under the strain of the American occupation, he repeatedly advanced the commercialization of female sexuality as emblematic. In late 1943, only two years after advocating the regulation of prostitution, this patriot recounted a bus ride he had recently taken in Port of Spain; what he claimed to have seen was nothing short of the demise of the "traditional" order. A wistful Gomes observed "a most amazing assortment: girls and mere children — children who had become experienced women overnight! As they entered the bus they spoke to uniformed figures on the sidewalk in a brogue that is certainly not of this land. Their speech was nasal and had a distinct drawl. . . . Beneath the brave gesture of rouge and paint most unaesthetically done, one saw fatigue, dissipation and even a glint of desperation. It was depressing in the extreme. Throughout that trip my impression was that here were human beings entirely uprooted and adrift."[99] Despite explicitly describing young women who sold their bodies to American servicemen, this essay ultimately addressed concerns that went beyond the subject of commercial sex. In these females, Gomes discerned a frightful new social creature produced by a new social crisis. They spoke differently, dressed differently, and in fact, possessed a new disposition. Tragic to the extreme, they struck him as girls only superficially successful in their search for independent womanhood.

Gomes's despair sounded a distinctly modernist note; he wrote of sex workers as manifestations of a new generation of "uprooted and adrift" people. Embodiments of the unmaking of the social order he had come to know, "prostitutes" signified for him the passing of a Trinidad that, as one of his columns had declared, he "was not likely to see again."[100] A year later, this patriot returned to the idea that the island had become a modern morass. Written just as the imperial and colonial government began championing the Welfare Department as the panacea for problems wracking Great Britain's colonies, Gomes used his *Trinidad Guardian* column to dramatize the enormity of the challenge faced by the hopeful social workers. Once again, he relied on a mise-en-scène of sex work for his anxious portrait of Trinidad. Local girls, he observed, had become so savvy about sex that the old boundaries between girlhood and womanhood had become invisible. Wearing "skirts so short," observed this column, "you wonder whether to smile at them or to regard the display as being tragic in the extreme." "Is it a woman that they encase," Gomes asked, "or a girl who, stylistically prepared, with the assistance of the abbreviated skirt enacts the women's role successfully?"[101]

The novel image of sexually precocious girls, moreover, was not the only source of disenchantment for this patriot; so, too, was the personage of young pimps. These men made for painfully glaring evidence of the emergence of a troubling modernity in Trinidad. A 1944 column captured Gomes's sense of what the appearance of these new men portended:

He comes within the area beneath the arc lights of the theater and with consummate savoire faire insinuates himself into a brief conversation with an uniformed foreigner. One hand goes into a pocket and the other stretches furtively to receive: there is the colorful flash of paper currency. Now I have been seeing that young fellow for years: indeed, I have watched him grow and am familiar with the domestic setting that has nurtured him. The family is a respectable one, all the brothers and sisters being fairly well placed. He had been very much attached to his mother when she was taken to hospital with her last illness. I remember him then as a shy and almost effeminate boy who brought flowers. I have spoken to him on several occasions and never once got the impression of dishonesty or vulgarity. He has been an orphan for a few years and now it seems that the current of life is sweeping him away. He returned in the direction whence he had come and presently the uniformed person dissolved. . . . The cup of gross ugliness and sordidness was running over. Port of Spain is a comparatively small city yet day by day it is becoming more and more a microcosm of big city suffering and woe.[102]

Here again, prostitution became little more than a trope to signify a dubious social transformation. Projecting this image of a transaction involving commercial sex onto the broader social canvas, Gomes meant to invoke not only a scene featuring a young man procuring sex for an American soldier but also a small island society shocked and shaken. A once pacific space, Trinidad saw its moral anchor dislodged in the course of its confrontation with occupying Americans. Gomes's young pimp, like young female prostitutes, provided a metaphor for a society robbed of youthful innocence. The colony had become a place, he suggests, where formerly girlish boys who once clung to their mothers had corruptly matured into calculatingly cool men who sold women's bodies. With the advent of Yankees in Trinidad, purchased sex supplanted genuine love. Sketched here was a society that had lost honesty, simplicity, and tenderness of spirit.[103]

Ralph De Boissiere's *Rum and Coca-Cola*, completed soon after the end of the occupation, represents prostitution and its practitioners in terms consistent with patriot discourse during the period.[104] Through the character Mopsy, a poor, ambitious colored woman, De Boissiere casts sex work as economically empowering but, in the end, morally dispiriting. Mopsy had been peddling sex on the streets even before the onset of base installation and, when questioned, accounted for her occupational choice with frank financial rationality: "If I could get work as a servant," she told her Swedish client, "I not makin' more than ten dollars at the very most, I still have to have a man if I want to live."[105] With the arrival of Americans, her sexual value skyrockets, and, for Mopsy, this facilitates communal leverage as well as personal mobility. On the day that Yankee contractors arrive to tear down shacks in her village, she agrees to go out with one of the white workers, Mat, in exchange for a respite that allows her neighbors to save their belongings and arrange new accommodations.

Mopsy, moreover, soon begins dating Mat, who provides her with a stipend of $40 a month and a home. Yet despite accumulating a houseful of furniture and savings of more than $2,000 in this arrangement, she gets frustrated with the American's racist, domineering ways. Thus when an older white Yankee named Robert Waters enters the scene, Mopsy takes up with him. More generous and sensitive than Mat, Waters sets her up in a rented house and gives her a stipend of $85 a week. Still, Mopsy feels no less exploited, especially when she learns that he was earning the grand salary of $250 a week. It is at this point that she accepts a stranger's offer of $30 to go to bed. A decisive transaction, it brings Mopsy to the painful and shameful realization that her life had been reduced to the mercenary exchange of sex. There and then she weeps—for the first time since she was twelve—and resolves to re-create herself. "She did not realize that a spirit of rebellion was growing within her; that the tears, pushing up like hardly flowering plants through the cracks in the concrete with which she had covered her heart, were not 'weakness' but a sign she would fight furiously against being dragged back into the old life."[106] Weeks later, with the encouragement of her seamstress friend, Mrs. Enriques, Mopsy opens a restaurant; achieving fast success, Mopsy's dreams of having "real money" finally materialize.

By the end of *Rum and Coca-Cola*, however, Mopsy's fortunes take a tragic turn. After falling for, marrying, and becoming pregnant by yet another white American, Wal Brown, she discovers that he was a swindler. Brown had gone back to the United States but promised to send for Mopsy so that they could settle as family up there. She soon learns, though, not only that Brown already had a wife back in the United States but also that he had another in Trinidad. The "trigamist" husband to whom she had been sending money had no intention of inviting her to America. A dejected Mopsy decides to take the life of their unborn child and then her own. In the end, she succeeds only in the first endeavor and winds up in a mental hospital.

Rum and Coca-Cola thus refuses any simple celebration of a local woman who sold her body for the Yankee dollar. Though Mopsy's financial fortunes affirm that bold, enterprising women could turn these foreigners into bountiful benefactors, her eventual fate as a devastated victim of a deceitful American accords with the novel's ultimate ambition to serve as a foundational nationalist fiction.[107] Committed to nation-building, De Boissiere could not admit a happy, productive heterosexual union between a nonwhite Trinidadian woman and a white American man. In spite of the protagonist's material gains through affairs with U.S. personnel, she loses much more. For a patriot like De Boissiere, Trinidadian hearts would find neither real love nor genuine happiness in Yankee hands.

CONCLUSION

Complex and ambiguous, women's engagements with sojourning U.S. personnel encapsulate the wider society during the years of occupation. These ties resisted easy categorizing, challenging confident distinctions between what these females might have experienced as labor and pleasure, savvy and vulnerability, and progress and disenchantment. What remained doubtless, however, was their subversiveness. Liaisons between local women and American men frequently flew in the face of the combined forces of white supremacy, male domination, and class privilege, troubling precepts essential to the social order. Ultimately, the stories of these affairs, fraught with uncertain and undecided struggles over status, desire, and material ambition, composed the story of occupied Trinidad.

Coda

Re-Membering Caliban and the Yankees

The Politics of History

Not long after Trinidad's raucous celebration of VJ (Victory over Japan) day, the American occupation began winding down; although the U.S. government retained rights to these installations for the next ninety-five years, it quickly and dramatically reduced troop strength once the war was over. By 1947, the Yankees had effectively gone home. These bases, however, still had plenty of history left in them, and a decade later fiery protest to reclaim the area under lease to the U.S. navy engulfed local politics. Spearheaded by Dr. Eric Williams, the leader of the governing People's National Movement (PNM) and Trinidad's new premier, this campaign to regain Chaguaramas marked the militant high point of postwar nationalist mobilization in the colony.[1] For one participant, indeed, it was "one of the greatest events in the history of the West Indies."[2]

By 1960, then, two decades after its initiation, the U.S. occupation returned to the center of Trinidadian history. In its retrospective reentrance, however, the episode assumed new character and meaning. Recalled in the course of a battle in which PNM patriots pit themselves against Yankee imperialists, occupied Trinidad was recast in a manner that threatened to shear it of any complexity. The expedience of the present simplified the recollection of the past experience, flattened a compellingly layered story. Yet all was not lost, for at the very moment that nationalist imperatives led to a Manichaean portrait of the wartime encounter, notes on more complex memories of the period emerged from other commentators. Espousing a politics that was nationalist and yet beyond it, they sowed the seeds for the kind of recovery undertaken in this book.

The political resurrection of the U.S. bases was rooted in an abiding faith in the idea of a federated British Caribbean. Tossed around since the end of the nineteenth century, the proposal for a West Indian federation finally took hold in the postwar years as Great Britain scrambled for an honorable way out of the financial and moral burden of empire. By 1956, following a series of conferences and negotiations, West Indian representatives and British officials had settled on an acceptable plan for unification. They set the inauguration of the federated unit for January 1958, elections for March, and the parliamentary opening for April 22. This constitutional and ceremonial program came off as scheduled, and all, it seemed, was well on the united West Indian front.

But one issue, the site of the capital for the new federation, descended into greater and greater bouts of uncertainty. In 1957, after some deliberation, West Indian leadership nominated Trinidad's northwestern peninsula. This, of course, was a potentially contentious choice, for according to the terms of the 1941 base agreement, the selected area remained under lease to the United States for the next eighty-two years. Americans soon ensured controversy, announcing in the middle of 1958 that they had no plans to release the naval site. To make matters worse, they effectively denied the very legitimacy of the new government by refusing to negotiate with West Indian representatives over the area. Chaguaramas, they insisted, was a "domestic British matter." It was a harsh slap in the face for the fledgling federal project.

If this show of arrogance was meant to seal the issue, it backfired. For although Barbadian Grantley Adams, the newly elected and first prime minister of the West Indian federation, accepted Americans' promise to review the issue in "say ten years," and British diplomats simply retreated from any debate, Eric Williams was in no mood for compromise.[3] Fresh from a triumphant foray into electoral politics, Trinidad's premier seized the impasse as a cause célèbre.[4] Though initially reluctant to press for the release of Chaguaramas, Williams made a volte-face by the middle of 1957. A review of the documents from the 1941 agreement, he claimed, exposed the falsity of Americans' position on the issue. The U.S. government, according to Williams the historian, had acquired the bases in the first place by bullying, and in light of this original injustice, he now insisted on the return of Chaguaramas. Thus began the belligerence, the "war for West Indian independence."

More than anything else, this was a war of words. By 1959 the PNM mouthpiece, the *Nation*, was converted into a base for the battle. Over the next year this organ, under the editorship of C. L. R. James, who had been invited back to Trinidad after more than twenty-five years away, blazed with denunciations of Americans' decision to retain Chaguaramas. The PNM's rhetorical assault was executed not only in print but also in open air. In July 1959, Williams gave his memorable "From Slavery to Chaguaramas" address before a large Arima crowd, and in it he rehearsed the Caribbean's post-Columbian history as the story of mercenary imperial warfare in which these islands served as little more than "garrisons, forts and military installations." Having set the 1941 base agreement within this historical frame, the author of *Capitalism and Slavery* rendered the treaty as simply one link in a long chain that began with fifteenth-century Spain and had now reached the twentieth-century United States. Williams's informal lecture ended with a call to action; in the war for Chaguaramas, he exhorted, West Indians held an opportunity to repudiate their colonial past, to close a chapter of history in which they traditionally featured as "passive agents."[5]

Redemptive action soon came. On April 22, 1960, a day the PNM had proclaimed West Indian Independence Day, approximately 20,000 people took to the streets of Port of Spain. Braving drenching rain, they marched through the city and finally arrived at the U.S. consulate. There, facing this concrete expression of American authority, party leaders demanded the return of Chaguaramas. Earlier that morning, demonstrators had assembled at Woodford Square, the downtown plaza that had been transformed into a virtual university by Williams's legendary displays of oratory and learning.[6] In the presence of a host of local and regional radicals and with a keen sense of theater, PNM representatives burned placards symbolizing "the seven deadly sins of colonialism." Mixed in this ashy heap of historical remains, not surprisingly, was the "1941 Anglo-American bases agreement." Williams had perorated, too, that morning, proclaiming to the marchers gathered in the overflowing square that, through their act of resistance, they had been reborn into a "new nation." His speech ended on a note of narrative closure: "As we surge forward confidently to meet the future," declared this eminent historian, "we bury the past."[7]

This war did mark the beginning of a burial, but it was hardly the colonizing power of the United States that was laid to rest. Although the PNM's campaign was successful insofar as it quickly compelled American officials to negotiate with Williams and to pledge to eventually give up Chaguaramas (by 1977 at the latest), more than anything else the denouement of the affair confirmed the persistence of U.S. hegemony. As both sides began bargaining in late 1960 and as Williams secured from Washington promises of funding for local development and educational programs, he abandoned what had been a vague position of ideological "neutralism." At a time when Fidel Castro's Cuba inspired great fear and fury in U.S. political circles, Trinidad's government, the premier now assured Washington, lined up smartly "West of the Iron Curtain." Just as telling, Williams and the PNM quickly purged C. L. R. James, turning the party's unabashedly Marxist political adviser into a persona non grata. When all was said and done, the battle for independence seemed to be little more than a gambit for aid from the United States.[8] A momentary boil of nationalist militancy quickly cooled into Cold War realpolitiks that reaffirmed the supremacy of America in its backyard.

Ironically, what was almost buried in the course of the struggle was a memory of the occupation that acknowledged how wittingly Trinidadians in the 1940s, not unlike Premier Williams, had negotiated Yankee power. In the midst of the PNM-led mobilization for Chaguaramas, wartime Trinidad was reimagined in a manner that threatened to erase any sense of a knowing, nuanced local engagement with U.S. occupiers. Williams's *History of the People of Trinidad and Tobago* (1962) is paradigmatic. Despite promising that the narrative of the base agreement and the occupation would "be told one day," this founding text of Trinidadian historiography prophesied that the story would brim with "bitterness" and reveal "almost total resistance to American demands." Such an argument (it should now be clear) was difficult to sustain, even for a scholar of Williams's caliber. Instructively, then, when he gestured toward substantiating this thesis of total resistance, Williams wound up turning to—of all historical actors—the colonial governor, Sir Hubert Young. Young, according to *History of the People*, was the "centre of opposition" to Americans. The paradox, of course, of presenting an officer of the British Empire as the embodiment of Trinidadian nationalist intransigence was not lost on Williams, and he quickly rationalized: Young, the text glossed, was "one of those strange characters that one encounters in the colonial history of the West Indies." The governor certainly might have been eccentric (even "slightly touched," as one peer believed), but the contradiction Williams faced derived less from Young's personal idiosyncrasy than from his own "retroactive nationalist logic."[9] The premier's tidy presentist demands ran up against a messy past.

From just over Williams's shoulder, though, emerged guides toward an alternative remembering of occupied Trinidad, one supple and subtle enough to accommodate the period's struggles and ambiguities. The name of C. L. R. James, not surprisingly, returns to the story here. In the appendix to the 1963 edition of *The Black Jacobins*, a sweeping update of West Indian history since the birth of Haiti titled "From Toussaint L'Ouverture to Fidel Castro," James included approximately two pages about the Chaguaramas struggle. Brevity notwithstanding, the topic was handled with characteristic complexity. (The entire essay actually boasted such efficiency; covering 165 years in only thirty pages it was, as David Scott aptly remarked, a "model of narrative economy.")[10] James figured the affair as a historic moment demonstrating a deep West Indian nationalism yet devoid of anti-American feeling. The rousing mobilization for Chaguaramas, he argued, was fueled not by "bitterness" but by a refreshingly affirmative energy. As James wrote, the "national upheaval" was "all the more remarkable" precisely because "people freely admitted that Trinidad had never enjoyed such financial opulence as when the Americans were there during the war."[11] Indeed, within the essay's broader argument, the fight for Chaguaramas stood as yet another instance of the exceptional savvy and sophistication of the region's people. Used to the modern world—better yet, modern from inception—West Indians, James proposed, knew better than to rashly repudiate America.

Within the appendix, moreover, was a bridge to another intellectual who, while not explicitly concerned with the occupation, provided a poignantly relevant frame for considering the broader question of America's place in the twentieth-century British West Indies. As James's discussion shifted from the nationalism manifest in Chaguaramas to the nationalism expressed in West Indian art, he invoked Barbadian writer George Lamming, "the most powerful and far ranging of the West Indian school," according to him. In citing Lamming, James had in mind the 1960 novel *A Season of Adventure*. But in that very year the young yet already highly acclaimed Lamming had published another work, *The Pleasures of Exile*, a book that contributed critically to contemplations of the significance of the United States in the Caribbean (and more broadly the world). A rangy, indeed almost unruly meditation on the relationships among literature, consciousness, and power, the collection of essays coheres as a tract on the cultural politics of British Caribbean decolonization. Yet, although England and its West Indian possessions stood as Lamming's express geographic referents, America was by no means peripheral. Not long after introducing the main theme as "the migration of the writer from the Caribbean to the dubious refuge of a metropolitan culture [that] is

London," the author accepted that "America is very much with us now." In essaying to recuperate Caliban—the achievement for which *Pleasures* is best known—Lamming, it turns out, had to wrestle with Yankees.

The book's concern with the United States should come as no surprise once its tributary relationship to the thinking of C. L. R. James is acknowledged. Few British West Indian intellectuals, after all, were as devoted to the study of "American Civilization" as this older Trinidadian, whom Lamming had met and befriended in London in the mid-1950s.[12] Befitting its benefactor, *Pleasures* presented an astute and sophisticated interpretation of the relationship between the British West Indies and the United States. The subject appeared early, indeed, in the first substantive chapter ("An Occasion for Speaking"). Recalling the publication of his debut novel, *In the Castle of My Skin* (1953), Lamming confessed that although alive to the money the novel might have earned in the United States, he, as a West Indian, cared nothing about the book's critical reception in the republic. "American judgment," he flatly stated, "could not IMPRESS ME." For Lamming, the United States counted as a material resource but meant little by way of cultural legitimacy. The reasoning underlying his attitude was simple yet important: in Lamming's mind the United States had not (yet) colonized the West Indies. The region's people, as a result, did not subscribe to a "myth" about American supremacy the way they did about England. On this account, indeed, Lamming concluded that "in a sense, America does not even exist."

This argument that British West Indians did not apprehend and experience the United States as a straightforward colonizer, as a plain old Prospero, was elaborated in a later chapter, "Ishmael at Home." (This essay, like the preceding one on *Black Jacobins*, drew direct inspiration from C. L. R. James; the title, in fact, reflects Lamming's likening of James to the intellectual protagonist in Herman Melville's *Moby Dick*, the nineteenth-century American classic James had famously analyzed.)[13] Directly addressing America or—as he put it in a riff on James—"evaluating the purposes of the Whale," Lamming produced a subtle and qualified set of assessments. He was at once hopeful, cautious, critical, and expectant, viewing the United States as a place of contingent desire and promise. It was, for him, the site of a yet unmade world that, if Americans were brave enough to allow it, West Indians could help make.

"The West Indies," declared *Pleasures*, "are lucky to be where they are: next door to America." Quickly, however, came a cascade of caveats, for the author had no illusions about the United States, especially about what he called the "calculated brutality" of its racism: "not the America of the Mason Dixie line or the colonizing policies in the guise of freedom and self-defense," and importantly, "not the America that is afraid of its own strength."[14] Indeed, the essay was emphatic that the United States ought to be inhabitable for West Indians; the government in Washington, urged Lamming, ought to feel sufficiently secure to open the doors of the republic to these islanders. In making this case for a United States favorable to Caribbean immigration, Lamming invoked the New World commonalities between the republic and the Antilles. The "human content" of the West Indies, he wrote, "bears a striking parallel with that expectation upon which America was launched in the result, if not method, of its early settlement."[15] The essay recalled, too, the tradition of West Indians finding and making their way in America, citing renowned thinkers and leaders like George Padmore, Eric Williams, and of course, C. L. R. James (the latter's essay on Melville he called "the most agonizing plea I have ever read from a man asking the simple human favor to go on living in a particular place"). But as the son of Barbadian peasants, the author was well aware that exemplary intellectuals were hardly alone in desiring to leave the islands for the United States. "A vast number of West Indians who flock to Britain," Lamming pointed out, "might have sailed next door if America were confident enough to risk that entry." These aspiring emigrants, according to him, were driven by basic wants, which he summed up by stealing a line from the *Tempest*: "It was Caliban's request: 'I must eat my dinner.'"[16] Indeed, *Pleasures*, a text that appeared not long after the McCarran-Walter Act effectively ended legitimate emigration from the region to the republic, was in this sense the author's plea on behalf of "hungry West Indians" who hoped to resettle in the United States. Fully aware of what they had done with America over the past half-century, Lamming was asking for more of the same.

Yet in the end, this essay meant to prescribe something more than a vision of America as a site of rescue for deprived West Indians. Lamming imagined a relationship more complex, more reciprocal, and ultimately enriching for the United States. Rather than just give, America, he promised, stood to benefit from the presence of West Indians. These migrants, he was convinced, would help renovate the republic, help America realize its often trumpeted ideals. They, after all, shared faith in the democratic vision vaunted by the likes of Walt Whitman, Herman Melville, and Mark Twain. West Indians, the essay insisted, were prepared to midwife the America that started "in the womb of promise, the America that started as an alternative to the old and privileged

Prospero." Of this America, the author pronounced, they "have a big stake in building"; in this kind of "cathedral," they were ready to "worship." Indeed, Lamming wagered that West Indians would "introduce some new psalms."[17]

Pleasures thus composed a critical imagining and engagement of America. Far from romantic, it never lost sight of the colonizing adventures and racist terrors of the United States. Yet neither did the text cast the republic simply as an evil empire to be resisted at all costs. Indeed, as evidenced in the author's turn to Whitman, the work held out hope in the ideal of American democracy. Still, this was not the same old exceptionalist story that attributed to the United States some especial monopoly on liberty. In Lamming's account, true democracy was not a gift made in America and destined to be exported to the rest of the world; it was, rather, the result of genuinely reciprocal relations between the United States and people beyond its borders. For Lamming, it was precisely through the struggles of these outsiders—West Indians in this case—to make something of America that democracy in the United States would flourish and achieve its ideals.

Thus was Lamming's vision in 1960. History, however, has no final acts, and by 1984, when he sat down to pen the introduction to the second edition of *Pleasures*, the author's way of seeing America had changed. Having witnessed the Bay of Pigs, Congo, the Dominican Republic, Vietnam, Grenada, and so much more, despair must have devoured Lamming's hope. In his now altered view, the United States had become for Caribbean people "a new and more fearsome thrust of imperial encirclement."[18]

Yet two decades later, in the face of calamities in Iraq and Afghanistan and shenanigans in nearby Venezuela, Lamming's vision of 1960 might be worth recuperating. As we migrants from *nuestra America* flock northward for "dinner" and find ourselves even more inextricably mixed up in America's business, it is clear that the achievement of genuine democracy here must become our business. The making of a brave new world in which Calibans, Yankees, and all manner of shipwrecked souls can prosper will depend on it.

Notes

ABBREVIATIONS

CO   Colonial Office Records, Public Records Office, Kew Gardens, London
CP   Colonial Paper, Government Publications, University of the West Indies,
      St. Augustine, Trinidad
DM   *Daily Mirror*
EN   *Evening News*
FO   Foreign Office Records, Public Records Office, Kew Gardens, London
LL   *Labor Leader*
NA   National Archives, College Park, Maryland
POSG *Port of Spain Gazette*
RG   Record Group
SG   *Sunday Guardian*
STSC *Sunday Times and Sporting Chronicle*
TG   *Trinidad Guardian*
TNT   *Trinidad News Tips*
UWI   University of the West Indies

INTRODUCTION

1 Although the strictest definition of "occupation" entails "taking possession"
   or "seizure, as by military conquest" (*Oxford English Dictionary*, 1989) locals'
   use of the term has the merit of emphasizing that U.S. citizens constituted an
   armed presence whose landing they had no part in sanctioning and reasonably
   no power to resist. Besides, had Great Britain surrendered to Nazi attacks, Trinidad certainly would have become a U.S. possession. One of the earliest scholarly
   uses of the phrase "American Occupation" appears in Lloyd Braithwaite, "Social
   Stratification in Trinidad," *Social and Economic Studies* 2 (1953): 78.

2 I have in mind the two texts that have done most to give the phrase "brave
   new world" its currency: *The Tempest* and *Brave New World*. See David Lindley,
   ed., *William Shakespeare's "The Tempest"* (Cambridge: Cambridge University
   Press, 2002), and Aldous Huxley, *Brave New World* (New York: Perennial Classics, 1998).

3 A note on usage: in this work I use "America" and "Americans"/"Yankees" interchangeably with "United States" and "U.S. citizens," respectively. While alert
to the imperialist history underlying this use of "America," I adopt the label
not only because it is what the historical actors used but more so because it
accords with the study's interest in how people beyond the United States—
British West Indians in this case—imagine the republic. For more on this idea
of "America" as an imaginary belonging to individuals who live outside but
encounter the United States through various channels, see Michael Geyer and
Charles Bright, "Where in the World Is America? The History of the United
States in a Global Age," in *Rethinking American History in a Global Age*, ed.
Thomas Bender (Berkeley: University of California Press, 2002), 63–97. For a
comparable conceptualization in the British Caribbean context, see Deborah
Thomas, "Modern Blackness: What We Are and What We Hope to Be," *Small
Axe* 12 (September 2002): 25–48.

4 "Base colony" was a label often used by British officials. The other British West
Indian base colonies were British Guiana, St. Lucia, Jamaica, Antigua, and the
Bahamas.

5 For a diplomatic history of the deal-making behind base construction in the
British West Indies, see William Roger Louis, *Imperialism at Bay: The United
States and the Decolonization of the British Empire, 1941–1945* (New York: Oxford
University Press, 1978); Fitzroy Baptiste, *War, Cooperation, and Conflict: The
European Possessions in the Caribbean, 1939–1945* (New York: Greenwood Press,
1988); and Cary Fraser, *Ambivalent Anti-Colonialism: The United States and the
Genesis of West Indian Independence, 1940–1964* (Westport, Conn.: Greenwood
Press, 1994).

6 See, for example, Lloyd Braithwaite, "Dollar Diplomacy," *New Dawn*, January
1941, 5.

7 For more on the U.S. strategic policy in the Caribbean during the first half of
the twentieth century, see Donald Yerxa, *Admirals and Empire: The United States
Navy and the Caribbean, 1898–1945* (Columbia: University of South Carolina
Press, 1991).

8 David Scott to Secretary of State, January 25, 1941, FO 371/26155. Indeed, with
respect to the other West Indian base colonies, save the Bahamas, wartime base
installation seemed to have had little impact.

9 The constitutional and political issues surrounding the transfer from Spanish
to English sovereignty are treated in James Millette, *Society and Politics in Colonial Trinidad* (Totowa, N.J.: Biblio Distribution Center, 1985). For a history of
Trinidad's constitution, see Hewan Craig, *The Legislative Council of Trinidad and
Tobago* (London: Faber & Faber, 1952), and Charles Reis, *A History of the Constitution or Government of Trinidad: From Earliest Times to Present Day, with Notes*
(Port of Spain: Author's personal press, 1929).

10 This précis draws on general histories and monographs that deal with pre-
twentieth-century colonial Trinidad. For general works, see Eric Williams, *His-*

tory of the People of Trinidad and Tobago (Port of Spain: PNM Publishing Co., 1962), and Bridget Brereton, *A History of Modern Trinidad, 1783–1962* (Exeter, N.H.: Heinemann, 1981). For a gendered perspective, see Rhoda Reddock, *Women, Labour, and Politics in Trinidad and Tobago: A History* (London: Zed Books, 1994). For the Spanish colonial period, see Linda A. Newson, *Aboriginal and Spanish Colonial Trinidad: A Study in Culture Contact* (New York: Academic Press, 1976). For the nineteenth century, the standard works are Donald Wood, *Trinidad in Transition* (London: Oxford University Press, 1968), and Bridget Brereton, *Race Relations in Colonial Trinidad, 1870–1900* (Cambridge: Cambridge University Press, 1979). More recent titles on those years include David Trotman, *Crime in Trinidad: Conflict and Control in a Plantation Society, 1838–1900* (Knoxville: University of Tennessee Press, 1986); Faith Smith, *Creole Recitations: John Jacob Thomas and Colonial Formation in the Late Nineteenth-Century Caribbean* (Charlottesville: University of Virginia Press, 2002); and Selwyn R. Cudjoe, *Beyond Boundaries: The Intellectual Tradition of Trinidad and Tobago in the Nineteenth Century* (Amherst: University of Massachusetts Press, 2003). Nineteenth-century immigration is addressed in Walton Look Lai, *Indentured Labor, Caribbean Sugar: Chinese and Indian Migrants to the British West Indies, 1838–1918* (Baltimore: Johns Hopkins University Press, 1993), and Kale Madhavi, *Fragments of Empire: Capital, Slavery, and Indian Indentured Labor Migration in the British Caribbean* (Philadelphia: University of Pennsylvania Press, 1998). For a history of "Levantine" migration to Trinidad, see David Nicholls, "Levantines in the Caribbean," *Ethnic and Racial Studies* 4, no. 4 (1981): 34–51. The early twentieth century has been conventionally treated as a "quiet period" and thus remains understudied in Trinidad and, indeed, the rest of the British West Indies. Efforts to fill the lacuna include Brinsley Samaroo, "Political and Constitutional Development in Trinidad" (Ph.D. diss., London University, 1969); Alvin Magid, *Urban Nationalism: A Study of Political Development in Trinidad* (Gainesville: University of Florida Press, 1988); Brian L. Moore and Swithin R. Wilmot, eds., *Before and after 1865: Education, Politics, and Regionalism in the Caribbean* (Kingston: Ian Randle, 1998); and Bridget Brereton and Kevin A. Yelvington, *The Colonial Caribbean in Transition: Essays on Postemancipation Social and Cultural History* (Gainesville: University Press of Florida, 1999).

11 "US Does Not Want to Rule Trinidad: Ethnic Potpourri," *TG*, August 25, 1942. See Governor Bede Clifford to Secretary of State, February 4, 1943, CO 295/627.

12 I use the term "Creole patriots" interchangeably with "nationalists." For similar usage, see David Brading, *First America: The Spanish Monarchy, Creole Patriots, and the Liberal States, 1492–1867* (New York: Cambridge University Press, 1991).

13 Though students of the British Caribbean have explored the cultural power of "Englishness," I have chosen "Britishness," a term that more aptly captures the imperial dimension of identity politics in these colonies. Englishness certainly

sits at the core of Britishness, but while West Indians could always reasonably aspire to be British, they could never be English. For a similar line of thinking, see Robert J. C. Young, *Colonial Desire: Hybridity in Theory, Culture, and Race* (New York: Routledge, 1995), 3. For analyses of the hegemony of Englishness in the region, see Belinda Edmondson, *Making Men: Gender, Literary Authority, and Women's Writing in Caribbean Narrative* (Durham: Duke University Press, 1999); Simon Gikandi, *Maps of Englishness: Writing Identity in the Culture of Colonialism* (New York: Columbia University Press, 1996); and Catherine Hall, *Civilising Subjects: Metropole and Colony in the English Imagination, 1830–1867* (Chicago: University of Chicago Press, 2002).

14   For elaboration on the point that Trinidad's late-nineteenth-century activists bred but did not embody nationalism, see Wood, *Trinidad in Transition*, 301, and Gordon Lewis, *Main Currents in Caribbean Thought: The Historical Evolution of Caribbean Society in Its Ideological Aspects, 1492–1900* (Baltimore: Johns Hopkins University Press, 1983), 307–14. Late-nineteenth-century critics like John Jacob Thomas were not Creole patriots but what I call "Crown patriots"; loyalty to a British community was paramount in their political imagination. See Smith, *Creole Recitations*, 22, and Juanita de Barros, " 'Race' and Culture in the Writings of J. J. Thomas," *Journal of Caribbean History* 27 (November 1993): 23–51.

15   For works that instructively frame nationalism as no less cultural than political, see Michel-Rolph Trouillot, *Haiti, State against Nation: The Origins and Legacy of Duvalierism* (New York: Monthly Review Press, 1990), and Partha Chatterjee, *The Nation and Its Fragments: Colonial and Postcolonial Histories* (Princeton, N.J.: Princeton University Press, 1993). Both imply that in the colonial world nationalism must be conceived of as the pursuit of self-government in the name of a cultural identity other than the colonizers'. For more on the definitional problems of nationalism in colonial polities, see Douglas Cole, "The Problem of 'Nationalism' and 'Imperialism' in British Settlement Colonies," *Journal of British Studies* 10 (May 1971): 160–82, and John Eddy and Deryck Schreuder, *The Rise of Colonial Nationalism: Australia, New Zealand, Canada, and South Africa First Assert Their Nationalities* (Boston: Allen & Unwin, 1988). See also Anne S. Macpherson, "Imagining the Colonial Nation: Race, Gender, and Middle-Class Politics in Belize, 1888–1898," in *Race and Nation in Modern Latin America*, ed. Nancy P. Appelbaum, Anne S. Macpherson, and Karin Alejandra Rosemblatt (Chapel Hill: University of North Carolina Press, 2003), 106–35.

16   See Si-lan Chen, *Footnotes to History* (New York: Dance Horizons, 1981).

17   Albert Gomes, *Through a Maze of Color* (Port of Spain: Key Caribbean Publications, 1975). Although members of Trinidad's Portuguese population were phenotypically "white," in many cases their inferior class position and everyday contact with nonwhites as retail merchandisers disqualified them from the prestige and privileges associated with whiteness. See Bridget Brereton, "White Elites in Trinidad, 1838–1950," in *The White Minority in the Caribbean*, ed. Howard Johnson and Karl Watson (Princeton, N.J.: Wiener, 1998), 87–138.

18 George Lamming, *The Pleasures of Exile* (London, 1960; reprint, Ann Arbor: University of Michigan Press, 1992). The quote comes from a recent contribution to the debate by Jonathan Goldberg, *Tempest in the Caribbean* (Minneapolis: University of Minnesota Press, 2004), 5. See also Diane Accaria-Zavala and Rodolfo Popelnik, eds., *Prospero's Isles: The Presence of the Caribbean in the American Imaginary* (New York: Oxford University Press, 2004). Earlier works in this vein include Roberto Fernandez Retamar, *Caliban and Other Essays* (Minneapolis: University of Minnesota Press, 1989); Houston Baker, "Caliban's Triple Play," *Critical Inquiry* 13 (Spring 1986): 182–96; Rob Nixon, "Caribbean and African Appropriations of *The Tempest*" *Critical Inquiry* 13 (Spring 1987): 557–78; Peter Hulme and William H. Sherman, eds., *The Tempest and Its Travels* (Philadelphia: University of Pennsylvania Press, 2000); Virginia Mason Vaughan and Alden T. Vaughan, eds., *Critical Essays on Shakespeare's "The Tempest"* (New York: G. K. Hall, 1998); and Sylvia Wynter, "Beyond Miranda's Meanings: Unsilencing the 'Demonic Ground' of Caliban's 'Woman,'" in *Out of the Kumbla: Caribbean Women Writers and Literature*, ed. Carol Boyce Davies and Elaine Savory Fido (Trenton, N.J.: Africa World Press, 1990, 213–43.

19 Both Fitzroy Baptiste and Cary Fraser have taken this view, but for the most part from the perspective of state actors. See Baptiste, *War, Cooperation, and Conflict*, and Fraser, *Ambivalent Anti-Colonialism*. For a study oriented toward intellectual history, see Michelle Stephens, *Black Empire: The Masculine Global Imaginary of Caribbean Intellectuals in the United States, 1914–1962* (Durham: Duke University Press, 2005).

20 In the Caribbean, this approach has been most consistent for Cuba. See, for example, Ada Ferrer, *Insurgent Cuba: Race, Nation, and Revolution, 1868–1898* (Chapel Hill: University of North Carolina Press, 1999), and Louis A. Pérez Jr., *On Becoming Cuban: Identity, Nationality, and Culture* (Chapel Hill: University of North Carolina Press, 1999). Paul A. Kramer makes this point in addressing Americanists; see his "Empires, Exceptions, and Anglo-Saxons: Race and Rule between the British and United States Empires, 1880–1910," *Journal of American History* 88 (March 2002): 1315–53.

21 Most prominent in this characterization of the United States were Rubén Darío and Jose Enrique Rodó. For discussion of Darío's "El Triunfo de Calibán," which first appeared in 1898, see Carlos Jáuregui, "Calibán: Icono del 98. A propósito de un artículo de Rubén Darío y 'El triunfo de Calibán,'" *Balance de un siglo (1898–1998)*, número especial, coordinación de Aníbal González, *Revista Iberoamericana* 184–85 (1998): 441–55. For Rodó, see Jose Enrique Rodó, *Ariel* (Austin: University of Texas Press, 1988).

22 Recent works that reflect a focus on diasporic connections between the British West Indies and the United States include Jason Parker, "Capital of the Caribbean: The African American–West Indian Harlem Nexus and the Transnational Drive for Black Freedom, 1940–1948," *Journal of African American History* 2 (Spring 2004): 98–117; Winston James, *Holding Aloft the Banner of Ethiopia:*

Caribbean Radicalism in Early Twentieth-Century America (New York: Verso, 1998); and Irma Watkins-Owens, *Blood Relations: Caribbean Immigrants and the Harlem Community, 1900–1930* (Bloomington: Indiana University Press, 1996). For relations between Cuban and U.S. blacks, see Lisa Brock and Digna Castañeda Fuertes, *Between Race and Empire: African-Americans and Cubans before the Cuban Revolution* (Philadelphia: Temple University Press, 1998).

23 Michel-Rolph Trouillot, *Silencing the Past: Power and the Production of History* (Boston: Beacon Press, 1995), 1.

24 The editor of the *Port of Spain Gazette*, for example, worried that local police officers had been instructed not to arrest unruly and criminal Americans; still he assured the commissioner of police that he would not make his concern public. See "Supplement to Section I on relations between American Armed Forces Personnel and the local population," June 1943, CO 971/23/5.

25 I turn especially to Samuel Selvon's *A Brighter Sun* (Harlow, Essex: Longman, 1952) and Ralph De Boissiere's *Rum and Coca-Cola* (Melbourne, 1956; reprint, London: Allison & Busby, 1984). Other fictional works in which the occupation is a key context include Earl Lovelace, *The Wine of Astonishment* (New York: Vintage, 1982); V. S. Naipaul, *Miguel Street* (London: Penguin, 1959); and Robert Antoni, *My Grandmother's Erotic Folktales* (New York: Grove Press, 2000). This list can include the case of a fictional detour in John O. Stewart's experimental anthropological narrative, *Drinkers, Drummers, and Decent Folk: Ethnographic Narratives of Village Trinidad* (Albany: State University of New York Press, 1989), chap. 3.

26 The very opening of *A Brighter Sun*, with its newspaper-like account of the day's events, betrays Selvon's realist orientation. For the documentary impulse behind Ralph De Boissiere's fiction, see Reinhard Sander, *Trinidad Awakening: West Indian Literature of the Nineteen Thirties* (New York: Greenwood Press, 1988). Indeed, Ken Ramchand advances both authors as writers of fiction who ought to inspire a revision of mid-twentieth-century West Indian history. Needless to say, I agree with Ramchand. See his "West Indian Literary History: Literariness, Orality, and Periodization," *Callaloo* 11 (Summer 1988): 95–110.

27 "Americans Are Coming," *TG*, November 17, 1940.

28 "Sites for US Bases in Trinidad," *TG*, January 23, 1941.

29 Trevor Christie, "Yankees in Trinidad," *Life*, April 1941, 16–23.

30 Ibid. Carpenters earned upward of $72 for a forty-eight-hour workweek. Foremen and supervisors were paid up to $150. Moreover, they earned "time and a half" for overtime labors.

31 In this book, racial classification consists of white or European, black or Afro-Trinidadian, Indian or Indo-Trinidadian, and Chinese. "Colored" refers to "mixed" people who are seen as carrying both white and nonwhite heritage. "People of color," on the other hand, is interchangeable with "nonwhite." According to the 1946 census, Trinidad had 15,283 whites, of which 9,711 were local-born. The colony had 261,485 blacks, 195,747 Indians, 78,775 coloreds,

5,641 Chinese, and 889 Syrians, Asiatics, and "others." See *Trinidad and Tobago Census* (Port of Spain, 1946), Government Publications, University of the West Indies, St. Augustine.

32 For the significance of the "subaltern" concept, see Ranajit Guha, preface to "Methodology," in *Selected Subaltern Studies*, ed. Ranajit Guha and Gayatri C. Spivak (New York: Oxford University Press, 1988), 35.

33 Albert Gomes, "That Trinidad Will Never Return," *SG*, November 28, 1943.

34 For a comparable case of a British Caribbean nationalist intelligentsia center-ing the "folk" in constructions of nationhood, see Deborah A. Thomas, *Modern Blackness: Nationalism, Globalization, and the Politics of Culture in Jamaica* (Dur-ham: Duke University Press, 2004).

35 The Western orientation of colonial nationalists has been a staple assump-tion of the relevant literature. Exemplary in this regard is Partha Chatterjee, *Nationalist Thought and the Colonial World: A Derivative Discourse?* (London: Zed Books, 1986).

36 Gomes, "That Trinidad."

37 The argument here resonates with that, for example, of Louisa Schein, an anthropologist whose work on the Chinese village of Xijiang examines per-formances of modernity by those "who are seen in one way or the other not to exemplify it" (Schein, "Performing Modernity," *Cultural Anthropology* 14 [August 1999]: 361–95).

38 For comprehensive overviews of the literature on U.S.–Latin American rela-tions, see Mark T. Berger, *Under Northern Eyes: Latin American Studies and U.S. Hegemony in the Americas, 1898–1990* (Bloomington: Indiana University Press, 1995). Also see the introduction to Gilbert M. Joseph, Catherine Le Grand, and Ricardo D. Salvatore, eds., *Close Encounters of Empire: Writing the Cultural His-tory of U.S.–Latin American Relations* (Durham: Duke University Press, 1998), and Louis A. Pérez Jr., "Intervention, Hegemony, and Dependency: The United States in the Circum-Caribbean, 1898–1980," *Pacific Historical Review* 51 (May 1982): 169–93. In a sense the "cultural turn" in the late 1980s encouraged a return to the earlier approach that rendered Latin Americans mostly objects of powerful American actors. See, for example, Amy Kaplan and David Pease, eds., *Cultures of United States Imperialism* (Durham: Duke University Press, 1993), and Mary A. Renda, *Taking Haiti: Military Occupation and the Culture of U.S. Imperialism, 1915–1940* (Chapel Hill: University of North Carolina Press, 2001).

39 In the case of Cuba, see almost everything by Louis A. Pérez Jr., esp. *Cuba between Empires, 1878–1902* (Pittsburgh: University of Pittsburgh Press, 1982) and *Cuba and the United States: Ties of Singular Intimacy* (Athens: University of Georgia Press, 1990). For Haiti, see Hans Schmidt, *The United States Occupa-tion of Haiti, 1915–1934* (New Brunswick, N.J.: Rutgers University Press, 1972), and Renda, *Taking Haiti*. For the Dominican Republic, see Eric Roorda, *The Dictator Next Door: The Good Neighbor Policy and the Trujillo Regime in the Do-minican Republic, 1930–1945* (Durham: Duke University Press, 1998), and Bruce

Calder, *The Impact of Intervention: The Dominican Republic during the U.S. Occupation of 1916–1924* (Austin: University of Texas Press, 1984).

40 A telling sign of the ambiguities involved in labeling this episode is the recent recuperation of the phrase "friendly invasion." See Steven High, "The Racial Politics of Criminal Jurisdiction in the Aftermath of the Anglo-American 'Destroyers-for-Bases' Deal, 1940–50," *Journal of Imperial and Commonwealth History* 32 (September 2004): 77–105.

41 The exception was Annette Palmer, "The United States and the Commonwealth Caribbean, 1939–45" (Ph.D. diss., Fordham University, 1979). There have been related studies beyond the case of Trinidad. See, for example, Howard Johnson, "The Anglo-American Caribbean Commission and the Extension of American Influence in the British Caribbean, 1942–45," *Journal of Commonwealth and Comparative Politics* 22 (June 1984): 180–203; Issac Dookhan, "Military Civilian Conflicts in the Virgin Islands during World War II," *Journal of Caribbean History* 24 (May 1990): 89–108; and Gail Saunders, "The 1937 Riot in Inagua, the Bahamas," *New West India Guide* 62 (Fall 1988): 129–45. The legal aspects of the bases-for-destroyers treaty are covered in North Burn, "United States Base Rights in the British West Indies, 1940–62" (Ph.D. diss., Princeton University, Fletcher School of Law and Diplomacy, 1964). In addition, since the early 1980s, several studies at the University of the West Indies, St. Augustine, have examined the social impact of the American occupation in Trinidad. Among the most informative are Joanne Forde, "The Social and Economic Impact of World War II on Trinidad and Tobago" (Caribbean Studies Project, UWI, St. Augustine, 1982); Merlyn Calliste, "The Impact of the American Base at Wallerfield" (Caribbean Studies Project, UWI, St. Augustine, 1993); and Vishoo Gopaul-Maharaj, "The Social Effects of the American Presence" (Master's thesis, UWI, St. Augustine, 1989). For British Guiana, see Roberta W. Kilkenny, "And So They Have Captured Demerara: A Preliminary Investigation of U.S. Guiana Relations during the Second World War" (paper presented at Conference of the Association of Caribbean Historians, Bahamas, 1986).

42 Professional history writing about the British West Indies remained episodic until the 1960s. For relevant historiographical review, see Barry Higman, *Writing West Indian Histories* (London: Macmillan Education, 1999), and Woodville Marshall and Bridget Brereton, "Historiography of Barbados, the Windward Islands, Trinidad and Tobago, and Guyana," in *General History of the Caribbean*, vol. 6, *Methodology and Historiography of the Caribbean*, ed. Barry Higman (London: Macmillan Education, 1999): 544–603. For an insightful earlier essay that deals exclusively with the historiography of Trinidad, see Anthony P. Maingot, "From Ethnocentric to National History Writing in the Plural Society," *Caribbean Studies* 9 (September 1969): 69–86.

43 Gordon K. Lewis, *The Growth of the Modern West Indies* (London: MacGibbon & Kee, 1968), 207.

44 Williams, *History of the People*, 243.

45 See, for example, the glowing Gordon Lewis review in *Caribbean Studies* 3 (January 1963): 100–105.

46 After Williams's *History of the People*, the idea of an interregnum between 1937 and 1955 emerges as a kind of article of belief within the literature, especially the politically oriented accounts. See Ivar Oxaal, *Black Intellectuals Come to Power: The Rise of Creole Nationalism in Trinidad and Tobago* (Cambridge, Mass.: Schenkman, 1968); Selwyn Ryan, *Race and Nationalism in Trinidad and Tobago: A Study of Decolonization in a Multiracial Society* (Toronto: University of Toronto Press, 1972); and more recently, Kirk Meighoo, *Politics in a "Half Made" Society: Trinidad and Tobago, 1925–2000* (Kingston: Ian Randle, 2003). Even studies that departed from Williams's political assumptions adopted his conventions of plotting, taking the years after 1937 as a period of decline hardly deserving of extensive examination. See Bukka Rennie, *The History of the Working Class in the Twentieth Century: The Trinidad and Tobago Experience* (Toronto: New Beginning Movement, 1973); Kelvin Singh, *Race and Class Struggles in a Colonial State: Trinidad, 1917–1945* (Calgary: University of Calgary Press, 1994); and Susan Campbell, "En'less Pressure: The Struggles of a Caribbean Working Class in Their International Context, 1919–1956" (Ph.D. diss., Queens University, 1995).

47 Braithwaite, "Social Stratification in Trinidad," 78.

48 The scholarship tends to treat occupied Trinidad as little more than a vessel of American-funded vice, and insofar as 1938 through 1955 figures as an era of perversity in the literature, these years marks the epitome.

49 This study nevertheless remains deeply indebted to reorientations within the broader literature on empire-making, particularly to the move away from Manichaean characterizations of relationships between the West and the rest. Most immediately, it incorporates the British West Indies into a growing body of writing on U.S.–Caribbean relations that troubles over the messy social and cultural terrain—as opposed to the (apparently, at least) less intractable areas of state and economy. This turn is well represented in Joseph, Le Grand, and Salvatore, *Close Encounters of Empire*. There were, of course, studies that glimpsed the future: Daniel Nugent, ed., *Rural Revolt in Mexico: U.S. Intervention and the Domain of Subaltern Politics* (Durham: Duke University Press, 1998) (originally published in 1988); William Roseberry, *Anthropologies and Histories: Essays in Culture, History, and Political Economy* (New Brunswick, N.J.: Rutgers University Press, 1989); and Charles Bergquist, *Labor and the Course of American Democracy: U.S. History in Latin American Perspective* (New York: Verso, 1996), esp. chap. 4. This book has also benefited greatly from the revitalization in the field of nationalism. At the center of this scholarship lies Benedict Anderson's *Imagined Communities: Reflections on the Origin and Spread of Nationalism* (New York: Verso, 1983). The long list of important works would include Philip Corrigan and Derek Sayer, *The Great Arch: English State Formation as Cultural Revolution* (New York: Blackwell, 1985); Chatterjee, *Nationalist Thought*; Homi K. Bhaba, ed., *Nation and Narration* (London: Routledge, 1990); Doris Sommer, *Founda-*

tional Fictions: The National Romances of Latin America (Berkeley: University of California Press, 1991); Peter Sahlins, *Boundaries: The Making of France and Spain in the Pyrenees* (Berkeley: University of California Press, 1989); Geoff Eley and Ronald Grigor Suny, eds., *Becoming National: A Reader* (New York: Oxford University Press, 1996); and Appelbaum, Macpherson, and Rosemblatt, *Race and Nation*. For Trinidad, this approach manifests in a dissertation by Daniel Segal, "Nationalism in a Colonial State: A Study of Trinidad and Tobago" (Ph.D. diss., University of Chicago, 1989).

50 Although this literature can be said to have gotten off to an auspicious start when C. L. R. James published *Beyond a Boundary* in 1963, it has not exactly flourished over the years. See, however, Errol Hill, *The Trinidad Carnival: Mandate for a National Theatre* (Austin: University of Texas Press, 1972); Gordon Rohlehr, *Calypso and Society in Pre-Independence Trinidad* (Port of Spain: G. Rohlehr, 1990); Donald Hill, *Calypso Callaloo: Early Carnival Music in Trinidad* (Gainesville: University of Florida Press, 1993); Stephen Stuempfle, *The Steelband Movement: The Forging of a National Art in Trinidad and Tobago* (Philadelphia: University of Pennsylvania Press, 1995); and John Cowley, *Carnival, Canboulay, and Calypso: Traditions in the Making* (Cambridge: Cambridge University Press, 1996).

51 Caribbeanists' uses of the concept of creolization tend to privilege Europe and Africa, straining to deal with Asia and generally neglecting the United States. See, for example, Verene A. Shepherd and Glen L. Richards, eds. *Questioning Creole: Creolisation Discourses in Caribbean Culture* (Kingston: Ian Randle, 2002).

52 See Frederick Cooper, *Colonialism in Question: Theory, Knowledge, History* (Berkeley: University of California Press, 2005), 3–32.

53 The allusion here is to Gyanendra Pandey, who in writing about Indian nationalism uses the term "fragment" to refer to "minority" groups who resist the homogenizing forces of nationalism. See "In Defense of the Fragment: Writing about Hindu-Muslim Riots Today," *Representations* 37 (Winter 1992): 27–55.

54 Such an approach has been favored within recent anthropological literature. An influential earlier work here is Brackette F. Williams, *Stains on My Name, War in My Veins: Guyana and the Politics of Struggle* (Durham: Duke University Press, 1991). See also Kevin A. Yelvington, ed., *Trinidad Ethnicity* (London: Macmillan, 1993); Viranjini Munasinghe, *Callaloo or Tossed Salad? East Indians and the Cultural Politics of Identity in Trinidad* (Ithaca: Cornell University Press, 2001); and Aisha Khan, *Callaloo Nation: Metaphors of Race and Religious Identity among South Asians in Trinidad* (Durham: Duke University Press, 2004).

55 See, for example, Arjun Appadurai, *Modernity at Large: Cultural Dimensions of Globalization* (Minneapolis: University of Minnesota Press, 1996). This sense of an "after-national" Caribbean pervades the work of David Scott; see, among his other writings, *Refashioning Futures: Criticism after Postcoloniality* (Princeton, N.J.: Princeton University Press, 1999). My point here is that in emphasizing a new break with nationalism, scholars run the risk of missing long-standing

queries and objections to nationalists' claims and ambitions. For parallel concerns about the postnational in the Caribbean, see Shalini Puri, *The Caribbean Postcolonial: Social Equality, Post-Nationalism, and Cultural Hybridity* (New York: Palgrave Macmillan, 2004).

56 The list of works that approach the region from this perspective would include, but hardly be limited to, C. L. R. James, *The Black Jacobins: Toussaint L'Ouverture and the San Domingo Revolution* (New York: Vintage, 1963); Eric Williams, *Capitalism and Slavery* (1944; reprint, Chapel Hill: University of North Carolina Press, 1994); Sidney Mintz, *Sweetness and Power: The Place of Sugar in Modern History* (New York: Viking, 1985); and more recently, Ferrer, *Insurgent Cuba*, and Mimi Sheller, *Consuming the Caribbean: From Arawaks to Zombies* (London: Routledge, 2003). An insightful discussion of the subject is found in Sidney Mintz, "Enduring Substances, Trying Theories: The Caribbean Region as Oikoumene," *Journal of the Royal Anthropological Institute* 2 (June 1996): 289–311.

57 Samuel Selvon, *An Island Is a World* (London: A. Wingate, 1955). A similar argument is implied in Beth Bailey and David Farber, *The First Strange Place: The Alchemy of Race and Sex in World War II Hawaii* (New York: Free Press, 1992).

58 See, for example, Richard Kuisel, *Seducing the French: The Dilemma of Americanization* (Berkeley: University of California Press, 1993); Rob Kroes, R. W. Rydell, D. F. J. Bosscher, and John F. Sears, eds., *Cultural Transmissions and Receptions: American Mass Culture in Europe* (Amsterdam: VU University Press, 1993); Reinhold Wagnleitner, *Coca-Colonization and Cold War: The Cultural Mission of the United States in Austria after the Second World War*, trans. Diana Wolf (Chapel Hill: University of North Carolina Press, 1994); Richard Pells, *Not Like Us: How Europeans Have Loved, Hated, and Transformed American Culture since World War II* (New York: Basic Books, 1997); Uta Poiger, *Jazz, Rock, and Rebels: Cold War Politics and American Culture in a Divided Germany* (Berkeley: University of California Press, 2000); Reinhold Wagnleitner and Elaine Tyler May, eds., *Here, There, and Everywhere: The Foreign Politics of American Popular Culture* (Hanover, N.H.: University Press of New England, 2000); Maria Höhn, *GIs and Fräuleins: The German-American Encounter in 1950s West Germany* (Chapel Hill: University of North Carolina Press, 2002); Petra Goedde, *GIs and Germans: Culture, Gender, and Foreign Relations, 1945–1949* (New Haven: Yale University Press, 2003); Victoria de Grazia, *Irresistible Empire: America's Advance through Twentieth-Century Europe* (Cambridge, Mass.: Belknap Press of Harvard University Press, 2005).

59 See roundtable "Cultural Transfer or Cultural Imperialism," in *Diplomatic History* 24 (Summer 2000): 465–516.

60 Ann Laura Stoler, "Intimidations of Empire: Predicaments of the Tactile and Unseen," in *Haunted by Empire: Geographies of Intimacy in North American History*, ed. Ann Laura Stoler (Durham: Duke University Press, 2006), 1.

61 The evidence here is quickly becoming overwhelming, thanks in part to the rise

of a diasporic perspective within academia in the late 1980s. See Kaplan and
Pease, *Cultures of United States Imperialism*; Brent Hayes Edwards, *The Practice
of Diaspora: Literature, Translation, and the Rise of Black Internationalism* (Cambridge, Mass.: Harvard University Press, 2003); Nikhil Pal Singh, *Black Is a
Country: Race and the Unfinished Struggle for Democracy* (Cambridge, Mass.: Har-
vard University Press, 2004); Penny M. Von Eschen, *Race against Empire: Black
Americans and Anticolonialism, 1937–1957* (Ithaca: Cornell University Press,
1997) and *Satchmo Blows Up the World: Jazz Ambassadors Play the Cold War*
(Cambridge, Mass.: Harvard University Press, 2004); Fanon Che Wilkins, "In
the Belly of the Beast: Black Radicalism, Africa, and the Global Search for Black
Power, 1957–1976" (Ph.D. diss., New York University, 2001); Mary L. Dudziak,
Cold War Civil Rights: Race and the Image of American Democracy (Princeton,
N.J.: Princeton University Press, 2000); and Brenda Gayle Plummer, ed., *Win-
dow on Freedom: Race, Civil Rights, and Foreign Affairs, 1945–1988* (Chapel Hill:
University of North Carolina Press, 2003).

62 The notion of an "excentric" approach has origins in postwar revisionist studies
of British imperialism in Africa and was meant to explain Great Britain's
imperial activity by examining events and crises in Africa itself. The focus,
therefore, was on the periphery rather than the center of empire. Though initially formulated as a moderating challenge to economically driven critiques of
European imperialism, this approach (the subject of endless scholarly debates)
or at least the phrase has reappeared in radical critiques of imperialism as a
synonym for stressing imperial processes at the "outpost." For an original formulation, see Ronald Robinson and John Gallagher, with Alice Denny, *Africa
and the Victorians: The Official Mind of Imperialism* (London: Macmillan, 1961).

63 The quote comes from Barnes's preface to the following studies: Leland Hamil-
ton Jenks, *Our Cuban Colony: A Study in Sugar* (New York: Vanguard, 1928), iv;
Bailey W. Diffie and Justine Whitfield Diffie, *Porto Rico: A Broken Pledge* (New
York: Vanguard, 1931); and Melvin Knight, *The Americans in Santo Domingo*
(New York: Vanguard, 1928).

CHAPTER I

1 L. E. Braithwaite, "We the Toilers," *New Dawn*, November 1940, 24.
2 For a discussion of the concept of political culture, see Lynn Hunt, *Politics, Culture, and Class in the French Revolution* (Berkeley: University of California Press,
1984), introduction, and Margaret Somers, "What's Political or Cultural about
Political Culture and the Public Sphere? Toward an Historical Sociology of the
Concept Formation," *Sociological Theory* 13 (July 1995): 113–44.
3 For France, see Hunt, *Politics*; for Cuba, see Ada Ferrer, *Insurgent Cuba: Race,
Nation, and Revolution, 1868–1898* (Chapel Hill: University of North Carolina
Press, 1999); for Haiti, see Laurent Dubois, *Avengers of the New World: The Story
of the Haitian Revolution* (Cambridge, Mass.: Belknap Press of Harvard Univer-
sity Press, 2004).

4 The phrase is taken from Chatterjee and reflects his indebtedness to Gramsci. See Partha Chatterjee, *Nationalist Thought and the Colonial World: A Derivative Discourse?* (London: Zed Books, 1986), esp. 43–52.

5 "Eve of a Divorce Bombshell," *TG*, December 13, 1931.

6 The exceptions here are C. L. R. James, *The Life of Captain Cipriani; or an Account of British Government in the West Indies* (London: Coulton, 1932); Hewan Craig, *The Legislative Council of Trinidad and Tobago* (London: Faber & Faber, 1952); Rhoda Reddock, *Women, Labour, and Politics in Trinidad and Tobago: A History* (London: Zed Books, 1994); and Leah Rosenberg, "Creolizing Womanhood: Gender and Domesticity in Early Anglophone Caribbean National Literatures" (Ph.D. diss., Cornell University, 2000).

7 Beatrice Greig, letter to editor, *DM*, July 24, 1932.

8 Hollis to Lord Passfield, November 21, 1930, CO 295 565/56479.

9 C. W. Greenidge, address to Legislative Council, December 11, 1931, *Hansard*, Government Publications, University of the West Indies, St. Augustine.

10 James, *Life of Captain Cipriani*, 98.

11 "Beloved Rebel" was the title of a biographical sketch of Cipriani. See *Caribbee*, February 1934, 8–10.

12 For more on Cipriani's political career, see Brinsley Samaroo, "Political and Constitutional Development in Trinidad" (Ph.D. diss., London University, 1969), and Kelvin Singh, *Race and Class Struggles in a Colonial State: Trinidad, 1917–1945* (Calgary: University of Calgary Press, 1994).

13 Hear, for example, Albert Gomes explaining pro-divorce activism: "Even though we detested the alien colonialist government as much as the medieval-minded church, we decided that in a proper order of priorities for progress in Trinidad the attenuation of the scope and authority of the church would have to take precedence" (*Through a Maze of Color* [Port of Spain: Key Caribbean Publications, 1975], 24).

14 The most thorough study of the *Beacon* group is Reinhard Sander's *Trinidad Awakening: West Indian Literature of the Nineteen Thirties* (New York: Greenwood Press, 1988). Still, Sander's normative assumptions about politics impose a limit on the book's appreciation for the group's oppositional activity. See also Hazel Carby, "Proletarian or Revolutionary Literary: C. L. R. James and the Politics of the Trinidadian Renaissance," *South Atlantic Quarterly* 87 (Winter 1988): 39–52, and Leah Rosenberg, "Creolizing Womanhood: Gender and Domesticity in Early Anglophone Caribbean National Literatures" (Ph.D. diss., Cornell University, 2000).

15 Greig, letter to editor.

16 David Scott, "The Sovereignty of the Imagination: An Interview with George Lamming," *Small Axe* 12 (March 2002): 92.

17 Alfred Mendes, "Revolt," *SG*, March 15, 1931.

18 *SG*, March 22, 1931. The "mendacity" charge appeared in a letter to the *POSG*, March 17, 1931.

19 Gomes, *Through a Maze*, 27; Reinhard Sander "Interview with Alfred Mendes,"

in *Kas-Kas, Interviews with Three Caribbean Writers in Texas: George Lamming, C. L. R. James, Wilson Harris*, ed. Ian Munro and Reinhard Sander (Austin: African and Afro-American Research Institute, 1972), 34–52.

20 Quote comes from Sinha Mrinalini, *Colonial Masculinity: The "Manly English-man" and the "Effeminate Bengali" in the Late Nineteenth Century* (New York: Manchester University Press, 1995), 8. This work has begun; see Rosenberg, "Creolizing Womanhood." For a recent study addressing the patriarchal claims of Caribbean nationalisms, see Kamala Kempadoo, *Sexing the Caribbean: Gender, Race, and Sexual Labor* (New York: Routledge, 2004).

21 Maynard Percival, "Divorce and Mr. Jerningham," *Beacon*, January/February 1932, 7–8.

22 Quote comes from Ralph Mentor, "An Appreciation of Mrs. B. Greig," *LL*, October 19, 1931. Long active in Trinidad's public life, Greig, as Rhoda Reddock has noted, had solid feminist credentials. See Reddock, *Women, Labour, and Politics*, 178–86. In 1927 she had made an ultimately unsuccessful bid to end the male exclusivity of the Port of Spain city council. See "Women in Council," *TG*, October 7, 1927.

23 "Give Us Divorce," *LL*, November 28, 1931.

24 Ibid. Greig's arguments resonated with those of women across the Americas; see, for example, Asunción Lavrin, *Women, Feminism, and Social Change in Argentina, Chile, and Uruguay, 1890–1940* (Lincoln: University of Nebraska Press, 1995). For comparison of introduction of divorce in Puerto Rico, see Eileen Suarez Findlay, "Love in the Tropics: Marriage, Divorce, and the Construction of Benevolent Colonialism in Puerto Rico, 1898–1910," in *Close Encounters of Empire: Writing the Cultural History of U.S.–Latin American Relations*, ed. Gilbert M. Joseph, Catherine Le Grand, and Ricardo D. Salvatore (Durham: Duke University Press, 1998), 139–72.

25 Indeed, anxiety about white supremacy was the subtext to a story carried on the front page of the *Trinidad Guardian* as the divorce bill was debated. The piece was essentially a warning of the "catastrophe" to come, since lots of women were awaiting the legislation so that they could divorce their "highly placed" husbands, who had taken a somewhat "lax" approach to matrimonial ties. That the mistresses were nonwhite is implied by the report's claim that many of the women in question had men employed in the Venezuela oil fields. Elsewhere I explore in detail the problems posed by interracial dating in colonial Trinidad. See Harvey Neptune, "White Lies: Race and Sexuality in Occupied Trinidad," *Journal of Colonialism and Colonial History* 2 (Spring 2001), 24–42.

26 Letter to the editor, *POSG*, December 30, 1931.

27 "The King Is Mightier Than the Pope," *LL*, December 19, 1931.

28 Deputation to the Secretary of State on the Trinidad Divorce Bill, February 4, 1932, CO 295 576. Hamel-Smith argued that it was mainly white transients (especially Americans in the oil industry), rather than resident whites, who favored legal divorce: "If a commission came out there and consulted the oil-

field managers and the people of the place," he warned, "they will soon real-ize [that] these [American] oil-field people will lose prestige with the laboring classes, both black and Indian."

29 "The Star Interviews Mr. Michael Hamel Smith," *Beacon*, March 1932, 2–3. The *Beacon* was not the only local publication to denounce the antidivorce dele-gation. The *Daily Mirror*, a recently founded progressive organ, mocked the delegation as "heroes," accusing them of "slander[ing]" Trinidad's blacks and making "amazing misrepresentations." See "How Trinidad Negroes Were Slan-dered," *DM*, April 17, 1932, and "Heroes," *DM*, April 24, 1932.

30 Gomes, *Through a Maze*, 25.

31 See Robert J. C. Young, *Colonial Desire: Hybridity in Theory, Culture, and Race* (New York: Routledge, 1995), 3.

32 This is now accepted within the literature; an earlier and then heterodox articu-lation can be found in Paul Gilroy, *"There Ain't No Black in the Union Jack": The Cultural Politics of Race and Nation* (London: Hutchinson Press, 1987).

33 The first quote represents an adaptation of the phrasing of Jean Comaroff and John Comaroff. See their *Of Revelation and Revolution: Christianity, Colonialism, and Consciousness in South Africa* (Chicago: University of Chicago Press, 1991), 6. The second quote is from the title of chapter 5 in Simon Gikandi's *Maps of Englishness: Writing Identity in the Culture of Colonialism* (New York: Columbia University Press, 1996).

34 Frantz Fanon, *The Wretched of the Earth* (New York: Grove Press, 1963).

35 As one observer put it, culture was measured by the capacity to appreciate "fine literature," to "parse and analyze," and to orate with "grace and facility" ("Liter-ary Corner," *STSC*, November 29, 1936).

36 "A West Indian Literature," *Beacon*, August 1933, 2–3.

37 For contemporary takes on Gomes's aggressive, even bullying character, see Owen Mathurin's review of his autobiography, "An Insider's View," *Caribbean Studies* 14 (December 1975): 73–83, and Arthur Calder-Marshall, *Glory Dead* (London: M. Joseph, 1939), chap. 4.

38 "West Indian Literature."

39 Frantz Fanon, *Black Skin, White Masks*, trans. Charles Lam Markmann (New York: Grove Press, 1967).

40 Hugh Stollmeyer, "Literary Clubs and Art," *Beacon*, October 1933, 68.

41 Hugh Stollmeyer, "The Time Has Come," *Beacon*, November 1933, 84.

42 "Notes of the Month," *Beacon*, September 1933, 25–27.

43 Ibid.

44 For discussions of "race consciousness" as oppositional, see Judith Jackson Fos-sett and Jeffrey A. Tucker, eds., *Race Consciousness: African-American Studies for the New Century* (New York: New York University Press, 1997), and Paula Stewart Brush, "Problematizing the Race Consciousness of Women of Color," *Signs* 27 (Autumn 2001): 171–98.

45 "Lecture by University Student," *POSG*, September 6, 1932. The lecturer had

recently returned from university in New York City and was the son of Aubrey Williams, a well-reputed Port of Spain figure.

46 For the notion of diaspora as detour, see Brent Hayes Edwards, *The Practice of Diaspora: Literature, Translation, and the Rise of Black Internationalism* (Cambridge, Mass.: Harvard University Press, 2003), introduction.

47 These phrases, mostly applied to Brazilian society, are equally suited, I submit, to racialization within the British Empire. See Michael George Hanchard, *Orpheus and Power: The Movimento Negro of Rio de Janeiro and Sao Paulo, Brazil, 1945–1988* (Princeton, N.J.: Princeton University Press, 1994).

48 Sydney Harland, "Race and Admixture," *Beacon*, July 1931, 25–29.

49 Dipesh Chakrabarty, "Postcoloniality and the Artifice of History: Who Speaks for 'Indian' Pasts?," *Representations* 37 (Winter 1992): 1–26.

50 Alfred Mendes, "Is the Negro Inferior?," *Beacon*, September 1931, 27.

51 Ralph Mentor, "Truth Is Mightier Than Fiction," *Beacon*, January/February 1931, 9–12, and June 1932, 11–13.

52 I have in mind, of course, C. L. R. James, *The Black Jacobins: Toussaint L'Ouverture and the San Domingo Revolution* (New York: Vintage, 1963), and Eric Williams, *Capitalism and Slavery* (1944; reprint, Chapel Hill: University of North Carolina Press, 1994).

53 C. L. R. James, "The Intelligence of the Negro: A Few Words with Dr. Harland," *Beacon*, August 1931, 6–10.

54 David Scott elaborates on the link between James's *Beacon* essay and *Black Jacobins*. See Scott, *Conscripts of Modernity: The Tragedy of Colonial Enlightenment* (Durham: Duke University Press, 2004), 79–81.

55 Nancy Cunard, ed., *Negro Anthology, Made by Nancy Cunard, 1931–1933* (London: Wishart & Co., 1934), 301. The quote comes from the preface to a poem Cunard had written; it was inspired by correspondence sent to her by Cruickshank and indeed was dedicated to the Afro-Trinidadian. For more on Cunard's anthology, see "Coda" in Edwards, *Practice of Diaspora*, 301–25.

56 For the pageant, see "Wilberforce Pageant Staged in Prince's Building: Life and Work of Great Emancipator," *TG*, August 9, 1933, and "Wilberforce Emancipation Centenary," *POSG*, August 8, 1933.

57 Stephen Haweis, "A Message and the Black Man," *Beacon*, October 1933, 67.

58 Alfred Cruickshank, "Reply to a Message," *Beacon*, October 1933, 67.

59 Louis A. Pérez Jr., "Incurring a Debt of Gratitude: 1898 and the Moral Sources of United States Hegemony in Cuba," *American Historical Review* 104 (June 1999): 356–98.

60 Nothing, I think, is more telling of the radical changes afoot in the region's politics between the late nineteenth century and the 1930s than the fact that in the 1890s British West Indian dissidents like Robert Love took the occasion of Emancipation Day to lecture on "the debt of the Negro Race" and to ask for the erection of statues to pay tribute to British "saints" such as James Phillippo and William Knibb. See B. W. Higman, "Remembering Slavery: The Rise, Decline, and Revival of Emancipation Day in the English-Speaking Caribbean,"

Slavery and Abolition 19 (April 1998): 90–105. For Trinidad, in particular, see
Bridget Brereton "The Birthday of Our Race: A Social History of Emancipation
Day in Trinidad, 1838–88," in *Essays Presented to Douglas Hall: Trade, Govern-
ment, and Society in Caribbean History, 1700–1920*, ed. B. W. Higman (Kingston:
Heinemann Educational Books Caribbean, 1983), 69–83. For a similar sense of
gratitude during emancipation celebrations in Belize, see Anne S. Macpherson,
"Imagining the Colonial Nation: Race, Gender, and Middle-Class Politics in
Belize, 1888–1898," in *Race and Nation in Modern Latin America*, ed. Nancy P.
Appelbaum, Anne S. Macpherson, and Karin Alejandra Rosemblatt (Chapel
Hill: University of North Carolina Press, 2003), 106–35.

61 The phrase is from Frances Fox Piven and Richard A. Cloward, *Poor People's
Movements: Why They Succeed, How They Fail* (New York: Pantheon, 1977).

62 W. M. Macmillan, *Warning from the West Indies: A Tract for Africa and the Empire*
(London, 1936; reprint, New York: Books for Publishing, 1971).

63 Report of the Labor Disturbances Commission, CP 109 1934. See also "Unem-
ployed Stage Hunger March in Sugar District," *TG*, July 21, 1934; "900 Laborers
Attack Sugar Estate Offices in Caroni," *TG*, July 25, 1934; "Unemployed March
on Port of Spain," *POSG*, July 21, 1934; "Unemployed Hunger March Fever
Spreads," *POSG*, July 22, 1934; "Labor Unrest Takes an Ugly Turn," *POSG*,
July 25, 1934.

64 "Labor Leaders Plead for Peace in Sugar Areas," *TG*, July 26, 1934.

65 O. Nigel Bolland, *On the March: Labour Rebellions in the British Caribbean, 1934–
39* (London: James Currey, 1995).

66 "Mounted Police Clash with Unemployed," *TG*, August 3, 1935.

67 "Unemployed Army Invade Government House," *TG*, August 2, 1935; "Unemployed Clash with Police," *POSG*, August 3, 1935.

68 "Unemployed Army."

69 "Unemployed Clash."

70 The same argument has been made for British West Africa. See S. K. B. Asante,
Pan-African Protest: West Africa and the Italo-Ethiopian Crisis, 1934–1941 (Lon-
don: Longman, 1977). For the response to the Ethiopian invasion in vari-
ous locales across the black diaspora, see Robert G. Weisbord, *Ebony Kinship:
Africa, Africans, and the Afro-American* (Westport, Conn.: Greenwood Press,
1973); William R. Scott, *The Sons of Sheba's Race: African-Americans and the
Italo-Ethiopian War, 1935–1941* (Bloomington: Indiana University Press, 1993);
Joseph E. Harris, *African-American Reactions to War in Ethiopia, 1936–1941*
(Baton Rouge: Louisiana State University Press, 1994). For Jamaica, see Ken
Post, *Arise Ye Starvelings: The Jamaican Labour Rebellion of 1938 and Its Aftermath*
(The Hague: Martinus Nijhoff, 1978). For response in France, see Edwards,
Practice of Diaspora. On Trinidad, see Kevin Yelvington, "The War in Ethio-
pia and Trinidad, 1935–36," in *The Colonial Caribbean in Transition: Essays on
Postemancipation Social and Cultural History*, ed. Bridget Brereton and Kevin
Yelvington (Gainesville: University Press of Florida, 1999), 189–225.

71 "Notes," *Caribbee*, September 1935, 4.

72 Yelvington, "War In Ethiopia."

73 Canon Max Farquhar was a respected West African–born Anglican clergyman.

74 Interview with Lloyd Braithwaite, 1988, Oral History Research Project, University of the West Indies, St. Augustine. In London, too, two former Queens Royal College students and masters, Eric Williams and C. L. R. James, also protested the invasion. See "Motion by Two Trinidad Men," *TG*, August 7, 1935.

75 "Hindus and Muslims Pledge Support," *People*, December 21, 1935, and "Afro-Indian Unity Stressed in Princes Town," *People*, December 28, 1935.

76 "Captain Cipriani Appeals for Sending of Aid to Ethiopia," *TG*, November 27, 1935.

77 Alfred M. Cruickshank, "Emperor Hailie Selassie I," *SG*, November 10, 1935.

78 "City Excited over Ethiopia's War," *TG*, October 5, 1935.

79 "Peter Denies Christ," *People*, October 19, 1935.

80 "Friends of Ethiopia Hold Mass Meeting in Arima," *TG*, November 11, 1935.

81 "Afro–West Indian League Holds Protest Meeting," *TG*, August 1, 1935.

82 Ibid. For a description of Francois, see Calder-Marshall, *Glory Dead*, 187.

83 "Mr. Godfrey Phillip Explains," *POSG*, August 2, 1935.

84 "Talk about African War," *People*, November 29, 1935.

85 See "Appeal Made for Ethiopia Fund at Mass Meeting," *SG*, November 3, 1935.

86 Ibid.

87 See James C. Scott, *Domination and the Arts of Resistance: Hidden Transcripts* (New Haven: Yale University Press, 1990).

88 "The Dog That Took His Hint," *TG*, January 5, 1936.

89 This episode has drawn an army of scholars. One of the best portraits and analyses is found in Singh, *Race and Class Struggles*. For the significance of the unrest as a catalyst for imperial reform, see Cary Fraser, "The Twilight of Colonial Rule in the British West Indies: Nationalist Assertion vs. Imperial Hubris in the 1930s," *Journal of Caribbean History* 30 (May and November 1996): 1–27. For a dissenting take on the prominence of the unrest within the historiography, see David Scott, "Political Rationalities of the Jamaican Modern," *Small Axe* 14 (September 2003), 1–22.

90 C. L. R. James, "From Toussaint L'Ouverture to Fidel Castro," appendix to *Black Jacobins: Toussaint L'Ouverture and the San Domingo Revolution* (New York: Vintage Books, 1989), 404.

91 Frederick Cooper, *Decolonization and African Society: The Labor Question in French and British Africa* (New York: Cambridge University Press, 1996), 57.

92 Ibid., 260.

93 "The Goose and the Gander," *People*, August 7, 1937. For samples of patriot criticisms, see "The Commission's Recommendations," *People*, February 24, 1940, and "Save Us from Nominated Officials," *People*, March 10, 1940. Rienzi's challenges to imperial agents appear in his interview with the Moyne Commission, CO 959 932. For an insightful discussion of Rienzi's somewhat strange political career, see Kelvin Singh, "Adrian Cola Rienzi and the Labour Movement in Trinidad (1925–1944)," *Journal of Caribbean History* 16 (November 1982): 11–35.

94 Richard E. Braithwaite, "The Petty Bourgeoisie," *People*, February 17, 1940.

95 The claim here resonates with that of other scholars who explore the contradictions and ambiguities of nationalism across the Americas. See Vera Kutzinski, *Sugar Secrets: Race and the Erotics of Cuban Nationalism* (Charlottesville: University Press of Virginia, 1993); Julie Skurski, "The Ambiguities of Authenticity in Latin America: *Dona Barbara* and the Construction of National Identity," *Poetics Today* 15 (Winter 1994), 605–42; and J. Michael Dash, *The Other America: Caribbean Literature in a New World Context* (Charlottesville: University Press of Virginia, 1998), esp. chap. 3. Illuminating essays on "primitivism" can be found in Elazar Barkan and Ronald Bush, *Prehistories of the Future: The Primitivist Project and the Culture of Modernism* (Stanford: Stanford University Press, 1995).

96 Part of the local argot, "Picong" means to insult in a jesting manner. See Robert Carlton Ottley, *Creole Talk: Trinibaganese of Trinidad and Tobago, Words, Phrases, and Sayings Peculiar to the Country* (Diego Martin, Trinidad: Crusoe Publications, 1981), 54.

97 Jean De Boissiere, "Culture: With Me Rum in Me Head," *Picong*, n.d. [ca. 1940], 18.

98 Useful histories of the early calypso include Gordon Rohlehr, *Calypso and Society in Pre-Independence Trinidad* (Port of Spain: G. Rohlehr, 1990); Donald Hill, *Calypso Callaloo: Early Carnival Music in Trinidad* (Gainesville: University of Florida Press, 1993); and John Cowley, *Carnival, Canboulay, and Calypso: Traditions in the Making* (Cambridge: Cambridge University Press, 1996). See also Michael Eldridge, "There Goes the Transnational Neighborhood: Calypso Buys a Bungalow," *Callaloo* 25 (Spring 2002), 620–38.

99 "Wash Pan Wash," *TG*, February 14, 1933. Herein lies the explanation for the appearance of several essays on the calypso in the tourist-oriented journal the *Trinidadian*. See Seepersad Naipaul, "Carnival, Calypso, and the Creole Troubadours," *Trinidadian*, February–March 1934, 13, and Bert Struthers, "Ballad Calypsos," *Trinidadian*, February–March 1935, 8.

100 Christobell Maynard, "A Biography of Lloyd Braithwaite: The Formative Years" (Caribbean Studies Thesis, UWI, St. Augustine, 1986).

101 "Trinidad Has Its Schools of Thought," *SG*, May 22, 1938.

102 "Are We Heading towards a West Indian Culture?," *People*, July 16, 1938.

103 Clarence Madoo, "The Trinidad Calypso," *SG*, October 16, 1938.

104 Carlisle Chang, "Painting in Trinidad," in *The Artist in West Indian Society: A Symposium*, ed. Errol Hill (St. Augustine: University of the West Indies, n.d. [ca. 1964]), 45.

105 "Art Takes Shape and Form in Trinidad," *SG*, January 17, 1933.

106 "Young Artists Find Expression: First Successful Show by Independents," *TG*, January 8, 1933, and "Independent Artists Hold a Show," *DM*, January 6, 1933. For more on art in the British Caribbean, see Veerle Poupeye, *Caribbean Art* (London: Thames and Hudson, 1998), and Boscoe Holder and Geoffrey MacClean, *The Art of Boscoe Holder* (Port of Spain: MacClean Publishing, 1995). For

Barbados, see Alissandra Cummins, Allison Thompson, and Nick Whittle, *Art in Barbados: What Kind of Mirror Image?* (Kingston: Ian Randle, 1998).

107   "Miss Chen Starts Something in Local Dance," *SG*, April 20, 1941.

108   Sylvia Chen, "The Past Is Not Good Enough," *SG*, April 4, 1941.

109   Si-lan Chen, *Footnotes to History* (New York: Dance Horizons, 1981), 268–87.

110   The phrase is taken from Scott, *Domination and the Arts of Resistance.*

111   Albert Gomes, "The Calypso," *SG*, January 29, 1939.

112   Quoted from Donald Hill, "Calypsonians Speak for the Record: An Ethnohistorical Study of the Trinidad Calypso, 1784–1950" (unpublished study, American University, St. Augustine, 1977), 2:35.

113   Lewis O'Sullivan, "The Calypso—To What Purpose?," *SG*, June 25, 1939.

114   He cited "Ole Lady Tay Lay Lay" and "Conga Bara."

115   Hugh Stollmeyer, "Calypso and Politics," *Beacon*, September 1939, 13–14.

CHAPTER 2

1   Frances Bernard to Secretary of State, October 16, 1861, Consular Despatches from Trinidad, West Indies, microfilm T 148, NA.

2   For insight into this period, see, for starters, Cyrus Veeser, *A World Safe for Capitalism: Dollar Diplomacy and America's Rise to Global Power* (New York: Columbia University Press, 2002); Mary A. Renda, *Taking Haiti: Military Occupation and the Culture of U.S. Imperialism, 1915–1940* (Chapel Hill: University of North Carolina Press, 2001); Emily S. Rosenberg, *Financial Missionaries to the World: The Politics and Culture of Dollar Diplomacy, 1900–1930* (Cambridge, Mass.: Harvard University Press, 1999); Thomas Miller Klubock, *Contested Communities: Class, Gender, and Politics in Chile's El Teniente Copper Mine, 1904–1951* (Durham: Duke University Press, 1998); G. M. Joseph, *Revolution from Without: Yucatan, Mexico, and the United States, 1880–1924* (Cambridge: Cambridge University Press, 1982); Thomas F. O'Brien, *The Revolutionary Mission: American Business in Latin America, 1900–1945* (New York: Cambridge University Press, 1996).

3   The phrase comes from Thomas C. Holt, *The Problem of Freedom: Race, Labor, and Politics in Jamaica and Britain, 1832–1938* (Baltimore: Johns Hopkins University Press, 1992).

4   The term "spreadeaglism" was used by locals in the late nineteenth century to refer to U.S. expansionism. See, for example, letter to the editor, *Public Opinion*, April 1, 1892, enclosed in letter by William Pierce to State Department, April 24, 1892, Consular Despatches from Trinidad, West Indies, microfilm T 148, NA.

5   On the significance of the United States to the nineteenth-century Jamaican banana industry, see Randolph Wilson Bartlett Jr., "Lorenzo D. Baker and the Development of the Banana Trade between Jamaica and the United States, 1881–1890" (Ph.D. diss., American University, 1977).

6   W. Macomb to Secretary of State, March 16, 1842, Consular Despatches from Trinidad, West Indies, microfilm T 148, NA.

7   For more on Barber, see Nikito Harwich-Vallenilla, *Asfalto y Revolución: La New York & Bermudez Company* (Caracas: Fundación para el Rescate del Acervo Documental Venezolano, Monte Avila Editores, 1992).

8   Barber Asphalt Paving Co., *Genuine Trinidad Asphalt: The Standard Pavement of America* (Washington, D.C.: Barber Asphalt Paving Co., 1885).

9   "Letter by Trinidadian," *POSG*, November 28, 1885.

10 For a history of the proposal, see Asphalt Concession, CP 84 1887.

11 Quotes come from "The Asphalt Question," *Public Opinion*, September 3, 1887, enclosed in Robinson to Secretary of State, September 21, 1887, CO 295/315.

12 "The Pitch Lake Monopoly," *San Fernando Gazette*, September 17, 1887.

13 See Fernando Coronil, *The Magical State: Nature, Money, and Modernity in Venezuela* (Chicago: University of Chicago Press, 1997).

14 T. B. Jackson, ed., *The Book of Trinidad* (Port of Spain: Muir Marshall, 1904), 65–67.

15 For a history of Trinidad's petroleum, see George E. Huggins, *A History of Trinidad Oil* (Port of Spain: Trinidad Express Newspapers, 1996), and Vernon Mulchansingh, "The Origins, Growth, and Development of the Oil Industry in Trinidad and Its Impact on the Economy, 1857–1965" (Ph.D. diss., Queens University of Belfast, 1967).

16 In the late nineteenth century, whites, as Bridget Brereton argues, were "by definition respectable" (*Race Relations in Colonial Trinidad, 1870–1900* [Cambridge: Cambridge University Press, 1979], 221).

17 For a sample of drillers' profiles, see Report from Foreign Service Posts, May 22, 1940, RG 84, box 16, NA.

18 Ralph Arnold, George A. Macready, and Thomas W. Barrington, *The First Big Oil Hunt, Venezuela, 1911–1916* (New York: Vantage Press, 1960).

19 Ibid., 36.

20 Letter to the editor, *TG*, December 5, 1941.

21 Letter from Division of Foreign Services, August 9, 1934, RG 59, box 1438, NA.

22 Ibid.

23 There is evidence, of course, of actual drunk "Yankee drillers," whom the local antiestablishment press was only too willing to highlight. See, for example, "Oil Driller on the Drunk," *Argos*, July 25, 1914.

24 For more on this, see Harvey Neptune, "White Lies: Race and Sexuality in Occupied Trinidad," *Journal of Colonialism and Colonial History* 2 (Spring 2001): 24–52.

25 Louis Meikle, *Confederation of the British West Indies versus Annexation to the United States of America: A Political Discourse on the West Indies* (London: S. Low, Marston & Co., 1912) (republished in 1969).

26 For a discussion of contemporary Latin American intellectuals' apprehensions of the United States, see John Reid, *Spanish American Images of the United*

States (Gainesville: University Press of Florida, 1977), and Fred Rippy, "Literary Yankeephobia in Hispanic America," *Journal of International Relations* 12 (July 1922), 351–71; also see Aims McGuinness, "Searching for Latin America: Race and Sovereignty in the Americas in the 1850s," in *Race and Nation in Modern Latin America*, ed. Nancy P. Appelbaum, Anne S. Macpherson, and Karin Alejandra Rosemblatt (Chapel Hill: University of North Carolina Press, 2003), 87–103.

27 Meikle, *Confederation*, 8.

28 See, for example, David Healy, *Drive to Hegemony: The United States in the Caribbean, 1898–1917* (Madison: University of Wisconsin Press, 1988).

29 W. T. Stead, *The Americanization of the World* (New York: H. Markley, 1902), 81.

30 In the midst of the disaster, U.S. marines came ashore to offer aid, and their unsolicited help triggered a controversy that led to the recall of the governor of Jamaica, James Sweetenham. See William Tilchin, "Theodore Roosevelt, Anglo-American Relations and the Jamaica Incident of 1907," *Diplomatic History* 19 (Fall 1995): 385–405, and Francis A. Coghlan, "The United States Navy and the Jamaica Earthquake," *Prologue* 8 (Spring 1976): 163–73. See also Zadie Smith, *White Teeth* (New York: Random House, 2000), 300.

31 See, for example, "Americanism in the West Indies," *Argos*, July 30, 1914.

32 Reid, *Spanish American Images*, 178.

33 Meikle, *Confederation*, 43.

34 "Confederation of the West Indies," *Mirror*, March 19, 1912. Meikle had studied at Howard University in Washington, D.C., then practiced medicine in Arkansas and Panama during the construction of the canal. He was living in Trinidad by the time of the book's publication.

35 Meikle, *Confederation*, 54.

36 Ibid., 43.

37 Ibid., 47.

38 Ibid., 176.

39 Ibid., 99.

40 Ibid., 176.

41 See Winston James, *Holding Aloft the Banner of Ethiopia: Caribbean Radicalism in Early Twentieth-Century America* (New York: Verso, 1998).

42 Official sources reveal that approximately 65,000 British West Indians had migrated to New York in the first two decades of the century. See Robert F. Foerster, *The Racial Problems Involved in Immigration from Latin America and the West Indies to the United States, a Report Submitted to the Secretary of Labor by Robert F. Foerster* (professor in economics at Princeton University) (Washington, D.C.: Government Printing Office, 1925). For literature on West Indian migration to the United States in this period, see—in addition to Winston James— Ira Reid, *The Negro Immigrant, His Background, Characteristics, and Adjustment, 1899–1937* (New York: Arno Press, 1939), and Irma Watkins-Owens, *Blood Relations: Caribbean Immigrants and the Harlem Community, 1900–1930* (Bloomington: Indiana University Press, 1996).

43 Consul Henry Baker, April 2, 1919, RG 59, box 7543, NA.

44 For the Harlem reference, see "West Indian Youths Welfare League," *People*, May 18, 1935. Tellingly, for a group of poor Afro-Trinidadians, it was neither London nor Liverpool but America's "blackest" terrain that inspired their imaginations.

45 "A Good Neighbor," *People*, November 28, 1936.

46 Barracks refer to the slumlike housing first provided by planters for agricultural workers; see Alfred Mendes, *Black Fauns* (London: New Beacon, 1935). For more on this body of fiction, see Reinhard Sander, *Trinidad Awakening: West Indian Literature of the Nineteen Thirties* (New York: Greenwood Press, 1988).

47 It is telling of America's significance that both Mendes's novels—*Black Fauns* and *Pitch Lake: A Story from Trinidad* (London: New Beacon, 1980)—open with references to the United States.

48 Mendes, *Black Fauns*, 34.

49 Ibid., 245.

50 Ibid., 244–48.

51 Ibid., 256.

52 Ibid.

53 "Exodus From Trinidad," *LL*, May 12, 1923.

54 Ibid. Similarly gendered claims were earlier issued by political dissidents. See, for example, "Women in the Northward Migration," *Argos*, May 20, 1913.

55 For more on imperialists' investments in patriarchal gender ideology in the British West Indies, see Catherine Hall, *Civilising Subjects: Metropole and Colony in the English Imagination, 1830–1867* (Chicago: University of Chicago Press, 2002).

56 For a gender-sensitive account of migration during the period, see Watkins-Owens, *Blood Relations*.

57 "Can Nine Cinemas Pay Port of Spain?," *SG*, December 5, 1937.

58 Report from Foreign Service Posts, January 5, 1939, RG 84, box 12, NA.

59 For other parts of the British Empire, see Charles Ambler, "Popular Films and Colonial Audiences: The Movies in Northern Rhodesia," *American Historical Review* 106 (June 2001): 81–105, and Rosaleen Smyth, "The Development of British Colonial Film Policy, 1927–1939," *Journal of African History* 20 (February 1979): 347–450.

60 The phrase "diasporic resource" is also employed in Jacqueline Nassy Brown, "Black Liverpool, Black America, and the Gendering of Diasporic Space," *Cultural Anthropology* 13 (August 1998): 291–325.

61 Alfredo Demorest to State Department, May 19, 1934, RG 59, box 622, NA. The banning of the 1933 film *Shanghai Lady* confirms that these principles, produced to regulate how "subject races" saw sexuality, race, and gender, were put into practice. This particular motion picture, the Board of Censors concluded, was unsuited for viewing in a colony like Trinidad that had "mixed races."

62 The literature on the overlapping of Hollywood cinema, sexuality, race, and censorship is enormous. An excellent place to start is Thomas Doherty, *Pre-Code*

Hollywood: Sex, Immorality, and Insurrection in American Cinema, 1930–1934 (New York: Columbia University Press, 1999).

63 Alfredo Demorest to State Department, January 7, 1933, RG 59, box 622, NA.

64 Ibid.

65 "Jotter's Notes," *Mirror*, July 11, 1910. For the racial motivations underlying the censorship of this fight, see Lee Grieveson, "Fighting Films: Race, Morality, and the Governing of Cinema," *Cinema Journal* 38 (Autumn 1998), 40–61.

66 Tito P. Achong, "Made to Order Patriotism: Americanism as Its Enemy," *LL*, September 18, 1926.

67 See Ian Jarvie, *Hollywood's Overseas Campaign: The North Atlantic Movie Trade, 1920–1950* (New York: Cambridge University Press, 1992), 118.

68 See, for example, the review of *Imitation of Life*, "Film with Color Appeal," *People*, October 12, 1935, and commentary on the Joe Louis–Max Schmeling bout, "That Fight," *People*, July 4, 1936.

69 "Why Green Pastures Film Was Banned," *STSC*, August 23, 1936.

70 "Correspondence," *STSC*, August 23, 1936.

71 Ibid.

72 "All's Well That Ends Well," *People*, September 27, 1936.

73 A debate carried out in very similar terms would erupt in 1943 over the showing of *Cabin in the Sky*.

74 "Mayor Opens Literary Club Conference," *TG*, December 1, 1935.

75 "Young West Indian Lectures on West Indian Federation," *TG*, June 29, 1933.

76 "City Not to Be Illuminated for Emancipation Day," *TG*, July 27, 1934.

77 "New Deal," *TG*, July 16, 1938.

78 "A Good Neighbor," *People*, November 28, 1936.

79 Arthur Calder-Marshall, *Glory Dead* (London: M. Joseph, 1939), 243.

80 "Unfounded Aspersion," *TG*, October 25, 1938.

81 "Trinidad Objects to Disloyalty to Britain Allegations," *SG*, October 23, 1938.

82 Ibid.

83 The term "banal imperialism" is adapted from Michael Billig, *Banal Nationalism* (London: Sage, 1995).

84 Letter to the editor, *TG*, October 26, 1938.

85 This statement was made by Vivian Henry, member of Cipriani's Trinidad Labor Party, as he addressed the members of the Moyne Commission and sought to refute Calder-Marshall's claims. See "Crowd Cheers Loyalty Statement at Royal Commission," *TG*, March 10, 1939.

86 Tito P. Achong, "Would Trinidad Like to Be American?," *People*, October 4, 1938.

87 "Is Mr. Calder-Marshall Wrong?," *People*, October 29, 1938.

88 Achong, "Would Trinidad Like to Be American?"

89 "Is Mr. Calder-Marshall Wrong?"

90 "Shall We Be Americanized?," *People*, January 20, 1940.

CHAPTER 3

1 "On Second Thoughts," *SG*, September 7, 1941. All money values referred to in this chapter are in local currency; a Trinidad dollar was equivalent to US$0.85.

2 Letter to the editor, *SG*, September 14, 1941.

3 Samuel Selvon, *A Brighter Sun* (Harlow, Essex: Longman, 1952), 135.

4 "Arima of Yesterday and Tomorrow," *SG*, December 28, 1941.

5 Ralph De Boissiere, *Rum and Coca-Cola* (Melbourne, 1956; reprint, London: Allison & Busby, 1984), 65.

6 Gail Saunders, "The 1942 Riot in Nassau: A Demand for Change?," *Journal of Caribbean History* 20 (May 1985): 117–46.

7 L. E. B. [Lloyd Braithwaite], "Yanks Are Coming," *New Dawn*, November 1940, 4.

8 "A Changing Situation," *New Dawn*, March 1941, 4.

9 "Legislature Debate on US Bases," *TG*, January 18, 1941.

10 "A Debate on the US Bases," *TG*, January 19, 1941.

11 Young's displeasure with the proceedings is everywhere in diplomatic correspondence. See, for example, Governor Young to Secretary of State, February 19, 1942, CO 967/135. See, indeed, the entire set of correspondences in this file.

12 "Labor Terms for US Army Base," *TG*, January 6, 1941.

13 "Whose People Are We?," *Vanguard*, August 23, 1941.

14 "The Yanks Have Come," *New Dawn*, April 1941, 19.

15 Enclosed in Governor Young to Secretary of State Lord Moyne, April 3, 1941, CO 971/2/1.

16 Selvon, *Brighter Sun*, 135.

17 Lord Moyne to Young, June 4, 1941, CO 971/2/1.

18 "Britain, America, and Wages," *Vanguard*, March 29, 1941.

19 Creech Jones to Secretary of State, July 26, 1941, CO 971/20/3.

20 League of Colored Peoples to George Hall, June 14, 1941, CO 971/2/1.

21 S Burns Weston to Joseph Morris, September 21, 1942, RG 43, box 28, NA; Walter White to AAAC, June 12, 1942, RG 43, box 49, NA. For more on the activities of the American West Indian Council on Caribbean Affairs, see Jason Parker, "Capital of the Caribbean: The African American–West Indian Harlem Nexus and the Transnational Drive for Black Freedom, 1940–1948," *Journal of African American History* 2 (Spring 2004): 98–117.

22 Trinidad trade unionists—with the important exception of Adrian Rienzi—agreed on February 2, 1940, not to strike during the war. See appendix to Joint Conciliation Board Oil Industry, 1941, CO 295 626.

23 "Wages and Blacklegs," *New Dawn*, February 1941, 4.

24 "American Base Workers Strike," *Vanguard*, June 14, 1941. See also Young to Secretary of State, June 10, 1941, CO 971/2/1.

25 Young to Secretary of State, May 20, 1941, CO 971/2/1.

26 James C. Shoulz, *History of the Trinidad Sector and Base Command*, vol. 5, *International Relations* (Washington, D.C.: Department of the Army, 1947), 93–102.

27 "Yanks Have Come."

28 Young to Secretary of State, May 20, 1941, CO 971/2/1.

29 De Boissiere, *Rum and Coca-Cola*, 57.

30 Governor Clifford to Secretary of State, November 19, 1942, CO 295 625.

31 Fitzroy Baptiste argues that base wages did not significantly exceed the local counterpart. See "Colonial Government, Americans, and Employment-Generation in Trinidad, 1939–44" (unpublished paper, n.d.).

32 Employees who worked at least twelve of fourteen days received a dependability bonus of 24 cents a day. See "Report on Events Connected with United States Bases," June quarter, 1943, CO 971/23/5.

33 Author interview with Frank Thomas, June 5, 1998, Queens, N.Y.

34 Sidney Smith, *Public Life and Sport: Jamaica, Grenada, and Trinidad* (Port of Spain: Trinidad Publishing Co., 1941), 107.

35 "Teachers Leaving Must Give Notice," *TG*, September 27, 1941; see also "Teachers Work As Carpenters on US Base," *SG*, September 7, 1941.

36 Gordon Grant and Co. to Lieutenant Commander Bushe, November 4, 1942, enclosed in Huggins to Secretary of State, December 12, 1942, FO 371/30718. This letter was intercepted by Trinidad's censors.

37 Sugar Manufacturers' Association to Secretary of State, September 15, 1942, CO 295 620/7049.

38 For a contrasting sense that base work introduced a more regimented sense of time, see Kevin Birth, *Any Time Is Trinidad Time: Social Meaning and Temporal Consciousness* (Gainesville: University Press of Florida, 1999), 32–34.

39 Selvon, *Brighter Sun*, 119–22.

40 Ibid.

41 Kenneth Ramchand, *An Introduction to the Study of West Indian Literature* (London: Nelson Caribbean, 1976), 67.

42 According to an American in the colony reporting naturally for a foreign publication, "A crowd of American soldiers of Southern antecedents threatened to lynch a Negro chauffeur for running down one of their number" (Trevor Christie, "Yankees in Trinidad," *Life*, April 1941, 16–23).

43 Letter to the editor, *TG*, November 20, 1941. For trial details, see "Murder Charge Hearing Opens at Fort Read," *TG*, November 19, 1941.

44 "US Police Official Gets 5 Years for Killing Guard," *TG*, May 7, 1943.

45 V. S. Naipaul, *Miguel Street* (London: Penguin, 1959), 185.

46 Peter J. Wilson, *Crab Antics: The Social Anthropology of English-Speaking Negro Societies of the Caribbean* (New Haven: Yale University Press, 1973).

47 Author interview with Alfred Lalla, August 9, 1998, Arima, Trinidad.

48 "West Indian Labor for Trinidad," *TG*, July 23, 1941.

49 "Labor Shortage," *SG*, March 9, 1941.

50 See, for example, *TG*, March 20, 1940.

51 Quote comes from an elected member of the legislature, A. C. Rienzi. See Janu-

ary 30, 1942, *Hansard*, Government Publications, University of the West Indies, St. Augustine.

52 "Yanks Have Come."

53 Report by A. V. Lindon, September 27, 1941, CO 295 625.

54 Young to Secretary of State, February 9, 1942, CO 295 625.

55 Quote comes from a telegram by Sugar Manufacturers' Association enclosed in West India Committee to Secretary of State, May 19, 1942, CO 295 625.

56 "Bill Issued for Labor Migration," *TG*, January 27, 1941.

57 Barbados had long been an important supplier of labor to Trinidad. See Bridget Brereton, *Race Relations in Colonial Trinidad, 1870–1900* (Cambridge: Cambridge University Press, 1979), 110–15.

58 "Extract from Enclosure to Trinidad Secret Despatch," September 9, 1943, CO 295 625 70497. See also "200 Bajan Laborers for US Army Base," *TG*, February 25, 1942.

59 "Thirty-Three Arrests Made in Arima Friday Night Disturbances," *SG*, April 5, 1942.

60 "Barbadian Labourers in Trinidad," *POSG*, April 15, 1942.

61 Young to Secretary of State, February 9, 1942, CO 295 625.

62 C. H. Thornley to Secretary of State, February 16, 1942, CO 967 135. Regarding Clifford, Thornley wrote that he "had many dealings with Americans" and that "Lady Clifford should be of great assistance to him in relations with Americans in Trinidad." For more on Clifford, see his memoirs, *The Honorable Sir Bede Clifford, Proconsul: Being Incidents in the Life and Career of the Honorable Bede Clifford* (London: Evans Bros., 1964).

63 "Conscription Discussed in Maiden Speech," *TG*, June 15, 1942.

64 Secretary of State to Clifford, January 15, 1943, CO 295 625.

65 H. Neal Fahey, *SG*, March 1, 1942.

66 Ralph Mentor, "Planters Demand Forced Labor," *POSG*, February 22, 1942.

67 "ID Cards for Residents," *TG*, August 15, 1942.

68 "Trinidad Starts Registering Today from 300 Centres," *TG*, August 26, 1942.

69 "Registration Closed Today at All Centres," *SG*, August 30, 1942.

70 Clifford to Secretary of State, May 14, 1943, CO 295 625.

71 See, for example, David Trotman, *Crime in Trinidad: Conflict and Control in a Plantation Society, 1838–1900* (Knoxville: University of Tennessee Press, 1986).

72 See, for example, correspondence in which the writer complained of "idlers" and "trouble dens" in Port of Spain and urged conscription, *TG*, July 28, 1942.

73 Editorial, *TG*, July 12, 1942.

74 Leonard Lyle to Secretary of State, April 20, 1943, CO 295 625.

75 The term was used to describe and discredit, for example, the Butler-led disturbances. See Trinidad and Tobago Disturbances Report of Commission, January 1938, Cmd. 5641, Parliamentary Papers, British Library, London. For earliest use of the word in England, see Geoffrey Pearson, *Hooligan: A History of Respectable Fears* (New York: Schocken Books, 1984).

76 C. B. Mathura, letter to the editor, *POSG*, May 17, 1942. As well, Phil Madison,

a well-known musician, wrote of the era's "strange children" who possessed an "extreme nervousness" (letter to the editor, *TG*, September 1, 1942).

77 For more on the concept of "moral panic," see Sonya Rose, "Cultural Analysis and Moral Discourses: Episodes, Continuities, and Transformations," in *Beyond the Cultural Turn: New Directions in the Study of Society and Culture*, ed. Victoria E. Bonnell and Lynn Hunt (Berkeley: University of California Press, 1999), 217–38. For similar application of the concept, see Stuart Hall, Charles Critcher, Tony Jefferson, John Clarke, and Brian Robert, *Policing the Crisis: Mugging, the State, and Law and Order* (New York: Holmes & Meier, 1978), and Joan Neuberger, *Hooliganism: Crime, Culture, and Power in St. Petersburg, 1900–1914* (Berkeley: University of California Press, 1993).

78 "Dismissed Worker Gets 3 Months for Throwing Stone," *TG*, September 19, 1942.

79 "Behaviour of Arima Young Men Condemned," *TG*, May 21, 1942.

80 "Gang Outrages Must Be Sternly Put Down," *TG*, October 9, 1942.

81 Letter to the editor, "Hooliganism in the City," *TG*, September 3, 1942.

82 Letter to the editor, "Miscreant," *TG*, October 10, 1942.

83 Letter to the editor, "JG," *TG*, September 12, 1942.

84 Jean De Boissiere, "Whose Hooligan Are You?," *Callaloo*, March 1944, 3.

85 "Drastic Measures to Control Hooliganism," *POSG*, November 12, 1942.

86 "Mayor against Special Meeting to Discuss Hooliganism," *TG*, October 30, 1942. Listen to *Lord Invader in New York*, CD 40450 (Folkways Recordings, 2000).

87 Tito Achong, *Report of the Mayor of Port of Spain* (Boston: Meador, 1943), 25.

88 The phrase "servant problem" comes from one of the few works dealing with the history of domestic workers in the region. See Elsa M. Chaney and Mary Garcia Castro, eds., *Muchachas No More: Household Workers in Latin America and the Caribbean* (Philadelphia: Temple University Press, 1989). Other relevant writings include Barry W. Higman, "Domestic Service in Jamaica since 1750," in *Essays Presented to Douglas Hall: Trade, Government, and Society in Caribbean History, 1700–1920*, ed. B. W. Higman (Kingston: Heinemann Educational Books Caribbean, 1983), 124–40, and Michele A. Johnson, "Decent and Fair: Aspects of Domestic Service in Jamaica, 1920–1970," *Journal of Caribbean History* 6 (November 1999): 83–106. For a parallel approach to the "domestic problem" in the postemancipation U.S. South, see Tera Hunter, *To 'Joy My Freedom: Southern Black Women's Lives and Labors after the Civil War* (Cambridge, Mass.: Harvard University Press 1997), esp. chap. 4.

89 Rhoda Reddock, *Women, Labour, and Politics in Trinidad and Tobago: A History* (London: Zed Books, 1994), 176.

90 De Boissiere, *Rum and Coca-Cola*, 65.

91 Albert Gomes, *All Papa's Children* (East Moseley, England: Cairi Publishing House, 1978), 32.

92 C. L. R. James, *Minty Alley* (London: New Beacon, 1971), 145.

93 Alfred Mendes, *Pitch Lake: A Story from Trinidad* (London: New Beacon, 1980).

94 "Domestics Hold Parley," *Vanguard*, March 9, 1941.

95 Report of West Indian Royal Commission, 1945, 481, Cmd. 6607, Parliamentary Papers, British Library, London. This report is also known as the Moyne Report.

96 "US Naval Bases," *TG*, March 7, 1941.

97 Adolphe Roberts, "Caribbean Headaches," *Nation*, September 20, 1941, enclosed in RG 43, box 29, NA. See also Christie, "Yankees in Trinidad."

98 Consul Claude Hall, Social Report, November 19, 1941, RG 84, box 25, NA.

99 "Extract from Enclosure to Trinidad Secret Despatch."

100 "Judge Says Jail to Washer Will Be Lesson to Others," *TG*, April 7, 1943.

101 De Boissiere, *Rum and Coca-Cola*, 74.

102 Ibid., 123.

103 Letter to the editor, "Servant Problem," *POSG*, November 13, 1943.

104 All quotes come from letters to the editor. See *TG*, November 19, 1943, and *SG*, November 21, 1943.

105 Iris Alcantara, letter to the editor, *SG*, November 21, 1943. For a similar sentiment, see letter to the editor, "Action Please," *SG*, November 21, 1943.

106 Quotes here come from letters to the editor by "justice," "broadminded," "fairplay," and Sam Lewis. See *SG*, November 21, 1943.

107 Albert Gomes, "That Trinidad Will Never Return," *SG*, November 27, 1943.

108 For "housewifization" in the context of colonial Trinidad, see Reddock, *Women, Labour, and Politics*. The ambiguity suggested in Gomes's account is consistent with the historiography on women and plantation labor in the postemancipation period. See Brereton, "Family Strategies, Gender and the Shift to Wage Labour in the British Caribbean," in *The Colonial Caribbean in Transition: Essays on Postemancipation Social and Cultural History*, ed. Bridget Brereton and Kevin Yelvington (Gainesville: University Press of Florida, 1999), 67–99, and Diana Paton, "The Flights from the Fields Reconsidered: Gender Ideologies and Women's Labor after Slavery in Jamaica," in *Reclaiming the Political in Latin American History: Essays from the North*, ed. Joseph Gilbert (Durham: Duke University Press, 2001), 175–204.

CHAPTER 4

1 Letter to the editor, *POSG*, June 23, 1946.

2 For origins of notions of restraint in Englishmen's dress, see David Kuchta, "The Making of the Self-Made Man: Class, Clothing, and English Masculinity, 1688–1832," in *The Sex of Things*, ed. Victoria de Grazia, with Ellen Furlough (Berkeley: University of California Press, 1996), 54–78.

3 For the intimate relationship between cricket and British colonial masculinity, see, of course, the classic C. L. R. James, *Beyond a Boundary* (1963; reprint, New York: Pantheon, 1984). See, too, Brian Stoddart, "Sport, Cultural Imperi-

alism, and Colonial Responses in the British Empire," *Comparative Studies in Society and History* 30 (October 1988): 649–73; Manthia Diawara, "Englishness and Blackness: Cricket as Discourse on Colonialism," *Callaloo* 13 (Fall 1990): 830–44; Arjun Appadurai, *Modernity at Large: Cultural Dimensions of Globalization* (Minneapolis: University of Minnesota Press, 1996); and Aviston Downes, "From Boys to Men: Colonial Education, Cricket, and Masculinity in the Caribbean, 1870–1930," *International Journal of the History of Sport* 22 (Spring 2005): 3–21.

4 For Trinidad, the historical literature on dress is barely existent and tends to deal with costuming in the context of masquerade. See, for example, Pamela Franco, "The 'Unruly Woman' in Nineteenth Century Trinidad Carnival," *Small Axe* 7 (March 2000): 60–76, and Bridget Brereton, *Race Relations in Colonial Trinidad, 1870–1900* (Cambridge: Cambridge University Press, 1979), chap. 8. For Jamaica, there is a growing corpus on the subject of dress. See Carol Tulloch, "Fashioned in Black and White: Women's Dress in Jamaica, 1880–1907," *Things* 7 (Fall 1997): 29–53, and Steeve Buckridge, *The Language of Dress: Resistance and Accommodation in Jamaica, 1760–1890* (Kingston: University of the West Indies Press, 2004). For a comprehensive and comprehensible introduction to the scholarly thinking on fashion, see Joanne Finkelstein, *Fashion: An Introduction* (New York: New York University Press, 1996). Also, for an insightful history of African American self-presentation and style, see Shane White and Graham White, *Stylin': African American Expressive Culture from Its Beginnings to the Zoot Suit* (Ithaca: Cornell University Press, 1998). For the African scene, see Hildi Hendrickson, *Clothing and Difference: Embodied Identities in Colonial and Post-Colonial Africa* (Durham: Duke University Press, 1996).

5 This sense of "making style" is used with the preposition "on." An individual who inexplicably does not acknowledge the presence of an old acquaintance, for example, could be accused of "making style on" that person.

6 The international influence of American film before World War II attracted scholarly attention quite early. See, for example, Eugene J. Harley, *World Wide Influences of Cinema* (Los Angeles: University of Southern California Press, 1940). Robert Sklar's classic *Movie-Made America: A Cultural History of the American Movies* (New York: Random House, 1975), esp. chap. 13, is also very helpful.

7 Jean De Boissiere, "Creole Style," *Picong*, n.d. [1940?], 36.

8 Rupert Gittens, "Old Clothes in the House," *New Dawn*, November 1941, 14.

9 Captain C. Longridge, "Jazz Music," *POSG*, November 22, 1931.

10 See, for example, the columns by J. D. Ramkeesoon, who wrote under the nom de plume "Clericus Ignotus." He condemned the "jollity of jazz," the "culture of pleasure," and the "fashion on film." See "Is Modern Youth Too Frivolous?," *SG*, May 14, 1939. Arthur Calder-Marshall, too, reported that during a symposium on the "trend of modern ideas," Rev. William H. Mayhew, a "popular priest," attacked the "tendency of the younger generation to attend

the cinema, rather than church, to wear cosmetics and smoke cigarettes." See Calder-Marshall, *Glory Dead* (London: M. Joseph, 1939), 174. Also, recounting the history of dance music in Trinidad, Audley Francis noted that initially many Trinidadians could not understand jazz and labeled it "monkey music." See "Trinidad's Swing Music," *Sport and Music Calvacade*, March 1944, 96.

11 The idea that black West Indian laborers were insufficiently oriented toward consumption, according to Thomas C. Holt, *The Problem of Freedom: Race, Labor, and Politics in Jamaica and Britain, 1832–1938* (Baltimore: Johns Hopkins University Press, 1992), 191, was central to imperial race-making in the mid-nineteenth century. At several points, the Report of West Indian Royal Commission, 1945, Cmd. 6607, Parliamentary Papers, British Library, London (hereafter cited as Moyne Report) observed that the experience of radio, cinema, and travel had stimulated in West Indians a keen desire for the commodities and lifestyles advertised by the Western world. Unlike Africans, it claimed, the region's inhabitants were "not living a simple life among [their] own people under a tribal organization"; rather, they were "now touching elbows with modern civilization" (Moyne Report, 490).

12 See CP 88, Report of the Wages Advisory Board, 1936. The board included three representatives of labor: Sarran Teelucksingh, Captain A. A. Cipriani, and dockworkers' organizer C. P. Alexander. Teelucksingh, according to historian Kelvin Singh, boycotted the board's sittings. See Singh, *Race and Class Struggles in a Colonial State: Trinidad, 1917–1945* (Calgary: University of Calgary Press, 1994).

13 Critics of Captain Cipriani's leadership accused him of "insulting" the colony's womanhood in signing the board's report. See "Reds Must Go," *People*, October 30, 1937. For discussion of this "bloomer's recommendation," also see Rhoda Reddock, *Women, Labour, and Politics in Trinidad and Tobago: A History* (London: Zed Books, 1994), 121. Ralph De Boissiere's virtual roman à clef of the 1930s also dramatizes this episode. See De Boissiere, *Crown Jewel* (Melbourne: Australasian Book Society 1956), 67.

14 Moyne Report, 283.

15 Ibid., 281.

16 Report of Major G. St. J. Orde-Browne on Labor Conditions in the West Indies, 31, Cmd. 6070, Parliamentary Papers, British Library, London.

17 For insightful discussions of colonial policy in this period, see J. M. Lee, *Colonial Development and Good Government: A Study of the Ideas Expressed by the British Official Classes in Planning Decolonization, 1939–1964* (Oxford: Clarendon, 1967), esp. chap. 2; Stephen Constantine, *The Making of British Colonial Policy, 1914–1940* (London: Cass, 1984); and Michael Havinden and David Meredith, *Colonialism and Development: Britain and Its Tropical Colonies, 1850–1960* (London: Routledge, 1993), esp. chaps. 7–10.

18 See, for example, Report of Social Welfare Officer, 1945, CP 33.

19 All quotations are taken from CP 23, Correspondence on the Subject of Agriculture, 1942. For Wakefield's full report, see Report of Agricultural Policy Com-

mittee of Trinidad and Tobago, Port of Spain, 1943, Government Publications, University of the West Indies, St. Augustine.

20 Canon Farquhar, letter to the editor, *TG*, July 16, 1941.

21 This point is stressed by Frederick Cooper in his analysis of British and French imperial labor policies in Africa. See Cooper, *Decolonization and African Society: The Labor Question in French and British Africa* (New York: Cambridge University Press, 1996).

22 T. S. Simey, *Welfare and Planning in the West Indies* (Oxford: Clarendon, 1946), 121.

23 Lloyd Braithwaite, "Social Stratification in Trinidad," *Social and Economic Studies* 2 (1953): 123.

24 Ibid., 143.

25 Letter to the editor, *TG*, August 6, 1941.

26 "Government Officers Set Men's Dress Reform Fashion," *TG*, September 16, 1941.

27 "Document from Tomorrow," *Observer*, August 1942, 12.

28 "Officials in Shorts," *TG*, September 17, 1941.

29 "Dress Reform Criticized," *TG*, September 17, 1941. Pujadas was the president of the Trinidad Law Association and was also connected to Cipriani's Trinidad Labor Party.

30 "No Decision on Dress Reform in South," *TG*, September 27, 1941. The quotation was attributed to alderman D. Chadee.

31 "Dj," letter to the editor, *TG*, September 17, 1941.

32 "Jitterbug," letter to the editor, *TG*, September 21, 1941.

33 "Critic," letter to the editor, *TG*, September 25, 1941.

34 "Officials in Shorts."

35 *People*, which advertised itself as the workers' organ, featured an advertisement for "latest two tone jitterbug shirts" (November 15, 1940). They were priced at $5.

36 David W. Stowe's history of swing provides endless evidence of the racial and moral panic that surrounded the jitterbug in the late 1930s and early 1940s. See Stowe, *Swing Changes: Big-Band Jazz in New Deal America* (Cambridge, Mass: Harvard University Press, 1994), esp. chap. 1.

37 "Jitterbug" also referred to the young swing music fans. For insightful discussions of the jitterbug and its cultural milieu, see Jean Stearns and Marshall Stearns, *Jazz Dance: The Story of American Vernacular Dance* (New York: Macmillan, 1968), 315–54.

38 Ibid., 30.

39 Quoted in Charles Espinet and Harry Pitts, *Land of the Calypso: The Origins and Development of Trinidad's Folk Song* (Port of Spain: Guardian Commercial Printery, 1944), 14.

40 Letter to the editor, "Is the Jitterbug Barbaric?," *TG*, October 15, 1941.

41 "Officials in Shorts."

42 John Buddhu, letter to the editor, *TG*, September 21, 1941.

43 "What about Teachers?," *TG*, September 19, 1941.

44 In an article titled, "From a Man's Viewpoint," a male writer complained that the latest women's fashions were nothing less than "frontal assaults on manhood," the "latest encroachment in our sphere of interests—this new attempt to wrest from our unsuspecting hands the last vestige of our independence and masculine authority" (*SG*, January 12, 1941).

45 "Women's Fashion and the Male," *TG*, January 16, 1941.

46 Jean De Boissiere, "Repressed Vagabondage," *Picong*, n.d., 35.

47 Letter to the editor, *TG*, September 18, 1941.

48 "Pepper Pot," *Teacher's Herald*, September 1941, 13.

49 "Professor Shaw," letter to the editor, *TG*, September 26, 1941.

50 "Dress Reform in Civil Service," *TG*, September 19, 1941, and "City Council Workers Allowed to Make Dress Reform," *TG*, September 26, 1941.

51 Eric Williams, *Capitalism and Slavery* (1944; reprint, Chapel Hill: University of North Carolina Press, 1994), 67–68.

52 The label was D. W. Rogers's. See introduction to Eric E. Williams, *Education in the British West Indies* (Port of Spain: Guardian Commercial Printery, 1946).

53 "Do You Know?," *Indian*, May 1941, 44.

54 "Document from Tomorrow," *Observer*, August 1942, 12. The personalities and politics informing this and other Indo-Trinidadian journals are the subject of Kris Rampersad's *Finding a Place: Indo-Trinidadian Literature* (Kingston: Ian Randle, 2002).

55 Some of the most useful examinations of these political statements include Bruce M. Tyler, "Black Jive and White Repression," *Journal of Ethnic Studies* 16 (Winter 1989): 30–66; Stuart Cosgrove, "Zoot Suit and Style Warfare," *History Workshop* 18 (Autumn 1984): 77–95; Steve Chibnall, "Whistle and Zoot: The Changing of a Suit of Clothes," *History Workshop* 20 (Spring 1985): 57–81; George Lipsitz, *Rainbow at Midnight: Labor and Culture in the 1940s* (Urbana: University of Illinois Press, 1994), chap. 3; Mauricio Mazón, *The Zoot Suit Riots: The Psychology of Symbolic Annihilation* (Austin: University of Texas Press, 1984); Robin D. G. Kelley, *Race Rebels: Culture, Politics, and the Black Working Class* (New York: Free Press, 1994), chap. 7; and Octavio Paz, *The Labyrinth of Solitude* (New York: Grove Press, 1961), chap. 1.

56 According to the local army publication, some of these black soldiers had "threatened violence" against army authorities back at their North Carolina camp over getting their uniforms in the "zoot cut style." See "Ack Acks, Good Soldiers, and Athletes," *TNT*, June 15, 1943.

57 "Zoot Suit Hits Island, Vanishes," *TNT*, March 15, 1943.

58 Along with Calloway, the cast included Lena Horne, Bill Robinson, and other African American talents.

59 "Cinema News," *SG*, November 21, 1943.

60 *Stormy Weather* attracted particularly intense public interest at that point

because its release coincided with strong local protests against censors' controversial decision to ban another film with a stellar African American cast, *Cabin in the Sky*. Thus an impassioned Albert Gomes decided to throw his critical weight behind *Stormy Weather*. See "Ubiquitous," "Green Pastures—Now Cabin in the Sky," *SG*, August 22, 1943. George "Beau" Brummel was the defining late-eighteenth-century British dandy; his dress, according to Susan Fillin-Yeh, "was predictive of the alluring risking behavior of dandies" (*Dandies: Fashion and Finesse in Art and Culture* [New York: New York University Press, 2001], 6).

61 "Good Programme Is Spoiled by Badly Behaved Audience," *SG*, October 3, 1943.

62 Mazón, *Zoot Suit Riots*.

63 Listen to *Calypso: Best of Trinidad, 1929–1952*, CD, conceived and compiled by Jean Michel Gilbert (CMG Ltd., 2004).

64 For a crucial contribution to this subject, see Dick Hebdige, *Subculture: The Meaning of Style* (New York: Routledge, 1979).

65 J. O'Neil Lewis, "Quaint Trinidadian Speech Has Historical Background," *SG*, January 4, 1945.

66 Letter to the editor, *SG*, January 21, 1945.

67 Letter to the editor, *SG*, February 6, 1945.

68 Letter to editor, *SG*, February 6, 1945.

69 Patrick Leigh Fermor, *The Traveler's Tree: A Journey through the Caribbean Islands* (London: J. Murray, 1950), 154–80.

70 Saga boys, especially their relationship to the steelband, are taken up briefly in Stephen Stuempfle, *The Steelband Movement: The Forging of a National Art in Trinidad and Tobago* (Philadelphia: University of Pennsylvania Press, 1995), 47–49. See, too, Jacob D. Elder, "Color, Music, and Conflict: A Study of Aggression in Trinidad with Reference to the Role of Traditional Music," *Ethnomusicology* 8 (May 1964): 128–36.

71 Stuempfle, *Steelband Movement*, 49.

72 "Saga Beggars," *EN*, February 23, 1945.

73 Most recent analyses of zoot suits and hepster culture have arrived at similar conclusions. Robin D. G. Kelley, for example, writes that the zoot suit "represented a subversive refusal to be subservient" (Kelley, *Race Rebels*, 166).

74 This discussion of Singh is based on an account by Derek Bickerton. Despite his later scholarly career as a critical figure in the field of Creole linguistics, Bickerton, who had been a journalist in the Caribbean in the 1950s, included no citations in this biography. See Bickerton, *The Murders of Boysie Singh: Robber, Arsonist, Pirate, Mass-Murderer, Vice and Gambling King of Trinidad* (London: A. Barker, 1962), 53.

75 Ibid., 57.

76 Ibid.

77 One report boasted that at this wedding, "guests were lavishly treated," "dancing was indulged until midnight," and music was played by John Buddy Williams and the George Mottoo Swing Band, a popular band from British Guiana. See *Indian*, August 1941, 14.

78 Fermor, *Traveler's Tree*, 175.

79 Earl Lovelace, *The Wine of Astonishment* (New York: Vintage, 1982), 22.

80 It is noteworthy that while the manliness of a saga boy is threatened, his gender
    is never suspect. This reminds us that patriarchal systems are rooted in age as
    well gender.

81 "Magistrate Ban on Zoot Suits Causes Widespread Criticisms," *TG*, Septem-
    ber 19, 1946.

82 J. O'Neil Lewis, "An Evening with the Hep Cats," *EN*, November 28, 1944.

83 "Vim," letter to the editor, *TG*, November 19, 1942.

84 A newspaper story reported that a Patrick Moore had fought with a boy who
    called him a saga boy; see "Court Briefs," *TG*, August 29, 1942.

85 "Wrist neck" refers to the collars that fit the neck snugly, almost completely
    covering it. Colonial officials tended to wear jackets with such collars.

86 Rev. Foster Hilliard, "Trinidad between Two Worlds," *Observer*, October 1943, 7.

87 "Saga Boys at Government House," *Indian*, March 1944, 3.

88 De Boissiere, "Cosquelle Is the Word for It," *Callaloo*, July 1944, 11–12.

89 Anthropologist Daniel Miller defines "cosquel" as a pejorative term "for some-
    thing overdone or juxtapositions which fail; it is . . . an attempt to style but a
    failure of taste" (Miller, *Modernity, an Ethnographic Approach: Dualism and Mass
    Consumption in Trinidad* [Oxford: Berg, 1994], 226). John Mendes's dictionary
    of Trinidadian speech defines "coskel" as being dressed in "outrageously mis-
    matched clothing, to have outlandish or bizarre taste in colors, décor or dress"
    (Mendes, *Cote Ce Cote La: Trinidad and Tobago Dictionary* [Arima, Trinidad:
    John Mendes, 1985], 38). For Robert Carlton Ottley, "kaskell" is "not in order"
    —as in "dat hat looking kaskell" (Ottley, *Creole Talk: Trinibaganese of Trinidad
    and Tobago, Words, Phrases, and Sayings Peculiar to the Country* [Diego Martin,
    Trinidad: Crusoe Publications, 1981], 16).

90 "Behind the Curtain," *SG*, December 15, 1945. In this column Gomes tellingly
    asks, "What are we to do with the young men and women whose contact with
    the bases has altered their values beyond any hope of adjustment?"

CHAPTER 5

1 "Carnival Revue," *TG*, May 5, 1944; "Behind the Curtain," *SG*, June 11, 1944;
   Jean De Boissiere, "Canned Carnival," *Callaloo*, August 1944, 4; Albert Gomes,
   Through a Maze of Color (Port of Spain: Key Caribbean Publications, 1975), 84.

2 Alfred Mendes, "Something Trinidadian on Stage," *TG*, June 11, 1944.

3 Ibid.

4 De Boissiere, "Canned Carnival."

5 Quotes come from, respectively, "Behind the Curtain," *SG* June 11, 1944, and
   "Review of 'Land of the Calypso,'" *TG*, May 20, 1944.

6 R. D. Napier Raikes, "Culture," *TG*, March 8, 1944.

7 For more on this subject in the Caribbean context, see Robin Moore, *Nationalizing Blackness: Afrocubanismo and Artistic Revolution in Havana, 1920–1940*

(Pittsburgh: University of Pittsburgh Press, 1997), and Peter Wade, *Music, Race, and Nation: Música Tropical in Colombia* (Chicago: University of Chicago Press, 2000).

8 Carnival, it must be remembered, was banned from 1942 until 1946.

9 Letter to the editor, *TG*, February 27, 1943. On the connection between litera-ture and nationalism, see, for starters, Benedict Anderson, *Imagined Communi-ties: Reflections on the Origin and Spread of Nationalism* (New York: Verso, 1983), and Homi K. Bhabha, ed., *Nation and Narration* (London: Routledge, 1990).

10 For "Paul Robeson" reference, see Donald Granado, letter to the editor, *TG*, September 11, 1944.

11 Letter to the editor, *TG*, March 13, 1943. Connor went on to act in movies and established himself as a key figure in the West Indian cultural scene in London during the 1950s. See David Scott, "The Sovereignty of the Imagination: An Interview with George Lamming," *Small Axe* 12 (March 2002): 121.

12 "Limbo and Bongo Danced during Lecture," *SG*, August 1, 1943. For a history of early steelband, see Stephen Stuempfle, *The Steelband Movement: The Forging of a National Art in Trinidad and Tobago* (Philadelphia: University of Pennsylvania Press, 1995). For useful popular work, see Hélène Bellour, Kim Johnson, and Milla Riggio, *Renegades: The History of the Renegades Steel Orchestra of Trinidad and Tobago* (Oxford: Macmillan Caribbean, 2002).

13 These issues are addressed in other studies. See Peter Wade, *Blackness and Race Mixture: The Dynamics of Racial Identity in Colombia* (Baltimore: Johns Hopkins University Press, 1993); Ada Ferrer, *Insurgent Cuba: Race, Nation, and Revolu-tion, 1868–1898* (Chapel Hill: University of North Carolina Press, 1999); and Kim Butler, *Freedoms Given, Freedoms Won: Afro Brazilians in Post-Abolition Sao Paulo and Salvador* (New Brunswick, N.J.: Rutgers University Press, 1998).

14 "Behind the Curtain," *SG*, September 26, 1943.

15 For a sense of De Boissiere's nostalgia for the late-nineteenth-century past, see *Land of Rising Inflexion* (Trinidad: Fraser's Printerie, [ca. 1943]).

16 Recall De Boissiere's satirical essay advocating rum drinking as culture. See Chapter 1.

17 "Bongo in Excelsis," *Callaloo*, October 1943, 41, and November 1944, 7.

18 "Candid Comments," *SG*, December 19, 1943.

19 "Candid Comments," *SG*, November 5, 1944.

20 Charles Espinet and Harry Pitts, *Land of the Calypso: The Origin and Development of Trinidad's Folk Song* (Port of Spain: Guardian Commercial Printery, 1944).

21 For more on the marginalization of Indo-Trinidadians, see Viranjini Muna-singhe, *Callaloo or Tossed Salad? East Indians and the Cultural Politics of Identity in Trinidad* (Ithaca: Cornell University Press, 2001).

22 Espinet and Pitts, *Land of the Calypso*, introduction.

23 Ibid., 35.

24 Ibid., 46–47.

25 Ibid.

26 Ibid., 31.

27 Ibid., 13.

28 Ibid., 57.

29 "Candid Talk," *TG*, March 23, 1945.

30 By independence in 1962 Trinidad would be identified as the Land of Steelband and Calypso.

31 Quote comes from "Behind the Curtain," *SG*, November 4, 1945.

32 See Donald Hill, "I Am Happy Just to Be in This Sweet Land of Liberty," in *Island Sounds in the Global City: Caribbean Popular Music and Identity in New York*, ed. Ray Allen and Lois Wilcken (Urbana: University of Illinois Press, 1998), 74–92. Quote is from Owen Mathurin, who wrote under the pseudonym "Pertinax," *EN*, February 19, 1994.

33 "Behind the Curtain," *SG*, September 9, 1944.

34 Henry Field, "US Problems in Trinidad," March 8–30, 1942, RG 43, box 57, NA.

35 The USO was the collaborative effort of several U.S. civic associations (including the Young Men's Christian Association, the Jewish Welfare, and the Salvation Army).

36 "Regular WVDI Schedule Soon," *SG*, March 14, 1943.

37 "Council Lodges Protest to WVDI Power Reduction," *TG*, December 10, 1947; letter to the editor, *TG*, December 9, 1947.

38 "Calypso: The Voice of the People," *TNT*, March 15, 1943.

39 Raymond Quevedo, *Attila's Kaiso: A Short History of Trinidad Calypso* (St. Augustine: Department of Extra Mural Studies, University of the West Indies, 1983), 70.

40 Ralph De Boissiere, "Calypso Is an Art," *TG*, March 4, 1944.

41 Quevedo, *Attila's Kaiso*, 63.

42 This affair, of course, was far more complicated, since there were several competing claims to the song. For an account of the twists and turns, see John Sforza, *Swing It! The Andrews Sisters* (Lexington: University Press of Kentucky, 1999). See, too, Gordon Rohlehr, *Calypso and Society in Pre-Independence Trinidad* (Port of Spain: G. Rohlehr, 1990), 360–64.

43 Espinet and Pitts point out that Americans paid as much as three times the old entrance fee; see *Land of the Calypso*, 21.

44 Roberts quoted in Rohlehr, *Calypso and Society*, 346.

45 Quevedo, *Attila's Kaiso*, 70.

46 "Calypso," *TNT*, March 15, 1942, 3.

47 Wenzell Brown, *Angry Men, Laughing Men: The Caribbean Caldron* (New York: Greenburg, 1947), 261.

48 "News from the Bases," *TG*, January 16, 1942.

49 For "psychic stripping" claim, see Rohlehr, *Calypso and Society*, 364–65; for the calypso as "protest," see, for example, Mimi Sheller, *Consuming the Caribbean: From Arawaks to Zombies* (London: Routledge, 2003), 163.

50 Quevedo, *Attila's Kaiso*, 77.

51 Ibid., 74–75.

52 Ibid.

53 Ibid., 73.

54 "Calypsoes and Kittens," *TG*, January 23, 1944.

55 Listen to Lord Invader, *Calypso in New York*, SFW CD 40454 (2000).

56 Lion's composition should thus be heard as an anticipation of Sparrow's 1956 classic, "Jean and Dinah."

57 Quevedo, *Atilla's Kaiso*, 80–81.

58 Ibid., 65.

59 Ibid., 19. Quevedo gives the date for this song as 1944. While this is possible, evidence points to late 1946 as more likely, as the calypso was played by a steelband in September 1946 and was the big "leggo" hit for the 1947 carnival. See "Steelbands Play Brahms and Tchaikovsky in Contest," *TG*, September 1946; "1947 Calypso Season Opens," *TG*, January 8, 1947; and "Behind the Curtain," *SG*, January 26, 1947.

60 "Behind the Curtain," *SG*, September 26, 1943.

61 Ibid. Espinet and Pitts make the same claim about "commercialism"; see *Land of the Calypso*, 21.

62 "Behind the Curtain," *SG*, January 16, 1944.

63 "Standards of Calypsoes Sung in City Tents," *EN*, January 22, 1944.

64 Robin D. G. Kelley, *Yo' Mama's Disfunktional! Fighting the Culture Wars in Urban America* (Boston: Beacon Press, 1997), chap. 2. Kelley, of course, had in mind the working class in the late-twentieth-century United States.

65 Vincent H. Clark, "Trinidad Culture Waxes on Despite Economic Woes," *TG*, December 12, 1945.

66 Quevedo, *Attila's Kaiso*, 78.

67 Eric Burger, "Lovers of Calypso Need a Sense of Proportion," *TG*, February 5, 1944.

68 "Calypsoes," *POSG*, January 26, 1944.

69 Letter to the editor, *TG*, January 29, 1944.

70 "Standards of Calypsoes."

71 "Police Warn Calypsonian," *TG*, January 22, 1944.

72 For the story about crashing the gates, see "Crowd Swarms Calypso Tents," *TG*, February 24, 1944. Recall, too, Lord Kitchener's remark about "natives" who could not get into the tent.

73 "Captain Cipriani Stops Calypso Drama," *TG*, January 25, 1944.

74 "Behind the Curtain," *TG*, December 31, 1944.

75 Quevedo, *Attila's Kaiso*, 81.

76 Alfred Mendes, "If Calypso Is Folksong, It Should Be Encouraged," *SG*, February 13, 1944; see, too, letter to the editor, *TG*, February 5, 1944.

77 All quotations are from Ralph De Boissiere's letter to the editor, *TG*, February 3, 1944.

78 Lyrics are cited in Paul Blanshard, *Democracy and Empire in the Caribbean: A*

Contemporary Review (New York: Macmillan, 1947), 258. "Picong" in Trinidad's argot refers to a speech aimed at ridicule.

79 The phrase comes from Gail Bederman, *Manliness and Civilization: A Cultural History of Gender and Race in the United States, 1880–1917* (Chicago: University of Chicago Press, 1995), 13.

80 "Behind the Curtain," *SG*, January 30, 1944.

81 Burger, "Lovers of Calypso."

82 McDonald Carpenter, "Calypsos Not Art," *TG*, February 8, 1944.

83 Brinsley Samaroo, foreword to Gomes, *Through a Maze*, xvi. For critical assessments of Gomes's autobiography as well as his political life, see Owen Mathurin, "An Insider's View," *Caribbean Studies* 14 (December 1975): 73–83, and Gordon Lewis, "Outsider's View," *Caribbean Studies* 14 (December 1975): 73–83.

84 McDonald Carpenter, "Europe's Culture Cast Our Own," *TG*, February 25, 1944.

85 See, for example, "Organize for a United Effort," *Observer*, October 1944, 10.

86 "Notes," *Observer*, March 1946, 6.

87 V. S. Naipaul, *The Middle Passage; Impressions of Five Societies: British, French, and Dutch in the West Indies and South America* (London: Vintage, 1962), 29–32.

88 The literature on V. S. Naipaul, not surprisingly, is enormous. The work that does most to locate him locally is Selwyn R. Cudjoe, *V. S. Naipaul: A Materialist Reading* (Amherst: University of Massachusetts Press, 1988). See, too, Stefano Harney, *Nationalism and Identity: Culture and the Imagination in a Caribbean Diaspora* (Atlantic Highlands, N.J.: Zed Books, 1996), chap. 6.

CHAPTER 6

1 For details on this case, see "Point Cumana Case Put Off," *TG*, February 26, 1943; "Point Cumana House Case," *POSG*, March 11, 1943; "Sentence to Be Passed Today," *TG*, April 2, 1943; "Point Cumana Bawdy House Appeal," *POSG*, August 24, 1943; "Point Cumana Beach House Conviction Upheld," *POSG*, September 11, 1943.

2 Marilyn Lake, "The Desire for a Yank: Sexual Relations between Australian Women and American Servicemen during World War II," *Journal of the History of Sexuality* 2 (October 1992): 621–33.

3 Despite a few oblique references by one interviewee, I have found no references to same-sex relationships. Suggestive, however, is Robert Antoni's fabulous narrative of the period, *My Grandmother's Erotic Folktales* (New York: Grove Press, 2000).

4 Although there was no legal barrier to interracial marriages, they were generally not accepted. See Lloyd Braithwaite, "Social Stratification in Trinidad," *Social and Economic Studies* 2 (1953): 95, and Vincent Tothill, *The Doctor's Office* (London: Blackie & Son, 1939). According to Tothill, an English doctor who lived and practiced in the colony during the 1930s, white women who mar-

ried men of color became total outcasts; on the other hand, white men who turned to women of color would be accepted among other whites once they left these partners. For the earlier period, see Bridget Brereton, *Race Relations in Colonial Trinidad, 1870–1900* (Cambridge: Cambridge University Press, 1979), 60–61. The relevant literature for other locales would include Ann Laura Stoler, *Carnal Knowledge and Imperial Power: Race and the Intimate in Colonial Rule* (Berkeley: University of California Press, 2002); Philippa Levine, *Prostitution, Race, and Politics: Policing Venereal Disease in the British Empire* (New York: Routledge, 2003); Kenneth Ballhatchet, *Race, Sex, and Class under the Raj: Imperial Attitudes and Policies and Their Critics, 1793–1905* (New York: St. Martin's Press 1980); Martha Hodes, *Sex, Love, Race: Crossing Boundaries in North American History* (New York: New York University Press, 1999); and Kevin J. Mumford, *Interzones: Black/White Sex Districts in Chicago and New York in the Early Twentieth Century* (New York: Columbia University Press, 1997).

5　This clever phrase comes from Petra Goedde, "Feature Review: Women and Foreign 'Affairs,'" *Diplomatic History* 23 (Fall 1999), 693–98.

6　Samuel Selvon, *A Brighter Sun* (Harlow, Essex: Longman, 1952), 65.

7　The literature on prostitution in Trinidad is scarce. See David Trotman, *Crime in Trinidad: Conflict and Control in a Plantation Society, 1838–1900* (Knoxville: University of Tennessee Press, 1986), 247–52, and Pamela Franco, "The 'Unruly Woman' in Nineteenth Century Trinidad Carnival," *Small Axe* 7 (March 2000): 60–76.

8　Robert Johnson, *History of the Trinidad Sector and Base Command*, vol. 1 (Washington, D.C.: Department of the Army, 1945), 76.

9　"Supplement to Section I on Relations between American Armed Forces Personnel and the Local Population," June 1943, CO 971/23/5. According to this document, "American sailors and soldiers maybe seen at almost all times of the day in friendly contact with the civilian population in the parks and squares of Port of Spain."

10　"US Soldier and Civilian Fight over Man," *TG*, October 5, 1941.

11　"Defense Opens in St. James Murder Trial," *TG*, November 21, 1941.

12　These testimonies remind us that calypsos about violent response to cuckoldry at the hands of American men were not necessarily fictive and fantastic. For a particularly melodious example, listen to "Yankee Man" by Lord Kitchener.

13　"Barataria Man on Trial in American Murder Case," *TG*, May 13, 1943, and "Santa Cruz Man Accused of Murdering American," *POSG*, May 15, 1943. For comparable studies of the volatile mix of U.S. soldiers, sex, and masculine violence, see Sonya Rose, "Sex, Citizenship, and the Nation in World War II Britain," *American Historical Review* 103 (October 1998), 1147–76; David Reynolds, *Rich Relations: The American Occupation of Britain, 1942–1945* (New York: Random House, 1995); Graham Smith, *When Jim Crow Met John Bull: Black American Soldiers in World War II Britain* (New York: St. Martin's Press, 1987); John Hammond Moore, *Over-Sexed, Over-Paid, and Over Here: Americans in Australia, 1941–45* (New York: University of Queensland Press, 1981); E. Daniel Potts and Annette Potts, *Yanks Down Under, 1941–45: The American Impact on Australia* (Melbourne: Oxford University Press, 1985); and Jacqueline Nassy Brown, "Black Liverpool, Black America, and the Gendering of Diasporic Space," *Cultural Anthropology* 13 (August 1998): 291–325.

14 The masculinist perspective of nationalist thought across the world has been the subject of several studies. For early examples, see George Mosse, *Nationalism and Sexuality: Middle Class Morality and Sexual Norms in Modern Europe* (New York: H. Fertig, 1985); Cynthia Enloe, *Making Feminist Sense of International Politics* (Berkeley: University of California Press, 1990); Andrew Parker, ed., *Nationalisms and Sexualities* (New York: Routledge, 1992); Kumari Jayawardena, *Feminism and Nationalism in the Third World* (London: Zed Books, 1986); Nira Yuval-Davis and Floya Anthias, eds., *Woman-Nation-State* (New York: St. Martin's Press, 1989); Nira Yuval-Davis, *Gender and Nation* (London: Sage, 1997); Kumkum Sangari and Sudesh Vaid, eds., *Recasting Women: Essays in Indian Colonial History* (New Brunswick, N.J.: Rutgers University Press, 1995); Natasha Barnes, "Representing the Nation: Gender, Class, and the State in the Anglophone Caribbean" (Ph.D. diss., University of Michigan, 1995); Donna Guy, *Sex and Danger in Buenos Aires: Prostitution, Family, and Nation in Argentina* (Lincoln: University of Nebraska Press, 1991); Lynn K. Stoner, *From Home to the Street: The Cuban Women's Movement for Legal Reform, 1898–1940* (Durham: Duke University Press, 1991); Susan K. Besse, *Restructuring Patriarchy: The Modernization of Gender Inequality in Brazil, 1914–1940* (Chapel Hill: University of North Carolina Press, 1996).

15 "Beach Scenes," *New Dawn*, October 1941, 20.

16 "Supplement to Section I." Not only American males betrayed this exoticizing orientation toward Trinidadian society. See Helen Follett, *Islands on Guard* (New York: Scribner's, 1943), 153.

17 For a discussion of Europeans who, in the Caribbean, "suffer tropicalization" and subsequently "go native," see Mimi Sheller, *Consuming the Caribbean: From Arawaks to Zombies* (London: Routledge, 2003), 118.

18 The concept of "moral topography" is taken most immediately from Peter Wade, *Blackness and Race Mixture: The Dynamics of Racial Identity in Colombia* (Baltimore: Johns Hopkins University Press, 1993), 56.

19 Martin Torrence, "This Is Inside Trinidad," *Esquire*, August 1941, 38.

20 "Waller Cruise News," *TNT*, January 1, 1943.

21 "White Lies," *TNT*, January 1, 1942.

22 "Humor," *TNT*, September 15, 1942.

23 Quote comes from a study of U.S. soldiers in wartime Hawaii. See Beth Bailey and David Farber, *The First Strange Place: The Alchemy of Race and Sex in World War II Hawaii* (New York: Free Press, 1992), 196.

24 *TNT*, July 18, 1942.

25 Letter by Mrs. E. F. Smallwood to U.S. consul, August 25, 1942, RG 84, box 30, NA.

26 The phrase comes from Cynthia Enloe, "It Takes Two," in *Let the Good Times*

Roll: Prostitution and the United States Military in Asia, ed. Saundra Sturdevant and Brenda Stoltzfus (New York: New Press, 1992), 22–38.

27   Stoler, *Carnal Knowledge*, 7.

28   U.S. Commander General Ralph Talbot, for example, advised the War Department against sending troops from the U.S. South for fear that they would "fraternize" with nonwhite Trinidadian women and, as a result, wound local sensibilities. See Johnson, *History of the Trinidad Sector*, 75.

29   Ben Bosquet and Colin Douglas, *West Indian Women at War: British Racism in World War II* (London: Lawrence and Wishart, 1991), 66. In a similar vein, two decades later in Vietnam, white soldiers would be warned not to "flaunt" their relationships with local women. See Harry Maurer, *Strange Ground: An Oral History of Americans in Vietnam, 1945–1975* (New York: H. Holt, 1989), 104.

30   James C. Shoulz, *History of the Trinidad Sector and Base Command*, vol. 5, *International Relations* (Washington D.C.: Department of the Army, 1947), 136.

31   Walter Weisbecker, "Mrs. Fahey Honored," *TNT*, August 15, 1942.

32   Surnames of senior hostesses included De la Bastide, Hart, Tardieu, and Pantin. See, for example, "News from the Bases," *TG*, February 24, 1942, and "Talk of Trinidad," *TG*, June 9, 1942.

33   "Dating Bureau," *TNT*, March 1, 1942.

34   Shoulz, *History of Trinidad*, 5:142.

35   See, for example, wedding announcements for Carmen D'heureaux and Mr. Elmer Rice, "Trinidad Girl Weds American," *SG*, September 13, 1942; Lt. William Kennedy and Theresa Marie Scheult, "US Officer to Wed Here," *SG*, January 17, 1943; and William Dennis Rogers and Theresa Mary Mendes, "Weddings," *SG*, March 29, 1942.

36   Ralph De Boissiere, *Rum and Coca-Cola* (Melbourne, 1956; reprint, London: Allison & Busby, 1984), 95.

37   Ibid., 96.

38   Ibid.

39   For more on antimiscegenation laws in the twentieth-century United States, see Peggy Pascoe, "Miscegenation Laws, Court Cases, and Ideologies of Race in Twentieth-Century America," in Hodes, *Sex, Love, Race*, 464–90.

40   Maj. Gen. Pratt to U.S. Consul, June 22, 1942, RG 84, box 30, NA.

41   Reynolds, *Rich Relations*, 276.

42   Rear Admiral Oldendorf to U.S. Consul, September 12, 1942, RG 84, box 30, NA.

43   "Marriage Ban Is Yet Another False Rumour," *TG*, October 22, 1942; "Marriage," *POSG*, October 21, 1942. While the *Port of Spain Gazette* did allude to the "color bar" in considering the army's marriage policy, the paper did not elaborate on the race issue. Moreover, its traditionally pious editorial line led it to support the army's position, with the editor charging that many of these marriages between visitors and local women were simply "illicit conveniences" and thus insupportable.

44   "Marriages Not to Be Banned," *SG*, October 25, 1942.

45   Rev. Ed Farrell to U.S. Consul, November 22, 1942, RG 84, box 30, NA. The couple got married anyway on March 7, 1943, and their daughter was born on August 17.

46   "Cipriani Defends Food Controller," *TG*, May 9, 1943.

47   Letter to the editor, *TG*, May 16, 1943.

48   Acting Governor to Secretary of State, April 9, 1942, CO 968 16/2. According to military historian Ulysses Lee, U.S. military officials figured that because of their racial constitution, black servicemen were particularly fit for the Caribbean's tropical climate. Further reflecting the dubious racial temper of the times, these officials, Lee also points out, were convinced that blacks were inefficient soldiers and thus best used in the inactive Caribbean theater, while white soldiers were relocated to other fronts fighting the decisive battles. See Lee, *The Employment of Negro Troops* (Washington, D.C.: Center of Military History, U.S. Army, 1994), 428.

49   Shoulz, *History of Trinidad*, 5:234.

50   See, for example, "Ack Acks Give $200 to Neediest Fund," *SG*, December 13, 1942.

51   "Trinidad Born United States Soldier Buys War Bond," *TG*, July 15, 1942.

52   "Rapsey Rhythm," *TNT*, December 1, 1942.

53   "Jive from a Bee Hive," *TNT*, January 1, 1943.

54   "Laventille News Meal," *TNT*, February 15, 1943.

55   "Laventille News Meal," *TNT*, December 1, 1942.

56   Gordon Rohlehr, *Calypso and Society in Pre-Independence Trinidad* (Port of Spain: G. Rohlehr, 1990), 345.

57   "Rapsey Rapsey-Dees," *TNT*, December 1, 1942.

58   "Jive from a Bee Hive."

59   Some marriages, for example, might have been prompted by the couple's desire to legitimize offspring. This is suggested in some records of marriages and childbirths. In many cases, the child's date of birth is much less than nine months after the date of marriage. See Reports from Foreign Service Posts, 1944, RG 84, box 41, NA.

60   Wenger to Taft, June 7, 1943, RG 338, box 165, NA.

61   "Rapsey Rapsey-Dees," *TNT*, December 15, 1942.

62   "Laventille News Meal," *TNT*, December 1, 1942.

63   "Rapsey Rapsey-Dees," *TNT*, December 15, 1942.

64   "Rapsey Rhythm," *TNT*, December 15, 1942.

65   This description is based on several reports: "American Soldiers in Disturbance," *POSG*, April 18, 1943; "Petition Sent to Mayor about US Troops," *TG*, April 22, 1943; Port of Spain City Council minutes, April 22, May 27, 1943, Port of Spain, Trinidad; and Governor Clifford to Secretary of State, May 14, 1943, FO 371 34107. For a secondary reference, see Annette Palmer, "Black American Soldiers in Trinidad: Wartime Politics in a Colonial Society," *Journal of Imperial and Commonwealth History* 14 (September 1986): 203–18.

66   "Five Soldiers Guilty in Laventille Trial," *TG*, June 16, 1943. That this episode

evinced conflict across the gender line within the Laventille community was suggested by the tendency of male dwellers to mercilessly malign black American soldiers while females came forward to defend them. Beatrice Sweeney, for example, corroborated three of the soldiers' alibis that they had been at a party in Port of Spain on the night in question. See "Alibi Defense in Riot Trial," *TG*, June 11, 1943.

67 "Laventille Man Jailed Assaulting US Soldier," *TG*, June 16, 1943.

68 "Alibi Defense in Riot Trial."

69 "Laventille Riot Echo," *POSG*, July 1, 1943.

70 "Charges of Rioting Fail," *POSG*, July 2, 1943.

71 In the mid-1960s, Mano Benjamin, who was then living in a village in central Trinidad called Biche, became frighteningly infamous when he was found guilty of torturing two young sisters. He would be popularly demonized as the "Beast of Biche," and decades later (when I was growing up), one whisper of the name "Mano" was enough to scare us children back into the house. See "Pauper's Funeral for 'Beast of Biche,'" *Trinidad Express*, March 3, 1998.

72 Take the case of George Blake, a local man who in late 1940 boldly assaulted his wife in a court where he was charged with failing to provide for her financially. Though committed in the magistrate's presence, Blake's assault earned him no more than a stern reprimand and a $10 fine. A year later, another Port of Spain man who beat up his wife for dating an American soldier was made to pay only $2.50. See "$10 Fine and Warning for Assaulting Wife in Court," *TG*, October 22, 1940. Most poignantly, perhaps, when Christopher Turton stabbed to death his wife who had taken up with an American man during the early months of the occupation, the jury recommended "strong mercy" and influenced the judge to let Turton off with a seven-year sentence. See "Jury Returns Verdict of Manslaughter," *TG*, February 5, 1942. Thus however jarring it might seem to our ears, the Lord Kitchener calypso in which a local man cuckolded by a visiting "Yankee man" promises to physically punish his woman ("ah going to beat yuh") would have struck the average listener in occupied Trinidad as unremarkable. Kitchener's composition would have seemed a tuneful fiction that strayed little from the social facts.

73 "Five Soldiers Guilty in Laventille Riot Trial."

74 This is a point stressed in the important work by Gail Hershatter, *Dangerous Pleasures: Prostitution and Modernity in Twentieth Century Shanghai* (Berkeley: University of California Press, 1997), esp. introduction.

75 There are, though, signs of change. See Kamala Kempadoo, *Sexing the Caribbean: Gender, Race, and Sexual Labor* (New York: Routledge, 2004). For insight regarding the trends and issues within scholarship on prostitution, see Timothy Gilfoyle, "Prostitutes in History: From Parables of Pornography to Metaphors of Modernity," *American Historical Review* 104 (February 1999): 117–41. For Latin America and the Caribbean, important works on the subject include Eileen J. Suarez Findlay, *Imposing Decency: The Politics of Sexuality and Race*

in Puerto Rico, 1870–1920 (Durham: Duke University Press, 1999); Sueann
Caulfield, *In Defense of Honor: Sexual Morality, Modernity, and Nation in Early
Twentieth-Century Brazil* (Durham: Duke University Press, 2000); and Guy, *Sex
and Danger in Buenos Aires.*

76 Arthur Calder-Marshall, *Glory Dead* (London: M. Joseph, 1939), 45.

77 Report of West Indian Royal Commission, 1945, 481, Cmd. 6607, Parliamentary Papers, British Library, London (Moyne Report), 543.

78 For the nineteenth century, see Franco, " 'Unruly Woman.' "

79 Wenger to Taft, June 7, 1943, RG 338, box 165, NA.

80 The evidence in newspapers is overwhelming, especially for late 1942 and
1943. See, for example, "Cumuto Man Gets 12 Months," *TG*, April 9, 1943;
court brief, *TG*, May 1, 1943; letter to editor, *TG*, May 19, 1943; court brief
TG, May 20, 1943; letter to the editor, *TG*, June 1, 1943; "15 Women in Bawdy
House Case," *SG*, August 8, 1943; and "San Juan Bawdy House Case Opens,"
SG, June 5, 1943.

81 "Park Street Jam," *TG*, April 9, 1942.

82 Letter to the editor, *TG*, October 26, 1943.

83 "Wrightson Road Demand Police Action," *TG*, October 26, 1944; see also
"Police Plan Special Action for Woodbrook Nuisance," *TG*, October 31, 1944.

84 Minutes of Arima City Council, January 6, 1942, Arima, Trinidad.

85 "Drastic Measures," *POSG*, November 12, 1942. Drivers also had to put up with
police officers, who now had the right to withhold or cancel their licenses on
the spot. Drivers' integral involvement in the business of sex in occupied Trinidad helps to account for the numerous clashes between them and American
soldiers.

86 "Plans to Combat Social Disease Here," *TG*, August 22, 1941, and "Councilors
Comment on Rat Nuisance in City," *TG*, August 22, 1941.

87 "White Slavery Must Be Stamped Out," *Vanguard*, February 20, 1943.

88 Henry Field, "US Problems in Trinidad," March 8–30, 1942, RG 43, box 57, NA.

89 *TNT*, June 12, 1942.

90 Quote comes from Torrence, "This Is Inside Trinidad." See, too, "History of
Medical Department Activities: Preventative Medicine," RG 338, box 3, NA.
According to this document, "The morale of the local colored females being
apparently low, and prostitution flourishing, the opportunity for sexual contacts
[for soldiers] was great."

91 Wenger was paired with British official Donald Williams. See "VD Specialists
Appointed to Tackle Growing Menace Here," *TG*, March 3, 1943. Wenger was
associated with the progressive movement and had been involved in this work
in Atlanta and Chicago. For more on his past, see Suzanne Poirier, *Chicago's
War on Syphilis, 1937–1940: The Times, the Trib, and the Clap Doctor* (Urbana:
University of Illinois Press, 1995).

92 "U.S. Government Policy on V.D. Control in the Caribbean," October 1943, RG
338, box 165, NA.

93 Wenger to Taft.

94 Ibid.

95 Ibid.

96 Jean De Boissiere, "Very Public School," *Picong*, n.d. Sa Gomes was and remains a major Port of Spain merchandise establishment.

97 Jean De Boissiere, "Glamorous Gomes," *Callaloo*, November 1945, 5.

98 Ibid.

99 "Behind the Curtain," *SG*, December 25, 1943.

100 "Behind the Curtain: That Trinidad Will Never Return," *SG*, November 28, 1943.

101 "Behind the Curtain," *SG*, October 1, 1944.

102 Ibid.

103 For more on Gomes's sense that Trinidad had become a place of "chaos and confusion," see "Behind the Curtain," *SG*, December 15, 1945.

104 De Boissiere, *Rum and Coca-Cola*.

105 Ibid., 11.

106 Ibid., 195.

107 Doris Sommer, *Foundational Fictions: The National Romances of Latin America* (Berkeley: University of California Press, 1991).

CODA

1 This story has been well documented. See Ivar Oxaal, *Black Intellectuals Come to Power: The Rise of Creole Nationalism in Trinidad and Tobago* (Cambridge, Mass.: Schenkman, 1968); Selwyn Ryan, *Race and Nationalism in Trinidad and Tobago: A Study of Decolonization in a Multiracial Society* (Toronto: University of Toronto Press, 1972); Bridget Brereton, *A History of Modern Trinidad, 1783–1962* (Exeter, N.H.: Heinemann, 1981); Cary Fraser, *Ambivalent Anti-Colonialism: The United States and the Genesis of West Indian Independence, 1940–1964* (Westport, Conn.: Greenwood Press, 1994); and Kirk Meighoo, *Politics in a "Half Made" Society: Trinidad and Tobago, 1925–2000* (Kingston: Ian Randle, 2003).

2 C. L. R. James, *The Black Jacobins: Toussaint L'Ouverture and the San Domingo Revolution* (New York: Vintage, 1963), 412.

3 Oxaal, *Black Intellectuals*, 131.

4 For more on the context surrounding the 1956 elections, see Ryan, *Race and Nationalism*, 154–64, and Meighoo, *Politics*, 35–44.

5 Eric Williams, *Forged from the Love of Liberty: The Selected Speeches of Dr. Eric Williams* (Port of Spain: Longman Caribbean, 1981), 308.

6 For Williams's legendary performances in the square, see Oxaal, *Black Intellectuals*, 98.

7 Williams, *Forged*, 314.

8 Oxaal, *Black Intellectuals*, 131; Brereton, *History*, 243.

9 Oxaal, *Black Intellectuals*, 129. The claim that Young was "slightly touched" was

made by an official in the Colonial Office as Young's removal from the governorship was under discussion. See Lord Moyne to Foreign Office, February 19, 1942, CO 967/135.

10 David Scott, *Conscripts of Modernity: The Tragedy of Colonial Enlightenment* (Durham: Duke University Press, 2004), 123.

11 James, *Black Jacobins*, 412.

12 The reference here is to James's book-length manuscript completed in 1950, "Notes on American Civilization," which was eventually published as *American Civilization* (Cambridge, Mass.: Blackwell, 1993). Lamming openly acknowledges the debt to James. See David Scott, "The Sovereignty of the Imagination: An Interview with George Lamming," *Small Axe* 12 (March 2002): 112.

13 C. L. R. James, *Mariners, Renegades, and Castaways: The Story of Herman Melville and the World We Live In* (Hanover, N.H.: University Press of New England, 2001).

14 George Lamming, *The Pleasures of Exile* (London, 1960; reprint, Ann Arbor: University of Michigan Press, 1992), 152. In 1955 Lamming lived in New York, and in this work he wrote wryly about Emmett Till, the boy who "raped a woman by looking at her longer than she thought necessary and appropriate" (204).

15 Ibid., 152.

16 Ibid., 154.

17 Ibid.

18 Ibid., "Introduction to 1984 edition."

Bibliography

ARCHIVAL SOURCES

England

Parliamentary Papers, British Library, London
  Report by the Parliamentary Undersecretary, the Hon. E. F. L. Wood, on His Visit
    to the West Indies and British Guiana, 1921, Cmd. 1679
  Report of Major G. St. J. Orde-Browne on Labor Conditions in the West Indies,
    1939, Cmd. 6070
  Report of the Commission of Enquiry in to the Trinidad and Tobago Disturbances,
    1937, 1938, Cmd. 5641
  Report of the West Indian Royal Commission, 1945, Cmd. 6607 (Moyne Report)
  West Indian Commission on Education, 1932, Cmd. 5641
Public Records Office, Kew Gardens, London
  Colonial Office Records
  CO 295, Trinidad Original Correspondence
  CO 950, West India Royal Commission, 1938–39
  CO 967, Colonial Office Private Papers Semiofficial and Personal
  Correspondence between the Secretary of State and Sir Hubert Young and Sir
    Bede Clifford, Governors
  CO 971, United States Bases Original Correspondence
  Foreign Office Records
  FO 371, Foreign Office, Political Departments, General Correspondence

Trinidad

Government Publications, University of the West Indies, St. Augustine
  Colonial Paper 23, Correspondence on the Subject of Agriculture Between the
    Government of Trinidad and Tobago and the Comptroller for Development
    and Welfare, British West Indies, 1942
  Colonial Paper 54, Correspondence on the Asphalt Concession, 1887
  Colonial Paper 88, Report of the Wages Advisory Board, 1936
  Hansard, 1930–1947 (Debates in the Trinidad and Tobago Legislative Council)

Report of the Mayor of Port of Spain, Port of Spain, 1943

Report of Agricultural Policy Committee of Trinidad and Tobago, Port of Spain, 1943

Trinidad and Tobago Census, Port of Spain, 1946

United States

Government Publications

Foerster, Robert F. *The Racial Problems Involved in Immigration from Latin America and the West Indies to the United States, a Report Submitted to the Secretary of Labor by Robert F. Foerster*. Washington, D.C.: Government Printing Office, 1925.

National Archives, College Park, Maryland

Consular Despatches from Trinidad, West Indies, microfilm, T 138

Record Group 43, Records of International Conferences, Commissions, and Expositions

Record Group 59, General Records of the Department of State

Record Group 84, Records of Foreign Service Posts

Record Group 165, Records of the War Department General and Special Staff

Record Group 226, Records of the Office of Strategic Services

Record Group 338, Files of the Antilles Department

Record Group 339, Caribbean Defense Command

Office of the Chief of Military History, Department of the Army, Washington, D.C.

Johnson, Robert. *History of the Trinidad Sector and Base Command*. Vol. 1. Washington, D.C.: Department of the Army, 1945.

Shoulz, James C. *History of the Trinidad Sector and Base Command*. Vol. 5, *International Relations*. Washington, D.C.: Department of the Army, 1947.

NEWSPAPERS AND JOURNALS

Argos

Beacon

Callaloo

Caribbee

Daily Mirror

East Indian Weekly

Evening News

The Indian

Labor Leader

The Mirror

New Dawn

Observer

People

Picong

Port of Spain Gazette

San Fernando Gazette

Sport and Music Cavalcade

Sunday Times and Sporting Chronicle

Teachers Herald

Trinidad Guardian

Trinidadian

Trinidad News Tips

INTERVIEWS

Holder, Boscoe, interview by author, Port of Spain, Trinidad, March 8, 1999
Ifill, Max, interview by author, Port of Spain, Trinidad, February 25, 1999
Lalla, Alfred, interview by author, Arima, Trinidad, August 9, 1998
Lewis, O'Neil, interview by author, Port of Spain, Trinidad, March 15, 1999
Thomas, Frank, interview by author, Queens, N.Y., June 5, 1998

PUBLISHED SOURCES

Books and Parts of Books

Accaria-Zavala, Diane, and Rodolfo Popelnik, eds. *Prospero's Isles: The Presence of the Caribbean in the American Imaginary.* New York: Oxford University Press, 2004.
Achong, Tito. *Report of the Mayor of Port of Spain.* Boston: Meador, 1943.
Ahye, Molly. *The Cradle of the Caribbean Dance: Beryl McBurnie and the Little Carib Theatre.* Port of Spain: Heritage Cultures, 1983.
Anderson, Benedict. *Imagined Communities: Reflections on the Origin and Spread of Nationalism.* New York: Verso, 1983.
Antoni, Robert. *My Grandmother's Erotic Folktales.* New York: Grove Press, 2000.
Appadurai, Arjun. *Modernity at Large: Cultural Dimensions of Globalization.* Minneapolis: University of Minnesota Press, 1996.
Appelbaum, Nancy P., Anne S. Macpherson, and Karin Alejandra Rosemblatt, eds. *Race and Nation in Modern Latin America.* Chapel Hill: University of North Carolina Press, 2003.
Arnold, Ralph, George A. Macready, and Thomas W. Barrington. *The First Big Oil Hunt: Venezuela, 1911–1916.* New York: Vantage Press, 1960.
Asante, S. K. B. *Pan-African Protest: West Africa and the Italo-Ethiopian Crisis, 1934–1941.* London: Longman, 1977.
Bailey, Beth, and David Farber. *The First Strange Place: The Alchemy of Race and Sex in World War II Hawaii.* New York: Free Press, 1992.
Ballhatchet, Kenneth. *Race, Sex, and Class under the Raj: Imperial Attitudes and Policies and Their Critics, 1793–1905.* New York: St. Martin's Press, 1980.
Banerjee, Sumanta. *Under the Raj: Prostitution in Colonial Bengal.* New York: Monthly Review Press, 2000.
Baptiste, Fitzroy. *War, Cooperation, and Conflict: The European Possessions in the Caribbean, 1939–1945.* New York: Greenwood Press, 1988.
Barber Asphalt Paving Co. *Genuine Trinidad Asphalt: The Standard Pavement of America.* Washington, D.C.: Barber Asphalt Paving Co., 1885.
Bardaglio, Peter W. *Reconstructing the Household: Families, Sex, and the Law in the Nineteenth-Century South.* Chapel Hill: University of North Caroline Press, 1995.
Barkan, Elazar, and Ronald Bush. *Prehistories of the Future: The Primitivist Project and the Culture of Modernism.* Stanford: Stanford University Press, 1995.

Bederman, Gail. *Manliness and Civilization: A Cultural History of Gender and Race in the United States, 1880–1917*. Chicago: University of Chicago Press, 1995.

Bellour, Hélène, Kim Johnson, and Milla Riggio. *Renegades: The History of the Renegades Steel Orchestra of Trinidad and Tobago*. Oxford: Macmillan Caribbean, 2002.

Berger, Mark T. *Under Northern Eyes: Latin American Studies and U.S. Hegemony in the Americas, 1898–1990*. Bloomington: Indiana University Press, 1995.

Bergquist, Charles. *Labor and the Course of American Democracy: U.S. History in Latin American Perspective*. New York: Verso, 1996.

Besse, Susan K. *Restructuring Patriarchy: The Modernization of Gender Inequality in Brazil, 1914–1940*. Chapel Hill: University of North Carolina Press, 1996.

Bhabha, Homi K. *The Location of Culture*. London: Routledge, 1994.

———, ed. *Nation and Narration*. London: Routledge, 1990.

Bickerton, Derek. *The Murders of Boysie Singh: Robber, Arsonist, Pirate, Mass-Murderer, Vice and Gambling King of Trinidad*. London: A. Barker, 1962.

Billig, Michael. *Banal Nationalism*. London: Sage, 1995.

Birth, Kevin. *Any Time Is Trinidad Time: Social Meaning and Temporal Consciousness*. Gainesville: University Press of Florida, 1999.

Blackburn, Robin, *The Overthrow of Colonial Slavery, 1776–1848*. London: Verso, 1988.

Blanshard, Paul. *Democracy and Empire in the Caribbean: A Contemporary Review*. New York: Macmillan, 1947.

Bliss, Katherine Elaine. *Compromised Positions: Prostitution, Public Health, and Gender Politics in Revolutionary Mexico City*. University Park: Pennsylvania State University Press, 2001.

Bolland, Nigel O. *On the March: Labour Rebellions in the British Caribbean, 1934–39*. London: James Currey, 1995.

Bonnell, Victoria E., and Lynn Hunt, eds. *Beyond the Cultural Turn: New Directions in the Study of Society and Culture*. Berkeley: University of California Press, 1999.

Bosquet, Ben, and Colin Douglas. *West Indian Women at War: British Racism in World War II*. London: Lawrence and Wishart, 1991.

Brading, David. *First America: The Spanish Monarchy, Creole Patriots, and the Liberal States, 1492–1867*. New York: Cambridge University Press, 1991.

Braithwaite, Lloyd. *Social Stratification*. Kingston: Institute of Social and Economic Research, University of the West Indies, 1975.

Brereton, Bridget. "The Birthday of Our Race: A Social History of Emancipation Day in Trinidad, 1838–88." In *Essays Presented to Douglas Hall: Trade, Government, and Society in Caribbean History, 1700–1920*, edited by B. W. Higman, 69–83. Kingston: Heinemann Educational Books Caribbean, 1983.

———. "Family Strategies, Gender, and the Shift to Wage Labour in the British Caribbean." In *The Colonial Caribbean in Transition: Essays on Postemanciaption Social and Cultural History*, edited by Bridget Brereton and Kevin A. Yelvington, 67–99. Gainesville: University Press of Florida, 1999.

———. *A History of Modern Trinidad, 1783–1962*. Exeter, N.H.: Heinemann, 1981.

———. *Race Relations in Colonial Trinidad, 1870–1900*. Cambridge: Cambridge University Press, 1979.

———. "White Elites in Trinidad, 1838–1950." In *The White Minority in the Caribbean*, edited by Howard Johnson and Karl Watson, 87–138. Princeton, N.J.: Wiener, 1998.

Brock, Lisa, and Digna Castañeda Fuertes. *Between Race and Empire: African-Americans and Cubans before the Cuban Revolution*. Philadelphia: Temple University Press, 1998.

Brown, Wenzell. *Angry Men, Laughing Men: The Caribbean Caldron*. New York: Greenburg, 1947.

Buckridge, Steeve. *The Language of Dress: Resistance and Accommodation in Jamaica, 1760–1890*. Kingston: University of the West Indies Press, 2004.

Burkett, Algernon. *Trinidad: A Jewel of the West, or 100 Years of British Rule*. London: Francis & Co., 1914.

Butler, Kim. *Freedoms Given, Freedoms Won: Afro Brazilians in Post-Abolition Sao Paulo and Salvador*. New Brunswick, N.J.: Rutgers University Press, 1998.

Calder, Bruce. *The Impact of Intervention: The Dominican Republic during the U.S. Occupation of 1916–1924*. Austin: University of Texas Press, 1984.

Calder-Marshall, Arthur. *Glory Dead*. London: M. Joseph, 1939.

Campbell, Carl. *The Young Colonials: A Social History of Education in Trinidad and Tobago, 1834–1962*. Barbados: University of the West Indies Press, 1996.

Cardoso, Enrique, and Enzo Faletto. *Dependency and Development in Latin America*. Trans. Marjory Mattingly Urquidi. Berkeley: University of California Press, 1978.

Caulfield, Sueann. *In Defense of Honor: Sexual Morality, Modernity, and Nation in Early Twentieth-Century Brazil*. Durham: Duke University Press, 2000.

Chaney, Elsa M., and Mary Garcia Castro, eds. *Muchachas No More: Household Workers in Latin America and the Caribbean*. Philadelphia: Temple University Press, 1989.

Chang, Carlisle. "Painting in Trinidad." In *The Artist in West Indian Society: A Symposium*, edited by Errol Hill, 37–55. St. Augustine: University of the West Indies, n.d. [ca. 1964].

Chatterjee, Partha. *Nationalist Thought and the Colonial World: A Derivative Discourse?* London: Zed Books, 1986.

———. *The Nation and Its Fragments: Colonial and Postcolonial Histories*. Princeton, N.J.: Princeton University Press, 1993.

Chen, Percy. *China Called Me: My Life inside the Chinese Revolution*. Boston: Little Brown, 1978.

Chen, Si-lan. *Footnotes to History*. New York: Dance Horizons, 1981.

Clifford, Bede. *The Honorable Sir Bede Clifford, Proconsul: Being Incidents in the Life and Career of the Honorable Bede Clifford*. London: Evans Bros., 1964.

Comaroff, Jean, and John Comaroff. *Of Revelation and Revolution: Christianity, Colonialism, and Consciousness in South Africa*. Chicago: University of Chicago Press, 1991.

Constantine, Stephen. *The Making of British Colonial Policy, 1914–1940*. London: Cass, 1984.

Cooper, Frederick. *Colonialism in Question: Theory, Knowledge, History*. Berkeley: University of California Press, 2005.

————. *Decolonization and African Society: The Labor Question in French and British Africa*. New York: Cambridge University Press, 1996.

Cooper, Frederick, and Ann Laura Stoler, eds. *Tensions of Empire: Colonial Cultures in a Bourgeois World*. Berkeley: University of California Press, 1997.

Coronil, Fernando. *The Magical State: Nature, Money, and Modernity in Venezuela*. Chicago: University of Chicago Press, 1997.

Corrigan, Philip, and Derek Sayer. *The Great Arch: English State Formation as Cultural Revolution*. New York: Blackwell, 1985.

Cowley, John. *Carnival, Canboulay, and Calypso: Traditions in the Making*. Cambridge: Cambridge University Press, 1996.

Craig, Hewan. *The Legislative Council of Trinidad and Tobago*. London: Faber & Faber, 1952.

Craig, Susan. *Smiles and Blood: Ruling Class Response to the Workers' Rebellion of 1937 in Trinidad and Tobago*. London: New Beacon, 1988.

Cudjoe, Selwyn R. *Beyond Boundaries: The Intellectual Tradition of Trinidad and Tobago in the Nineteenth Century*. Amherst: University of Massachusetts Press, 2003.

————. *V. S. Naipaul: A Materialist Reading*. Amherst: University of Massachusetts Press, 1988.

Cummins, Alissandra, Allison Thompson, and Nick Whittle. *Art in Barbados: What Kind of Mirror Image?* Kingston: Ian Randle, 1998.

Cunard, Nancy. *Negro Anthology, Made by Nancy Cunard, 1931–1933*. London: Wishart & Co., 1934.

Dash, J. Michael. *The Other America: Caribbean Literature in a New World Context*. Charlottesville: University Press of Virginia, 1998.

De Boissiere, Jean. *Land of Rising Inflexion*. Trinidad: Fraser's Printerie, [ca. 1943].

De Boissiere, Ralph. *Crown Jewel*. Melbourne: Australasian Book Society, 1956.

————. *Rum and Coca-Cola*. Melbourne, 1956. Reprint, London: Allison & Busby, 1984.

De Grazia, Victoria. *Irresistible Empire: America's Advance through Twentieth-Century Europe*. Cambridge, Mass.: Belknap Press of Harvard University Press, 2005.

De Leon, Raphael. *Calypso from France to Trinidad: 800 Years of History*. Port of Spain: Imprint Books, 1988.

Diffie, Bailey W., and Justine Whitfield Diffie. *Porto Rico: A Broken Pledge*. New York: Vanguard, 1931.

Doherty, Thomas. *Pre-Code Hollywood: Sex, Immorality, and Insurrection in American Cinema, 1930–1934*. New York: Columbia University Press, 1999.

Dubois, Laurent. *Avengers of the New World: The Story of the Haitian Revolution*. Cambridge, Mass.: Belknap Press of Harvard University Press, 2004.

Dudziak, Mary L. *Cold War Civil Rights: Race and the Image of American Democracy*. Princeton, N.J.: Princeton University Press, 2000.

Eddy, John, and Deryck Schreuder. *The Rise of Colonial Nationalism: Australia, New Zealand, Canada, and South Africa First Assert Their Nationalities*. Boston: Allen & Unwin, 1988.

Edmondson, Belinda. *Making Men: Gender, Literary Authority, and Women's Writing in Caribbean Narrative*. Durham: Duke University Press, 1999.

Edwards, Brent Hayes. *The Practice of Diaspora: Literature, Translation, and the Rise of Black Internationalism*. Cambridge, Mass.: Harvard University Press, 2003.

Elder, J. D. *From Congo Drum to Steelband: A Sociohistorical Account of the Emergence and Evolution of the Trinidad Steel Orchestra*. St. Augustine: University of the West Indies Press, 1969.

Eley, Geoff, and Ronald Grigor Suny, eds. *Becoming National: A Reader*. New York: Oxford University Press, 1996.

Enloe, Cynthia. *Making Feminist Sense of International Politics*. Berkeley: University of California Press, 1990.

Espinet, Charles, and Harry Pitts. *Land of the Calypso: The Origin and Development of Trinidad's Folk Song*. Port of Spain: Guardian Commercial Printery, 1944.

Fanon, Frantz. *The Wretched of the Earth*. New York: Grove Press, 1963.

Farred, Grant, ed. *Rethinking C. L. R. James*. Oxford: Blackwell, 1996.

Fermor, Patrick Leigh. *The Traveler's Tree: A Journey through the Caribbean Islands*. London: J. Murray, 1950.

Ferrer, Ada. *Insurgent Cuba: Race, Nation, and Revolution, 1868–1898*. Chapel Hill: University of North Carolina Press, 1999.

Fillin-Yeh, Susan, ed. *Dandies: Fashion and Finesse in Art and Culture*. New York: New York University Press, 2001.

Findlay, Eileen J. Suarez. *Imposing Decency: The Politics of Sexuality and Race in Puerto Rico, 1870–1920*. Durham: Duke University Press, 1999.

Finkelstein, Joanne. *Fashion: An Introduction*. New York: New York University Press, 1996.

Follett, Helen. *Islands on Guard*. New York: Scribner's, 1943.

Foulkes, Julia L. *Modern Bodies: Dance and American Modernism from Martha Graham to Alvin Ailey*. Chapel Hill: University of North Carolina Press, 2002.

Fraser, Cary. *Ambivalent Anti-Colonialism: The United States and the Genesis of West Indian Independence, 1940–1964*. Westport, Conn.: Greenwood Press, 1994.

Geyer, Michael, and Charles Bright. "Where in the World Is America? The History of the United States in a Global Age." In *Rethinking American History in a Global Age*, edited by Thomas Bender, 63–97. Berkeley: University of California Press, 2002.

Gikandi, Simon. *Maps of Englishness: Writing Identity in the Culture of Colonialism*. New York: Columbia University Press, 1996.

Gilroy, Paul. *"There Ain't No Black in the Union Jack": The Cultural Politics of Race and Nation*. London: Hutchinson Press, 1987.

Goedde, Petra. *GIs and Germans: Culture, Gender, and Foreign Relations, 1945–1949*. New Haven: Yale University Press, 2003.

Goldberg, Jonathan. *Tempest in the Caribbean*. Minneapolis: University of Minnesota Press, 2004.

Gomes, Albert. *All Papa's Children*. East Moseley, England: Cairi Publishing House, 1978.

————. *Through a Maze of Color.* Port of Spain: Key Caribbean Publications, 1975.

Guha, Ranajit, and Gayatri C. Spivak, eds. *Selected Subaltern Studies.* New York: Oxford University Press, 1988.

Guy, Donna. *Sex and Danger in Buenos Aires: Prostitution, Family, and Nation in Argentina.* Lincoln: University of Nebraska Press, 1991.

Hall, Catherine. *Civilising Subjects: Metropole and Colony in the English Imagination, 1830–1867.* Chicago: University of Chicago Press, 2002.

Hall, Stuart, Charles Critcher, Tony Jefferson, John Clarke, and Brian Robert. *Policing the Crisis: Mugging, the State, and Law and Order.* New York: Holmes & Meier, 1978.

Hanchard, Michael George. *Orpheus and Power: The Movimento Negro of Rio de Janeiro and Sao Paulo, Brazil, 1945–1988.* Princeton, N.J.: Princeton University Press, 1994.

Harley, Eugene J. *World-Wide Influences of Cinema.* Los Angeles: University of Southern California Press, 1940.

Harney, Stefano. *Nationalism and Identity: Culture and the Imagination in a Caribbean Diaspora.* Atlantic Highlands, N.J.: Zed Books, 1996.

Harris, Joseph E. *African-American Reactions to War in Ethiopia, 1936–1941.* Baton Rouge: Louisiana State University Press, 1994.

Harwich-Vallenilla, Nikita. *Asfalto y Revolución: La New York & Bermúdez Company.* Caracas: Fundación para el Rescate del Acervo Documental Venezolano, Monte Avila Editores, 1992.

Havinden, Michael, and David Meredith. *Colonialism and Development: Britain and Its Tropical Colonies, 1850–1960.* London: Routledge, 1993.

Healy, David. *Britain, 1832–1938.* Baltimore: Johns Hopkins University Press, 1992.

————. *Drive to Hegemony: The United States in the Caribbean, 1898–1917.* Madison: University of Wisconsin Press, 1988.

Hebdige, Dick. *Subculture: The Meaning of Style.* New York: Routledge, 1979.

Hendrickson, Hildi. *Clothing and Difference: Embodied Identities in Colonial and Post-Colonial Africa.* Durham: Duke University Press, 1996.

Hershatter, Gail. *Dangerous Pleasures: Prostitution and Modernity in Twentieth Century Shanghai.* Berkeley: University of California Press, 1997.

Herskovits, Melville, and Frances Herskovits. *Trinidad Village.* New York: Octagon, 1948.

Higman, B. W., ed. *Essays Presented to Douglas Hall: Trade, Government, and Society in Caribbean History, 1700–1920.* Kingston: Heinemann Educational Books Caribbean, 1983.

————. *General History of the Caribbean.* Vol. 6, *Methodology and Historiography of the Caribbean.* London: Macmillan Education, 1999.

————. *Writing West Indian Histories.* London: Macmillan Education, 1999.

Hill, Donald. *Calypso Callaloo: Early Carnival Music in Trinidad.* Gainesville: University of Florida Press, 1993.

————. "I Am Happy Just to Be in This Sweet Land of Liberty." In *Island Sounds in the Global City: Caribbean Popular Music and Identity in New York*, edited by Ray Allen and Lois Wilcken, 74–92. Urbana: University of Illinois Press, 1998.

Hill, Errol. *The Trinidad Carnival: Mandate for a National Theatre*. Austin: University of Texas Press, 1972.

———, ed. *The Artist in West Indian Society: A Symposium*. St. Augustine: University of the West Indies, n.d. [ca. 1964].

Hodes, Martha, ed. *Sex, Love, Race: Crossing Boundaries in North American History*. New York: New York University Press, 1999.

Höhn, Maria. *GIs and Fräuleins: The German-American Encounter in 1950s West Germany*. Chapel Hill: University of North Carolina Press, 2002.

Holder, Boscoe, and Geoffrey MacClean. *The Art of Boscoe Holder*. Port of Spain: MacClean Publishing, 1995.

Holt, Thomas, *The Problem of Freedom: Race, Labor, and Politics in Jamaica and Britain, 1832–1938*. Baltimore: Johns Hopkins University Press, 1992.

Huggins, George E. *A History of Trinidad Oil*. Port of Spain: Trinidad Express Newspapers, 1996.

Hulme, Peter, and William H. Sherman, eds. *The Tempest and Its Travels*. Philadelphia: University of Pennsylvania Press, 2000.

Hunt, Lynn. *Politics, Culture, and Class in the French Revolution*. Berkeley: University of California Press, 1984.

Hunter, Tera. *To 'Joy My Freedom: Southern Black Women's Lives and Labors after the Civil War*. Cambridge, Mass.: Harvard University Press, 1997.

Huxley, Aldous. *Brave New World*. New York: Perennial Classics, 1998.

Jackson, T. B., ed. *The Book of Trinidad*. Port of Spain: Muir Marshall, 1904.

Jackson Fossett, Judith, and Jeffrey A. Tucker, eds. *Race Consciousness: African-American Studies for the New Century*. New York: New York University Press, 1997.

James, C. L. R. *American Civilization*. Cambridge, Mass.: Blackwell, 1993.

———. *Beyond a Boundary*. 1963. Reprint, New York: Pantheon, 1984.

———. *The Black Jacobins: Toussaint L'Ouverture and the San Domingo Revolution*. New York: Vintage, 1963.

———. *Mariners, Renegades, and Castaways: The Story of Herman Melville and the World We Live In*. Hanover, N.H.: University Press of New England, 2001.

———. *Minty Alley*. London: New Beacon, 1971.

James, Winston. *Holding Aloft the Banner of Ethiopia: Caribbean Radicalism in Early Twentieth-Century America*. New York: Verso, 1998.

Jarvie, Ian. *Hollywood's Overseas Campaign: The North Atlantic Movie Trade, 1920–1950*. New York: Cambridge University Press, 1992.

Jayawardena, Kumari. *Feminism and Nationalism in the Third World*. London: Zed Books, 1986.

Jenks, Leland Hamilton. *Our Cuban Colony: A Study in Sugar*. New York: Vanguard, 1928.

Johnson, Howard, and Watson Karl, eds. *The White Minority in the Caribbean*. Princeton, N.J.: Wiener, 1998.

Jones, James H., *Bad Blood: The Tuskegee Syphilis Experiment*. New York: Free Press, 1981.

Joseph, Gilbert, ed. *Reclaiming the Political in Latin American History: Essays from the North*. Durham: Duke University Press, 2001.

——. *Revolution from Without: Yucatan, Mexico, and the United States, 1880–1924*. Cambridge: Cambridge University Press, 1982.

Joseph, Gilbert, and Daniel Nugent, eds. *Everyday Forms of State Formation: Revolution and the Negotiation of Rule in Modern Mexico*. Durham: Duke University Press, 1994.

Joseph, Gilbert M., Catherine Le Grand, and Ricardo D. Salvatore, eds. *Close Encounters of Empire: Writing the Cultural History of U.S.–Latin American Relations*. Durham: Duke University Press, 1998.

Kaplan, Amy, and David Pease, eds. *Cultures of United States Imperialism*. Durham: Duke University Press, 1993.

Kelley, Robin D. G. *Race Rebels: Culture, Politics, and the Black Working Class*. New York: Free Press, 1994.

——. *Yo' Mama's Disfunktional! Fighting the Culture Wars in Urban America*. Boston: Beacon Press, 1997.

Kempadoo, Kamala. *Sexing the Caribbean: Gender, Race, and Sexual Labor*. New York: Routledge, 2004.

Khan, Aisha. *Callaloo Nation: Metaphors of Race and Religious Identity among South Asians in Trinidad*. Durham: Duke University Press, 2004.

Klubock, Thomas Miller. *Contested Communities: Class, Gender, and Politics in Chile's El Teniente Copper Mine, 1904–1951*. Durham: Duke University Press, 1998.

Knight, Franklin, *The Caribbean: Genesis of a Fragmented Nationalism*. New York: Oxford University Press, 1990.

Knight, Melvin. *The Americans in Santo Domingo*. New York: Vanguard, 1928.

Kroes, Rob, R. W. Rydell, D. F. J. Bosscher, and John F. Sears, eds. *Cultural Transmissions and Receptions: American Mass Culture in Europe*. Amsterdam: VU University Press, 1993.

Kuchta, David. "The Making of the Self-Made Man: Class, Clothing, and English Masculinity, 1688–1832." In *The Sex of Things*, edited by Victoria de Grazia, with Ellen Furlough, 54–78. Berkeley: University of California Press, 1996.

Kuisel, Richard. *Seducing the French: The Dilemma of Americanization*. Berkeley: University of California Press, 1993.

Kutzinski, Vera. *Sugar Secrets: Race and the Erotics of Cuban Nationalism*. Charlottesville: University Press of Virginia, 1993.

La Feber, Walter. *The New Empire: An Economic Interpretation of American Expansionism, 1860–98*. Ithaca: Cornell University Press, 1963.

Lamming, George. *The Pleasures of Exile*. London, 1960. Reprint, Ann Arbor: University of Michigan Press, 1992.

Lamont, Norman. *Problems of Trinidad: A Collection of Speeches and Writings*. 1932. Reprint, Port of Spain: Pan-Caribbean Publications, 1982.

Langley, Lester. *Banana Wars: An Inner History of the American Empire, 1900–1934.* Lexington: University Press of Kentucky, 1985.

Lavrin, Asunción. *Women, Feminism, and Social Change in Argentina, Chile, and Uruguay, 1890–1940.* Lincoln: University of Nebraska Press, 1995.

Lee, J. M. *Colonial Development and Good Government: A Study of the Ideas Expressed by the British Official Classes in Planning Decolonization, 1939–1964.* Oxford: Clarendon, 1967.

Lee, Ulysses. *The Employment of Negro Troops.* Washington, D.C.: Center of Military History, U.S. Army, 1994.

Levine, Philippa. *Prostitution, Race, and Politics: Policing Venereal Disease in the British Empire.* New York: Routledge, 2003.

Lewis, Gordon K. *The Growth of the Modern West Indies.* London: MacGibbon & Kee, 1968.

———. *Main Currents in Caribbean Thought: The Historical Evolution of Caribbean Society in Its Ideological Aspects, 1492–1900.* Baltimore: Johns Hopkins University Press, 1983.

Lindley, David, ed. *William Shakespeare's "The Tempest."* Cambridge: Cambridge University Press, 2002.

Lipsitz, George. *Rainbow at Midnight: Labor and Culture in the 1940s.* Urbana: University of Illinois Press, 1994.

Look Lai, Walton. *Indentured Labor, Caribbean Sugar: Chinese and Indian Migrants to the British West Indies, 1838–1918.* Baltimore: Johns Hopkins University Press, 1993.

Louis, William Roger. *Imperialism at Bay: The United States and the Decolonization of the British Empire, 1941–1945.* New York: Oxford University Press, 1978.

Lovelace, Earl. *The Wine of Astonishment.* New York: Vintage, 1982.

Macaulay, Neil. *The Sandino Affair.* Chicago: Quadrangle Books, 1967.

Macmillan, W. M. *Warning from the West Indies: A Tract for Africa and the Empire.* 1936. Reprint, New York: Books for Publishing 1971.

Madhavi, Kale. *Fragments of Empire: Capital, Slavery, and Indian Indentured Labor Migration in the British Caribbean.* Philadelphia: University of Pennsylvania Press, 1998.

Magid, Alvin. *Urban Nationalism: A Study of Political Development in Trinidad.* Gainesville: University of Florida Press, 1988.

Martin, Linda, and Kerry Segrave, eds. *The Servant Problem: Domestic Workers in North America.* Jefferson, N.C.: McFarland and Co., 1985.

Maurer, Harry. *Strange Ground: An Oral History of Americans in Vietnam, 1945–1975.* New York: H. Holt, 1989.

Mazón, Mauricio. *The Zoot Suit Riots: The Psychology of Symbolic Annihilation.* Austin: University of Texas Press, 1984.

McClintock, Anne. *Imperial Leather: Race, Gender, and Sexuality in the Colonial Conquest.* New York: Routledge, 1995.

McGuinness, Aims. "Searching for Latin America: Race and Sovereignty in the

Americas in the 1850s." In *Race and Nation in Modern Latin America*, edited by Nancy Appelbaum, Anne Macpherson, and Karin Alejandra Rosemblatt, 87–103. Chapel Hill: University of North Carolina Press, 2003.

Meighoo, Kirk. *Politics in a "Half Made" Society: Trinidad and Tobago, 1925–2000.* Kingston: Ian Randle, 2003.

Meikle, Louis. *Confederation of the British West Indies versus Annexation to the United States of America: A Political Discourse on the West Indies.* London: S. Low, Marston & Co., 1912.

Mendes, Alfred. *Black Fauns.* London: New Beacon, 1935.

———. *Pitch Lake: A Story from Trinidad.* London: New Beacon, 1980.

Mendes, John. *Cote Ce Cote La: Trinidad and Tobago Dictionary.* Arima, Trinidad: John Mendes, 1985.

Miller, Daniel. *Modernity, an Ethnographic Approach: Dualism and Mass Consumption in Trinidad.* Oxford: Berg, 1994.

Millette, James. *Society and Politics in Colonial Trinidad.* Totowa, N.J.: Biblio Distribution Center, 1985.

Mintz, Sidney. *Sweetness and Power: The Place of Sugar in Modern History.* New York: Viking, 1985.

Moore, Brian L., and Swithin R. Wilmot, eds. *Before and after 1865: Education, Politics, and Regionalism in the Caribbean.* Kingston: Ian Randle, 1998.

Moore, John Hammond. *Over-Sexed, Over-Paid, and Over Here: Americans in Australia, 1941–45.* New York: University of Queensland Press, 1981.

Moore, Robin. *Nationalizing Blackness: Afrocubanismo and Artistic Revolution in Havana, 1920–1940.* Pittsburgh: University of Pittsburgh Press, 1997.

Mosse, George. *Nationalism and Sexuality: Middle Class Morality and Sexual Norms in Modern Europe.* New York: H. Fertig, 1985.

Mrinalini, Sinha. *Colonial Masculinity: The "Manly Englishman" and the "Effeminate Bengali" in the Late Nineteenth Century.* New York: Manchester University Press, 1995.

Mumford, Kevin J. *Interzones: Black/White Sex Districts in Chicago and New York in the Early Twentieth Century.* New York: Columbia University Press, 1997.

Munasinghe, Viranjini. *Callaloo or Tossed Salad? East Indians and the Cultural Politics of Identity in Trinidad.* Ithaca: Cornell University Press, 2001.

Munro, Ian, and Reinhard Sander, eds. *Kas-Kas, Interviews with Three Caribbean Writers in Texas: George Lamming, C. L. R. James, Wilson Harris.* Austin: African and Afro-American Research Institute, 1972.

Naipaul, V. S. *The Middle Passage; Impressions of Five Societies: British, French, and Dutch in the West Indies and South America.* London: Vintage, 1962.

———. *Miguel Street.* London: Penguin, 1959.

Neuberger, Joan. *Hooliganism: Crime, Culture, and Power in St. Petersburg, 1900–1914.* Berkeley: University of California Press, 1993.

Newson, Linda A. *Aboriginal and Spanish Colonial Trinidad: A Study in Culture Contact.* New York: Academic Press, 1976.

Nugent, Daniel, ed. *Rural Revolt in Mexico: U.S. Intervention and the Domain of Subaltern Politics.* Durham: Duke University Press, 1998.

O'Brien, Thomas F. *The Revolutionary Mission: American Business in Latin America, 1900–1945.* New York: Cambridge University Press, 1996.

Ottley, Robert Carlton. *Creole Talk: Trinibaganese of Trinidad and Tobago, Words, Phrases, and Sayings Peculiar to the Country.* Diego Martin, Trinidad: Crusoe Publications, 1981.

Oxaal, Ivar. *Black Intellectuals Come to Power: The Rise of Creole Nationalism in Trinidad and Tobago.* Cambridge, Mass.: Schenkman, 1968.

Parker, Andrew, ed. *Nationalisms and Sexualities.* New York: Routledge, 1992.

Pascoe, Peggy. "Miscegenation Laws, Court Cases, and Ideologies of Race in Twentieth-Century America." In *Sex, Love, Race: Crossing Boundaries in North American History,* edited by Martha Hodes, 464–90. New York: New York University Press, 1999.

Paz, Octavio. *The Labyrinth of Solitude.* New York: Grove Press, 1961.

Pearson, Geoffrey. *Hooligan: A History of Respectable Fears.* New York: Schocken Books, 1984.

Pells, Richard. *Not Like Us: How Europeans Have Loved, Hated, and Transformed American Culture since World War II.* New York: Basic Books, 1997.

Pérez, Louis A., Jr. *Cuba and the United States: Ties of Singular Intimacy.* Athens: University of Georgia Press, 1990.

———. *Cuba between Empires, 1878–1902.* Pittsburgh: University of Pittsburgh Press, 1982.

———. *On Becoming Cuban: Identity, Nationality, and Culture.* Chapel Hill: University of North Carolina Press, 1999.

Piven, Frances Fox, and Richard A. Cloward. *Poor People's Movements: Why They Succeed, How They Fail.* New York: Pantheon, 1977.

Plummer, Brenda G. *The Psychological Moment: The United States and Haiti.* Athens: University of Georgia Press, 1990.

———. *Rising Wind: Black Americans and U.S. Foreign Affairs, 1935–1960.* Chapel Hill: University of North Carolina Press, 1996.

Poiger, Uta. *Jazz, Rock, and Rebels: Cold War Politics and American Culture in a Divided Germany.* Berkeley: University of California Press, 2000.

Poirier, Suzanne. *Chicago's War on Syphilis, 1937–1940: The Times, the Trib, and the Clap Doctor.* Urbana: University of Illinois Press, 1995.

Post, Ken. *Arise Ye Starvelings: The Jamaican Labour Rebellion of 1938 and Its Aftermath.* The Hague: Martinus Nijhoff, 1978.

———. *Strike the Iron: A Colony at War—Jamaica, 1939–1945.* Atlantic Highlands, N.J.: Humanities Press, 1981.

Potts, E. Daniel, and Annette Potts. *Yanks Down Under, 1941–45: The American Impact on Australia.* Melbourne: Oxford University Press, 1985.

Poupeye, Veerle. *Caribbean Art.* London: Thames and Hudson, 1998.

Prakash, Gyan, ed. *After Colonialism: Imperial Histories and Postcolonial Displacements.* Princeton, N.J.: Princeton University Press, 1994.

Pratt, Mary Louise. *Imperial Eyes: Travel Writing and Transculturation*. New York: Routledge, 1992.

Puri, Shalini. *The Caribbean Postcolonial: Social Equality, Post-Nationalism, and Cultural Hybridity*. New York: Palgrave Macmillan, 2004.

Quevedo, Raymond. *Attila's Kaiso: A Short History of Trinidad Calypso*. St. Augustine: Department of Extra Mural Studies, University of the West Indies, 1983.

Ramchand, Kenneth. *An Introduction to the Study of West Indian Literature*. London: Nelson Caribbean, 1976.

Rampersad, Kris. *Finding a Place: Indo-Trinidadian Literature*. Kingston: Ian Randle, 2002.

Reddock, Rhoda. *Elma Francois: The NWCSA and The Worker's Struggle for Change in the Caribbean*. London: New Beacon, 1988.

———. *Women, Labour, and Politics in Trinidad and Tobago: A History*. London: Zed Books, 1994.

Regis, Louis. *The Political Calypso: True Opposition in Trinidad and Tobago, 1962–1987*. Gainesville: University of Florida Press, 1999.

Reid, Ira. *The Negro Immigrant, His Background, Characteristics, and Adjustment, 1899–1937*. New York: Arno Press, 1939.

Reid, John. *Spanish American Images of the United States*. Gainesville: University Press of Florida, 1977.

Reis, Charles. *A History of the Constitution or Government of Trinidad: From Earliest Times to Present Day, with Notes*. Port of Spain: Author's personal press, 1929.

Renda, Mary A. *Taking Haiti: Military Occupation and the Culture of U.S. Imperialism, 1915–1940*. Chapel Hill: University of North Carolina Press, 2001.

Rennie, Bukka. *The History of the Working Class in the Twentieth Century: The Trinidad and Tobago Experience*. Toronto: New Beginning Movement, 1973.

Retamar, Roberto Fernandez. *Caliban and Other Essays*. Minneapolis: University of Minnesota Press, 1989.

Reynolds, David. *Rich Relations: The American Occupation of Britain, 1942–1945*. New York: Random House, 1995.

Robinson, Ronald, and John Gallagher, with Alice Denny. *Africa and the Victorians: The Official Mind of Imperialism*. London: Macmillan, 1961.

Rodney, Walter. *A History of the Guyanese Working People, 1881–1905*. Baltimore: John Hopkins University Press, 1981.

Rodó, José Enrique. *Ariel*. Austin: University of Texas Press, 1988.

Rohlehr, Gordon. *Calypso and Society in Pre-Independence Trinidad*. Port of Spain: G. Rohlehr, 1990.

Roorda, Eric. *The Dictator Next Door: The Good Neighbor Policy and The Trujillo Regime in the Dominican Republic, 1930–1945*. Durham: Duke University Press, 1998.

Roseberry, William. *Anthropologies and Histories: Essays in Culture, History, and Political Economy*. New Brunswick, N.J.: Rutgers University Press, 1989.

Rosenberg, Emily S. *Financial Missionaries to the World: The Politics and Culture of Dollar Diplomacy, 1900–1930*. Cambridge, Mass.: Harvard University Press, 1999.

Rowe, William, and Vivian Schelling. *Memory and Modernity: Popular Culture in Latin America*. New York: Verso, 1991.

Ryan, Selwyn. *Race and Nationalism in Trinidad and Tobago: A Study of Decolonization in a Multiracial Society*. Toronto: University of Toronto Press, 1972.

Sahlins, Peter. *Boundaries: The Making of France and Spain in the Pyrenees*. Berkeley: University of California Press, 1989.

Said, Edward. *Culture and Imperialism*. New York: Random House, 1993.

Sander, Reinhard. *Trinidad Awakening: West Indian Literature of the Nineteen Thirties*. New York: Greenwood Press, 1988.

Sangari, Kumkum, and Sudesh Vaid, eds. *Recasting Women: Essays in Indian Colonial History*. New Brunswick, N.J.: Rutgers University Press, 1995.

Schmidt, Hans. *The United States Occupation of Haiti, 1915–1934*. New Brunswick, N.J.: Rutgers University Press, 1972.

Scott, David. *Conscripts of Modernity: The Tragedy of Colonial Enlightenment*. Durham: Duke University Press, 2004.

———. *Refashioning Futures: Criticism after Postcoloniality*. Princeton, N.J.: Princeton University Press, 1999.

Scott, James C. *Domination and the Arts of Resistance: Hidden Transcripts*. New Haven: Yale University Press, 1990.

———. *Weapons of the Weak: Everyday Forms of Peasant Resistance*. New Haven: Yale University Press, 1985.

Scott, William R. *The Sons of Sheba's Race: African-Americans and the Italo-Ethiopian War, 1935–1941*. Bloomington: Indiana University Press, 1993.

Selvon, Samuel. *A Brighter Sun*. Harlow, Essex: Longman, 1952.

———. *An Island Is a World*. London: A. Wingate, 1955.

Sforza, John. *Swing It! The Andrews Sisters*. Lexington: University Press of Kentucky, 1999.

Sheller, Mimi. *Consuming the Caribbean: From Arawaks to Zombies*. London: Routledge, 2003.

Shepherd, Verene A., and Glen L. Richards, eds. *Questioning Creole: Creolisation Discourses in Caribbean Culture*. Kingston: Ian Randle, 2002.

Simey, T. S. *Welfare and Planning in the West Indies*. Oxford: Clarendon, 1946.

Singh, Kelvin. *Race and Class Struggles in a Colonial State: Trinidad, 1917–1945*. Calgary: University of Calgary Press, 1994.

Singh, Nikhil Pal. *Black Is a Country: Race and the Unfinished Struggle for Democracy*. Cambridge, Mass.: Harvard University Press, 2004.

Sklar, Robert. *Movie-Made America: A Cultural History of the American Movies*. New York: Random House, 1975.

Smith, Faith. *Creole Recitations: John Jacob Thomas and Colonial Formation in the Late Nineteenth-Century Caribbean*. Charlottesville: University of Virginia Press, 2002.

Smith, Graham. *When Jim Crow Met John Bull: Black American Soldiers in World War II Britain*. New York: St. Martin's Press, 1987.

Smith, Sidney. *Public Life and Sport: Jamaica, Grenada, and Trinidad*. Port of Spain: Trinidad Publishing Co., 1941.

Smith, Zadie. *White Teeth*. New York: Random House, 2000.

Sommer, Doris. *Foundational Fictions: The National Romances of Latin America*. Berkeley: University of California Press, 1991.

Stead, W. T. *The Americanization of the World*. New York: H. Markley, 1902.

Stearns, Jean, and Marshall Stearns. *Jazz Dance: The Story of American Vernacular Dance*. New York: Macmillan, 1968.

Stephens, Michelle. *Black Empire: The Masculine Global Imaginary of Caribbean Intellectuals in the United States, 1914–1962*. Durham: Duke University Press, 2005.

Stewart, John O. *Drinkers, Drummers, and Decent Folk: Ethnographic Narratives of Village Trinidad*. Albany: State University of New York Press, 1989.

Stocking, George W., Jr. *Race, Culture, and Evolution: Essays in the History of Anthropology*. New York: Free Press, 1968.

Stoler, Ann Laura. *Carnal Knowledge and Imperial Power: Race and the Intimate in Colonial Rule*. Berkeley: University of California Press, 2002.

———. "Intimidations of Empire: Predicaments of the Tactile and Unseen." In *Haunted by Empire: Geographies of Intimacy in North American History*, edited by Ann Laura Stoler, 1–22. Durham: Duke University Press, 2006.

Stoner, Lynn K. *From Home to the Street: The Cuban Women's Movement for Legal Reform, 1898–1940*. Durham: Duke University Press, 1991.

Stowe, David W. *Swing Changes: Big-Band Jazz in New Deal America*. Cambridge, Mass.: Harvard University Press, 1994.

Stuempfle, Stephen. *The Steelband Movement: The Forging of a National Art in Trinidad and Tobago*. Philadelphia: University of Pennsylvania Press, 1995.

Sturdevant, Saundra, and Brenda Stoltzfus, eds. *Let the Good Times Roll: Prostitution and the United States Military in Asia*. New York: New Press, 1992.

Thomas, Deborah A. *Modern Blackness: Nationalism, Globalization, and the Politics of Culture in Jamaica*. Durham: Duke University Press, 2004.

Thomas, Roy, ed. *The Trinidad Labor Riots: Perspectives Fifty Years Later*. St. Augustine: University of the West Indies Press, 1987.

Torgovnick, Marianna. *Gone Primitive: Savage Intellects, Modern Lives*. Chicago: University of Chicago Press, 1990.

Tothill, Vincent. *The Doctor's Office*. Foreword by Owen Rutter. London: Blackie & Son, 1939.

Trotman, David. *Crime in Trinidad: Conflict and Control in a Plantation Society, 1838–1900*. Knoxville: University of Tennessee Press, 1986.

Trouillot, Michel-Rolph. *Haiti, State against Nation: The Origins and Legacy of Duvalierism*. New York: Monthly Review Press, 1990.

———. *Silencing the Past: Power and the Production of History*. Boston: Beacon Press, 1995.

Vaughan, Virginia Mason, and Alden T. Vaughan, eds. *Critical Essays on Shakespeare's "The Tempest."* New York: G. K. Hall, 1998.

Veeser, Cyrus. *A World Safe for Capitalism: Dollar Diplomacy and America's Rise to Global Power*. New York: Columbia University Press, 2002.

Von Eschen, Penny M. *Race against Empire: Black Americans and Anticolonialism, 1937–1957.* Ithaca: Cornell University Press, 1997.

———. *Satchmo Blows Up the World: Jazz Ambassadors Play the Cold War.* Cambridge, Mass.: Harvard University Press, 2004.

Wade, Peter. *Blackness and Race Mixture: The Dynamics of Racial Identity in Colombia.* Baltimore: Johns Hopkins University Press, 1993.

———. *Music, Race, and Nation: Música Tropical in Colombia.* Chicago: University of Chicago Press, 2000.

Wagnleitner, Reinhold. *Coca-Colonization and Cold War: The Cultural Mission of the United States in Austria after the Second World War.* Trans. Diana Wolf. Chapel Hill: University of North Carolina Press, 1994.

Wagnleitner, Reinhold, and Elaine Tyler May, eds. *Here, There, and Everywhere: The Foreign Politics of American Popular Culture.* Hanover, N.H.: University Press of New England, 2000.

Watkins-Owens, Irma. *Blood Relations: Caribbean Immigrants and the Harlem Community, 1900–1930.* Bloomington: Indiana University Press, 1996.

Weisbord, Robert G. *Ebony Kinship: Africa, Africans, and the Afro-American.* Westport, Conn.: Greenwood Press, 1973.

White, Shane, and Graham White. *Stylin': African American Expressive Culture from Its Beginnings to the Zoot Suit.* Ithaca: Cornell University Press, 1998.

Williams, Brackette F. *Stains on My Name, War in My Veins: Guyana and the Politics of Struggle.* Durham: Duke University Press, 1991.

Williams, Eric. *Capitalism and Slavery.* 1944. Reprint, Chapel Hill: University of North Carolina Press, 1994.

———. *Education in the British West Indies.* Port of Spain: Guardian Commercial Printery, 1946.

———. *Forged from the Love of Liberty: The Selected Speeches of Dr. Eric Williams.* Comp. Paul K. Sutton. Port of Spain: Longman Caribbean, 1981.

———. *History of the People of Trinidad and Tobago.* Port of Spain: PNM Publishing Co., 1962.

Williams, Raymond, *The Sociology of Culture.* Chicago: University of Chicago Press, 1981.

Wilson, Peter J. *Crab Antics: The Social Anthropology of English-Speaking Negro Societies of the Caribbean.* New Haven: Yale University Press, 1973.

Wood, Donald. *Trinidad in Transition.* London: Oxford University Press, 1968.

Wynter, Sylvia. "Beyond Miranda's Meanings: Unsilencing the 'Demonic Ground' of Caliban's 'Woman.'" In *Out of the Kumbla: Caribbean Women Writers and Literature,* edited by Carol Boyce Davies and Elaine Savory Fido, 213–43. Trenton, N.J.: Africa World Press, 1990.

Yelvington, Kevin A., ed. *Trinidad Ethnicity.* London: Macmillan, 1993.

Yerxa, Donald, *Admirals and Empire: The United States Navy and the Caribbean, 1898–1945.* Columbia: University of South Carolina Press, 1991.

Young, Robert J. C. *Colonial Desire: Hybridity in Theory, Culture, and Race.* New York: Routledge, 1995.

Yuval-Davis, Nira. *Gender and Nation*. London: Sage, 1997.

Yuval-Davis, Nira, and Floya Anthias, eds. *Woman-Nation-State*. New York: St. Martin's Press, 1989.

Articles

Ambler, Charles. "Popular Films and Colonial Audiences: The Movies in Northern Rhodesia." *American Historical Review* 106 (June 2001): 81–105.

Baker, Houston. "Caliban's Triple Play." *Critical Inquiry* 13 (Spring 1986): 182–96.

Braithwaite, Lloyd. "Social Stratification in Trinidad." *Social and Economic Studies* 2 (1953): 5–175.

Brown, Jacqueline Nassy. "Black Liverpool, Black America, and the Gendering of Diasporic Space." *Cultural Anthropology* 13 (August 1998): 291–325.

Brush, Paula Stewart. "Problematizing the Race Consciousness of Women of Color." *Signs* 27 (Autumn 2001): 171–98.

Campones, Oscar V. "1898 and the Nature of the New Empire." *Radical History Review* 73 (Winter 1999): 128–38.

Carby, Hazel V. "Policing the Black Woman's Body in an Urban Context." *Critical Inquiry* 18 (Summer 1992): 738–55.

———. "Proletarian or Revolutionary Literary: C. L. R. James and the Politics of the Trinidadian Renaissance." *South Atlantic Quarterly* 87 (Winter 1988): 39–52.

Chakrabarty, Dipesh. "Postcoloniality and the Artifice of History: Who Speaks for 'Indian' Pasts?" *Representations* 37 (Winter 1992): 1–26.

Chibnall, Steve. "Whistle and Zoot: The Changing of a Suit of Clothes." *History Workshop* 20 (Spring 1985): 57–81.

Coghlan, Francis A. "The United States Navy and the Jamaica Earthquake." *Prologue* 8 (Spring 1976): 163–73.

Cole, Douglas. "The Problem of 'Nationalism' and 'Imperialism' in British Settlement Colonies." *Journal of British Studies* 10 (May 1971): 160–82.

Cooper, Frederick. "Conflict and Connection: Rethinking Colonial African History." *American Historical Review* 99 (December 1994): 1475–1545.

Cosgrove, Stuart. "Zoot Suit and Style Warfare." *History Workshop* 18 (Autumn 1984): 77–95.

De Barros, Juanita. "'Race' and Culture in the Writings of J. J. Thomas." *Journal of Caribbean History* 27 (November 1993): 23–51.

Diawara, Manthia. "Englishness and Blackness: Cricket as Discourse on Colonialism." *Callaloo* 13 (Fall 1990): 830–44.

Dookhan, Issac. "Military Civilian Conflicts in the Virgin Islands during World War II." *Journal of Caribbean History* 24 (May 1990): 89–108.

Downes, Aviston. "From Boys to Men: Colonial Education, Cricket, and Masculinity in the Caribbean, 1870–1930." *International Journal of the History of Sport* 22 (Spring 2005): 3–21.

Elder, Jacob D. "Color, Music, and Conflict: A Study of Aggression in Trinidad with

Reference to the Role of Traditional Music." *Ethnomusicology* 8 (May 1964): 128–36.

Eldridge, Michael. "There Goes the Transnational Neighborhood: Calypso Buys a Bungalow." *Callaloo* 25 (Spring 2002): 620–38.

Franco, Pamela. "The 'Unruly Woman' in Nineteenth Century Trinidad Carnival." *Small Axe* 7 (March 2000): 60–76.

Fraser, Cary. "The Twilight of Colonial Rule in the British West Indies: Nationalist Assertion vs. Imperial Hubris in the 1930s." *Journal of Caribbean History* 30 (May and November 1996): 1–27.

Gienow-Hecht, Jessica C. E. "Shame on U.S.? Academics, Cultural Transfer, and the Cold War: A Critical Review" *Diplomatic History* 24 (Summer 2000): 465–516.

Gilfoyle, Timothy. "Prostitutes in History: From Parables of Pornography to Metaphors of Modernity." *American Historical Review* 104 (February 1999): 117–41.

Goedde, Petra. "Feature Review: Women and Foreign 'Affairs.'" *Diplomatic History* 23 (Fall 1999): 693–98.

Grieveson, Lee. "Fighting Films: Race, Morality, and the Governing of Cinema." *Cinema Journal* 38 (Autumn 1998): 40–61.

High, Steven. "The Racial Politics of Criminal Jurisdiction in the Aftermath of the Anglo-American 'Destroyers-for-Bases' Deal, 1940–50." *Journal of Imperial and Commonwealth History* 32 (September 2004): 77–105.

Higman, B. W. "Remembering Slavery: The Rise, Decline, and Revival of Emancipation Day in the English-Speaking Caribbean." *Slavery and Abolition* 19 (April 1998): 90–105.

Jáuregui, Carlos. "Calibán: Icono del 98. A propósito de un artículo de Rubén Darío y 'El triunfo de Calibán.'" *Balance de un siglo (1898–1998).* Número especial. Coordinación de Aníbal González. *Revista Iberoamericana* 184–85 (1998): 441–55.

Johnson, Howard. "The Anglo-American Caribbean Commission and the Extension of American Influence in the British Caribbean, 1942–45." *Journal of Commonwealth and Comparative Politics* 22 (June 1984): 180–203.

———. "Oil, Imperial Policy, and the Trinidad Disturbances, 1937." *Journal of Imperial and Commonwealth History* 4 (September 1975): 29–53.

Johnson, Michele A. "Decent and Fair: Aspects of Domestic Service in Jamaica, 1920–1970." *Journal of Caribbean History* 6 (November 1999): 83–106.

Kramer, Paul A. "Empires, Exceptions, and Anglo-Saxons: Race and Rule between the British and United States Empires, 1880–1910." *Journal of American History* 88 (March 2002): 1315–53.

Lake, Marilyn. "The Desire for a Yank: Sexual Relations between Australian Women and American Servicemen during World War II." *Journal of the History of Sexuality* 2 (October 1992): 621–33.

Levine, Philippa. "Venereal Disease, Prostitution, and the Politics of Empire: The Case of British India." *Journal of the History of Sexuality* 4 (July 1994): 579–602.

Lewis, Gordon K. "Outsider's View." *Caribbean Studies* 14 (December 1975): 73–83.

———. "Review." *Caribbean Studies* 3 (January 1963): 100–105.

Maingot, Anthony P. "From Ethnocentric to National History Writing in the Plural Society." *Caribbean Studies* 9 (September 1969): 69–86.

Mallon, Florencia E. "The Promise and Dilemma of Subaltern Studies: Perspectives from Latin American History." *American Historical Review* 99 (December 1994): 1491–1516.

Mathurin, Owen. "An Insider's View." *Caribbean Studies* 14 (December 1975): 73–83.

Mintz, Sidney. "Enduring Substances, Trying Theories: The Caribbean Region as Oikoumene." *Journal of the Royal Anthropological Institute* 2 (June 1996): 289–311.

Neptune, Harvey. "White Lies: Race and Sexuality in Occupied Trinidad." *Journal of Colonialism and Colonial History* 2 (Spring 2001): 24–52.

Nicholls, David. "Levantines in the Caribbean." *Ethnic and Racial Studies* 4, no. 4 (1981): 34–51.

Nixon, Rob. "Caribbean and African Appropriations of *The Tempest*." *Critical Inquiry* 13 (Spring 1987): 557–78.

Palmer, Annette. "Black American Soldiers in Trinidad: Wartime Politics in a Colonial Society." *Journal of Imperial and Commonwealth History* 14 (September 1986): 203–18.

Pandey, Gyanendra. "In Defense of the Fragment: Writing about Hindu-Muslim Riots Today." *Representations* 37 (Winter 1992): 27–55.

Parker, Jason. "Capital of the Caribbean: The African American–West Indian Harlem Nexus and the Transnational Drive for Black Freedom, 1940–1948." *Journal of African American History* 2 (Spring 2004): 98–117.

Pearse, Andrew. "Mitto Sampson on Calypso Legends of the Nineteenth Century." *Caribbean Quarterly* 4 (March/June 1956): 250–62.

Perez, Louis A., Jr. "Incurring a Debt of Gratitude: 1898 and the Moral Sources of United States Hegemony in Cuba." *American Historical Review* 104 (June 1999): 356–98.

———. "Intervention, Hegemony, and Dependency: The United States in the Circum-Caribbean, 1898–1980." *Pacific Historical Review* 51 (May 1982): 169–93.

Prakash, Gyan. "Subaltern Studies as Postcolonial Criticism." *American Historical Review* 99 (December 1994): 1475–91.

Ramchand, Ken. "West Indian Literary History: Literariness, Orality, and Periodization." *Callaloo* 11 (Summer 1988): 95–110.

Rippy, Fred. "Literary Yankeephobia in Hispanic America." *Journal of International Relations* 12 (July 1922): 351–71.

Rose, Sonya. "Sex, Citizenship, and the Nation in World War II Britain." *American Historical Review* 103 (October 1998): 1147–76.

Saunders, Gail. "The 1937 Riot in Inagua, the Bahamas." *New West India Guide* 62 (Fall 1988): 129–45.

———. "The 1942 Riot in Nassau: A Demand for Change?" *Journal of Caribbean History* 20 (May 1985): 117–46.

Schein, Louisa. "Performing Modernity." *Cultural Anthropology* 14 (August 1999): 361–95.

Scott, David. "Political Rationalities of the Jamaican Modern." *Small Axe* 14 (September 2003): 1–22.

———. "The Sovereignty of the Imagination: An Interview with George Lamming." *Small Axe* 12 (March 2002): 72–200.

Singh, Kelvin. "Adrian Cola Rienzi and the Labour Movement in Trinidad (1925–1944)." *Journal of Caribbean History* 16 (November 1982): 11–35.

Skurski, Julie. "The Ambiguities of Authenticity in Latin America: *Dona Barbara* and the Construction of National Identity." *Poetics Today* 15 (Winter 1994): 605–42.

Smyth, Rosaleen. "The Development of British Colonial Film Policy, 1927–1939." *Journal of African History* 20 (February 1979): 347–450.

Somers, Margaret. "What's Political or Cultural about Political Culture and the Public Sphere? Toward an Historical Sociology of the Concept Formation." *Sociological Theory* 13 (July 1995): 23–76.

Stoddart, Brian. "Sport, Cultural Imperialism, and Colonial Responses in the British Empire." *Comparative Studies in Society and History* 30 (October 1988): 649–73.

Summerfield, Penny. "Gender and War in the Twentieth Century." *International History Review* 19 (Spring 1997): 3–16.

Thomas, Deborah. "Modern Blackness: What We Are and What We Hope to Be." *Small Axe* 12 (September 2002): 25–48.

Tilchin, William. "Theodore Roosevelt, Anglo-American Relations, and the Jamaica Incident of 1907." *Diplomatic History* 19 (Fall 1995): 385–405.

Tulloch, Carol. "Fashioned in Black and White: Women's Dress in Jamaica, 1880–1907." *Things* 7 (Fall 1997): 29–53.

Tyler, Bruce M. "Black Jive and White Repression." *Journal of Ethnic Studies* 16 (Winter 1989): 30–66.

Wolfe, Patrick. "History and Imperialism: A Century of Theory from Marx to Postcolonialism." *American Historical Review* 102 (April 1997): 388–420.

UNPUBLISHED WORKS AND DISSERTATIONS

Baptiste, Fitzroy. "Colonial Government, Americans, and Employment-Generation in Trinidad, 1939–44." Unpublished paper, n.d.

Barnes, Natasha. "Representing the Nation: Gender, Class, and the State in the Anglophone Caribbean." Ph.D. diss., University of Michigan, 1995.

Bartlett, Randolph Wilson, Jr. "Lorenzo D. Baker and the Development of the Banana Trade between Jamaica and the United States, 1881–1890." Ph.D. diss., American University, 1977.

Burn, North. "United States Base Rights in the British West Indies, 1940–62." Ph.D. diss., Princeton University, Fletcher School of Law and Diplomacy, 1964.

Calliste, Merlyn. "The Impact of the American Base at Wallerfield." Caribbean Studies Project, University of the West Indies, St. Augustine, 1993.

Campbell, Susan. "En'less Pressure: The Struggles of a Caribbean Working Class in Their International Context, 1919–1956." Ph.D. diss., Queens University, 1995.

Elder, J. D. "Evolution of the Traditional Calypso of Trinidad and Tobago: A Socio-Historical Analysis of Social Change." Ph.D. diss., University of Pennsylvania, 1966.

Forde, Joanne. "The Social and Economic Impact of World War II on Trinidad and Tobago." Caribbean Studies Project, University of the West Indies, St. Augustine, 1982.

Gopaul-Maharaj, Vishoo. "The Social Effects of the American Presence." Master's thesis, University of the West Indies, 1989.

Hill, Donald, "Calypsonians Speak for the Record: An Ethnohistorical Study of the Trinidad Calypso, 1784–1950." Vol. 2. Unpublished study, American University, St. Augustine, 1977.

Kilkenny, Roberta W. "And So They Have Captured Demerara: A Preliminary Investigation of U.S. Guiana Relations during the Second World War." Paper presented at Conference of the Association of Caribbean Historians, Bahamas, 1986.

Mulchansingh, Vernon. "The Origins, Growth, and Development of the Oil Industry in Trinidad and Its Impact on the Economy, 1857–1965." Ph.D. diss., Queens University of Belfast, 1967.

Palmer, Annette. "The United States and the Commonwealth Caribbean, 1939–45." Ph.D. diss., Fordham University, 1979.

Paris, L. G. W., "The Socio-economic Effects of the American Occupation of Trinidad, 1939–45." Thesis, University of the West Indies, St. Augustine, 1972.

Rosenberg, Leah. "Creolizing Womanhood: Gender and Domesticity in Early Anglophone Caribbean National Literatures." Ph.D. diss., Cornell University, 2000.

Samaroo, Brinsley. "Political and Constitutional Development in Trinidad." Ph.D. diss., London University, 1969.

Segal, Daniel. "Nationalism in a Colonial State: A Study of Trinidad and Tobago." Ph.D. diss., University of Chicago, 1989.

Singh, Sandra. "Lloyd Braithwaite: A Biography." Caribbean Studies thesis, University of the West Indies, St. Augustine, 1987.

Wilkins, Fanon Che. "In the Belly of the Beast: Black Radicalism, Africa, and the Global Search for Black Power, 1957–1976." Ph.D. diss., New York University, 2001.

DISCOGRAPHY

Calypso: Best of Trinidad, 1929–1952. CD. Conceived and compiled by Jean Michel Gilbert. CMG Ltd. 2004.

Lord Invader. *Calypso in New York.* SFW CD 40454. 2000.

Lord Invader in New York. CD 40450. Folkways Recordings. 2000.

Index